CHARLES DE GAULLE
The Crucial Years, 1943–1944

CHARLES DE GAULLE

▶ *The Crucial Years, 1943 – 1944*

by ARTHUR LAYTON FUNK

NORMAN

UNIVERSITY OF OKLAHOMA PRESS

By Arthur Layton Funk

Source Problems in Twentieth Century History (New York, 1953)
Charles de Gaulle: The Crucial Years, 1943–1944 (Norman, 1959)

The publication of this volume has been aided by grants from the FORD FOUNDATION *and the* GUGGENHEIM FOUNDATION.

LIBRARY OF CONGRESS CATALOG CARD NUMBER: 59–7956

To G. S. F.

▶ *Introduction*

This account covers a dramatic and complex period of American foreign relations. When Pétain's Vichy government emerged after the defeat of France, a unique problem in foreign relations was posed by those Frenchmen who chose dissidence in preference to loyalty to the venerable Marshal. The term *dissidence* is used to include all individuals in France, in the French colonies, in England, in the United States, or elsewhere who, as patriotic French citizens, endeavored to liberate France through channels other than those provided by Vichy; and while the word is not common, it is the only one which succinctly and adequately encompasses all the diverse French groups which resisted German aggression. The word *dissidence* is larger in scope than *resistance*, which popularly implies (but not necessarily correctly) the underground that operated essentially in France; *dissidence*, on the other hand, suggests those who organized themselves outside of the country itself. By the time France was liberated, all French dissident groups had rallied behind General de Gaulle and the Committee of National Liberation; this record therefore spans the period during which De Gaulle, originally excluded from North Africa by the Allies, gradually gained control of the dissident movement and became head of the French Provisional government.

There have been many books on aspects of French dissidence, but most of the disinterested historical studies have concentrated on the dramatic events of the first two years of the war or on the reorganization of France after the liberation. American relations with Vichy have been described in detail by William L. Langer in *Our Vichy Gamble*, and the North African invasion has been treated carefully by the French historian Kammerer, but both Langer and Kammerer terminate their studies with Admiral Darlan's death in December, 1942. Several excellent volumes have been devoted to the origins of the Fourth Republic, but they all deal in cursory fashion with the wartime years. For this reason the present study concentrates on the 1943–44 period, in the hope of filling a gap in the history of France and of American foreign relations; the book should serve as a sequel to *Our Vichy Gamble* and as an introduction to histories of the Fourth Republic.

Comprehension of wartime developments, so difficult to understand while the war was in progress, is not facilitated by the many memoirs which have appeared in the last ten years. Within the volumes prepared by Churchill, Hull, Leahy, Eisenhower, Sherwood (*Roosevelt and Hopkins*), Duff Cooper, Stettinius, and Grew can be found an exhaustive presentation of American and British points of view. On the French side, General de Gaulle, General Giraud, and two commissioners, Emmanuel d'Astier de la Vigerie and Jacques Soustelle, have written memoirs of historical significance; and De Gaulle's volumes have special interest for historians by reason of the large number of documents he has published as appendices. Although the war archives of neither France, Great Britain, nor the United States have yet been opened to the public, the general lines of policy are clear enough; it remains to future historians to fill in a host of unspectacular details.

Franco-American wartime relations provide a problem concerning which a definitive, impartial and honest appraisal is difficult to achieve. It is a problem which is permeated with bitter rivalries and conflicts and which has been obscured throughout by some of the most malevolent propaganda of World War II. All of this was rendered more complex by the interaction of British, American, and Russian interests with French ambitions. And above all, the events in North Africa and France evolved as they did in accordance with what Churchill and Roosevelt and De Gaulle and their adherents thought about national interest, imperialism, strategy, and the ends of the war. No participant has told the whole truth in his memoirs about what happened. The present narrative constitutes an effort to work through the conflicting arguments, facts, propaganda, and accomplishments and in so doing to render justice equally to the French and the American points of view.

While this volume emphasizes the United States' position, it is of course impossible in many cases to separate American from British or even from Russian policy when that policy represented an Allied decision. American attitudes sometimes developed in conjunction with, and sometimes as a reaction to, British points of view, and an attempt has been made to describe the British position (and, to a lesser degree, the Soviet) where it has a bearing on that of the United States. In similar fashion, while this account makes no pretension of being a complete history of the French Committee of National Liberation, sufficient detail concerning the Committee's activities and policies has been provided to serve as a background against which the development of American attitudes may be understood. Policy is not made in a vacuum, and the reader must have the same sort of information at his disposal as (and if possible more of it than) those who made decisions during the war.

It might be argued that British policy—or even Russian—should be given equal consideration with United States policy in a study of this sort. But much as De Gaulle was indebted to Churchill's government during his three years in London, American influence became predominant once the Fighting French leader arrived in Algiers. The invasion of North Africa was essentially an American operation; American forces were in the majority in Morocco, Algeria, and Tunisia; and it was the United States which assumed responsibility for rearming the French. British influence regained significance during the liberation of France, but even then the American position, characterized by Roosevelt's stubborn determination not to recognize the French Committee, was the one which prevailed. So far as the Soviets are concerned, Russian influence was less important than Anglo-American, and, in any case, the historian unfortunately has few Soviet documents with which to work.

The writer has been permitted access to some French and American material not generally accessible and is particularly indebted to the State Department for its consideration and assistance in permitting study of many documents from its archives. Many gaps have been filled through interviews and correspondence with individuals who played significant roles during the war. Among those who have been interviewed in connection with this project are the following:

Emmanuel d'Astier de la Vigerie: leader of the resistance movement *Libération;* later commissioner of interior in the French Committee of National Liberation.

General François d'Astier de la Vigerie: head of Free French Air Force, 1942–43; military delegate in London, 1944.

General Béthouart: head of French Military Mission in Washington, 1943–44; chief of staff of national defense, 1944–45.

René Capitant: head of *Combat,* the Gaullist movement in North Africa; later minister of education in the Provisional government.

General René Chambe: *chef de cabinet militaire* of General Giraud, 1943–44.

Maurice Couve de Murville: commissioner of finance in the French Committee of National Liberation.

General Charles de Gaulle: chairman of the French Committee of National Liberation; first head of the postwar French Provisional government.

Maurice Dejean: commissioner of foreign affairs in the French National Committee, 1940–42.

Admiral R. Fenard: head of French Naval Mission in Washington, 1943–45.

Colonel Julius Holmes: political adviser on Eisenhower's staff at Allied headquarters, North Africa, and later with SHAEF.

Lieutenant Commander Tracy Kittredge, U.S.N.R.: attached to Admiral Stark's staff in London and responsible for liaison with French National Committee.

Alexis Léger: former secretary-general in French Foreign Office; resided in Washington during the war.

Jacques Lemaigre-Dubreuil: member of North African resistance group, "The Five"; adviser of General Giraud.

Harold Macmillan: British representative on Eisenhower's staff with rank of ambassador, 1943; later British delegate on the Italian Advisory Commission.

René Massigli: commissioner of foreign affairs on the French Committee of National Liberation, 1943-45.

H. Freeman Matthews: chargé d'affaires at Vichy; later political adviser to Eisenhower, Hull, and Roosevelt.

John J. McCloy: assistant secretary of the army; responsible for civil administration policy.

Robert Murphy: civil adviser on Eisenhower's staff with rank of ambassador, 1943; delegate on Italian Advisory Commission, 1944; political adviser with SHAEF, 1944-45.

Colonel Paul Paillole: head of the French Army counterintelligence and military security, 1942-45.

Gaston Palewski: *chef de cabinet* of General de Gaulle, 1942-45.

André Poniatowski: member of advisory staff of General Giraud, 1941-43.

Samuel Reber: State Department official responsible for negotiations with Admiral Robert; later on Murphy's staff in North Africa.

General Rivet: head of the French Army intelligence service, 1943-44.

Jacques Soustelle: commissioner of public information in the French National Committee, 1942-43; director of the *Direction Générale de Recherche et Renseignement,* 1943-45; minister of information, 1945-46.

René Thibault: member of General de Gaulle's staff; editor of documents published by De Gaulle in his memoirs.

Edwin C. Wilson: American representative to the French Committee of National Liberation, with rank of ambassador, 1944-45.

The writer is also indebted to the following for assistance and co-operation: Dr. Kent Roberts Greenfield, chief historian in the U. S. Army Office of Military History; M. Henri Michel, secretary-general of the *Comité d'Histoire de la Deuxième Guerre Mondiale;* Mr. Taylor Parks of the State Department Division of Historical Policy Research; Colonel Cossé Brissac, director of the French *Service Historique de l'Armée;* Miss Elizabeth Campbell, deputy press librarian at the Royal Institute of International Affairs, London, who rendered valuable assistance in making available material from the Institute's remarkable clipping service; the librarians at the University of Florida Library and at the Bibliothèque de Documentation Internationale Contemporaine, Paris, where most of the research was accomplished; my wife, whose typing and sympathetic understanding may have faltered but never failed; and the Guggenheim Foundation, whose grant permitted a year's leave of absence from the University of Florida for work on the project.

ARTHUR LAYTON FUNK

Madras, India
January 5, 1959

▶ Contents

▶ *Illustrations*

CHARLES DE GAULLE
The Crucial Years, 1943–1944

▶ 1. The Background, 1940–1942

Washington and Vichy

ONE OF the curious anomalies to emerge from World War II exists in the fact that while Frenchmen deeply respect the name of Franklin D. Roosevelt and Americans enthusiastically honor Charles de Gaulle as France's great liberator, both Roosevelt and De Gaulle, holding tenaciously to diametrically opposed views about France, regarded each other with suspicion and mistrust. To President Roosevelt, France was a dismembered, defeated country, leaderless and bankrupt, whose disposition must await the war's unpredictable end; for De Gaulle, she was a bewildered victim whose temporary deviation from the road of traditional grandeur could be corrected by placing her trust in the leader of Fighting France. When De Gaulle met the President for the first time in January, 1943, at the Casablanca Conference, he endeavored to persuade Roosevelt that he possessed the moral, if not the legal right, to represent the French people. Joan of Arc, he argued, had never received any more formal investment from the people than he to lead France against her enemies. But De Gaulle's vivid presentation of his case increased the President's hostility, and the analogy with St. Joan served only to provide anecdotal material which the President later employed skillfully in denigrating De Gaulle to hundreds of listeners. In his many retellings of the story, Roosevelt twisted De Gaulle's arguments to make them appear as if the General had arrogantly portrayed himself as a twentieth-century Maid of Orléans.

The interchange between De Gaulle and the President at Casablanca took place over two and one-half years after De Gaulle had dramatically flown from Bordeaux, armed only with his stubborn determination to bring France back into the war. Long before they met, each had solidified his thinking into a pattern which inevitably brought them into conflict—a conflict in which not only Americans and French were to be entangled, but in which British interests were so powerfully involved that dangerous strains were produced between French and British and between British and Americans. The story of relations between the Fighting French and the United States moves with the predestined tragic pace of Euripidean drama; once the positions had been assumed, every action, every chance occurrence, every speech pushed the protagonists into situations from which neither could extricate himself with ease or dignity.

It was only in 1943, shortly after the Casablanca Conference, that De Gaulle, having become chairman of the French Committee of National Liberation, had to be seriously considered in connection with American policy. Before that time, during which De Gaulle's activities were largely a British preoccupation, the United States had maintained only casual and intermittent relations with the Free French and, because of its recognition of Vichy, assumed that such relations possessed minor importance so far as American interests were concerned. When finally, through its unique contacts in North Africa, the United States found itself impelled to take French dissidence into account, it developed relations with Admiral Darlan and General Giraud and shut its eyes to the growing influence of Gaullism. An account of American relations with De Gaulle, Giraud, and other Frenchmen who broke with the Vichy government, from the Casablanca Conference to the end of the war, constitutes the substance of the present study. Details of American dealings with Vichy and with Darlan and Giraud during the North African invasion have been so adequately recounted that there is no need for anything but a cursory repetition in this chapter for the sake of those unfamiliar with the detailed studies already in print.

American attitudes toward France developed as a result of the situation emerging from the fact that for two years after the beginning of World War II the United States did not enter the conflict. Americans read their newspapers with interest and alarm when Hitler's panzer divisions engulfed a defenseless Poland in 1939, and they breathed easier during the eventless winter of the Phony War; but they watched with increased and disturbed awareness the ease with which Germany broke

4

the resistance of Norway, of the Low Countries, and finally of France in the terrible months of May and June, 1940. They deplored the abject surrender of the newly formed Pétain government, just as they applauded the gallant appeal of the obscure Brigadier General, Charles de Gaulle, who called on Frenchmen everywhere not to lay down their arms. But if this wave of sympathy for the collapse of a great power demonstrated an American sentiment which was pro-French and pro-British, it by no means meant that in 1940 Americans were prepared to abandon the comfortable neutrality which permitted them the luxury of outrage with few of the risks.

Since there was no question of armed intervention by the American people, official circles in Washington were soon required to decide whether there could be any advantage in breaking with the Pétain government. The policy makers did not question that the United States' interests would best be served by the ultimate defeat of Germany. If Germany seized the French fleet, they reasoned, she would be in a position to dominate the Mediterranean; if she controlled the Mediterranean, she could march into North Africa and effectively make use of Atlantic ports, and at Dakar she would possess a well-equipped base from which to exploit the northern coast of Brazil and the West Indies. If France collaborated closely, she might object neither to a German occupation of North Africa nor to German use of French possessions in the Western Hemisphere—Guadeloupe and Martinique in the French West Indies, French Guiana in South America, and Saint Pierre and Miquelon, the two tiny islands off the coast of Newfoundland. Under the terms of the armistice which Pétain and Hitler had concluded on June 22, 1940, the German occupation of North Africa could not take place because the French fleet, while immobilized, remained under French command. North Africa remained unoccupied and was to be permitted a token French force of about 150,000 men under regular French command.

Out of these considerations evolved the Vichy policy, whose adherents argued successfully that no material benefits would follow a break with Pétain. The policy involved two basic elements: support of the Pétain regime in helping to prevent further German incursions and protection of American interests vis-à-vis French possessions which were situated so as to affect the defense of the United States. A case could be made for Pétain, aged and defeatist though he was, as defender of French integrity; and it could even be argued (as no less a person than De Gaulle admitted) that Admiral Darlan, as minister of marine in the French cabinet, would never willingly relinquish the French Navy to the Germans. But when, in the summer of 1940, Pierre Laval obtained the portfolio of foreign affairs, no one could with assurance guarantee that France would avoid a policy of the most abject collaboration.

By the end of 1940, however, it appeared to President Roosevelt and to Secretary of State Cordell Hull that Vichy policy was proving itself to be quite justifiable; an outward demonstration of support in the appointment of an ambassador seemed appropriate. The choice finally fell on Admiral William D. Leahy, some of whose limitations in political experience were offset by his unquestioned loyalty to the President. The President did not ask the Admiral to seek among the grass roots of France to determine whether the Pétain government represented the elements with which the United States should maintain contact. He was not asked to cultivate Free Masons, Jews, Socialists, or Communists; he was told to maintain close relations with Marshal Pétain, to associate with high officers in the French Navy, and to persaude them that collaboration or German use of the French fleet was inimical to their own interests and might forfeit the good will of the United States.[1] In the eighteen months that Leahy remained at Vichy, he endeavored to carry out the President's wishes. His task was simplified by the fact that many Frenchmen could see, without too much American persuasion, that minimum co-operation and preservation of the fleet was to France's interest. The result was that instead of Leahy's persuading the French, it was the French who persuaded Leahy that some resistance to the Germans existed within the framework of the Vichy government. This was true, but Leahy was in no position to judge the extent, the nature, or the value of the resistance as compared to other types of clandestine activity. Thus he came away from France with the conviction that important seeds of resistance existed within the structure of the Pétain administration and that there was no need for an exterior, "illegal" resistance such as De Gaulle had established in London. Had Admiral

[1] William D. Leahy, *I Was There*, 443–46.

Leahy, when he was recalled from Vichy in April, 1942, retired from active service, his reactions and attitudes would signify little in the history of Franco-American relations; but, in 1942, Leahy came to be President Roosevelt's military attaché and close adviser, a member of the inner White House entourage, and the President's personal representative at meetings of the United States Joint Chiefs of Staff and of the Anglo-American Combined Chiefs of Staff. Leahy's inflexible and conservative temperament produced in him a disinclination to alter his opinions readily, and in 1943 and 1944 he would tend to assume that conditions in France remained as they had been when he was there in 1941. This lag in current intelligence would cause him to argue that De Gaulle had no support in France at a time when the major underground networks had clearly demonstrated their willingness to affiliate with Fighting France.

The second fundamental ingredient of American policy toward the Vichy regime involved the prevention of potential Nazi use of French possessions as bases for operations against the United States. American planners were particularly concerned about Dakar, the port nearest South America on the bulge of French West Africa, and the islands of Martinique and Guadeloupe in the West Indies. Dakar could provide an important base for amphibious operations, while submarines could refuel and rearm at Martinique and perhaps obtain possession of the $245,000,000 worth of gold bullion which had been shipped there from France. It must be noted that none of the areas in the New World had rallied spontaneously to the Free French. Undoubtedly, if the United States had intervened in De Gaulle's favor, the West Indies, French Guiana, and Saint Pierre–Miquelon would have accepted Gaullist representatives, since many of the inhabitants of the French possessions disliked the Vichy regime. But Washington had already committed itself to a different tack, preferring the safety of the *status quo* to the uncertainties and dangers of a radical shift in political orientation.

An important arrangement was therefore worked out with Admiral Robert, the highest-ranking French officer in the Western Hemisphere, who by his command over a small fleet based on Martinique represented Vichy's authority in the western Atlantic. Two visits by Rear Admiral John W. Greenslade in August and November, 1940, persuaded Robert, with the approval of Vichy, that he should immobilize his ships and accept an American naval observer in exchange for promises of economic support.[2]

While the arrangements with Admiral Robert seemed to safeguard American defenses in the Caribbean, they did nothing to offset the danger of a Nazi penetration into North and West Africa. These areas differed from Martinique in that they were not susceptible to an American occupation, and therefore some other means of pressure had to be sought. This became particularly important after the failure of the Gaullist-British expedition against Dakar in September, 1940, because it was then unmistakably clear that the British had not the force to mount an amphibious operation in Africa and that De Gaulle lacked the popular backing there to effect a voluntary rallying of the population. Out of the arguments over means of safeguarding North Africa, two main theories emerged. One, generally supported in England and later by the American Board of Economic Warfare, urged a boycott and blockade of North Africa; the other, of which the State Department was largely the architect, envisaged the shipment of goods to North Africa with the idea of developing French good will toward America and of bolstering the determination of the inhabitants to resist. It was felt that General Maxime Weygand, who since September 9, 1940, had held the post of delegate general in North Africa, would be sympathetic to American overtures and would predispose civilians and troops in French possessions to resist a German invasion and even to provide the spearhead for a counterattack against the Axis.

The mission to Weygand was entrusted to tall, affable, forty-four-year-old Robert D. Murphy, a career diplomat who as counselor at the American Embassy in Paris had witnessed the ordeals of the Popular Front, the collapse of the Reynaud government, and the rise of Pétain to power. After two visits to North Africa, Murphy came to an agreement with Weygand on February 26, 1941, whereby the United States contracted to send to North Africa economic assistance for which it would be paid out of blocked funds. To insure that the goods would not be reshipped and used by the Axis, the United States was to be permitted to appoint consuls in North Africa who would supervise the shipments.[3]

---

[2] Admiral Georges Robert, *La France aux Antilles de 1939 à 1943,* 79–85.

If the plan worked, North Africa should be able to achieve some measure of economic independence, which, it was hoped, would inspire General Weygand to build up his army against the day when it could fight once more against Germany. There were some who feared that Weygand was a slender reed upon which to lean as leader of French resistance. Not only had the British abandoned the attempt to lure Weygand into dissidence, but Murphy also reported to Washington that Weygand's loyalty to the Marshal was complete. The United States nevertheless chose to place the weight of its economic influence with the people who turned to Vichy for approval of the steps they took. Months would pass before the world could know where Frenchmen looked for leadership in the struggle for liberation—to the armistice army and its legitimate chiefs in North Africa or to the handful of men, led by General de Gaulle, with their headquarters in London, who called themselves the Free French.

The Free French

Out of the confusion and defeatism that reigned at Bordeaux during the dark days of France in June, 1940, there emerged one voice which virtually alone appealed to the government and to the French people to continue resistance overseas. At the time he flew from France to London on June 17, 1940, Charles de Gaulle was forty-nine years old and only recently promoted to the rank of brigadier general. He was well known in professional military circles as an expert on tanks and as an impassioned advocate of a warfare of movement, but he had never made an effort to play politics or to attract a popular following. His rapid rise during the invasion of France to the post of undersecretary of national defense had resulted from the patronage of the Premier, Paul Reynaud, who was an admirer of De Gaulle's concepts of strategy and armament, and not from public pressure. It would be difficult to imagine a person more poorly equipped to catch the popular imagination. Serious, reserved, an awkward public speaker, lacking the human and personal grace—sometimes thought of as showmanship—which endears a political personality to his adherents, General de Gaulle was ill-cast for the

[3] William L. Langer, *Our Vichy Gamble,* 128–35; text in Appendix I, 399–400.

role destiny chose for him. But, if he lacked warmth and facility, he possessed other qualities which forced the French people to revive their faith in themselves and their leadership; his pride, his will to resist, and his courage contrasted vividly with the servility, the defeatism, and the malleability that had characterized so many prewar politicians.

At first De Gaulle thought of himself only as leading a military force, and his formal agreement with the British government signed on August 7, 1940, spoke simply of a French group of volunteers to be organized and employed against the common enemies. De Gaulle, as supreme commander, would accept the general directives of the British command. The only civilian groups envisaged in the agreement were "the administrative services necessary for the organization of his forces."

But as time wore on, it became clear that De Gaulle was destined to do more for France than represent her in a last-stand battle. No political or military personage with greater authority and prestige than De Gaulle arrived from France to supersede him as representative of the French will-to-resist. No well-known parliamentarian like Herriot, Lebrun, or Jeanneney, no former minister like Reynaud, Daladier, Blum, Paul-Boncour, or Mandel, no general officer like Weygand, Gamelin, or Georges saw fit to escape from France to take the responsibility for forming a government-in-exile; those who were abroad and available —Jean Monnet, René Mayer, and Pierre Cot—expressed sympathy but declined to associate themselves with De Gaulle's forces. De Gaulle was left, virtually by default, to continue alone as head of his movement in England.

Later in the summer of 1940, when parts of the French Empire began to rally to De Gaulle, he was forced to evolve even further from military to political thinking. Although in September the failure of an expedition against Dakar prevented any immediate thought of rallying French West Africa, other areas of the French Empire—the New Hebrides, Chad, French Equatorial Africa, the Cameroons, the Marquesas Islands, French India, and New Caledonia—rallied to the Free French before the end of the year. To De Gaulle it was clear that a central authority which would integrate the administration of these scattered possessions had to be proclaimed, that this authority must justify its right vis-à-vis Vichy, and that it must possess civilian and political as well as military attributes. When Pétain appeared to relinquish his independence by his conference with Hitler at Montoire, De Gaulle seized the occasion as justification of his publication on October 27, 1940, of the Brazzaville Manifesto, the basic charter of Free France. The most important parts are the following:

> France is undergoing the most terrible crisis of her history. Her frontiers, her empire, her independence and even her soul, are threatened by destruction. . . .
>
> Now, a truly French government no longer exists. In effect, the organism at Vichy, which assumes this name, is unconstitutional and subject to the invader. In its state of servitude, this organism cannot be, and is not other than an instrument used by the enemies of France against the honor and the interest of the country. It is thus necessary that a new power assume the charge of directing the French war effort. Events have imposed this sacred duty on me. I will not fail.
>
> I will exercise my powers in the name of France and solely to defend her and I make a solemn engagement to render an account of my acts to the representatives of the French people when it will be possible for them to judge freely.
>
> To help me in my task, I am establishing on this day a Council of Defense of the Empire. This Council, composed of men who already exercise authority over French territories or who symbolize the highest moral and intellectual values of the nation, represents the country and the empire which fight for their life. . . .

A few days later the Manifesto was amplified by a Declaration which, by describing Vichy's unconstitutional acts, further guaranteed that Free France was the true depository of French Republicanism. It pointed out that in spite of Vichy's attempts, the constitution remained legally in effect and that, "under these conditions, all Frenchmen, and especially all free Frenchmen, are released from all obligation toward the pseudo-government at Vichy."[4]

The consequences of the position De Gaulle had taken would be far reaching. The Free French refused from then on to consider themselves as a "movement" whose aim was simply to fight side by side with Great

[4] Charles de Gaulle, *L'appel*, vol. I of *Mémoires de guerre*, 303-16.

Britain against the Axis; they claimed to represent nothing less than France. The Brazzaville theory rendered an understanding with the United States quite difficult so long as Washington continued to recognize Vichy. If De Gaulle were to insist that he be accorded the rights and honors of a sovereign nation and if he refused to be treated only as the head of a military movement, he would place upon the United States the necessity of making an all-or-none decision. So long as the United States kept out of the war and had no need of special privileges in the territories De Gaulle controlled, the fine distinctions inherent in the Free French manifesto remained relatively unimportant. But the time was not far distant when American good will could be extremely valuable to the cause of Free France, and the pretensions to sovereignty made by De Gaulle ran badly afoul of President Roosevelt's favorite doctrine of postponing political decisions until after the war.

It should not be assumed that the United States alone felt that General de Gaulle's claims to represent France were unsubstantial. If De Gaulle by his unambiguous denunciation of Vichy was able to attract some groups, he nevertheless forfeited the support of many Frenchmen who were persuaded neither of Pétain's complete bankruptcy nor of De Gaulle's qualifications to replace him. Among his own followers, the chief of the Free French Navy, Admiral Muselier, believed De Gaulle's actions to be extreme and dictatorial. Many Frenchmen who were living outside of France and were therefore free to join the Free French were alienated by De Gaulle's vigorous hostility to Pétain, and they refused to associate themselves with the London group. Even in England, which had broken with Vichy and was faced with no alternative but to deal with De Gaulle's council, there was uneasiness before the implication that De Gaulle would be more disposed to protect what he considered French interests than to fight the war.

The first serious clash between De Gaulle and the British developed during the spring of 1941 in the Near East, during the joint invasion which ousted General Dentz, the Vichy high commissioner and commander in chief in Syria, and his troops from Syria and Lebanon. De Gaulle feared that French influence in the area would be destroyed by the British, who he believed would take credit for granting the former French mandates their independence. He was particularly furious because the British determined to maintain military control of the region. An agreement was ultimately reached whereby De Gaulle grudgingly conceded the supremacy of British command, with the understanding that the French would have control in administrative and political areas. De Gaulle's position was weakened, however, by his inability to recruit more than a few thousand of Dentz's forces to serve in the ranks of Fighting France. He was thus scarcely able to demand that the security of Syria be turned over completely to his charge. De Gaulle named as Delegate General to administer Free French interests in the Middle East, General Georges Catroux, former governor general in Indochina and an officer of wide colonial and administrative experience, who, although senior in rank to De Gaulle, had placed himself voluntarily under his orders. On September 27, 1941, Catroux published a Declaration of Syrian Independence, and it appeared that the delicate arrangements in Syria and Lebanon had reached a balance which would preclude further disagreements. But the balance would not be long maintained: national ferment in the two Levant states, held in check by inexperienced administrators, would in a matter of months bring even more serious strains between De Gaulle and the Allies.

When De Gaulle returned to London in September, 1941, his stature had altered vastly from what it had been when he sailed against Dakar a year previously. His stubborn and impetuous defense of Free French interests in Syria, his arbitrary and dictatorial mien, and his reported overtures for Russian and United States support had generated in Winston Churchill and the Foreign Office important doubts about their wisdom in committing themselves to De Gaulle as leader of the Free French. Sensitive to this criticism, De Gaulle concluded that the demands of world-wide administration justified the formation of a "government" comparable to those governments-in-exile of Poland and Czechoslovakia already residing in London. The French problem was unique, however, in that neither De Gaulle nor his principal associates could claim any popular mandate or any authority which was generally recognized in international law. On the other hand, De Gaulle had already negotiated specific agreements with Great Britain and was in fact administering areas more vast than those of any true government-in-exile. If legalists required some justification and precedent for the formation of the French

National Committee, they could find a parallel in the Czechoslovak National Committee of World War I, which had been accepted by Great Britain "as a trustee" of Czechoslovak interests. The Free French employed the same formula:

> Important colonial territories . . . have rallied to Free France. . . . This fact requires that General de Gaulle and Free French authorities exercise over these territories and their forces the powers of a government. But General de Gaulle has always solemnly proclaimed that he exercises these powers only in an essentially temporary capacity, as trustee [*gérant*] of the French patrimony, and that he submits in advance to a national representation whenever it can be freely brought together.[5]

On September 24, 1941, De Gaulle established the French National Committee, which would remain the central organ of his movement until June, 1943, when the seat of French external resistance shifted from London to Algiers. Ten commissioners, including René Pleven, Hervé Alphand, General Le Gentilhomme, Admiral Muselier, and André Diethelm, were appointed as chiefs of administrative departments roughly corresponding to cabinet distribution in the French government; but General de Gaulle retained in his own hands legislative authority as well as supreme command over Free French forces.

Establishment of the French National Committee created no flurry in Washington. Even though the negotiations with Tokyo rapidly flowed toward their crucial phase, the theories of peace and isolationism still reigned. Relations with Marshal Pétain and Admiral Robert continued to be cordial. Admiral Leahy remained at Vichy. However much the liberal press might laud the patriotic labors of General de Gaulle, official Washington had its reasons for remaining aloof.

Washington and De Gaulle

Long before the United States entered the war an informal Free French representation had developed in America, but the arrangements were so contradictory and changeable that they confused not only the

[5] De Gaulle to Pleven, 22 Sept. 1941 (in De Gaulle, *Mémoires*, I, 481–82).

State Department but the French community as well. Most Frenchmen in the United States, although they regarded Vichy with suspicion, were slow to lose faith in Pétain and slower still to place their trust in De Gaulle. In 1940 a Gaullist organization, France Forever, had been founded in New York by Eugène Gentil, Henry d'Ornano, and Eugène Houdry, and while the Vichy regime foundered into collaboration, France Forever spread throughout the United States and before the end of the war had established fifty-two chapters. A French-language newspaper, *Pour la Victoire,* edited by the celebrated journalist Geneviève Tabouis and former Deputy Henri de Kerillis, although not an organ of France Forever, tended toward pro-Gaullist sympathies until the end of 1942. But the majority of well-known and influential Frenchmen living in America, including Jules Romains, Henry Bernstein, Alexis Léger, Jacques Maritain, Pierre Cot, Pierre Mendès-France, Raoul de Roussy de Sales, and many others, preferred to guard their independence and were extremely wary of publicly affiliating themselves with the Gaullists. The American public was witness to countless disagreements among the *émigrés,* who carried their argumentative individualism to extremes in their internecine disputes over the proper attitude to assume in regard to the struggle against Germany. French opinion extended all the way from the collaboration of the actual Vichy representatives, such as Ambassador Henry-Haye, through the various shades of independent thinking to the belligerency of the ardent Gaullists in France Forever.

Into this welter of attitudes De Gaulle failed in 1940 to inject any positive leadership which would channel French opinion in favor of Free France. He was officially represented in the United States only by a former Embassy secretary, Jacques de Siéyès, who had broken his allegiance to Pétain after the fall of France. Another diplomat who resigned from the Embassy, Maurice Garreau-Dombasles, was also designated by De Gaulle as his "delegate" in the United States; but lacking clearcut authorization and an official status at the State Department, neither Siéyès nor Garreau-Dombasles was able to represent the Free French in ways that would promote the interests of the movement.

After the United States had demonstrated its determination to help the belligerent nations by its passage, in March, 1941, of the Lend-Lease

Act, De Gaulle reached the long-postponed conclusion that his representation in America must be established on a firmer basis. To accomplish this, he sent to Washington one of his earliest and most trusted adherents, René Pleven, a young, pliable, and persuasive businessman who had worked closely with Jean Monnet on the Anglo-French Coordinating Committee in 1940. When he arrived in Washington in June, Pleven found a great deal more antagonism to the Free French than he had imagined possible. Although he succeeded in seeing Harry Hopkins, Morgenthau, Stimson, and Henry Wallace, he never was able to obtain an interview with either Hull or the President, both of whom seemed to be motivated in their refusals by a personal objection to Pleven as an envoy. When Pleven argued with Undersecretary of State Sumner Welles on October 1 for a Lend-Lease agreement, he was coldly informed that Lend-Lease arrangements would be difficult because such contracts were made only with governments and a direct delivery of supplies to the Free French would be tantamount to recognition. Welles declared that the matter was under study, but he gave Pleven no reason to become sanguine about early recognition.[6]

Before long, however, the United States did agree to include the Free French in Lend-Lease allocations. On November 11, 1941, Roosevelt wrote to Lend-Lease Administrator Stettinius:

> In order for you to arrange for Lend-Lease aid to the French Volunteer Forces (Free French) by way of re-transfer from His Majesty's Government . . . I hereby find that the defense of any French territory under control of the Free French is vital to the defense of the United States.[7]

The State Department also agreed to accept the credentials of a Free French representative in Washington, even though the United States was unwilling to reciprocate by accrediting an American diplomat to the Free French. De Gaulle appointed Adrien Tixier, director of the International Labor Bureau, whose reputation as a labor leader in France

---

[6] De Gaulle, *Mémoires*, I, 182–83, 471–85; Raoul de Roussy de Sales, *L'Amérique entre en guerre*, 202, 210; William L. Langer and S. Everett Gleason, *The Undeclared War*, 509, 581–82.

[7] L. M. Goodrich and M. J. Carroll, eds., *Documents on American Foreign Relations*, IV, 178, 1n.

and whose unquestioned patriotism (he had been wounded in World War I) would tend to allay suspicions in the United States that De Gaulle was opposed to democratic ideals.

Shortly after Pearl Harbor, relations with the Free French took a new and unexpected turn over the Saint Pierre–Miquelon incident. Saint Pierre and Miquelon are two small French islands off the coast of Newfoundland, inhabited by a small population of rugged fishermen. The islands possessed no strategic importance except for a radio transmitter which, by sending weather reports to Vichy France, might be helping U-boats in the Atlantic. There was no reason why these islands should not be rallied to De Gaulle, for there was good evidence that the inhabitants, if free from Admiral Robert's administrative control, would gladly shift to the Free French; but Great Britain and Canada were unwilling for De Gaulle to take this step unless the United States concurred. Negotiations among the powers failed to convince Washington that De Gaulle's intervention was necessary, and by early December arrangements had been reached whereby Admiral Robert would permit Canada to proctor the transmissions. On December 13, Roosevelt assured Pétain that the United States had no intention of abrogating the Havana Convention of 1940, which guaranteed maintenance of the *status quo* in the Western Hemisphere. Meanwhile, the Free French naval chief, Admiral Muselier, who had under his command three corvettes and the submarine *Surcouf* in the vicinity of the islands, stood ready to carry out the landing; but first, through inquiries at Ottawa, he attempted to make sure of Allied approval. When he learned that Washington was thoroughly opposed to the project, he notified Free French headquarters to that effect. De Gaulle, ascertaining finally and definitely on December 17 that Washington would not consent, agreed that the Free French would take no further action.

Six days later, on Christmas Eve, Hull learned to his astonishment that Muselier had rallied the islands. If there was any one thing the venerable, sharp-spoken Secretary of State despised, it was failure to abide by a given word, and this clear-cut sample of De Gaulle's lack of trustworthiness seemed not only to corroborate what he had heard about Free French underhandedness, but convinced him that the Gaullists should be completely eliminated from future consideration. Hull's fury over the incident departed completely from the limits of reason; he stormed at Roosevelt and at Churchill, who had come to Washington shortly before Christmas for the "Arcadia" Conference; and he issued a denunciatory note about the "so-called Free French," a note which provoked so much sympathy for De Gaulle that it left an impression contrary to what Hull anticipated—all of which did nothing to reduce the Secretary's peevishness.

De Gaulle's motives were the same as those which drove him to defy the British in Syria: he feared the slightest encroachment of foreign influence in territories the integrity of which he had sworn to protect. He had an intense, fanatical jealousy concerning French sovereignty, which left him completely unreasonable in the face of foreign, even though Allied, interventions. Although in his memoirs De Gaulle refers to the incident as "almost infinitesimal in itself," he adds wryly, "Perhaps, for my part, I did provoke it to stir things up, as when you throw a stone into a pond."[8] He justifies his action by affirming that the Foreign Office notified him that Canada, "in agreement with the United States if not at their instigation," had decided to land a force on Saint Pierre. It was this information that ended De Gaulle's hesitation and impelled him, without consulting the National Committee, to order Muselier to act.

Although Churchill deprecated the importance of the move and Roosevelt was disinclined to make an issue over what he referred to as a "teapot tempest," Hull would never rid himself of the sensation of distrust he felt thereafter for De Gaulle. Even though the incident was smoothed over, Hull almost resigned in the course of the negotiations. During the discussions which Roosevelt and Churchill held between December 22 and January 14, 1942, at Washington (the "Arcadia" Conference), Hull proved himself pettish to a degree which first amused but finally irritated the President, who saw that his Secretary of State had lost his sense of proportion to the point of nearly producing a rupture

---

[8] De Gaulle, *Mémoires*, I, 184. Compare this with the comment of Daniel Barlone, a Gaullist stationed at Free French headquarters, in a diary entry dated 26 Dec. 1941: "De Gaulle suspected the existence of an understanding in regard to our Atlantic possessions between the United States and Vichy. . . . It was therefore decided to throw a stone into the frog-pond. If the frogs croaked, he thought, it would be because an agreement had been made. . . . And how the frogs croaked!" (*La route des sommets*, 47.)

between himself and the Prime Minister over a relatively minor problem. Thereafter Roosevelt became more and more inclined to eliminate Hull from top-level discussions when French matters were raised. He came to consider the State Department's Robert Murphy as his own personal emissary in North Africa, and he tended to handle French political matters through the Joint Chiefs of Staff. He even refused to permit Hull to attend the Casablanca Conference, where French questions were thoroughly aired. While the responsibility for the Saint Pierre–Miquelon incident is indisputably De Gaulle's, Hull, by his uncontrolled irritation and irascibility, contributed to the cross-purposes and overlapping which were to characterize American policy toward the French.

After Pearl Harbor: Policy toward Vichy

The entry of the United States into the war obviously altered the framework of relations both with Vichy and with the Free French. Whereas up until Pearl Harbor the American public had made no vociferous denunciations of the Vichy policy nor any impressive demonstrations on behalf of De Gaulle, there gradually began to develop among civic leaders the disturbing impression that continued recognition of Pétain and refusal to recognize De Gaulle implied that the United States condoned Fascism and totalitarianism and rejected the friends who had been battling against Hitler and the Axis since the earliest days of the war. Leahy had long since become repelled by Pétain's spinelessness and was fully in accord with the policy that brought about his recall shortly after Laval returned to Vichy in April, 1942.

It appeared that Washington was on the verge of breaking finally with Pétain's discredited regime and was ready to embark on a new course vis-à-vis the French. The State Department, however, continued to support the Vichy policy by arguing that the advantages of maintaining American agents in North Africa and the building of pro-American good will among the inhabitants more than overbalanced the aid to the enemy which might have trickled to the Axis from American shipments. These arguments, which finally prevailed, were supported by the War Department and by Admiral Leahy, who in July, 1942, had returned to Washington to become the President's chief of staff and personal representative to the Joint Chiefs of Staff. They knew that plans were going ahead for an amphibious operation in North Africa which required co-operation from American and French agents, who for a long time had planned for this eventuality.

The State Department and the War Department nursed another reasonable justification for not breaking with Vichy. Although no great effort was made after Leahy's return to reiterate the old argument about bolstering weak-kneed Vichyites and keeping the fleet out of German hands, there were nevertheless several advantages in maintaining the contact. An Axis occupation of Dakar and Martinique still provided the most important potential danger to the United States. As long as those areas remained neutral the United States had nothing to fear; but a severance of relations with Vichy, now that Laval was in power, might have opened the way for unobstructed German penetration of those strategic points.

As it was, the War and State Departments were in the process of successfully renegotiating an agreement with Admiral Robert at Martinique. There were those, like Secretary of the Navy Knox, who wanted to occupy Martinique and Guadeloupe and others who would have turned them over to De Gaulle, but in the end, the advocates of a negotiated neutrality prevailed. Out of the discussions emerged a compromise policy, which, like many compromises, possessed contradictions within itself that would make it occasionally difficult to justify. In territories such as Martinique, where American armed strength could be brought to bear and Vichy's could not, the United States would negotiate directly with the local authority for an arrangement which would be favorable both to the United States and to the Governor. The policy had advantages: it would permit negotiations with Vichy or Gaullist representatives, depending on which held the power, without any commitments to support either Pétain or De Gaulle; it would make possible a continuing arrangement in case France fell completely under German control; and it would carry no guarantee to a central French authority that the United States after the war would support a return of all French possessions to the *status quo ante bellum*. On the other hand, this policy of local arrangements was so contrary to French thinking and usage that it could never satisfy or be understood by French authorities. France and the French Empire were administratively centralized and integrated to a degree that no local official could conceive of functioning without obtaining his powers from higher authority. When the United States attempted to implement the policy by negotiating with Admiral Robert, the Admiral continually referred to Vichy and negotiated in accordance with the instructions he received. The policy may have served as a face-saving device for the United States, but it did not persuade local French authorities to alter their habitual orientation. It was curious to find how, in December, 1942, after the deal with Darlan, American officials from the President down justified the need for this arrangement in terms of the French insistence on a chain of authority from a central power. It appeared that the experts in the State Department knew a great deal about the French official mind late in 1942 but had not yet learned these elemental facts a few months earlier when the policy of local arrangements had been formulated.

In regard to Martinique, the "local arrangements" negotiations were started by Admiral John H. Hoover during a visit on May 9, 1942, and were continued by a State Department representative, Samuel Reber. The negotiations were carried on during the next six months while preparations for the North African invasion were being made, and they were not terminated until after the landings. The United States then broke relations with Vichy; and since Robert would not consider himself authorized to sign, the settlement was transformed into a gentlemen's agreement which Robert, although he continued to report to Vichy, nevertheless kept faithfully until he was ousted several months later. The agreement immobilized Robert's ships and planes by transferring vital parts to Casablanca; in return, the United States guaranteed to respect French sovereignty in the West Indies and in Guiana, to unblock French funds, and to permit the shipment of supplies to the islands.

Another reason for the United States' preservation of contacts with Vichy was military: intelligence information was being made available to the Allies by the co-operation of French agents. Secretary Hull and others used this argument to justify the policy, but because of its secret aspects no one was (or is) in a position to evaluate the importance of the information obtained. Even Professor William L. Langer, in his discussion of underground contacts in *Our Vichy Gamble,* covers the question with brevity and presents no concrete evidence of the value of these associations.[9] Pro-Gaullist journalists tended to ridicule this argument by insinuating that Vichy (and Germany) was able to propagandize by means of these contacts to an extent which more than overbalanced the value of information received. There was, however, good reason in 1941 and 1942 for American military and diplomatic officials to believe in the importance of the information they were obtaining. The American military attaché at Vichy, Colonel Robert Schow, and the Naval attaché, Thomas G. Cassady (of the OSS), had intimate contacts with members of the French *Deuxième Bureau,* which, in spite of the fact that the Germans had disbanded it, continued to operate a clandestine service behind the façade of a *Société d'Entreprises des Travaux Ruraux* (TR). The *Société* was approved by Weygand and administered by Colonel Perruche and Commandant Paillole. It was Paillole, an experienced and capable intelligence officer, along with Colonel Baril, who maintained the principal contacts with Schow.

These contacts permitted the British and Americans to learn of plans under discussion in 1941 and 1942 for the French Army to co-operate with an Allied landing in France. Whether or not the Armistice Army could have helped the Allies effectively in 1942, many officers in the State Department and in the army, who were aware of the contacts, believed that the French military resistance provided a valuable and effective potential ally, that French intelligence and counterespionage were bringing in important data, and that the good faith of the Frenchmen involved was beyond question. Although the OSS had accurate information about the strength of Gaullist resistance movements in France, many American (and British) officers felt sure that the relations with the professional military men would be more valuable than contacts with De Gaulle's essentially civilian agents. As time went on, especially after the Germans occupied all of France and the Resistance became more thoroughly Gaullist, this opinion would have to be revised; but in 1942 it provided a justification for the maintenance of contacts with Vichy.

[9] *Our Vichy Gamble,* 172–73. Cf. *The Memoirs of Cordell Hull,* II, 1192.

After Pearl Harbor: Policy toward De Gaulle

If United States policy had to be reconsidered early in 1942, so, at about the same time, but for different reasons, did De Gaulle recognize the necessity of reorienting the policy of the Free French. Up until this time De Gaulle had struggled largely to rally elements of the French Empire, to build up his armed forces, and to protect the sovereignty of French territory. Although the Free French maintained clandestine relations with France, during 1940 and 1941 these contacts had been secondary to De Gaulle's main efforts. But after the beginning of 1942, De Gaulle became more conscious of the anti-Pétainist resistance movements that were springing up in France, and he gradually came to wonder whether the future strength of his movement could be built on support in France rather than on aid from England and America.

De Gaulle's changed outlook could not have come easily to him. Brought up in an extremely conservative environment, trained to think in military terms, and despising the hurly-burly of partisan politics, De Gaulle was by nature inclined to an authoritarian, apolitical attitude not dissimilar to that of Marshal Pétain and of General Giraud, whose rival he was to become. Yet De Gaulle, unlike Pétain and Giraud, was intelligent and flexible enough to comprehend that if a political evolution was necessary to achieve the liberation of France, he must educate himself in the direction required.

What convinced De Gaulle of the need for this reorientation was the rising strength of resistance movements throughout France. These movements were not, like the ones previously described, made up of patriotic elements within the French Army who believed they were carrying out the Marshal's secret wishes; they were essentially civilian, leftist organizations that despised Pétain and his Fascist authoritarianism.

After the beginning of 1942, contacts between De Gaulle's headquarters and metropolitan France became increasingly frequent. Perhaps more than anyone else, Jean Moulin, former prefect of Eure-et-Loir, who conferred with De Gaulle in December, 1941, persuaded the General that he must attempt to capture the support of a united resistance. Before he was arrested and executed by the Gestapo, Moulin almost achieved his objective in France—to which he had returned in January,

23

1942—of unifying the various movements, particularly in the South, and of aligning them behind De Gaulle.

The backing of Free France by the Resistance resulted in some significant changes, one of which was an increasing influence of civilians in the National Committee. Admiral Muselier had been eliminated from control of the Free French Navy in March, 1942, after a severe crisis during which Muselier, with some British sympathy, had attempted to obtain control of the Committee. With Muselier gone, the civilians moved into the ascendant aided by the influence of two gifted individuals who joined the Committee in 1942: Jacques Soustelle, a young, brilliant ethnologist who for a while had represented De Gaulle in Mexico and had been instrumental in obtaining a powerful Free French transmitter which was installed at Brazzaville, was called to London to take over the Commissariat of Information; in July, André Philip came out of France to accept the post of commissioner of interior and labor. A socialist, Philip had been on the executive committee of a clandestine union associated with the resistance group *Libération* and had come to London with the sanction of Léon Blum and Félix Gouin as a representative of the Socialist party, which had declared for De Gaulle on June 15. Philip was thus the first bona fide member of the metropolitan Resistance to hold a seat on the French National Committee, and he typified the direction in which Free France was moving. Although his excitability and his nervous enthusiasm and occasionally uncouth mannerisms impaired Philip's efficiency as an administrator, De Gaulle hoped that his joining the Committee would improve its status in France and its relations with the Allies. On the Committee, Soustelle and Philip, together with André Diethelm and René Pleven, provided a bloc which consistently argued for the need of standing by political ideals and not bowing to military exigency. Their detractors occasionally suggested that their political ambition motivated them somewhat more than their ideals.

If the Committee was becoming dominated by civilians, this did not mean that its military enterprises had lost significance. It was in June, 1942, that General Koenig's small band of volunteers, operating in conjunction with British forces in Libia, put up such a stubborn and brilliant defense against the Germans at Bir Hacheim that, although they had to withdraw, they knew they had convinced themselves and the world that Frenchmen could stand up to Hitler's *Wehrmacht*. This demonstration of combativeness, together with wide support of the Resistance in France, led to the movement's assuming a new title, *La France Combattante*, or Fighting France. As the men of the Resistance were not "free" in the sense of belonging to a group outside France, the change made clear, to those who cared to investigate, the altered nature of the movement.

De Gaulle's relations with America possessed great possibilities for improvement in 1942. As Washington shied away from Vichy and as the Resistance came over to the Free French, the way could have been opened for a real *rapprochement*. Early in the year the disagreeable turmoil over Saint Pierre–Miquelon had subsided as a result of Hull's reluctant consent to let the matter rest, and difficulties in New Caledonia had been smoothed over. Friction had developed in New Caledonia when the Gaullists feared that General Patch intended to occupy the island instead of working with the Free French authorities, but although a native insurrection for a while placed the French in a very delicate situation, the affair was resolved satisfactorily. On February 28, 1942, the United States made a declaration in regard to the situation in New Caledonia, which by its terms gave more recognition to the Free French than any previous American pronouncement. The statement said that the United States recognized that island possessions in the Pacific "are under the effective control of the French National Committee established in London" and went on to affirm that the United States would cooperate "with no other French authority."[10] It would have appeared, with this step, that the time was propitious for De Gaulle to push his advantage in Washington.

At the American capital, however, Gaullist stock was not high. Particularly in the State Department, not only Secretary Hull, but also his counselors on policy, Adolf Berle, James Dunn, and Raymond Atherton, as well as Undersecretary Welles, had not yet become convinced that Gaullism was widely accepted in France. One reason for this attitude

[10] Goodrich and Carroll, eds., *Documents on American Foreign Relations*, IV, 634. The United States also recognized the Free French "effective control" of French Equatorial Africa on 4 Apr. 1942 (*ibid.*, 634–35).

could be found in the fact that the official Free French representative in Washington, Adrien Tixier, had been unable to attract to Free France several distinguished Frenchmen who were well known to State Department officials. One such Frenchman was Camille Chautemps, the former French premier, who had been a member of the first Pétain cabinet until he was ousted by Laval late in 1940. Chautemps made his way to the United States and, still on the Vichy payroll, acted in Washington as a personal and unofficial representative of Pétain. Another distinguished statesman in the American capital was Alexis Léger, for a long time secretary-general at the Quai d'Orsay, who had been removed from office by Reynaud in 1940. Léger had found employment as a consultant at the Library of Congress in Washington and continued to be received in diplomatic circles, where he had many acquaintances. Since both these men were far more experienced and well known than De Gaulle and were generally held in respect, their opinions on French matters carried considerable weight. Both expressed admiration for De Gaulle, but neither had become associated with his movement. Some elements in the State Department felt that if Chautemps, Léger, Pierre Cot, a former French air minister also in the United States, or Jacques Maritain, the distinguished French philosopher, would work together, it might be possible to form a French organization that Washington could recognize.

Opposed to these influences, Tixier was handicapped not only because of confusion between himself and Étienne Boegner, son of the president of Protestant churches in France, over control of the Free French delegation, but because he had severe doubts concerning the depth of De Gaulle's republican convictions. Both he and Boegner went to London in the spring of 1942, and neither was reassured by the cross-purposes and antagonisms that they found within the movement. Boegner was subjected to one of De Gaulle's nationalistic tantrums. He told De Roussy de Sales later that De Gaulle seemed like "a phenomenon of patriotism which, whenever you touch on anything French, electrocutes you instantly with a violent discharge."[11] Reports on these differences and misunderstandings were sent regularly to Washington, which also recorded the hostile comments of General Odic of the French Air

[11] De Roussy de Sales, *L'Amérique entre en guerre*, 269.

Force, who, having come to London to join the Free French, could not reach terms with De Gaulle about the nature of his employment. In this untoward situation De Gaulle decided to send someone to the United States who could persuade Tixier that French labor groups were sincerely behind the National Committee and who might persuade Léger to accept the portfolio of foreign affairs of the French Committee.

The man he chose for this mission was Emmanuel d'Astier de la Vigerie, a leader of the Resistance, who, having come secretly to London in May, was dispatched to Washington in June. Although he was unable to bring Léger into the Free French movement, D'Astier did do much to assuage Tixier's doubts. In the State Department he encountered hostility in Adolf Berle, but with Welles and others he succeeded in working out a *modus vivendi* to permit closer liaison between the French Committee and American representatives.[12] Since the United States wished to avoid all impressions that the Committee was given political representation, it was considered undesirable to operate through the Embassy in London; but no objection was seen to using American military personnel to effect a permanent relationship with the Gaullists. Out of D'Astier's discussions finally came the appointment, on July 9, of Brigadier General C. L. Bolté, Eisenhower's assistant chief of staff, and Admiral Harold Stark, commander of naval forces in Europe, as representatives to consult with the French Committee on all matters relating to the conduct of the war. Stark's capable aide, Lieutenant Commander Tracy B. Kittredge, whose long residence in France gave him an extensive knowledge of French matters, kept important records and memoranda of American dealings with De Gaulle in the course of the following year.

Although D'Astier saw Justice Frankfurter and Harry Hopkins while he was in Washington, he was unable to see the President, who anticipated the arrival of Churchill in several days. Since Churchill's visit would throw open the question of military operations in 1942 and 1943, both D'Astier's and Churchill's stay in Washington may have been instrumental in Roosevelt's expressing a wish, late in June, to have De

---

[12] Emmanuel d'Astier de la Vigerie, *Sept fois sept jours*, 81–85; D'Astier, *Les dieux et les hommes*, 29–30; De Gaulle, *Mémoires*, I, 237; *Journal Officiel, Débats* (1946), III, 2623; interview with D'Astier.

Gaulle come to Washington.[13] He was dissuaded by the British, who, although they complained continually about De Gaulle's actions, never seemed eager to permit him to develop close, personal relations with high-ranking Americans. It is possible that Churchill and Eden, much as they distrusted De Gaulle, preferred to keep him under observation in London rather than permit him to wander into the Russian or the American fold. Since no commitments had at this time been made to General Giraud, one can only speculate whether or not De Gaulle, if he had seen Roosevelt, could have promoted a sympathetic understanding between himself and the President.

With De Gaulle in the Near East during August and September, no new problems developed between the United States and Fighting France, and on the surface matters seemed to be progressing satisfactorily. The Bolté-Stark mission had been established, negotiations for mutual aid were successfully terminated in September, and on October 6 the President authorized direct Lend-Lease aid to the Fighting French. In September long discussions took place in London between Resistance leaders who had recently come from France and Americans representing Stark, Bolté, and the OSS. The OSS Planning Group was convinced of the value of De Gaulle's connections in France and recommended co-operation.[14] But the OSS seems not at this time to have had the influence in Washington to counter top-level decisions made by Roosevelt and the Joint Chiefs of Staff, and perhaps the reports never came to the attention of anyone high enough in the administration to permit significant action to be taken.

De Gaulle could not definitely know (although he suspected) that in September the final arrangements were being made to invade North Africa. De Gaulle possessed a fairly accurate idea of Allied plans by the end of August,[15] but he was uncertain about such details as President Roosevelt's authorization to introduce General Giraud into the operation with the idea of rallying Vichy's North African army. In any event, De Gaulle determined to make another personal appeal to the President. He sent him a long letter dated October 26, 1942, this time

[13] Hull, *Memoirs*, II, 1162.
[14] Langer, *Our Vichy Gamble*, 296–300.
[15] Dejean to De Gaulle, 16 Aug. 1942 (De Gaulle, *Mémoires*, II, 355); De Gaulle to Pleven and Dejean, 27 Aug. 1942 (*ibid.*, 360–61).

by the hand of André Philip, who, like D'Astier, would demonstrate the solidarity of the Resistance behind the London Committee. Since this letter set forth De Gaulle's position effectively and may have influenced the President's attitude, its more important passages are worth a careful reading:

> . . . I did what seemed necessary to keep France from abandoning the struggle and to appeal to all Frenchmen inside and outside of France to continue the fight. Is this to say that my companions and I posed at any moment as the Government of France? By no means. On the contrary, we have considered ourselves and proclaimed ourselves to be an essentially provisional authority, responsible to a future national representative body, and applying the laws of the Third Republic. . . .
>
> We are told that we should not play politics. . . . We do not recoil from the word "political" if it concerns rallying not simply a few troops but the whole French nation in the war; or if it means discussing French interests with our Allies at the same time that we defend them for France against the enemy. After all, who besides ourselves can represent these interests? . . .
>
> . . . Without asking to be recognized as the Government of France, we believe we should be approached each time there is a question of France's general interests; or of French participation in the war; or of the administration of French territories which the war's progress gradually brings into a position to rejoin the fight, yet which have not yet been able to rally to us spontaneously. . . .
>
> I am told that members of your entourage fear that in recognizing our existence you will compromise the possibility that certain elements, mostly military, who are now attached to the Vichy Government, may soon re-enter the war. But, do you believe that you should ignore the French who do fight, letting them become discouraged in isolation, so that you can draw others into the struggle? On the other hand, what danger for France could compare to the fact that the Allies might provoke her own division by favoring the formation of several rival groups, the one neutralized by an agreement of the Allies themselves, the others fighting separately for the same Fatherland! . . .
>
> . . . All this is why I ask you to accept the idea of a general and direct examination of the relations between the United States and Fighting France.[16]

[16] De Gaulle to Roosevelt, 26 Oct. 1942 (*ibid.*, 381–85).

Although De Gaulle's letter represented a straightforward appraisal of his position, it was not entirely calculated to assuage the President's doubts about him. Roosevelt never concluded that De Gaulle could be trusted, and the mere promise that De Gaulle made and repeated many times—that he had no intention of claiming the authority of a French government—did not convince the President or his advisers.

Preparations for "Torch"

At the same time that De Gaulle's special emissaries, D'Astier and Philip, were attempting to persuade the Americans that they should back De Gaulle, Roosevelt and Churchill were working out plans for the next offensive with little regard for Fighting French interests. With his preference for a flank attack, Churchill had long been uneasy about the tentative decision made in April, 1942, to invade France from across the channel, and in June he reopened the question of a North African operation in discussions with Roosevelt and the Joint Chiefs in Washington. As a result, the thinking turned to a project for which Roosevelt had long nurtured a predilection: an attack in Tunisia and Algeria sometime before the end of 1942. A month later, Harry Hopkins, General Marshall, and Admiral King, in London for further deliberations, reached an agreement with Churchill to embark on the North African operation, now known by the code-name "Torch." The decision was made on July 25, just sixteen days after Admiral Stark and General Bolté had been authorized to deal directly with De Gaulle and two days after De Gaulle had engaged in long conversations with Eisenhower, Marshall, and King. General Eisenhower, designated commander of the operation, shortly set up his headquarters in London.

In carrying out an invasion of North Africa, the Allies were confronted with a unique situation in that the country could not be considered conclusively either friend or enemy. As long as French commanders remained loyal to Vichy, they were bound to resist any attack on North Africa, whether German, British, or American. Many of them detested the British and had no love for Americans. Few were pro-German, but many admired the regimentation and discipline that had been imposed as a result of Pétain's "national revolution." Nevertheless, in the two years that Americans had ranged about in North and West Africa as a consequence of the Murphy-Weygand agreement, an impressive amount of evidence had come to hand which suggested that a landing could be achieved with no more than token resistance. This evidence had been accumulated by Lieutenant Colonel Solborg, representing the Co-ordinator of Information (later the OSS), Lieutenant Colonel Eddy (U.S.M.C.) of Naval Intelligence, and Robert Murphy in his capacity of chargé d'affaires at Algiers and supervisor of the consuls sent to North Africa to watch over the program of economic aid. Solborg, Eddy, and Murphy had made a wide variety of contacts with influential army officers, administrators, and civilians, many of whom enthusiastically favored any American project that would promote a re-entry of North Africa into the war. Of the civilians, one of the most significant, because of his ability to travel unrestrictedly between North Africa and France, was a French capitalist, Jacques Lemaigre-Dubreuil, president of one of the leading French vegetable-oil firms, *Huiles Lesueur*.

Nothing in Lemaigre-Dubreuil's career suggested any leanings except toward the conservative right, and it was not surprising that after France's defeat he should have maintained close contacts with Laval and Hitler's representative, Otto Abetz, and with members of Pétain's entourage: Pierre Pucheu, minister of the interior who was later executed for collaboration, and Jacques Barnaud, in charge of Franco-German economic relations. To permit supervision of his vegetable-oil projects in North Africa, Lemaigre-Dubreuil had obtained a passport which enabled him to move back and forth without interference between Africa and France.

While he continued to cultivate his interests simultaneously at Vichy and at Algiers, Lemaigre-Dubreuil did his best to influence Murphy to accept a concept of French resistance which was anti-Gaullist. He understood, as many did not, the true significance of Gaullism, which aimed not only at sovereign power as a provisional government but at economic and political reforms along the lines of Léon Blum's Popular Front government of 1936. If the Allies ever liberated France, it was of primordial importance to him that they should do so in conjunction with a resistance movement that was anti-Gaullist and anti-German but not necessarily anti-Vichy.

The arguments for this position were received with hostility neither by Murphy nor by his superiors in Washington. Murphy by disposition was inclined to blame France's prewar feebleness on the vacillations and errors of the Popular Front, and he numbered among his French friends more aristocrats, Roman Catholics, and conservatives than he did Free-Masons, Jews, Socialists, and Communists. Later, Murphy would become the target of vicious attacks alleging that his Fascist inclinations had prompted him to advise Eisenhower to appease Darlan and the Vichy appointees in North Africa. This does Murphy an injustice, for he was neither as forceful in his influence over Eisenhower nor as inventive in his political convictions as some editors seemed to believe. An article favorable to Murphy, written in 1944, quoted him as saying that he had merely carried out the directives issued to him by the State Department and the military authorities and that he had acted as a "diplomatic messenger boy."[17] Walter Lippmann characterized Murphy as "a most agreeable and ingratiating man whose warm heart causes him to form passionate personal and partisan attachments rather than cool and detached judgments."[18]

Murphy reported that while few Gaullists had influence in North Africa, there were nevertheless many anti-German elements who were prepared to collaborate with the Allies, and he persuaded Roosevelt, predisposed in any case to by-pass the Free French, that De Gaulle must be completely excluded from participation in Operation "Torch." As planning for the invasion progressed, the President emphasized continuously to Churchill that De Gaulle must have nothing to do with it, even insisting that the Free French receive no notification until after the landings had taken place. "I am very apprehensive," Roosevelt wrote the Prime Minister, "in regard to the adverse effect that any introduction of De Gaulle into the invasion situation would have on our promising efforts to attach a large part of the French African forces to our expedition."[19]

In time, the complex operations of resistance groups in North Africa

[17] Kingsbury Smith, "Unrevealed Facts about Robert Murphy," *American Mercury*, Vol. LIX, No. 251 (Nov., 1944), 528–36.

[18] *N. Y. Herald Tribune*, 19 Jan. 1943.

[19] Langer, *Our Vichy Gamble*, 290. Cf. Winston S. Churchill, *The Hinge of Fate* (vol. IV of *The Second World War*), 605–606.

came to be centralized in a Committee of Five: Lemaigre-Dubreuil; Jean Rigault, a slender, taciturn individual with tremendous capacities for work; Colonel van Heck, head of the *Chantiers de la Jeunesse;* Tarbé de Saint-Hardouin, a career diplomat; and Henri d'Astier de la Vigerie, brother of the Resistance leader, a persuasive Royalist and Gaullist. When in April, 1942, General Henri Honoré Giraud escaped from the German prison of Königstein, where he had been imprisoned since 1940, it seemed that no individual more suitable for The Five's purposes could be found. He appeared to have every qualification. His patriotism and his hate for the Germans, from whom he had escaped in both world wars, were proverbial; he wore five stars to De Gaulle's one; and he was known as a daring commander with a long military experience in North Africa. He was not celebrated, however, either as a liberal or as a statesman.

As soon as he had returned to France, Giraud disquieted Vichy by his industrious efforts to learn what military dispositions had been made by the army command to resist further German encroachments in the unoccupied zone. Disturbed by such energy. Laval had forced Giraud to sign a prepared statement on May 4 in which the General declared his loyalty to the Marshal. The note said in part:

> I am fully in agreement with you. I give you my word as an officer that I will do nothing which could in any way hinder your relations with the German Government or upset the work which you have entrusted Admiral Darlan or President Pierre Laval to accomplish under your high authority.
> My past is the guarantee of my loyalty.[20]

When this testimonial was later made public by Vichy, it proved to be a source of great embarrassment to Giraud and his American supporters and a useful propaganda instrument for his Gaullist rivals. Giraud never took much trouble to insist that he had signed under pressure, nor did he take vigorous steps to give publicity to a second letter, written at the time of the North African landings, which repudiated the first and advised Pétain: "I am sure moreover of your deepest wishes,

[20] Albert Kammerer, *Du débarquement africain au meurtre de Darlan*, 106.

but more free than you, I am able to go to Africa to prepare what you will achieve yourself in France." The salutary close of this communication did not, however, suggest that Giraud anticipated a sharp break with the Vichy regime. "I ask," he wrote, "that you kindly hold me in your esteem and consider me always as one of your most devoted and respectful subordinates."[21] Even as late as November, 1943, Giraud would find himself attacked because he had never published an unambiguous declaration that he had severed all connections with Marshal Pétain.

Giraud's Pétainist sympathies comprised but one of several reasons why Washington should have hesitated before coming to terms with him. The American negotiators should have thought more seriously about the qualifications needed in a French leader. The need, presumably, was for a commander who would issue orders to French troops not to fire on the Americans and the British as they landed. It would have been much more reasonable for this purpose to have conspired with the North African Commander in Chief, General Juin, rather than with a general who, regardless of his prestige, had no place in the normal command hierarchy. General Juin later maintained that he might have co-operated; but Murphy had by the time of the landings become too involved in his commitments to Giraud, and he never approached Juin. There was, furthermore, no need for a French military commander to take charge of operations against the Germans. Although Giraud believed he was being brought to North Africa to assume an active military command, Eisenhower neither needed nor desired additional advice at the supreme command level; and the Combined Chiefs of Staff were completely uninterested in Giraud's strategic concepts. A third possibility, the need of a chief behind whom to rally a great wave of non-Gaullist combatants, was equally not accomplished in the choice of General Giraud. Giraud possessed no popular following, no organization, no social imagination, no interest in politics, no program. It was unthinkable, although Murphy and some officials may have believed it, that a popular liberation movement dedicated to the destruction of Fascism and totalitarianism could be nurtured on the same ideological sustenance that remained sterile in North Africa under Marshal Pétain.

[21] *Ibid.*, 230–31.

If, finally, what the Americans wanted in Algiers was a competent administrator who would keep matters running smoothly while the fighting against the Axis continued, they could hardly have made a poorer choice. Giraud prided himself on his reputation as a fighting general. "I do not make politics," he loved to say, "I make war." With his nearly fanatical concern over troops and weapons, tactics and strategy, Giraud was disposed to leave administrative matters, even those connected with the maintenance and supply of his own troops, to take care of themselves. In problems of civil administration he had no interest whatsoever.

Whatever the arguments against Giraud's selection may have been, Lemaigre-Dubreuil was authorized to seek out the General and propose to him that he join forces with the dissident group in North Africa. These negotiations, it should be noted, had started in May, 1942, before the decision to mount Operation "Torch" had been made. At the same time he was negotiating with Lemaigre-Dubreuil, Giraud also established contact with President Roosevelt and gained the impression that he was the Allied choice for commander in chief in the liberation of France. The two independent themes—planning for "Torch" and arrangements with The Five in North Africa—converged in September when Murphy reported to Roosevelt, who soon after dispatched him to England in order that Eisenhower could be brought up to date on the North African conspiracy. Out of these discussions emerged the arrangements for Eisenhower's representative, General Mark Clark, to undertake a secret voyage to North Africa. There he was to confer directly with General Charles Mast, a long-standing friend of Giraud's who had been a fellow prisoner at Königstein and who, after his release, had been given command of the Nineteenth Army Corps at Algiers. The meeting, attended by Clark, Mast, Murphy, van Heck, Rigault and others, took place at Cherchel on October 22, and while it sealed the determination on Eisenhower's part to co-operate with the dissident French groups, it also marked the beginning of a long series of misunderstandings between the French and the Allies in North Africa. When a memorandum of the Cherchel Conference reached Giraud via Lemaigre-Dubreuil, the French General drew up on October 27 an "agreement in principle" which contained his understanding of what had been decided. This document reveals that Giraud believed he would become commanding general as soon at the Allies had landed and that he would have the right to set the date of the operation, which would be combined with a landing in southern France. That Eisenhower remained unaware of Giraud's conception of the operation gives some suggestion of the difficulties in store for him.

Lemaigre-Dubreuil and especially Rigault saw quite clearly, now that the Americans had accepted Giraud's leadership, that his participation in the projected operation would not safeguard French sovereignty unless a political as well as a military accord was reached. Just as De Gaulle had fought to keep the Free French army independent of British command in 1940, they also hoped to keep Giraud and the North African army from absorption by an occupation force that would leave the French no independence of action and no guarantees concerning their political status in North Africa. In Algiers, Murphy was placed in the cheerless position of having to find an answer that would satisfy Giraud's memorandum of October 27, as well as a formula which would guarantee the political status of North Africa. Since the landings were now but a week distant and a submarine would soon be standing by to rush Giraud to Gibraltar, there was no time for clearance from Washington. Not knowing whether he would be supported, Murphy wrote Giraud three letters on November 2, the first of which had been drafted earlier after consultations with Lemaigre-Dubreuil and Rigault. In this he said:

> . . . It is well understood that French sovereignty should be re-established as soon as possible over all territories, metropolitan as well as colonial, over which the French flag waved in 1939.
>
> The Government of the United States considers the French nation as an ally and will treat it as such.
>
> I add that in case of military operations on French territory (either metropolitan or colonial) in all instances where the French collaborate, the American authorities will in no way intervene in affairs which are solely the province of the national administration or which derive from the exercise of French sovereignty. . . .

In regard to Giraud's taking command, Murphy became less committal: he took cognizance of Giraud's point of view and then added, "I am communicating your suggestion to the General Staff of the American Army and I am certain that an acceptable formula will be found."

The second letter assured Giraud that the United States would bring military and civilian supplies to North Africa, and the third guaranteed that the operation would be "essentially American under American command" and that no "dissident French elements," i.e., Gaullists, would participate.[22]

It is the section of the first letter, quoted above, which carried the greatest political significance. In the name of the United States and without prior approval from Washington, Murphy had given guarantees which in many ways ran counter to the President's personal ideas. Although at this time he had not entirely formulated his thinking on imperialism and trusteeships, Roosevelt had never been inclined to grant guarantees regarding the future of French colonial areas. The promise that France would be treated as an ally carried with it the implication that French commanders would be invited to share in decisions on strategy, a promise which Roosevelt, Churchill, and the Combined Chiefs of Staff would not readily support. Finally, recognition of sovereignty in areas occupied by Allied forces was never officially accorded by Washington until after the French Provisional government was installed at Paris in 1944.

The Invasion of North Africa

On November 8, 1942, over 100,000 troops—practically all American —landed in the vicinities of Casablanca, Oran, and Algiers; but the original conception of the operation, from the point of view of Murphy, Giraud, and The Five, was incapable of being put into effect. In the first place, Giraud was not brought to Algiers in time. At Eisenhower's temporary headquarters at Gibraltar, to which he had been brought by submarine and plane, the unpleasant truth dawned on Giraud that he had been completely misinformed about the nature of the expedition

[22] The section of the letter here quoted was drafted during conversations of Murphy with Tarbé de Saint-Hardouin, Lemaigre-Dubreuil, and Rigault on 15, 18, 19 Oct. 1942 (Crusoe [pseudonym of Lemaigre-Dubreuil], *Vicissitudes d'une victoire*, 115–16). Text in Kammerer, *Du débarquement africain*, 654; English version in Langer, *Our Vichy Gamble*, 333.

and his relation to it. By the time a working agreement had been achieved between Eisenhower and Giraud, events unfolding in Algiers had moved so rapidly that an entirely novel situation confronted the Allied commander of operations, General Clark. When Clark and Giraud finally reached North Africa on November 9, they discovered that while Algiers was safely in Allied hands as a result of the audacious activity of Murphy's conspirators and of General Juin's co-operation, fighting still continued at Oran and in Morocco which Giraud's prestige was powerless to stop. Although General Mast and General Émile Béthouart collaborated fully with the Americans, they were incapable of preventing resistance to the Allied landing forces. Giraud had no influence whatsoever.

A completely unanticipated improvisation followed the news that Admiral Darlan, commander in chief of all Vichy land, sea, and air forces, was in Algiers. Disillusioned on account of Giraud's incapacity to meet the emergency, Clark turned to Darlan, whom on November 10 he persuaded to order a cease-fire. By the time this order was received and obeyed at Oran and in Morocco, French resistance had been almost completely reduced by the American attacks, but General Clark and the commanders in North Africa believed that thousands of American lives had been saved by Darlan's order and that he alone could provide the authority in civil and military affairs that would safeguard communications during the remainder of the campaign. General Giraud's irascibility had so alienated Clark that he was disinclined to consider Giraud any longer as a candidate for the post of French high commissioner in North Africa.

Darlan appeared to be the only alternative. Through him it might have been possible to rally Tunisia and French West Africa and to bring the French fleet forth from Toulon. Negotiations with Governor General Boisson, carried on by General Jean Marie Bergeret, former Vichy minister for air, who had flown to Algiers shortly before the landings, did bring French West Africa under Allied control by November 23; but the hopes of obtaining Tunisia collapsed when German troops landed there unopposed. The French fleet, refusing to respond to Darlan's halfhearted appeals, was scuttled in the harbor on November 27. Meanwhile Eisenhower, having journeyed to Algiers on November 14 to obtain a firsthand view of the muddled situation, approved an agreement with Darlan, who in turn promised to retain Giraud as commander in chief of ground and air forces.

The decision to deal with Darlan had not been an easy one, but it was made on the basis of entirely military considerations. If the "Darlan deal" would prove to have been politically shortsighted and would provoke horror-stricken disapproval among liberals in England and America, it would be difficult to trace out an alternate course which Eisenhower could have pursued. In spite of his long and enterprising activity in North Africa, Robert Murphy had failed to provide what the army commanders needed: a trustworthy civil administration which would safeguard the rear. Giraud had proved inadequate, and none of the conspirators—Lemaigre-Dubreuil, Rigault, D'Astier, or the others—had prestige or experience enough to warrant their being placed at the head of civil affairs. Of the army officers with whom Murphy had collaborated, the highest-ranking, General Mast and General Béthouart, were held in such disdain by their Vichy-appointed fellow officers, who considered them traitors, that they were for the moment useless as administrators. It may be that the generals were poorly advised by their political counselors, but, had Murphy advised against Darlan, whom, other than De Gaulle, could he have suggested in his place?

Although both Roosevelt and Churchill reacted negatively to the arrangement, they both agreed that the commander in the field should be supported. To assuage his uneasiness, Roosevelt seized upon an anecdote he had heard—that in times of danger you could hold the devil's hand until you crossed the bridge. Winston Churchill, with his commitments to De Gaulle, fretted restlessly under the press attacks which every day became more violent. On November 17 he cabled Roosevelt:

I ought to let you know that very deep currents of feeling are stirred here by the arrangement with Darlan. The more I reflect upon it the more convinced I become that it can only be a temporary expedient justifiable solely by the stress of battle. We must not overlook the serious political injury which may be done to our cause, not only in France but throughout Europe, by the feeling that we are ready to make terms with the local Quislings. A permanent arrangement with Darlan on the formation of a Darlan Government in French North Africa would not be understood by the great masses of ordinary people whose simple loyalties are our strength.[23]

In Washington, Cordell Hull was also trying to persuade the President to make a statement about Darlan, and he sent a note to Roosevelt on the same day the President received the Prime Minister's wire. Convinced of the urgency of the situation, the President put the two together, doctored them a bit, and that afternoon announced at his press conference, using Churchill's words, that the "Darlan deal" was nothing but a "temporary expedient." The President wrote Hull that he thought "it will take all right."[24] For a while it did.

Once the fighting had ended, Eisenhower needed a basic instrument which would define the relations between the French and the Allies. Darlan found himself in no position to bargain; once having committed himself to co-operation, he was willing, in order to obtain recognition in the American camp, to make extreme concessions. The document he finally approved, which came to be known as the Clark-Darlan Agreement, was drawn up in less than a week by Murphy, Colonel Julius Holmes, and Freeman Matthews. By this agreement the Allies were granted control and command of airports, harbor and port defenses, fortifications, and arsenals; control of military telecommunication facilities; information on all military installations; the right of requisition; extraterritorial rights for Allied personnel; and wide emergency powers in case the internal situation threatened disorder.

If the foregoing rights virtually gave the Allied commander in chief the power to occupy all North Africa, other terms of the agreement guaranteed the preservation of the *status quo ante bellum*. The French land, air, and naval forces remained intact, under French command, to co-operate with the Allies against the Axis and to maintain internal security. It is to be noted that no clause prescribed that French forces should operate under the command of the Allied commander; they were to act in co-operation with him, with the sole restriction that the French command should notify the Allies of all military movements.

From the political point of view, the most important clause of the

23 Churchill, *Hinge of Fate*, 630.
24 Hull, *Memoirs*, II, 1199–1200.

Clark-Darlan Agreement was that which left the Vichy administration in North Africa intact. Nowhere in the agreement could be found a stipulation which in the least implied that the French would be required to expunge Fascist elements from the governmental structure. If the High Commissioner chose to maintain in office the Vichy-appointed governors—Noguès, Boisson, and Chatel; if he kept anti-semitic laws patterned on Hitler's Nuremberg decrees in effect; or if he took no steps to liquidate the *Service d'Ordre Légionnaire* (SOL), the North African version of the *Schutzstaffel*, there could be no justification for Allied interference unless it could be shown that such policies endangered military operations.

In spite of the fact that French administration was not to be altered, hundreds of problems involving civil matters were nevertheless of necessity directed at Allied headquarters. Eisenhower attempted to expand the civil affairs section of his staff, but the chief burden of dealing with nonmilitary problems fell on the shoulders of Robert Murphy. After the beginning of 1943 this responsibility was shared with the British representative, Harold Macmillan, appointed to Eisenhower's staff in December. The arrangement was not entirely satisfactory. Murphy and Macmillan were not in a position to adjudicate disputes, take security measures, sign contracts, or take other than advisory actions to reform or improve administrative arrangements. They could only appeal to, persuade, or cajole French administrators. They possessed a veto power, but since its use involved a recourse to military headquarters, they were reluctant to invoke it unless justified by a situation of unusual urgency. As representatives of foreign policy, neither Macmillan nor Murphy could be entirely clear from day to day what that policy would be, nor were they sure whether they should intervene on their own initiative or only upon directives from Washington and London. Furthermore, any intervention would presume that Murphy and Macmillan would be agreed on policy, while future events would reveal that American and British attitudes did not always coincide.

Regardless of its drawbacks, the Clark-Darlan Agreement served the Allies for the entire time of their stay in North Africa. Since it provided the harbor facilities, airports, and communication networks which Eisenhower needed, Washington never responded with any enthusiasm to French insistence that the agreement be revised. It was generally understood that if the Committee of National Liberation, formed in June, 1943, obtained Allied recognition, a revision of the Clark-Darlan Agreement would naturally follow. But no revision had been effected even by August, 1944, when the Committee had returned to France as the French Provisional government and the war had moved far away from the Mediterranean theater.

Once having committed himself to the deal with Darlan, Eisenhower exposed himself to devastating criticism on the part of Allied correspondents, who, chafing under censorship and not too occupied with news from the front, peered inquiringly at every aspect of French and Allied administration in North Africa. They saw a vast population of underprivileged Arab natives with no political rights; Jews persecuted under Vichy laws which remained in effect; prisons and concentration camps filled with Communists, Jews, anti-Vichy political prisoners, and Spanish Republicans; Fascist organizations—the *Légion des Anciens Combattants* and the SOL effectively bullying the population and carrying on their petty graft through the *groupements;* and all of the French officials, civil and military, who for two years under Vichy had permitted these conditions to flourish, still in office. All this the American and British correspondents observed and, in spite of censorship, managed to report in their newspapers until the liberal press in both countries, and the Gaullists in London, became livid in their denunciation of Anglo-American follies.

It seems that the errors could have been easily rectified. One need only dismiss Darlan and the Vichy-appointed governors, Boisson, Noguès, and Chatel, and all other petty officials guilty of collaboration; replace them with liberal Republicans; free the political prisoners; abrogate all Vichy legislation, particularly that which was anti-Semitic; and disband the para-military organizations. Why could this not have been done? The answer is partially to be found in the terms of the Clark-Darlan Agreement. But recommendations were also easier to make than to implement.

The difficulty of replacing officials was perfectly demonstrated in the case of Eisenhower's attempt to find a new governor general to succeed Yves Chatel in Algeria. Darlan suggested Marcel Peyrouton, who had been minister of the interior at Vichy but had demonstrated his anti-collaborationist convictions when he brought about Laval's dismissal in December, 1940, and again when he resigned from his post as ambassador to Argentina on Laval's return to office in 1942. Neither Murphy nor Eisenhower had any objections, and they requested the State Department, on December 9, to facilitate Peyrouton's transportation from Buenos Aires to Algiers. The State Department knew, what apparently Murphy and Eisenhower did not, that Peyrouton's reputation for repressive measures at Vichy, for anti-Semitism, and for sympathies with police-state organization, made him abhorred among French liberals who were at all informed. In spite of the Department's protests, Murphy and Eisenhower pushed the request until, on December 28, War Department orders reached Peyrouton permitting him to proceed to Algiers. When, two weeks later, Giraud appointed him governor general of Algeria, a storm of protest broke out in the British and American press. Eisenhower later admitted that in spite of Peyrouton's acknowledged abilities as an administrator, the appointment was a mistake.[25]

In practice, Darlan was more liberal than the members of his Imperial Council, the officer corps of the army, and hundreds of minor administrators. He comprehended clearly enough what program had to be pursued in North Africa in order to assuage American and British opinion; but also, for he was an intelligent and efficient administrator, he did not underestimate the difficulties of his position. Darlan's critics have not deprecated either his intelligence or his personal capacities as an administrator. The question was, rather, should Darlan have been there at all? Can an ideological war be won with "temporary expedients"? Was there no better solution? The Gaullists in London thought there was.

De Gaulle and the Invasion

De Gaulle's immediate reaction to the landings in North Africa was not entirely hostile. Until November 14, when the arrangement with Admiral Darlan was announced, no one at Carlton Gardens, De Gaulle's London headquarters could gather a clear impression of what had tran-

---

[25] Dwight D. Eisenhower, *Crusade in Europe*, 131. Peyrouton was arrested in Nov., 1943. He spent over four years in prison but was acquitted in Dec., 1948.

spired, and De Gaulle assumed that General Giraud would soon be supplanting Juin, Noguès, and Boisson as the ranking French commander in North Africa. While De Gaulle was unenthusiastic about the selection of Giraud, he felt that the choice was more unfortunate than vicious. But De Gaulle was not unwilling to co-operate with General Giraud, and he immediately sought Allied approval to send a mission which might include Pleven and Colonel Billotte, representing the French National Committee, together with Emmanuel d'Astier and François de Menthon, representing the Resistance in France. Although neither Churchill nor Roosevelt objected to the proposal, the plan was abruptly dropped when the news was broadcast that Darlan would head the North African administration in place of Giraud.

De Gaulle was furious. In a bitter rage he wrote to Admiral Stark: "I understand that the United States buys the treachery of traitors, if this appears profitable, but payment must not be made against the honor of France." Stark tactfully returned the letter to De Gaulle, suggesting that a mistake must have been made; and next day De Gaulle's *chef de cabinet,* Gaston Palewski, brought Stark an apology. The effect of Stark's gesture was destroyed a few days later, however, when the sense of De Gaulle's message was published in the London press. This kind of publicity, presumably the handiwork of Jacques Soustelle's Commissariat of Information, did not improve Stark's admiration for De Gaulle as a diplomat or man of honor.[26]

When De Gaulle learned early in December that General Giraud had been appointed commander in chief of land and air forces, he believed that some sort of military liaison could be achieved if it should prove possible to collaborate with Giraud and Eisenhower but not with Darlan. For this mission De Gaulle chose the third of the D'Astier brothers, François, a general in the French Air Force who had rallied to De Gaulle after the Darlan deal. Besides trying to improve military liaison, General d'Astier was to get in touch with his brother Henri in

---

[26] "Selected Documents from Correspondence of Adm. Harold R. Stark, U.S.N., Commander, U. S. Naval Forces in Europe (COMNAVEU)," from the historical monograph Kittredge, U.S.N.R., Part II, Appendix B, 1, 22–23. (Cited hereafter as COMNAVEU *United States–French Relations, 1942–1944* (multolithed), prepared by Lt. Cdr. Tracy B. Documents.) See also Jacques Soustelle, *De Londres à Alger* (vol. I of *Envers et contre tout*), 369–72; Barlone, *La route des sommets,* 110–14; Churchill, *Hinge of Fate,* 630–31.

Algiers and bring him funds (about $35,000) which would help to build up the Fighting French organization in Algeria. When D'Astier arrived in Algiers on December 19, he found that neither Giraud nor Eisenhower would work with him without Darlan's consent and co-operation. Since this was impossible from both Darlan's and D'Astier's point of view, the General was forced to leave North Africa with some abruptness three days after he arrived.

Another possible method of effecting *de facto* co-operation between De Gaulle and Giraud was by way of their respective secret services. Many of De Gaulle's agents, operating under the *Bureau Central de Renseignements et d'Action* (BCRA), headed by Colonel Passy, duplicated the work of the resistant army intelligence services continuing its functions within the Vichy framework. When the Nazis occupied France after the North African invasion, Colonel Rivet, Colonel Villeneuve, Colonel Ronin, and Commandant Paillole transferred headquarters of their espionage operations to North Africa under General Giraud. Before going to Algiers, Paillole, having worked his way across Spain to Gibraltar, came to London to try to construct a formula for co-operation of his counterespionage operations with those of Passy. Such co-operation might have provided a nucleus from which Giraud and De Gaulle could have developed fuller co-ordination of their efforts; but as time revealed an unresolvable difference in aim and function between the Gaullist and the Giraudist secret service structure, the two organizations provided a basis more of rivalry and friction than of collaboration.

Between November 14 and 18, De Gaulle nursed his bitterness against the Americans, but when the President affirmed that Darlan was but a "temporary expedient," De Gaulle concluded that only a direct contact with President Roosevelt would dissipate some of the misunderstandings which the North African adventure had generated. Since André Philip had not yet returned to London, it might be useful, De Gaulle thought, to have him get back to Washington (he was then at Ottawa) if the President would receive him. The message was transmitted via Stark to the President, who immediately agreed to see Philip as soon as he could manage to reach the capital.

The interview, which took place on November 20, marked the first occasion on which Roosevelt had personally received a Free French representative. Had De Gaulle's emissary possessed the tact and diplomatic skill of General Catroux, he might have mended some of the ruptures that events had produced in Free French–American relations. But Philip and Tixier (who accompanied him) were politicians rather than statesmen, and, sincere and patriotic as they may have been, in their bitterness they completely lost sight of the larger views which might have helped their mission. De Roussy de Sales, who knew both men and received a firsthand report of the interview, asserts that "they made an absolutely deplorable impression on the President, who found them filled with personal ambition and totally incomprehensible." De Roussy de Sales thought they must have cut a strange figure, since they "are almost caricatures of French leftist politicians," and "by stupidity or natural rudeness" Philip avoided any congratulations on the North African landings but instead launched into a tirade of recriminations. Tixier later reported that Philip ranted and railed, condemning the White House, the State Department, and the American Army, brandishing an accusing finger under Roosevelt's nose like an avenging preacher. Instead of permitting Roosevelt to explain the nature of the Darlan deal, Philip placed him on the defensive. The President curtly justified the arrangement as a military necessity and explained that Eisenhower would retain or dismiss Darlan accordingly as he produced what Eisenhower required, but several times he reiterated that he would still be glad to see De Gaulle if he cared to visit Washington. Stark later received a wire from the President: "Why did you insist that I receive that man Philip? He had not a word of appreciation."[27]

In spite of Philip's botched execution of his mission, a firm arrangement for De Gaulle to fly to Washington was achieved shortly after the interview. Roosevelt stood on a narrow technicality: he would not *invite* De Gaulle to come because an invitation would imply a recognition of De Gaulle's status as head of the London Committee; but, on the other hand, if De Gaulle would himself take the initiative and express a desire to come, the President would make the facilities available and would

[27] De Roussy de Sales, *L'Amérique entre en guerre*, 360–67, 372; De Gaulle, *Mémoires*, II, 408–12; Barlone, *La route des sommets*, 115–17; Pierre and Renée Gosset, *La deuxième guerre*, 197.

reserve the time for an appointment. Although there later developed some difficulties among his entourage over this point, De Gaulle did not demur at the arrangement, and before the end of November, Roosevelt had promised to reserve the necessary time after January 9. Since Churchill and the President had already reached an agreement (on November 26) to meet in North Africa around the middle of January, it is clear that Roosevelt had no personal hesitation about conferring with De Gaulle before he left for the Casablanca Conference. At first Roosevelt had been prepared to see De Gaulle at once, but he postponed the visit until January on the advice of the Joint Chiefs.

On December 18 the President wrote to Sumner Welles: "I think I can see General de Gaulle on January 10th or the morning of the 11th, but I greatly doubt if I can see him after that until about February first."[28]

Arrangements were then concluded for De Gaulle's trip to Washington. The President had asked Admiral Stark to be present when he saw De Gaulle, and the evening before his departure for Washington on December 16, Stark called on De Gaulle and had a long conversation with him. De Gaulle elaborated on his role as leader of the Fighting French; explained his inability to work with Darlan even though he could co-operate with Giraud, Juin, and Béthouart; and summed up the grievances he held against the United States for its contradictory policy in relation to Darlan. He was irritated particularly that Darlan should be able to communicate with Admiral Robert, with Admiral Godefroy at Alexandria, and with Vichy diplomatic agents throughout the world. In the course of these remarks De Gaulle touched on the justifications for his assuming leadership of the Free French. These comments are best described in the words of Lieutenant Commander Kittredge, who was present and took notes at the conversation:

[De Gaulle] was also convinced that French culture, intelligence and capacities of leadership were so widely diffused in France that when any elite or governing class failed France, through decadence or defeatism, new individuals were always projected upward out of the French masses, to give enlightened and inspired leadership to "eternal France"; that

28 Elliott Roosevelt, ed., *F.D.R.: His Personal Letters*, II, 1380; De Gaulle, *Mémoires*, II, 428.

this had been true through the centuries from the time of Charlemagne to that of Hitler. Thus de Gaulle referred to the rise of the Capetian royal house, to Joan of Arc, to Henri IV, to the revolutionary leaders (1789-93), to Napoleon, finally to Poincaré and Clemenceau; de Gaulle added—"perhaps this time I am one of those thrust into leadership by circumstances, and by the failure of the other leaders."

Admiral Stark was much impressed by this historical and philosophical analysis and suggested that de Gaulle, on meeting Roosevelt (a great student of French history and politics), should attempt to make the President understand his concepts.[29]

Shortly before Christmas the final plans were completed. An army transport plane was put at the disposal of De Gaulle and his party, who were to board the plane on December 26, pick up General Catroux at Accra on December 28, and be in Washington well before the appointment now scheduled for January 8 or 9. Shortly before the time arranged for the takeoff, just as De Gaulle was preparing to leave for the airport, an urgent message from the Prime Minister asked him to postpone the flight. An unpredictable and badly timed event had intervened to frustrate De Gaulle's prospects of reaching an understanding with the President. Word had come from Algiers that Admiral Darlan had been assassinated on Christmas Eve.

Giraud Succeeds Darlan

The murder of Admiral Darlan solved nothing. If it removed a noxious personality who typified the execrable qualities of the Vichy regime, it brought consequences in its wake, unanticipated by the conspirators, which worked to the detriment of the Fighting French. Most immediate and inauspicious, the assassination destroyed all possibility of an early *rapprochement* between Roosevelt and De Gaulle. At the White House a spontaneous and uninformed reaction expressed itself in the conviction that Gaullists must have been responsible for the assassination. Admiral Leahy took unconcealed satisfaction in dispatching a blunt cable to London to the effect that De Gaulle had better be

[29] Robert Sherwood, *Roosevelt and Hopkins: An Intimate History,* 956; COMNAVEU Documents, II, 65–69. This conversation is not mentioned by De Gaulle in his *Mémoires.*

At a crucial time, the Free French National Committee in session: reading from bottom left, General Volin (Air), M. Pleven (Economy, Finance, and Colonies), General de Gaulle, M. Dejean (Foreign Affairs), General le Gentilhomme (War), and M. Diethelm (Interior).

The four men who shaped the destiny of France during World War II: General Henri Honoré Giraud, North African high commissioner, President Franklin D. Roosevelt, General Charles de Gaulle, leader of the Fighting French, and Prime Minister Winston Churchill meet the press after the Casablanca Conference in January, 1943.

kept at home. The cancellation was translated into diplomatic terms for delivery at Carlton Gardens, but the suspicion lurking behind the crisp tone of the message presaged antagonisms and obstacles in future American relations with the Gaullists. When it was learned soon afterward that Henri d'Astier de la Vigerie had been arrested for implication in the assassination, De Gaulle appeared definitely to be linked to the plot because it was remembered that D'Astier's brother, General François d'Astier, had left a large sum of money with him when he had visited Algiers as De Gaulle's personal emissary a few days before the murder. Although it was uncorroborated and circumstantial, the evidence was nevertheless accepted as fact by many officials in Washington in the days following Darlan's death, and its disagreeable shadow lingered for a long time to prevent the development of better relations between Roosevelt and the Fighting French.

Before Leahy's cables reached London, Prime Minister Churchill, suspecting that American policy might need reconsideration, had asked General de Gaulle to delay his departure for forty-eight hours. Shortly thereafter the American cancellation came through, and De Gaulle had no other alternative than to accept the postponement.

Admiral Leahy dispatched another cable on that same Christmas afternoon—this time to Eisenhower—authorizing him "to appoint Giraud" as Darlan's successor. The wording of this message leaves no doubt that Roosevelt, whatever his democratic sympathies may have been, considered that Eisenhower was dictator in Algiers. Under the terms of the Clark-Darlan Agreement, Eisenhower could scarcely "appoint" a French official, and had he done so, he would have been subjected to vociferous accusations about more Allied interference in purely French affairs. Eisenhower and Giraud had been on their way to the front when they were recalled to Algiers by the crisis. General Bergeret, as Giraud's deputy, immediately wired Noguès and Boisson to proceed to Algiers for an emergency meeting of the Imperial Council, which, whether Roosevelt was aware of it or not, assumed that it alone possessed the authority to designate Darlan's successor. A minor crisis could have developed if Noguès had insisted that he should succeed to the post of high commissioner. Eisenhower made it unquestionably clear that he would not abide retention of Noguès in this position and that for the American command Giraud was the only acceptable candidate. Noguès stood on ground much too unstable to permit him to contest this position.

With President Roosevelt's message on the record, as well as Eisenhower's unambiguous pronouncement that Giraud was the only acceptable candidate, the Imperial Council proceeded on December 26 to the task of electing a successor to Admiral Darlan. To nobody's surprise, the choice fell unanimously on General Henri Honoré Giraud, who was immediately invested with the authority of high commissioner in French Africa and of commander in chief of the ground, naval, and air forces.

This manifestation of Roosevelt's union with Giraud was accomplished with such unseemly speed that the American and British public, like Hamlet lamenting his mother's hasty remarriage, could complain of the dexterity with which Giraud had been posted to the High Commissariat. Those who reflected on the event could have wished that time had been permitted for a more leisurely reappraisal of the entire North African policy, for an examination of the possibility of breaking more completely with Vichy, and even for a reconsideration of the desirability of introducing De Gaulle into the North African picture. The election of Giraud had taken place without the British having been consulted, without discussion by the Combined Chiefs of Staff, and certainly without participation of the State Department. Roosevelt had been motivated partly by a desire to support Eisenhower but more by the desire to keep in North Africa a leader favorable to the United States and effectively anti-Gaullist. If Roosevelt was motivated by a persistent suspicion that Gaullists had plotted the assassination of Darlan, it was indeed unfortunate that the concatenation of events made such uncertainties plausible; for the injection of General Giraud into high office meant not only a continuation of the Vichy ideology but its administration in the hands of a man far more politically inept than the murdered Admiral.

General Giraud was no better a choice on December 26 than he had been on November 8. He still bore a superficial resemblance to the ideal French leader; he was a courageous soldier, patriotic, anti-German, pro-Ally, and untainted by having held a post under Vichy, but he possessed drawbacks which over the months would operate to his own—and to American—disadvantage. Probably the most serious of Giraud's shortcomings was his incapacity and distaste for politics. He completely lacked a comprehension of the concepts, techniques, theories, and methods whereby men work together to establish the social structure under which they live. It is not true that Giraud inclined toward totalitarianism; but his attitudes might be explained by pointing out that he basically understood only one type of social structure: the organization of an army. He could understand the operation of directives, orders, discipline, courts-martial, and allegiance, but he was mystified by their civilian counterparts—democratic legislation, morale, trials by jury, and loyalty to abstract concepts. Nor did he have the flexibility and imagination to realize that in order to insure the support of his democratic Allies he must abandon the notion that North Africa should be governed like a military outpost. General de Gaulle may originally have been equally authoritarian and restricted in his personal outlook, but he had evolved in his two years of leading Fighting France to an appreciation of the necessity of basing his movements on the principles and ideals of the Third Republic. Here he possessed an advantage over the older general that could not be overcome, regardless of the amount of American support of Giraud. Nothing, and no one, seemed to be able to persuade Giraud that he must abandon his dogmatic rigidity and permit his thinking to evolve in the direction of the concepts for which many people believed the war was being fought.

Out of Giraud's inflexibility emerged innumerable administrative deficiencies. The men with whom Giraud surrounded himself were primarily army colleagues—General Bergeret, General Prioux, and General Chambe—who, however personable they may have been as individuals, were habituated to thinking in military rather than in political terms. The result was a complete concentration on military phases of administration, while the civil side took care of itself with a minimum of direction from the High Commissioner. If the Vichy pattern continued, if the ancient face of Marshal Pétain was still to be seen posted on North African walls, if Darlan's administrators remained in office, and if the reforms started by Darlan were not vigorously pushed, it was a consequence of Giraud's apathy in civil affairs rather than the result of a considered policy.

Giraud's disdain for civil matters left him a prey to his advisers, for it was characteristic of him that he tended to place faith, rather naïvely, in a few individuals who he believed were capable of managing the civilian end of his affairs. The free hand he gave to Lemaigre-Dubreuil and Rigault, and later to Jean Monnet, enabled these men to move Giraud from one extreme to the other, although they failed to impress upon him the need of developing his own political philosophy. This uncritical trust, coupled with a disinclination to operate through bureaucratic channels, an occasional impetuosity in adhering to personal conclusions which the facts scarcely justified, and a directness which bordered on tactlessness, rendered Giraud an unpredictable and poor champion of the French Resistance. Yet his precipitate elevation to the High Commissariat could not be readily undone. The President had chosen his champion; he would have to make out as well as he could with what he had.

Observers who had resented the deal with Darlan now turned expectantly toward General Giraud to introduce a series of much-needed reforms. Giraud's reaction to his opportunity was the measure of the man; he immediately made arrangements for a tour of inspection in French West Africa, the most heavily populated of the areas under his control and consequently the most fertile region for recruiting troops. He made no immediate changes among the civil or military administrators who had held office under Darlan.

Giraud's total preoccupation with rearmament, recruiting, and the Tunisian campaign meant that he left the administrative direction of civil affairs to his deputy, General Bergeret, whose experience in political matters and whose grasp of democratic concepts was as limited as Giraud's. Charged with the responsibility of unearthing the group behind Darlan's assassination, Bergeret accepted with some gullibility a police report that the conspiracy included also a threat to the lives of General Giraud and Robert Murphy. The report included the names of over a dozen persons, some of whom had helped the Allies during the landings. Bergeret and Giraud approved the list, and during the night of December 29 the *Gardes Mobiles* arrested twelve of the accused men.

It would have been difficult to have discovered a more inept way for Giraud to enter upon his administration as *haut commissaire*. If the

General can be defended by the argument that he was not personally responsible, he cannot escape the charge that in permitting a subordinate to carry out steps so redolent of those of a police state, he must himself be Fascist or administratively incompetent. The tumult over the arrests, kept alive by correspondents, by members of the psychological warfare section, and by some Frenchmen, ultimately persuaded General Giraud that the men should be released. He later apologized for the indignity of the arrests, and even went so far as to send Professor René Capitant, a militant and outspoken Gaullist, to London to explain that the situation in Algiers was not so bad as it seemed. No apologies, of course, could correct the general impression of ill faith, and bad administration that spread widely as a result of the incident. Even President Roosevelt, who was scheduled to leave in less than two weeks for his conference with Churchill, could not guess at the uproar that would develop in the press as a result of Giraud's inept and fumbling moves.

▶ 2. Casablanca

American and British Policies Prior to the Casablanca Conference

THE CHANGE in North African administration produced by Darlan's assassination impelled both the British and American governments to seek more satisfactory bases for their relations with the French. Although the precipitate elevation of Giraud to the highest French post in North Africa may have somewhat confounded Churchill, he nevertheless gallantly informed Eisenhower and President Roosevelt that "we entirely agree with this solution."[1] In the secret deliberations of the British government, however, concern was expressed that American policy was directed at building up a French administration in North Africa which, by its grip on the heavily populated areas there, could have no other aim than to keep the Fighting French, and consequently British influence, outside of the French final settlement. It is possible that Churchill personally would not have regretted the departure of General de Gaulle as head of the London movement, but he could not regard disinterestedly or with pleasure the construction of a regime under American sponsorship from which the British were entirely excluded. Nor could he disregard the hammering of the British press, which supported De Gaulle and was becoming increasingly critical of the way affairs were handled in North Africa.

Churchill's government resolved on two important measures—one an immediate practical approach, the other a long-range shift in policy. The practical approach was concerned essentially with an effort to accelerate the arrival of Harold Macmillan at Algiers, where he would have a voice in the day-to-day deliberations on French policy. Although Macmillan's appointment as representative to Allied headquarters had been

[1] 27 Dec. 1942, *Hinge of Fate*, 645.

54

made in December, his arrival at Algiers was delayed until January 4, over a week after Darlan's death. Head of the Macmillan book-publishing firm, the British delegate was a Conservative, a distinguished Member of Parliament, and a personal friend of Churchill's. He had comprehensive and tolerant views, possessed a delightful sense of humor, and could upon occasion exert a charm as ingratiating as that of Churchill himself. Macmillan was senior in age, rank, and experience to his American counterpart, Robert Murphy, and he comprehended what his own government wished to accomplish more clearly than Murphy understood the United States' aims. Considerable hopes were pinned on Macmillan's ability to influence the developments in North Africa in a direction acceptable to British aims.

The long-range British policy was deliberated in London early in January. The Foreign Office emerged with a proposal suggesting that America and Great Britain support the formation of a French provisional organ which would be headed by some figure of international prestige, untainted by connections with either Vichy or the Popular Front, whom Giraud, De Gaulle, Robert, and Godefroy, commander of the immobilized French fleet at Alexandria, could accept without aspiring to the leadership themselves. The names of Louis Marin, Lebrun, Herriot, and Jeanneney were suggested, although it was not known whether these individuals were available or could be smuggled out of France. This body would not be recognized as a provisional government, but it would maintain relations with foreign governments, be treated as an Allied power, and be accepted as one of the United Nations. The advantages of this scheme were several: it would provide a legal basis which neither De Gaulle nor Giraud could claim, it would centralize and improve the French war effort, and it would dispose of the embarrassing and sometimes trying differences between the American and British governments.[2]

The British proposal reached Washington while Roosevelt and his aides were endeavoring to clarify in their own minds what American policy should be. The Americans found themselves not particularly

[2] Report of a British official in Washington, quoted in Col. Passy, *Missions secrètes* (vol. III of *Souvenirs*), 262–67; COMNAVEU Documents, II, 86; Harry C. Butcher, *My Three Years with Eisenhower*, 232; Hull, *Memoirs*, II, 1206–1207.

dissatisfied with the existing situation. After long and difficult nego-tiations with Admiral Robert at Martinique they had attained an ar-rangement there which satisfied their requirements for security. Dakar was now under American control, and Governor General Boisson was proving entirely co-operative. There was no immediate danger that Hitler would threaten America by domination of Africa and the West Indies, and by keeping these colonial areas under American military observation, with no strong ties to any legitimate French authority, the way would be open for negotiations after the war with a properly con-stituted French government, for arrangements which might perma-nently guarantee American security. No advantage was seen in Wash-ington in permitting these areas to rally to a central French authority— Gaullist or other. As the idea was expressed in a memorandum of the time:

> . . . no French political authority can exist or be allowed to create itself outside of France. It is the duty of the United States and Great Britain to preserve for the people of France the right and opportunity to deter-mine for themselves what government they will have, and the French people as well as the world must receive that solemn assurance. . . . It is im-portant to prevent the use which Darlan made of Pétain's authority from being developed into a legitimacy recognized or fostered by the Allies.[3]

President Roosevelt felt much more strongly about the idea of mili-tary security than many people realized. Even though he approved of the Clark-Darlan Agreement, he consistently acted as if he assumed that North Africa was an occupied province, that Eisenhower was in complete charge, and that the French were to be permitted independence only as long as they behaved themselves and co-operated in the war effort. It is possible that the President was poorly informed about actual conditions in North Africa and understood imperfectly how little had been accomplished in removing the more malodorous remnants of Vichydom, but he was at this time much less basically concerned with such political and social problems than he was with military phases of the invasion. It is noteworthy that in preparation for the Casablanca

[3] Unsigned memorandum dated 24 Dec. 1942, quoted in Sherwood, *Roosevelt and Hopkins*, 680-81.

Conference the President discussed policy with the Joint Chiefs of Staff rather than with representatives of the State Department, and he made a point of keeping his Secretary of State from attending the Conference. The President's thinking was, as Butcher cogently put it, "180 degrees opposed" to the Prime Minister's, and the British proposal did not obtain the courtesy of a reply.[4]

It was no wonder that reflections of these differences at high level should have reached the public. Secretary of State Hull, as well as Admiral Leahy, had long been convinced that the Foreign Office and the Free French were partners in a conspiracy to install De Gaulle as master of North Africa, and although the State Department had not been a party to Giraud's selection, its officials accepted Giraud as the only available counterbalance to De Gaulle. Washington correspondents received information from the President, Admiral Leahy, Secretary of State Hull, and lesser authorities, conducive to the conclusion that no acceptance of De Gaulle, Giraud, or anyone else as a political leader was contemplated in Washington.

During the first two weeks of January, 1943, the press attacks on both sides of the Atlantic fomented an uneasy but widespread fear that a serious cleavage existed between Washington and London which threatened the effective prosecution of the war. It was not known, of course, that Churchill and Roosevelt had long since concluded arrangements which would bring them together with the full panoply of their military advisers at Casablanca in Morocco on January 14. Yet the journalistic storm, intensified by unconfirmed rumors that Marcel Peyrouton would shortly join Giraud, had reached such proportions that on the same day the Casablanca Conference opened, the British minister of information, Brendan Bracken, felt constrained to make a public denial that any rift existed between the United States and the United Kingdom. It may have been that a rift did not exist, but no official who knew of the diversity of points of view in regard to the French could with any honesty affirm that there was complete harmony between the two governments. What they could affirm was a hope that as a result of personal discussions at the highest level, a policy acceptable to everyone would soon be worked out.

[4] Butcher, *My Three Years with Eisenhower*, 232, 234.

General Giraud's Aspirations Prior to Casablanca

One of the basic hopes cherished by General Giraud, ever since his first contact with the Americans, pertained to the equipping of the forces which he assumed would come under his command after the North African landings. As soon as he had been appointed commander in chief of French ground and air forces in North Africa, Giraud ordered his staff officers to make a tally of the requirements of the African army. The Franco-German Armistice of 1940 had permitted approximately 150,000 troops to remain in North Africa, with another 75,000 in West Africa. Under General Weygand and General Juin, clandestine recruiting had augmented these figures by another 75,000, comprising troops disguised as workers, policemen, and members of the youth organization, *Chantiers de la Jeunesse.* Giraud thus concluded he could ultimately build up a modern force of 300,000 men if he had the equipment. Although the French had hidden a considerable quantity of arms from the Italo-German Armistice Commission, the African forces boasted no more than one hundred tanks, fewer than three hundred guns of a caliber greater than 75 mm., and only a few thousand vehicles. All of this equipment dated from 1940 at the latest, had been imperfectly maintained, and lacking antiaircraft guns and electronic equipment, was utterly inadequate for modern warfare. The troops of which Giraud could dispose were mostly natives—black Senegalese from West Africa, Moroccan Tabors and Goumiers—all of them contingents celebrated for their fighting qualities but whose personnel was limited in education and technical instruction in mechanized warfare. With fewer than 100,000 Europeans available in North Africa, there was a serious deficiency of trained personnel; officers, mechanics, and supply, medical, maintenance, communication, and transportation experts were lacking.

The figures on which Giraud's computations were based might be questioned. With the inefficiency that conditions in North Africa imposed, accounting systems could not be entirely accurate, and it was suspected by some that 250,000 would be a better figure than 300,000. Giraud insisted, however, that it should be possible to equip and train eleven divisions (of which three would be armored) and also to build up an air force of 1,000 planes. In the first weeks of December, 1942, detailed plans for the formation of these divisions were drawn up at Giraud's headquarters for submission to the Americans.[5]

Eisenhower was more than a little embarrassed by Giraud's ardor. The French General, who under the terms of the Clark-Darlan Agreement operated independently from Allied headquarters, continued to order the French Army up to the Tunisian front, where, inadequately clothed, poorly supplied, and armed with antiquated rifles, its men suffered enormous casualties and in some instances hindered rather than helped the campaign. Toward the end of January many French troops had to be withdrawn for reorganization and training. Of the 50,000 French who saw action in the Tunisian Campaign, almost one-third became casualties. This intense and enthusiastic effort to re-enter the fight against the Germans could not help but evoke sympathy and admiration among the Americans, but Eisenhower possessed so little matériel of his own that he was incapable of turning over appreciable amounts to the French. The equipping of the French was a problem for Washington, and Giraud was advised to send a mission to the United States to raise the question at the staff level.

Giraud determined to send as heads of his mission two men whose excessive aid to the Allies during the invasion had brought them a temporary ostracism among pro-Pétainist officials: General Béthouart and Jacques Lemaigre-Dubreuil. Béthouart was to handle the essentially military questions and remain in Washington as permanent military delegate, while Lemaigre-Dubreuil was to take care of Lend-Lease, production priorities, and shipping allotments and then return to Algiers. Departing from Algiers around December 15, the mission was en route when Darlan was assassinated, and by the time Béthouart and Lemaigre-Dubreuil arrived in Washington they learned that they represented Giraud not only as French commander in chief but as high commissioner in North and West Africa as well.

The reception that Béthouart received in Washington did not give him much hope for optimism. On December 29 he and Lemaigre-Dubreuil saw the President as well as Admiral Leahy. Leahy commented that they "urged on me that French troops in North Africa be given a

---

[5] Marcel Vigneras, *Rearming the French* (special study in *The United States Army in World War II*), 25–30.

priority over our own forces in the matter of military equipment. This attitude was extremely disconcerting in view of the fact that there was not a sufficient number of American troops in Africa to hold the French under control in that great area by force of arms."[6] There was, of course, good reason for the President and Leahy to be noncommittal. They knew, as the French delegates did not, that Roosevelt, Churchill, the Combined Chiefs of Staff, and the major theater commanders would in two weeks be discussing the entire range of tactical and strategic commitments at Casablanca. Disposition of French matters could wait until then.

At the State Department, Lemaigre-Dubreuil made out somewhat more successfully. On January 9, the day that President Roosevelt left unobtrusively for Casablanca, he conversed with Secretary Hull in the presence of Ray Atherton and Samuel Reber. Lemaigre-Dubreuil made an earnest appeal for State Department backing. He argued that the Clark-Darlan Agreement should be modified to conform with Murphy's earlier commitment to Giraud, and he intimated that if General Giraud were provided with sufficient support, the General could relegate De Gaulle's political aspirations to a secondary place. Lemaigre-Dubreuil also suggested that Giraud issue a statement which would undercut the claims De Gaulle had made in his Brazzaville Declaration of two years earlier. Such a statement would affirm Giraud's position as trustee of French interests until the end of the war.[7]

Upon reflection after this discussion with the Secretary of State, Lemaigre-Dubreuil concluded that a declaration by Giraud would hardly suffice to balance the pretensions that De Gaulle had been making unless it became clear that Giraud was supported by the United States. When he saw Atherton two days later, he suggested that Giraud's statement be followed by a declaration from the President saying that he recognized Giraud as an ally and as trustee of French interests. It is not likely that anyone in the State Department believed the President would go this far, and it was understood that before the Department submitted any memoranda to the President, Lemaigre-Dubreuil would have to obtain Eisenhower's approval.

[6] *I Was There*, 142; Crusoe, *Vicissitudes d'une victoire*, 78–86.
[7] Department of State, *Memorandum of conversation*, 9 Jan. 1943.

It occurred to Hull that if Lemaigre-Dubreuil was anxious to obtain sanction for his proposal, there could be no more opportune moment than the present, when Eisenhower, Giraud, and the President were all together at Casablanca. Hull was quick to realize that if the President subscribed to the Frenchman's proposal, it would in fact place a considerable barrier to De Gaulle's usurping authority in North Africa. In any case, Hull decided that Lemaigre-Dubreuil could plead his cause more effectively in North Africa, and on January 16, without revealing that the Casablanca Conference was then in progress, he took steps to facilitate Lemaigre-Dubreuil's flight back to Algiers, where, he said, a surprise awaited him.[8]

On his arrival in North Africa, Lemaigre-Dubreuil soon learned of Giraud's whereabouts, and he persuaded Colonel Julius Holmes of Eisenhower's staff to authorize his flight to Casablanca. He arrived there three days before the end of the Conference. He had just enough time.

De Gaulle–Giraud Relations before the Conference

The positions that British and American policy makers had taken and the hopes that Lemaigre-Dubreuil entertained on General Giraud's behalf did not permit much optimism in regard to the Gaullists' early introduction into North Africa. De Gaulle had not hesitated, however, to make contacts with General Giraud. Before it was known that Giraud would succeed to Darlan's post, De Gaulle had dispatched a message on Christmas Day via American military headquarters in London, proposing to Giraud that they meet on French soil to discuss means of effecting the unification of their forces. The message was delivered to Giraud on December 27, and two days later he replied, stating that he approved of unification but that the atmosphere was unfavorable at this time for a personal encounter.

Giraud did not exaggerate. It will be remembered that on December 30 the Algerian police had forcibly detained several Gaullists, who it was reported possessed information about a plot to murder Giraud and Murphy. While the charges against these men were exaggerated, the

[8] Crusoe, *Vicissitudes d'une victoire,* 84–89; interview of author with Lemaigre-Dubreuil.

general uneasiness in Algiers did not lull General Giraud's apprehensions in regard to Gaullists, and he found no enthusiasm at Allied headquarters or among his own entourage for a visit from the Fighting French leader. Furthermore, Giraud was far more interested in the military matters that demanded much of his time, and he was anxious to learn from a personal inspection of West Africa what kind of forces were available there. Although his replies to De Gaulle appeared brusque and noncommittal, Giraud undoubtedly believed that concern for his own army of 100,000 took precedence over discussions that might add two divisions more or less to his total forces. To Giraud's soldierly mind, the question of union was fundamentally the question of joining two armies.

Not having received a satisfactory reply to their advances, Fighting French headquarters drew up a communiqué to express the Gaullist position, and without first consulting with either the British or the Americans, they abruptly published their statement on January 2, 1943. In this declaration De Gaulle made public his overtures to Giraud (he had sent Giraud another proposal on New Year's Day) and announced that the solution to the confusion at Algiers should be:

> . . . the establishment in French North and West Africa—as in all other French territories overseas—of a temporary and enlarged central power founded on national union, inspired by the spirit of war and of liberation, with laws that are the laws of the Republic, to last until such time as the nation has made known her will.

A release on policy published in the Gaullist newspaper *La Marseillaise* on January 3 also made it clear that the Fighting French believed that political unification should precede military union, but it was also known that De Gaulle would not reach agreement with Giraud unless men like Boisson and Noguès were removed from their influential administrative posts. When on January 16 it was announced that Marcel Peyrouton would succeed Chatel in Algeria, the Gaullists felt that a conspiracy to keep Vichy in power could hardly be denied.

Giraud continued to be evasive in his replies, not answering the January 1 note for four days and then regretting that he was completely engaged until the end of the month. De Gaulle immediately transmitted a third message on January 7. By the time he received this message in Algiers, Giraud had learned that he would shortly have the opportunity of meeting President Roosevelt at the Casablanca Conference. Under these circumstances he could discover no advantage in a consultation with De Gaulle, but he did agree, just before he left Algiers for Casablanca, to accept a Fighting French military liaison officer as soon as one could be sent from London.

De Gaulle felt that the last response from Giraud was encouraging, and he made plans to send Colonel Billotte and Major Pelabon immediately to Algiers. On January 17 he asked the Americans to transmit a fourth message to Giraud, stating that the officers were on their way and that a meeting between himself and Giraud should not be delayed any longer. On the same day De Gaulle received via the Foreign Office a message from Churchill inviting him to proceed at once to participate in the Casablanca Conference, where he would have an opportunity to confer with Giraud.

To De Gaulle this was an altogether different matter. He had no objection to negotiations, conferences, or exchanges of mission with Giraud, so long as these proceeded between Frenchmen without Allied interference; but all of De Gaulle's nationalist pride and shame at his position as "prisoner of the English" welled up in him to reject the curt summons from a foreigner to meet another Frenchman on French soil in "the atmosphere of an exalted Allied forum." He transmitted to Foreign Secretary Eden a flat, peremptory, and unqualified rejection of the Prime Minister's invitation. Nor did he, incidentally, take pains to inform his National Committee either of the invitation or of his action concerning it. The hopeful exchanges that had been passing between De Gaulle and Giraud were now pushed to the background by the British and American injection of themselves into the negotiations. De Gaulle's blind suspicions caused him to reach the conclusion that the Americans had purposely delayed his messages and had influenced Giraud to respond coolly to his proposals.[9]

Aggrieved and irascible, the sulking De Gaulle kept to his tent. No one could estimate how much or what kind of cajolery would be required to bring him forth.

[9] De Gaulle, *Mémoires*, II, 437–38.

Churchill and Roosevelt at Casablanca

Not far from Casablanca, on a rise overlooking the Atlantic, lies the tiny residential suburb of Anfa, composed almost entirely of sumptuous, well-furnished villas. Early in January, 1943, the Allied forces had requisitioned the entire area; surrounded it with barbed wire; provided it with cooks, orderlies, and guards; and prepared it for the arrival of the President and the Prime Minister, their Chiefs of Staff, and their experts on geography, logistics, and all the technical matters necessary for the waging of modern warfare. Neither Hull nor Eden took part in the Conference, for, since Roosevelt had not wished Hull to be present, Churchill had been forced to agree reluctantly that Eden should be left in London. Admiral Leahy, who had fallen ill on the way to the meeting, was also unable to attend.

The major work of the Conference included the planning, by the British and American high-ranking officers who comprised the Combined Chiefs of Staff, of the campaigns to follow upon the conquest of Tunisia. Roosevelt and Churchill did not generally interfere with the work of the Combined Chiefs but devoted their own attentions primarily to over-all strategy and to political matters. If the description of the conference which follows permits the impression that the French problem received the exclusive attention of the policy makers, it should be borne in mind that military discussions, the invasions of Sicily and Italy, the question of unconditional surrender, and other matters took up most of the Conference's attention. On the other hand, the French problem proved to have many more facets and to be much more difficult to resolve than Roosevelt had anticipated. Difficulties with the French kept the Conference going until January 24, although it had been originally planned to finish on January 21.

In coming to Anfa, Roosevelt had probably been prepared to argue for the *status quo* in North and West Africa. He had not yet met General Giraud, but his antipathy to De Gaulle would have inclined him to avoid any measures which would bring the two generals together under an arrangement permitting De Gaulle to obtain political mastery over such a significant and heavily populated part of the French Empire. Still, if the two French leaders wished to unify their forces in such a

Roosevelt's "willing bridegroom" (Giraud) and Churchill's "temperamental bride" (De Gaulle) met to inspect a guard of honor in North Africa on May 30, 1943.

Culver Service

On June 14, 1944, for the first time since the Germans occupied his country, General de Gaulle stepped on French soil. Here, he greets General Montgomery and inspects some of the British troops who fought in the recapture of Normandy.

way that the war effort would be assisted, Roosevelt could not, either from personal conviction or in the face of public opinion, stand in the way. Soon after his arrival at Anfa on January 14, following his first conversations with Churchill, Macmillan, and Murphy, the President saw that the problem was more pressing than he had realized. He learned that public opinion and the pro-Gaullist press in England had made such a commotion about the Darlan affair and the exclusion of the Free French that Churchill felt constrained to take some positive step which would ease the pressure. To Roosevelt, with his great faith in the efficacy of personal contacts and in his own ability to mediate the most troublesome conflicts, the solution was apparent: bring the two Frenchmen together and see what will happen. "We'll call Giraud the bridegroom," he suggested to Churchill, "and I'll produce him from Algiers, and you get the bride, De Gaulle, down from London, and we'll have a shotgun wedding."[10]

After two days of discussion, the Prime Minister admitted that it might be desirable to invite De Gaulle to Casablanca. If the Prime Minister agreed reluctantly (as the President seemed to believe), it could have been that Churchill, knowing De Gaulle's irascible temperament, feared an explosion that would cause De Gaulle irreparable harm and permanently destroy his chances of coming into the North African picture. Such an eventuality would diminish British prestige and possibly produce further breaks in the stretched fabric of Anglo-American harmony. Churchill had to weigh the advantage of keeping De Gaulle in London against the disadvantage of creating ill will in the President. Concluding that the latter course was the more hazardous, the Prime Minister sent off a dispatch on January 16, inviting De Gaulle to the Conference. De Gaulle's disdainful rejection of this invitation has already been described.

In spite of the President's confidence that he had chosen the best possible way of handling French differences, his advisers did not share his optimism. Robert Murphy and General Eisenhower told the President about some of the difficulties they were beginning to have with Giraud: his impetuosity and independence in ordering French troops

[10] Roosevelt press conference of 12 Feb. 1943, in Samuel I. Rosenman, comp., *Public Papers and Addresses of Franklin D. Roosevelt, 1943,* 83.

to the front, his ambition to take over the inter-Allied supreme command, and his lack of interest in civil administration.

If the President did not immediately grasp the significance of Eisenhower's report, Harry Hopkins instantly saw that such a state of affairs at Giraud's headquarters would produce no amelioration in the North African social conditions which had so incensed Allied correspondents and that Giraud could be easily duped by the socially and politically conscious retinue of General de Gaulle. Unless the United States was prepared to turn North Africa completely over to the Free French, it would be necessary for General Giraud to establish a civil cabinet capable of formulating a program that would be democratic, liberal, and not patterned on Vichy. There was in Washington, Hopkins recalled, a Frenchman who might serve on such a cabinet: Jean Monnet, a man who, like Hopkins himself, shunned publicity, yet possessed extraordinary acumen together with a genius for discovering sources of weakness and imaginative ways of overcoming them. Monnet, who had been head of the Anglo-French Co-ordinating Committee in 1940, had been the author of the dramatic political-union scheme which Churchill proposed to Reynaud; later, in Washington with the British Supply Council, he had devised the slogan, "the Arsenal of Democracy," and with America in the war, he had worked on the "Victory Program" and on Hopkins' Munitions Assignments Board. Although Monnet's backgrounds were big business and high finance, Hopkins had faith that Monnet, "the little howitzer of great ideas," was the man who could provide Giraud with the necessary guidance; and he strongly recommended to the President that Giraud be persuaded to invite him to Algiers.

On January 17, General Giraud arrived at Anfa, accompanied by two staff officers, Colonel de Linarès and Captain Beaufré. It is indicative of Giraud's character that he brought only a small military staff and left the chiefs of the North African civil administration, such as Rigault, Tron, and Pose, in Algiers. (Lemaigre-Dubreuil was, so far as Giraud knew, still in Washington.) The only civilian (although a reserve officer) among his advisers was André Poniatowski, a tank expert who had acted as liaison between London and Vichy in 1942 and who had come to North Africa, offering his services to Giraud, soon after the invasion.

On the afternoon of the seventeenth a schedule was arranged whereby General Giraud would see both Roosevelt and Churchill. General Mark Clark conducted Giraud to the President's villa, where the conversation lasted for about an hour. According to Clark, "the President didn't like to make use of an interpreter and tried to conduct the conversation in French. This was a dismal failure since Giraud merely became more and more puzzled as the President rattled on in his rusty French." Giraud is more generous, stating that the President greeted him, *"parlant très facilement français."* The discussion was an agreeable one, turning on personal matters, but Giraud did not fail to bring up the question uppermost in his thinking. He asked for equipment for 300,000 men, and he placed a request, in accordance with instructions from M. Tron, his financial adviser, for a re-evaluation of the rate of exchange in North Africa. Giraud was pleased with his reception—*"J'ai un partenaire très compréhensif"*—for Roosevelt promised to take up all the matters with his advisers.[11] Roosevelt availed himself of the opportunity to observe the personality which had led Murphy and Eisenhower to doubt Giraud's administrative capacities. According to the President's son Elliott, the interview "was a vast disappointment to Father. . . . Father showed by his questions that he felt Giraud underestimated his job seriously."

True to his promise to Giraud, President Roosevelt brought up next day at the plenary session of the Combined Chiefs of Staff, which Churchill also attended, the proposal that arms and equipment for North and West African troops be provided for General Giraud's use. The British members received this suggestion with little enthusiasm. They could anticipate that these deliveries would be made at the expense of equipment earmarked for the United Kingdom, they could see that Giraud would muster eleven strong divisions to De Gaulle's two, and they could see the whole French war effort oriented toward Washington. Yet when the President personally put forth the proposal, it was difficult for the British, themselves very dependent on American production, to raise objections. Knowing the President's attitude toward De Gaulle, they could not very well argue that the Free French were more deserving of this equipment than Giraud.

11 Henri Giraud, *Un seul but, la victoire,* 90–91; Mark W. Clark, *Calculated Risk,* 148.

In the absence of their champion, the British found themselves in an awkward position. Roosevelt unmercifully badgered Churchill about his inability to produce "the temperamental bride." He wrote to Hull that the bride "has become quite high-hat about the whole affair and doesn't want to see either of us, and shows no intention of getting into the bed with Giraud."[12] Churchill may have lacked enthusiasm for De Gaulle's coming to Casablanca, but neither did he enjoy being made the butt of the President's remarks; and after Roosevelt jokingly suggested that he ought to terminate De Gaulle's subsidies, the Prime Minister determined to send a stronger note to London. If he did not threaten to cut off De Gaulle's ration, he at least decided to make it clear that the invitation came as much from Roosevelt as from himself and that a refusal would involve another serious crisis between De Gaulle and the British.[13]

After two days of intensive discussion, the French political question was no nearer to a solution. No reply had been received from London about the possibility of De Gaulle's coming, and the poorly timed announcement of Peyrouton's appointment as governor of Algeria promised to produce incurable resentment at Carlton Gardens. Churchill, piqued, tormented by Roosevelt about De Gaulle's nonappearance, could foresee that British influence in the North African area might gradually melt away. He determined to see Giraud once more. During the afternoon interview between the French General and the President, Churchill strode in and dramatically announced that De Gaulle would have to choose between coming and losing his British subsidies. Giraud had the impression that the scenario had been prepared, which, considering that the message had gone off two days previously, indeed it had been.

[12] Hull, *Memoirs*, II, 1207.

[13] Churchill, *Hinge of Fate*, 680–81. Churchill maintains that this dispatch "dismisses forever" Elliott Roosevelt's allegation that the Prime Minister opposed De Gaulle's coming to Casablanca (Elliott Roosevelt, *As He Saw It*, 89, 92, 99). Yet it should be noted that Churchill does not cite his first telegram of January 16, the text of which is published in French by De Gaulle (*Mémoires*, II, 437), nor does he emphasize the fact that the Conference had been in session four days before the second note was sent. Churchill's lack of reference to Roosevelt in the first note particularly irked De Gaulle (*ibid.*, 75), who had long been trying to see Giraud. Note also a reference to three invitations in Hull, *Memoirs*, II, 1208.

On January 21, while the President went off by jeep to review American troops, Giraud occupied himself in discussing matters of supply with General Somervell, head of the service forces. The American problem, to locate the shipping with which to transport arms and equipment to North Africa, was particularly difficult in the light of commitments to England, Russia, and China which strained convoy resources to the utmost. Giraud had offered to put 160,000 tons of French shipping into the Allied Shipping Pool and expected that a certain percentage of this would be applied to French civilian and military needs. No clear-cut decision, however, emerged from his conversations on convoy allotments.

On the same day, while absorbed in estimates and calculations concerning military requirements, Giraud was interrupted by the unexpected and not, from his point of view, entirely desirable arrival of his civilian emissary to Washington, Jacques Lemaigre-Dubreuil. Whether he wished to or not, Giraud would soon have to discuss the sensitive question of French sovereignty.

The Sovereignty Question

What Lemaigre-Dubreuil wished to accomplish, and what Giraud failed to appreciate, was no less than an abrogation of the Clark-Darlan Agreement and recognition of Giraud as the sole representative of French interests, not simply in North Africa but in the entire French Empire.[14] This would mean not only that De Gaulle would be by-passed but that the Allies, having accepted French sovereignty in North Africa, would be required to negotiate with the French as equals for the use of facilities instead of receiving them, as they so far had done, under the terms of the Clark-Darlan pact. It should be pointed out, in fairness to Lemaigre-Dubreuil, that the Gaullists also were in favor of a modification of the Clark-Darlan Agreement, although obviously not at the price of their own exclusion from North Africa. When Giraud told Lemaigre-Dubreuil of his accomplishments thus far—the promise of rearmament and the adjustment of the exchange rate—the industrialist

[14] Lemaigre-Dubreuil describes his role in Crusoe, *Vicissitudes d'une victoire,* 87–98. Some information was also received from conversations with Lemaigre-Dubreuil, André Poniatowski, General François d'Astier, and Julius Holmes.

saw at once that Giraud had overlooked what in his judgment was most significant: an understanding with the Americans concerning Giraud's political powers, such as those established in the Murphy letters of November 2 which the Clark-Darlan Agreement had suspended. The two men discussed the matter heatedly, but their backgrounds and interests were so diverse that it was impossible for each to sympathize with the other's point of view.

Lemaigre-Dubreuil devoted the evening of his arrival to the redaction of a memorandum which set forth the terms of what he would consider to be a satisfactory political arrangement. This memorandum would in effect include the points discussed at the State Department, which were to be cleared by Eisenhower; but obviously a direct contact with the President would make such clearance unnecessary. The memorandum would place in force the Murphy letter of November 2 which recognized French sovereignty, recognized the French as an ally, and affirmed that "American authorities will in no way intervene in affairs which are solely the province of the national administration or which derive from the exercise of French sovereignty." The memorandum would further state that both the American and British governments recognized in the "Commander-in-Chief, with his headquarters at Algiers [i.e., Giraud] the right and duty of preserving all French interests in the military, economic, financial, and moral plane." Lemaigre-Dubreuil somewhat naïvely believed that by omitting the political plane, his document might be palatable to the British.

During the next few days the memorandum was slightly revised by General Giraud until it achieved the following form:

1. The intervention of the Anglo-American troops on the 8th of November on French territory in Africa, brought about at the demand of the French who, since 1940, have wanted to take up the fight against Germany, was the first act of liberation of an oppressed nation accomplished by the United Nations.

2. The form of the relations between France and the Foreign powers temporarily occupying part of French territory, the post-war consequences of the association of France and the United States in the fight against Germany, the military, economic and financial aid given to France, have all been defined in letters exchanged between the Consul, Mr. Murphy,

in the name of President Roosevelt, and General Giraud, before the landing. They remain in force. However, the paragraph dealing with the military question and with the Inter-Allied Command is excepted.

3. Because of the fact that the French nation and the French people are the only ones who may fix their representation and designate their government, and because it is impossible for the French in the motherland to pronounce freely her will, France no longer possesses a government.

In the interests of the French people, in order to safeguard France's past, her present and her future, the Government of the United States and the Government of Great Britain recognize in the Commander in Chief, with his headquarters at Algiers, the right and duty of preserving all French interests in the military, economic, financial and moral plane. They bind themselves to aid him by all the means in their power until the day when, in complete freedom, the French people and the French nation, shall be able to designate their regular government.

General Eisenhower and Minister Murphy will work out with the French Commander in Chief, with his headquarters at Algiers, the details of the present understanding. In so doing, they will be governed by the conversations exchanged in Washington between the 28th of December and the eleventh of January, by the representatives of General Giraud and the State Department, and the decisions which have been made by President Roosevelt, Mr. Churchill, and General Giraud in the interview at Casablanca between the seventeenth and twenty-fourth of January, 1943.[15]

General Giraud promised Lemaigre-Dubreuil that he would submit the memorandum to President Roosevelt if he had an opportunity during their next conversation. Meanwhile Lemaigre-Dubreuil could do nothing but wait.

De Gaulle and the Conference

In London, General de Gaulle continued to nurse his resentment against Churchill for his interference in French affairs, against the Americans for their support of Giraud, and against Giraud for his slavish quasi allegiance to Vichy. On January 16 his resentment was deepened

[15] A. L. Funk, "The 'Anfa Memorandum': An Incident of the Casablanca Conference," *Journal of Modern History*, Vol. XXVI, No. 3 (Sept., 1954), 249–50.

by the announcement that Marcel Peyrouton, reputed to have signed De Gaulle's death warrant when he was Vichy's minister of the interior, had been installed as governor of Algeria. In spite of this staggering knowledge, De Gaulle had sent Giraud on January 17 a message in regard to exchange of liaison officers. He had not received a reply to this message when, on January 19, Churchill's strong and urgent note was handed to him. He could only conclude that Giraud was now a prisoner of the Americans just as he was a prisoner of the British.

Although De Gaulle had not publicized his invitation to the Conference, General Catroux learned of it and with his habitual level-headed good judgment attempted to persuade De Gaulle that he should go. Catroux finally obtained a grudging consent on De Gaulle's part to permit the National Committee to discuss the question on the following day, January 20. Ultimately Diethelm and Soustelle, who strongly opposed the General's departure, lost out to the advice of the military that De Gaulle should accept the invitation. That De Gaulle took with him to Casablanca General Catroux and Admiral d'Argenlieu, but no civilian advisers, suggests that he was considering a discussion of military coordination rather than political liaison. (In June, 1944, the same argument would bring De Gaulle back to London from Algiers on the eve of the Normandy landings.)

After taking leave of the members of his National Committee, De Gaulle proceeded to call on the Foreign Secretary, who urged him to leave at once. Bad weather intervened, however, and the General was not able to take his plane until the following evening. He arrived finally at Casablanca on January 22, by which time, according to the original plans, the Conference was to have terminated.

President Roosevelt was anxious to meet De Gaulle as soon as possible, and an appointment was scheduled for the same evening, after the President's dinner for the Sultan of Morocco. The interview was not auspicious in regard to improved relations with Free France. De Gaulle's initial hostility had been aggravated by his reception: he was virtually under observation at all times, was not free to pass about at will, and during his interview with the President was under the close and constant surveillance of armed secret-service men. Roosevelt, on the other hand, had no inclination to listen patiently while De Gaulle elaborated on his problems. The President endeavored to charm De Gaulle, speaking to him in French, and to clarify his own position in regard to North Africa. De Gaulle, remembering his conversation with Admiral Stark a month previously, tried to justify his role as leader of the Free French in terms of France's ability, which had been proved historically, to produce an individual who without legal backing was able in time of emergency to assume the leadership. Neither the President nor the General, as a result of mutual interruptions, made their points clear, and Roosevelt brought away the impression that De Gaulle believed himself to be a latter-day Joan of Arc. De Gaulle's allusion to Joan of Arc became the basis of one of the President's favorite anecdotes. In its many retellings it was elaborated and distorted; and when it finally came to De Gaulle's attention, it made him so indignant, it was reported, that he never wanted to meet Roosevelt again. It should not be believed, however, that the failure of this meeting provided the basis for future difficulties between the two men. Those difficulties, which arose from entirely different and conflicting attitudes toward France and French colonial possessions, had long antedated the Casablanca Conference. Had De Gaulle been more pliant, more informal, more co-operative, he might have smoothed the rough edges of the President's animosity, but he could never have erased the friction created by their contrasting points of view.[16]

After De Gaulle had taken his leave of President Roosevelt, Winston Churchill and Harold Macmillan returned to the President's villa for further discussions. Both the Prime Minister and the President agreed for the moment to refrain from interference and to let the two French generals attempt to work out their own solutions.

On the following morning, Giraud proceeded to De Gaulle's villa for lunch, and the discussion lasted through the afternoon. All of the bitterness and rancor that had been generated by the Gaullists against the North African regime since November 15 foamed to the surface. De Gaulle employed the same arguments he had used in his letter of

[16] Roosevelt, *As He Saw It,* 112–14; De Gaulle, *Mémoires,* II, 79; Sherwood, *Roosevelt and Hopkins,* 685–86, 691, 956; Churchill, *Hinge of Fate,* 682; and Pendar, *Adventure in Diplomacy,* 144. For versions of the "Joan or Arc anecdote" see Kerillis, *I Accuse de Gaulle,* 115; Hull, *Memoirs,* II, 1208; and Jacques Soustelle, *D'Alger à Paris* (vol. II of *Envers et contre tout),* 129–30.

October 5 to President Roosevelt: that Fighting France had developed a *mystique,* as representative of the Resistance, which rendered it unthinkable that any other group should pose as the focus of the French effort. Giraud was not convinced. A *mystique* and two divisions did not overbalance his own potential army of eleven or twelve divisions, *mystique* or no. From the military point of view—and Giraud was incapable of thinking in other terms—De Gaulle should come to North Africa with his troops and affiliate himself with Giraud's army in a subordinate capacity. This arrangement was one which would be acceptable to Roosevelt, whom Giraud did not wish to offend; but any other settlement, which would permit De Gaulle an influence superior to the weight of his divisions, Giraud knew would be no more acceptable to the Americans than to himself.

Robert Murphy had already suggested a solution which might have avoided a great many difficulties:

> ... in my first conversation with de Gaulle after his arrival I suggested that he come to North Africa without making elaborate conditions in advance. He said that he was not able to take this decision because he was 'a prisoner of his committee.' He also said that he doubted that more than 10% of the North African French would support him at that time. The suggestion was de Gaulle's and not mine although I was convinced of its accuracy. I pointed out to him that General Giraud was not interested in politics and that if a satisfactory working relationship could be worked out between the two men, Giraud would be happy to handle the military end of things leaving de Gaulle pretty much a free hand politically. I believe the idea appealed to de Gaulle but he apparently could not decide that way for reasons best known to himself.[17]

What probably prevented De Gaulle from coming immediately to Algiers was the lack of a guarantee that certain individuals whom Free French propaganda had long attacked would be purged. For De Gaulle and his group to come to North Africa as subordinates of Giraud would mean that they would have to range themselves side by side with the

[17] Robert Murphy to the author, 2 May 1951. De Gaulle attributes the estimate of 10 per cent to Murphy (*Mémoires,* II, 83).

Vichy appointees: Noguès, Boisson, Peyrouton, and Bergeret. This they could not possibly do, for the spirit of the Fighting French movement was generated from its antipathy to everything Vichy stood for. This Giraud apparently could not grasp.

One other compromise plan was discussed by the two generals. This was a modification of the suggestion that was basic to the new British policy—that a committee be formed which would be headed by some distinguished Frenchman under whom both De Gaulle and Giraud would be willing to subordinate themselves. The British had brought up this plan during the early days of the Conference, but the lack of specific information on the location and availability of French leaders made it impossible to pursue the project very far. During the discussions, however, Hopkins had mentioned the name of Jean Monnet, and Churchill wondered at the possibility of bringing General Alphonse Georges out of France. President Roosevelt had broached this solution with Giraud, suggesting that "maybe we could get someone else out of France or someone who has taken refuge in Switzerland." Members of Giraud's staff entertained the possibility of a variation on this theme, the formation of a triumvirate in which De Gaulle would handle political affairs, Giraud military affairs, and Catroux colonial matters; although when Giraud brought up the proposal with Catroux he became somewhat vague about the identity of the third person: "I don't know yet," he said, "perhaps General Georges." But De Gaulle would have nothing to do with a triumvirate and rejected the idea with habitual brusqueness. "Bonaparte had two things," he told Giraud, "a plebiscite and victories. You have neither."

The two generals had reached a deadlock. Giraud refused to purge his administrative personnel, and De Gaulle refused to come to Africa in a subordinate capacity. All suggested compromises had fallen on barren ground, and since there appeared to be no other possible solutions, they took leave of each other. "We separated," writes Giraud, "correctly if not coldly."[18]

[18] *Un seul but, le victoire,* 107; General Georges Catroux, *Dans la Bataille de Méditerranée,* 320. De Gaulle attributes the Giraud–De Gaulle–Georges triumvirate idea to Churchill (*Mémoires,* II, 78).

The Conference Comes to an End

With the Conference scheduled to terminate the following day, Allied leaders despaired of effecting a reconciliation between the Frenchmen. On the other hand, the major work of the meeting—the decisions on military strategy—had been successfully concluded on January 23, when the Combined Chiefs of Staff reached a number of final decisions in regard to "Husky" (the invasion of Sicily), aid to Russia, the antisubmarine program, and the build-up for the Normandy invasion. It should be noted, however, that while the Combined Chiefs had discussed French rearmament and the use of French troops, they had reached no formal conclusions. Similarly, while the American Joint Chiefs and, individually, Generals Marshall and Somervell had discussed the problem in detail, none had arrived at a definite commitment or final plans. Marshall had in fact urged that the American Chiefs set forth "a policy with respect to the contemplated employment of the French forces in North Africa and the scale of equipment to be provided," but by the end of the Conference no such policy had been adopted. Marshall left for Washington with the understanding that the question was still undecided.

On the evening of January 23, Murphy and Macmillan learned the disappointing news that in spite of the afternoon's discussions the French leaders had been unable to reach a compromise. It had been hoped that a communiqué could be issued which would reveal the end of French differences. Although they had hoped that it would be unnecessary to intervene, the two Allied diplomats decided to do what they could to locate some common ground before the press conference which had been scheduled for noon the next day. But throughout the evening of the twenty-third, De Gaulle remained adamant in his refusal to subscribe to a statement which in his judgment did not reflect the actual state of relations between the two French groups.

Sunday, January 24, was the final day of the Conference. The Combined Chiefs of Staff had completed their work, and the joint British-American communiqué required only a few final touches. Everything was in readiness for meeting the correspondents, except for a settlement of the French issue, on which Murphy and Macmillan reported that while the two French generals were willing to co-operate, neither would agree to subordinate himself to the other. Frenetic negotiations continued throughout the morning. Admiral d'Argenlieu tried to persuade Giraud that it was his entourage of Bergeret, Boisson, and Peyrouton which rendered it impossible for the Gaullists to accept a conciliatory attitude. Giraud felt the position was exaggerated, and he remained "stupefied at such stubbornness."

While they were working over the final version of the official communiqué, Hopkins told the President that he thought "we could get an agreement on a joint statement issued by de Gaulle and Giraud—and a picture of the two of them. Bob [Murphy] and I [Hopkins] then told Macmillan that Churchill had to bring de Gaulle around." Thus it was arranged that Churchill should attempt to persuade De Gaulle and Roosevelt should put pressure on Giraud. It is not unlikely that Hopkins and Murphy had already drafted a proposed communiqué to which it was believed the French generals could not object.

Late in the morning De Gaulle went to see Churchill at his villa. Convinced of the futility of further sojourn at Anfa, De Gaulle had already made his preparations to leave and thought of his visit to the Prime Minister as a courtesy call in which to make his farewells. Churchill could see in his abrupt departure only a complete loss of British prestige in North and West Africa; he insisted, even threatened, that he would expose De Gaulle to adverse public opinion and to Parliament if he did not prove co-operative in the matter of the communiqué. Coercion only intensified De Gaulle's intransigence. Bristling, he informed the Prime Minister that he was free thus to dishonor himself and unceremoniously walked off to take his farewell of the President.[19]

Meanwhile, arrangements had been made for Giraud to see the President at about 11:00 A.M. By this time Giraud had drawn up a memorandum which reflected the points discussed between himself and the President, General Marshall and General Somervell. The text, in French, had been written with some care in collaboration with Robert Murphy.

[19] Giraud, *Un seul but, la victoire*, 108; Churchill, *Hinge of Fate*, 692–93; Sherwood, *Roosevelt and Hopkins*, 693–94. De Gaulle characterizes his meeting with Churchill as "la plus rude de nos rencontres" of the entire war (*Mémoires*, II, 84).

Since the memorandum became a basic document in further relations with the French, the official translation of the text which the President approved is given in full. The marginal comments were those made by Roosevelt.

Okay

1. Under the military plan, it has been agreed between the President of the United States and General Giraud that the French forces will receive, by priority, the equipment which is indispensable to them and that this shall be made up of the most modern material.

2. In subsequent talks with General Marshall and General Somervell, it was agreed in principle that the delivery would amount to material for three armored divisions and eight motorized divisions as well as for a first-line air force consisting of 500 fighters, 300 bombers, and 200 transport planes, and that of this equipment there would be delivered during the weeks to come 400 trucks, and equipment for two armored regiments, three reconnaissance battalions, three battalions of tank destroyers, and three motorized divisions and such of the aviation equipment as can come by air. The details are to be worked out with the Commander in Chief Allied Forces.

Okay in principle, work out with Eisenhower and Somervell.

3. In regard to transport, it has been agreed with General Somervell that the supplying of French Africa would be assured by a monthly allocation of 65,000 tons (50,000 tons of wheat, 12,000 tons of sugar, 3,000 tons of material) and that the shipment of this material would be made before next summer. France would furnish to the inter-Allied pool a share of 165,000 tons of shipping and the Allies would furnish the remainder for the delivery to be completed within the agreed time. The aviation material would be sent (coal and fuel excepted) as far as possible, by air.

Okay

4. Under the political plan, it was agreed between the President of the United States, the Prime Minister of Great Britain and General Giraud that it was to their common interest for all the French fighting against Germany to be reunited under one authority, and that every facility would be given to General Giraud in order to bring about this reunion.

Okay as amended

5. In connection with this, it has been agreed by the President of the United States that the exchange would be brought to 50 francs to the dollar in order to ameliorate the existing differences with the exchange rate given to the territories placed under the control of General de Gaulle (it being the strong hope that, in the latter territories, the rate will be lowered from 43 to 50 francs to the dollar).

78

6. It has also been agreed that the necessary propaganda (for France in the French language) should be carried on from the African territory by the French authorities and that, for this reason, conferences should be held regarding the use of short-wave radio stations.[20]

Amend

Shortly before he left for his final meeting with the President, Giraud was accosted by Lemaigre-Dubreuil, who wished to accompany the General so that he could present the memorandum which he had drawn up to cover the political points discussed at the State Department in Washington. Giraud refused this request, but agreed to take the Lemaigre-Dubreuil document along with him.

At about half-past eleven, while De Gaulle was still with Churchill, Giraud went in to see the President. He agreed willingly enough that Frenchmen should be unified and expressed his readiness to sign a communiqué jointly with De Gaulle. Then the General and the President turned to the other (military) memorandum concerning questions of rearmament which had been discussed during the Anfa Conference. The version used was the English translation. In Murphy's words: "I happened to have a copy of it at the moment of the discussion which I provided as General Giraud had not brought his copy along with him."[21]

President Roosevelt went over the military memorandum point by point, with Murphy translating for Giraud's benefit, and he commented "okay" or "okay in principle" at the various passages. It has been suggested that "oui en principe" to the French mind is more specific and binding than the English equivalent. This seems to be a fine distinction, for the real difference in interpretation concerned the degree to which a binding commitment was desired by the French and by the Americans. With their world-wide commitments, the Americans tended to accord French rearmament a low priority, whereas to General Giraud the agreement in principle was his only chance of remaining in the war. Giraud therefore tended to interpret "oui en principe" as a commitment,

[20] Murphy telegram of 1 Feb. 1943 (State Dept., 740.0011 Eur. War 1939/27641). Cf. text in Vigneras, *Rearming the French*, 38. French text in René Richard and Alain de Sérigny, *La bissectrice de la guerre*, 231–32.

[21] Letter of Murphy to the writer, 2 May 1941; Funk, "The 'Anfa Memorandum,' " *Journal of Modern History*, Vol. XXVI, No. 3 (Sept., 1954), 250–51. This episode, while a minor one, presented an opportunity for Gaullist propagandists to cite it as evidence that Giraud was completely a tool of the Americans.

and he experienced great chagrin and disappointment at the slowness with which the program was later implemented.

The President also signed Lemaigre-Dubreuil's political memorandum without making any modifications in the text. In this instance he must have signed without giving any thoughtful consideration to the implications of what he was doing. Certainly the President's French was adequate to comprehend the significance of the text, but he definitely must not have realized that he was approving a statement on behalf of the British government which no British representative—not even the Prime Minister—had seen. He must have missed the point that while the Murphy letters of November 2 "remained in force" the memorandum abrogated the Clark-Darlan Agreement, which Roosevelt not only supported but felt should be interpreted even more stringently by Eisenhower. Later, when Secretary of War Stimson pointed out to him certain implications of the document, President Roosevelt told him "a good story about it." Stimson writes:

> I retaliated by telling him I knew all about this one because Hull had told me it was an agreement "signed over a drink" by the President, at which he laughed and virtually admitted that the other covenants in the paper might have been accomplished the same way.[22]

It should be reiterated that neither of the memoranda had received prior approval of either the Joint or the Combined Chiefs of Staff. These were not recommendations from Roosevelt's military advisers. General Giraud had drawn up with Murphy's help what in his opinion had been agreed during his conversations with the President and with Generals Marshall and Somervell. This summary was then shown to President Roosevelt, who, without consulting either of the generals, precipitately approved the document. This is not to say that Giraud purposely misrepresented the facts, for Machiavellianism was unknown to him, but it does indict the President for overhasty and ill-considered action. When one recalls that on this same morning he propounded his "unconditional surrender" concept of the war, one is forced to conclude

[22] Henry L. Stimson and McGeorge Bundy, *On Active Service in Peace and War,* 558–59.

that it was indeed his day for baiting the British Prime Minister. The gesture of all-out support of Giraud can be explained only in the light of personal antipathy to De Gaulle's stubbornness and a desire to permit his champion—the willing bridegroom—to obtain every advantage in the inevitable struggle for French political domination of North Africa.

When General Giraud left President Roosevelt's villa about noon, General de Gaulle entered. De Gaulle reaffirmed his position, that he would not accept a place subordinate to Giraud and that he would not sign a meaningless joint communiqué. The President did his utmost to bring De Gaulle under the influence of the Rooseveltian charm. It was a matter of public opinion, he argued; the world must not be permitted to see that the Allies were divided among themselves. What the masses required, he pointed out, was drama. Catroux, who was present, remarks dryly that the President's French did not quite do justice to the occasion. He used the word *drame* for "drama," but with its connotations of tragedy to the French mind, it must have been a curiously ironic comment.[23] At this point Churchill entered the villa, and a moment later Harry Hopkins, who had intercepted Giraud's departure, ushered General Giraud back in for a four-way discussion. Hopkins says:

> The President was surprised at seeing Giraud but took it in his stride. De Gaulle was a little bewildered. Churchill grunted. But the President went to work on them with Churchill backing him up vigorously.[24]

The pressure was now applied in earnest. The generals had to agree, did they not, that they both sought a common aim, the liberation of France? They agreed that they were willing to maintain liaison (a decision which had already been reached between them, it will be remembered, before the Casablanca Conference). Should they not be willing, then, to sign a brief statement committing them at least to those two propositions? "Write just twenty words, and sign them," admonished Roosevelt. "You will satisfy public opinion." This finally the generals agreed to do, placing their signatures to a brief, noncommittal communiqué:

23 Catroux, *Dans la bataille de Méditerranée,* 322; De Gaulle, *Mémoires,* II, 85.
24 Sherwood (quoting Hopkins' notes), *Roosevelt and Hopkins,* 693.

We have met, we have talked. We have registered our entire agreement on the end to be achieved, which is the liberation of France and the triumph of human liberties by the total defeat of the enemy.

This end will be attained by the union in war of all Frenchmen, fighting side by side with their Allies.

But President Roosevelt was not yet satisfied that the joint communiqué and the generals' promise to continue negotiations provided enough "drama" for the masses. The generals must meet the press, who were at this moment waiting outside on the lawn for the President and the Prime Minister. The four men emerged to greet the astonished correspondents. Two additional chairs were drawn up, and the two French generals sat in alternating seats, for the benefit of photographers, with Roosevelt and Churchill. Then the President brought forth another suggestion for further "drama": he asked Giraud and De Gaulle to stand up and shake hands. It took some time to convince De Gaulle, but finally the pictures were taken to provide the world with visual proof that at Casablanca the two French groups had reached a sincere accord. The shotgun wedding had come off, and some of the pictures recorded, through their facial expressions, what the participants thought of their union.

At the conclusion of the Anfa Conference, De Gaulle returned to London, where he arrived on the morning of January 26 and immediately began conferences with his Committee. Giraud returned to Algiers, while Roosevelt and Churchill drove to Marrakech, where they relaxed for a day at the villa of the American consul, Kenneth Pendar. From there Roosevelt flew back to the United States by way of Liberia and Brazil, while Churchill proceeded to Cairo and to Turkey for conversations with President Inönü.

President Roosevelt was confident that he had settled the problem of French differences. Shortly after his return to Washington he told a group of newspaper editors:

> Well, as to the future of France, I think everybody is agreed that we must not exercise any influence by any act or deed today—by recognizing this, that, or the other individual as to what that future has got to be. It has got to be chosen by the people of France at the end of the war. . . .

And that is why you have the great effort by de Gaulle to be recognized as what he calls *L'esprit de France, L'âme de France.* . . . Nobody is going to do that, because it would give an unfair advantage. Giraud wants to be recognized as the representative of France all over the world. I said, "No. That will give you an unfair advantage. Let France choose her own government. In the meanwhile, run your own little bailiwick wherever you may happen to be."[25]

But the difficulties had only begun. De Gaulle would not be content to let local officials run their "own little bailiwicks" so long as he had means at his disposal to claim the allegiance of the entire French Empire. A wide and unbridgeable gulf stretched between the President and the leader of Fighting France; it would not be crossed for many months.

American Policy Following the Conference

If President Roosevelt had not solved every aspect of the French problem at Casablanca, he had at least made certain aspects of his policy abundantly clear. He had committed himself thoroughly to General Giraud, and he was prepared to hinder De Gaulle from gaining political or military control of North Africa. Whatever misgivings he may have entertained about Giraud as an individual, he had become determined to provide arms and equipment so that his forces could re-enter the European conflict as soon as possible. From this moment until after the war, considerations of rearmament and employment of French troops must of necessity enter into any discussion of American policy toward the French.

Upon his return from Casablanca, President Roosevelt began to formulate his attitudes more and more precisely. He brought together a number of related ideas which urged him to an inevitable conclusion which supported the policy of local arrangements and nonrecognition which had been developed during the previous years. He never forgot the danger to the United States that resided in the bulge of Africa, and now that North and West Africa were safely in American hands and the threat of German occupation was no longer present, he began to

[25] Rosenman, comp., *Public Papers and Addresses of F. D. Roosevelt, 1943,* 86.

explore means whereby the United States would not again have to tremble at the thought of a hostile power so close to the Western Hemisphere. Less than a month after he left Casablanca, the President remarked during a press conference:

> It has been a great menace, more than we realize it in this war, the fact that the Germans had it in their power to take over Dakar and use it as a raider and submarine base. It's a direct threat against Brazil and this continent, the West Indies, and so forth.
>
> And I think when the war is over, we have got to take certain steps. First, to demilitarize western Africa all the way down. And second, possibly to have a strong point either in Dakar or Bathurst, where we will have sufficient air strength, and sufficient Navy, and sufficient air fields, and so forth, to prevent any aggressor nation in the future from re-establishing a threat against this continent.
>
> Well, as to details I have no idea; it isn't worth talking about. But you have an objective.[26]

Obviously these comments were not to be construed as constituting official United States policy, but the safeguarding of West Africa was nevertheless an idea which permeated the President's thinking and which he developed frequently among his close associates.

If the President was interested in France's postwar position in her colonies because of security reasons, he also entertained certain apprehensions from humanitarian motives about France's right to continue to exploit her colonies. His justification could go back to the Atlantic Charter, but he became more emphatic on the subject after he had an opportunity to examine colonialism at firsthand in Africa during his trip to Casablanca. In the British colony of Gambia he had seen disease "rampant," no education, "pitiful" agriculture, and no possibility of self-government; and he was no more impressed by what he learned about French imperialism.[27] It is not unlikely that the President concurred with Harry Hopkins' ideas on the subject: that this nation "should state unequivocally its belief in the political and economic freedom of

[26] *Ibid.*, 86–87.
[27] Press conference of 5 Feb. 1944 (Rosenman, comp., *Public Papers and Addresses of F. D. Roosevelt, 1944–45*, 68–70).

all people throughout the world, even though that might spell the doom of all the Colonial Empires."[28] At Casablanca, President Roosevelt brought up the subject of imperialism again and again, to Winston Churchill's embarrassed discomfort, and he emphasized it especially during his dinner with the young Sultan of Morocco, Sidi Mohammed Ben Youssef, who took away the impression from Roosevelt's comments that America would support an independence movement in Morocco.

The President's son, Elliott Roosevelt, in his book devoted to recollections of his father's conversations, records that at Casablanca Roosevelt devoted a good proportion of his rambling observations to the postwar world and to the position of colonial empires. According to this source, the President said:

> He [De Gaulle] made it quite clear that he expects the Allies to return all French colonies to French control immediately upon their liberation. You know, quite apart from the fact that the Allies will have to maintain military control of French colonies here in North Africa for months, maybe years, I'm by no means sure in my own mind that we'd be right to return France her colonies *at all, ever,* without first obtaining in the case of each individual colony some sort of pledge, some sort of statement of just exactly what was planned, in terms of each colony's administration. . . . *How* do they belong to France? Why does Morocco, inhabited by Moroccans, belong to France? Or take Indo-China. The Japanese control that colony now. Why was it a cinch for the Japanese to conquer that land? The native Indo-Chinese have been so flagrantly downtrodden that they thought to themselves: Anything must be better, than to live under French colonial rule! Should a land belong to France? By what logic and by what custom and by what historical rule? . . . Don't think for a moment, Elliott, that Americans would be dying in the Pacific tonight, if it hadn't been for the shortsighted greed of the French and the British and the Dutch. Shall we allow them to do it all, all over again? . . . When we've won the war, I will work with all my might and main to see to it that the United States is not wheedled into the position of accepting any plan that will further France's imperialistic ambitions, or that will aid or abet the British Empire in *its* imperial ambitions.[29]

[28] Sherwood, *Roosevelt and Hopkins,* 924. (This opinion was set down by Hopkins in 1945.)
[29] *As He Saw It,* 115–16.

The entire accuracy of Elliott Roosevelt's version of the President's remarks may be held in question by reason of the book's many errors of fact, which suggest that the conversations were reproduced later from the author's memory rather than taken down verbatim at the time; but it is reasonable to suppose that the record, which is corroborated by other sources, represents in a general way the President's casual, thinking-out-loud approach to the question.

Although Roosevelt was far from formulating official American policy at this time, he was by no means isolated in his ideas about imperialism, for the same point of view was emerging in careful State Department studies at about the same time. The President may have been expressing, consciously or unconsciously, in his own words the conclusions that were gradually being developed into the form of a definite foreign policy. Leo Pasvolsky, Green Hackworth, and Stanley Hornbeck had long been working on a formulation of policy to demonstrate that the United States supported steps that would permit colonial areas to move toward independence. Many officials in the State Department interested themselves in the conference of the Institute of Pacific Relations held at Quebec in December, 1942, where debates on postwar international "trusteeships" over colonial areas brought forth some provocative ideas that were incorporated into State Department planning on the United Nations. By the time of the Casablanca Conference, Secretary Hull was attempting to persuade the suspicious British of the merits of a colonial policy which the Allies might adopt to implement the Atlantic Charter; and when Anthony Eden came to Washington in March, 1943, a draft of this policy, which closely paralelled the ideas the President had been turning over, was ready for serious discussion.[30]

Since General de Gaulle had proved himself stubbornly opposed, particularly in Syria, to any modification of the French Empire, it becomes immediately apparent that an American anti-colonial policy must produce a head-on collision with De Gaulle. Since Roosevelt had no intention of trying to implement his ideas during the war but wished to bring them up at the final peace conference, he would not want any French group to achieve such a strong position that it could contest

[30] Hull, *Memoirs*, II, 1234–36.

the underlying philosophy of anti-colonialism. Although it is possible he might have been willing to discuss the matter amiably with any Frenchman who showed himself sympathetic to his ideas, the President knew that man was not De Gaulle. The Fighting French leader believed that as trustee he must return to France with an unimpaired empire, and no more than Churchill for the British Empire, would he be willing to officiate at the liquidation of French possessions. In their staunch defense of colonialism, Churchill and De Gaulle, in spite of their many differences, walked on common ground; and Churchill may have seen in De Gaulle a potential ally in the eventuality of being faced, one day toward the end of the war, by a Russian and American determination to end the reign of colonial powers.

It would be an exaggeration to insist that Roosevelt opposed De Gaulle because he had designs on the French Empire, particularly in view of the fact that the President's ideas at the beginning of 1943 were not formulated clearly enough to be taken as definite policy. Official pronouncements had, indeed, many times affirmed that the United States looked to the total restoration of the French Empire. But, already disposed to oppose De Gaulle or any other pretender toward French sovereign power, the President's general ideas of security and humanitarianism confirmed him in the decision already taken.

President Roosevelt, while inclined toward a genial Francophilism, had lost faith in France as a great power. Not only had he been disillusioned by the rapid collapse of the country in 1940, but he had been confirmed in his judgment by the weak-kneed acquiescence to the Japanese occupation of Indochina, which thereafter threatened the American position in the Philippines.

That De Gaulle mouthed heady phrases about grandeur and honor did not mean that France herself after the war would revive her industry and morale to the point that would render her capable of resuming the responsibilities of a great power. If, after the war, she proved herself strong, American policy could adjust itself to that fact; until then the President could see no reason why the United States should use its influence to build up a new regime artificially or permit it to use the billion dollars' worth of blocked francs in America, when it was not clear that any advantage would result from such a policy.

If aid to the Free French, or to Giraud, or to anyone else, could help shorten the war, American assistance would be forthcoming to permit French troops to re-enter the fight; but this should not permit, according to Roosevelt, the build-up of any movement which could pretend to represent France at the peace conference or hope to participate in the councils of the mighty three.

In the light of events after the war, Roosevelt's policy would seem to have been shortsighted. If France had been rearmed and De Gaulle supported, France might not have abandoned the Western bloc, permitted Communists to obtain a toehold in the government, or allied with Russia. But Roosevelt was not thinking in terms of blocs and balance of power; he anticipated a new Holy Alliance in which Russia, England, and the United States would co-operate for world peace and the good of mankind. In this idealistic world it did not greatly matter whether France was strong or weak.

Although in the last analysis it was the President of the United States who pronounced on foreign policy, it was not always possible, in the day-by-day implementation of foreign affairs, to place the responsibility in quite so specific a fashion. In case the President, for one reason or another, failed to define his policy with precision, or was too occupied with other matters to give it his personal attention, policy could become a makeshift affair worked out by the not always co-operating State and War Departments, by the Joint Chiefs of Staff, or by theater headquarters.

A rather delicate balance existed between military and political affairs. The President was generally disinclined to interfere with military decisions, and when the military situation coincided with his political convictions, he believed that no advantage would be served by his intervention. Such was the case after the Casablanca Conference. Roosevelt believed he had sized up the situation and settled it at the policy level by approving the rearmament of Giraud's North African forces; the military details could now be worked out by Marshall and Eisenhower, and the political measures by Hull and Murphy.

By leaving the matter thus, the President placed the burden of decision with characteristic unconcern on those who were least capable of achieving a disinterested estimate of the situation. Eisenhower and his staff were first of all preoccupied with the North African campaign and were neither inclined nor prepared to evaluate the political orientation of every French soldier in North Africa. Allied headquarters knew that the French officers with whom they came in contact cooperated and that many were passionately disposed to get into the war and fight Germans. They knew that Giraud and his officers were willing to work with them to train and rearm a sizable number of North African troops. They knew that Giraud through his *Deuxième Bureau* maintained intelligence and counterespionage networks in France that were potentially capable of providing important military information. That many of these officers had remained in France or in North Africa after the Armistice did not suggest to Eisenhower's headquarters that they were Fascists or collaborators. Nor was it the task of the American (or British) military command to pass judgment on this point, except where security and espionage were concerned. If Gaullist propaganda—that every Frenchman tainted by Vichy was a traitor—had to be verified, it was a political and not a military appraisal which was involved.

A unique relationship, so far as political decisions were concerned, existed between Eisenhower, as Allied commander in the North African theater, and the White House. Eisenhower bore certain responsibilities to the President as commander in chief of American armed forces, but he also served as an Allied commander receiving orders from the Combined Chiefs of Staff, who in turn took political direction from the British and American chiefs of state. Under such cumbersome organization, it is little wonder that confusion regarding policy occasionally developed at Eisenhower's headquarters. In general, Eisenhower attempted to avoid formulating policy and looked to the White House, through his political adviser, Robert Murphy, or to the Combined Chiefs for policy direction. He, of course, from time to time made recommendations in the political area, and occasionally, lacking specific direction, he had to interpret existing pronouncements as best he could and implement a policy he believed to be in Allied interests. Under such circumstances misunderstandings sometimes occurred in situations where United States and British policy were in conflict.

Although Eisenhower represented a combined Anglo-American command, President Roosevelt upon occasion sent him direct instructions and sent copies to the British Prime Minister. Since Churchill's consistent policy was to avoid clashes with the United States, the Prime Minister invariably concurred, even though he may have held serious reservations (as in the case of the Darlan deal and the Giraud rearmament program) concerning the wisdom of American schemes. Through personal conversations, or by the intermediary of Harold Macmillan, Churchill was generally able to convey to Eisenhower the British position; it was then Eisenhower's responsibility to evaluate the directives and advice he received from the British government, the Combined Staffs, the Joint Chiefs and War Department, the State Department, and the White House on policy matters. The responsibility was a heavy one, especially for a man whose training had been along military rather than political lines. It was especially difficult because of a tendency existing in American circles to grant the theater commander as much local autonomy as possible; this resulted occasionally in a sort of political "buck-passing" between Washington and the field. It is to Eisenhower's credit that he emerged so successfully in the political area, for the most part avoiding entanglements with the British and French and at the same time earning their trust and respect.

In the case that political advice was desired in Washington or in Algiers, it would most logically have emerged from the office of Robert Murphy. Yet Murphy was in a singularly poor position to render disinterested advice for at least half a dozen reasons: as a civilian he had no authority in military matters; he was committed by ties of friendship to many former Vichy officials with whom he had worked before the landings; he was in no position to evaluate the Gaullist movement because the Gaullists were not strong in North Africa; his contacts were for the most part not representative of the "grass roots" nor were they with the "political" Resistance in France; he assumed, under the Clark-Darlan Agreement, that he was not to interfere in strictly French administrative matters; and he had no specific instructions from Washington about what he was supposed to do. These last two points probably loomed large in Murphy's thinking and were quite misunderstood by the liberal press in the United States which bitterly castigated Murphy as the architect of America's "Fascist" policy. But for Murphy it was not so simple. He knew, as the journalists did not, that President Roosevelt had given his accolade to Giraud, and until informed to the contrary, Murphy would have to assume that such was the American policy which he was obliged to support. Certainly Murphy was aware of the fact that Giraud's political naïveté, his lack of administrative capacity, and his susceptibility to abrupt decisions made him a much poorer high commissioner than the politically acute Darlan; but what could he do? If he used his influence to persuade Giraud to liberalize his administration and to rid himself of some of his advisers, he could be charged with interfering in French affairs. If he simply reported on conditions, he had the right to expect that Washington would take action; but the White House and the State Department were slow to respond.

There were loud cries in the liberal journals at the time for Murphy's recall. If this had been done, it would have implied that American policy had changed, that the United States was withdrawing support from General Giraud and was, by implication, inclined to favor De Gaulle. If Murphy had been recalled, he presumably would have to be replaced by a higher-ranking official who would by his prestige give emphasis to this reorientation of policy. But if there were no reorientation of policy, what benefit would be derived from the appointment of a new political adviser to Eisenhower? The change would suggest that the government had lost confidence in its agents in North Africa, and such a slur could hardly be justified unless a change of policy went with it.

The Anfa Memorandum Revised: Political

The two parts of the Anfa memorandum—those hastily approved documents which seemed to set forth basic American policy—included sections involving political and military commitments. The United States appeared to be prepared to recognize Giraud as trustee of all French interests, to treat him as an ally, and to provide him with vast quantities of arms as soon as possible. From the British point of view the consequences of such a policy were staggering: De Gaulle would be relegated to a secondary role, and British influence in French matters would suddenly be reduced to a minimum. When he learned of the document's existence on his return from Turkey, Churchill decided to spend a few days at Algiers, where he landed on February 5, to find out more about this unexpected turn in American policy.[31]

The Prime Minister found himself in a delicate position. His carefully maintained attitude of being fed up with De Gaulle had been, however unintentionally, put to the test; if his protestation of dislike and distrust was a bluff, it had been called. If he allowed the Anfa memorandum to go unchallenged, it would imply that Great Britain and the United States agreed to underwrite Giraud's headquarters in North Africa as the principal agency through which the Allies would deal with France. But since American strength would continue to be preponderant in North Africa, such recognition would in a sense surrender completely to the President the major influence over the French in connection with strategy and postwar planning. On the other hand, if he raised too violent objections to the memorandum, Churchill might jeopardize some of the good will and co-operation with the President that had been an outstanding achievement at Anfa. What Churchill had to do was to counteract the effect of the memorandum without letting it appear to the Americans that he was pushing De Gaulle to usurp authority in North Africa at Giraud's expense.

The least Churchill could do was to insist that De Gaulle be kept on a plane of equality with Giraud, and this was the line of argumentation he took with Robert Murphy, with whom he was closeted for a long discussion on the evening of February 5. The Prime Minister pointed out that Great Britain had long-standing commitments to De

---

[31] Was De Gaulle in Algiers at this time? In their memoirs, Butcher, Churchill, and Admiral Cunningham refer to a luncheon party on Feb. 5 at which De Gaulle, together with Giraud, Peyrouton, Boisson, and Noguès, was present (Butcher, *My Three Years with Eisenhower*, 255; Churchill, *Hinge of Fate*, 723; Admiral Andrew Browne Cunningham, *A Sailor's Odyssey*, 518). General de Gaulle personally told the writer that it would have been impossible for him to have gone to Algiers at this time and in his *Mémoires* says nothing of this matter except that a proposed trip to Libya after Casablanca was vetoed by the British (II, 86). I have received letters from Sir Alexander Cadogan, Sir Alan Brooke, and Sir Kenneth Anderson, who also attended the luncheon. Each found a diary entry concerning the luncheon but no mention of De Gaulle's presence. Sir Alan Brooke comments: "You see that I did not mention de Gaulle. I feel certain I should have mentioned him if he had been there, and do not remember his being present on that occasion." Robert Murphy, who was also present, wrote the author: "To the best of my recollection and I believe I am accurate, de Gaulle returned to London from Casablanca and did not, repeat not, visit Algiers at that time. I am sure this is correct."

Gaulle and simply could not abandon him precipitately; on the other hand, Churchill denied any desire to impede Giraud, whose regime he was willing to help for the sake of maintaining communications and local security in North Africa. Murphy and Churchill, after going over the troublesome memorandum sentence by sentence, agreed that the President really did not wish to recognize Giraud as trustee of all French interests but only of those which Giraud controlled in North and West Africa. The discussion with Churchill must have been somewhat embarrassing to Murphy because it was he who had made the rather extravagant promises to Giraud on November 2 which the present memorandum purported to place once more in effect. Murphy was too clearheaded a diplomat to make an animated defense of the document, however, particularly since he knew how dismayed Eisenhower would be to find the Clark-Darlan Agreement abandoned and a new set of negotiations to be undertaken; and he knew perfectly well that the President and the State Department had consistently avoided recognition of any element as trustee of all French interests. He thus acquiesced that the sentence "They remain in force" be expunged from a revised version.

After the memorandum had been carefully revised, Giraud no longer retained any exclusive claim to French sovereignty. The new version declared:

> . . . it was agreed between the President of the United States, the Prime Minister of Great Britain, and General Giraud that it was to their common interest for all French fighting against Germany to be reunited under one authority and that every facility would be given to General Giraud *and to the French National Committee under General de Gaulle* in order to bring about this union.[32]

What now remained to be done was to bring Giraud and the President into agreement on the new version. Giraud could have only one objection: did the revised version jeopardize in any way the commitment to supply him with arms? When Murphy next morning assured

[32] Murphy dispatch to State Dept., 6 Feb. 1943 (740.0011 Eur. War 1939/27641); Funk, "The 'Anfa Memorandum,' " *Journal of Modern History,* Vol. XXVI, No. 3 (Sept., 1954), 251–52; Crusoe, *Vicissitudes d'une victoire,* 102.

him that military equipment was not in the least involved, Giraud not only gave his approval but thanked Murphy for altering the document so that the Prime Minister could sign it.

On February 9, Giraud wrote to Murphy asking him "in what way President Roosevelt is willing to confirm that he recognizes the commander in chief residing at Algiers as the trustee of French interests in the United States as well as in other countries of American influences?" This was a shrewd move, because at the time, while De Gaulle had Adrien Tixier at Washington representing Fighting France, Giraud was represented only by General Béthouart and Admiral Fenard, heads of his military and naval missions, who were authorized to deal solely with military affairs. The establishment at Washington of a Giraudist civil representative, and the appointment of Giraudist delegates in Latin America, could still provide Giraud with a political advantage over De Gaulle.

Washington made no difficulties over the changed status of the Anfa memorandum. The State Department acquiesced to the alterations on February 11 and approved the Giraud civil mission, although it pointed out that he would have to make his own arrangements with the countries of "American influences." Roosevelt undertook no defense whatsoever of the original document and made only unimportant changes in the final draft which was returned to Giraud in essentially the same form it had left Churchill's hands on February 5. The affair was thus carried off with no serious fractures in Anglo-American relations, and the status of recognition returned to the basic understandings at Anfa, as understood prior to the President's approval of the memorandum. On February 7, Macmillan and Murphy held a joint press conference during which they emphasized for the sake of skeptical correspondents that there were no differences between the United States and Great Britain. Their statement was, in fact, as far as official policy toward De Gaulle's and Giraud's political regimes was concerned, basically correct; it was essentially in keeping with the President's desire to see a unified French war effort but no commitments to anyone as representing a French government. This did not apply, however, to the policy of military aid.

The Anfa Memorandum Revised: Military

The promise of military aid given by the President to General Giraud at Anfa ran into difficulties almost before Roosevelt had returned to Washington. It will be remembered that the President had placed his "okay" on a paper which promised material for eleven divisions to be delivered to Giraud "in the weeks to come." In typically Rooseveltian fashion the President had handed the paper to Giraud and cheerfully neglected to inform the War Department, the British, or even Generals Marshall and Somervell, who had left Casablanca before the final day of the Conference. Murphy did not transmit a copy to the State Department until February 1, after the President and his party had returned to Washington.

Marshall first learned of the President's commitment when General Béthouart, who had been wired a copy from Giraud's headquarters, called on February 3 to talk over ways in which the allocations would be carried out. Marshall knew, of course, that the eleven-division program had been discussed at Anfa, but he had no idea that the President had committed the government to make specific deliveries in the immediate future; and he realized that to inject a French program into the tight schedule of deliveries to China, Russia, and England would upset priorities, production deadlines, and shipping arrangements that had been allocated before the Casablanca conference. Marshall saw that to send equipment at the expense of all other commitments without consulting the Chief of Staff, the Chief of the Supply Services, or the Combined Chiefs of Staff could produce misunderstandings unless agreement was reached at the highest level. He immediately informed War Secretary Stimson, who quickly obtained a copy of the memorandum from Béthouart. When Stimson saw the President that afternoon, he chided him for the characteristic administrative action which had produced such unnecessary confusion. Roosevelt good-naturedly agreed with the Secretary of War, but while he entertained him with anecdotes on the way the papers had been signed, he revealed no inclination to back down on the principle of a rearmament program for the French.

The real significance of the President's act reposed in the fact that he had made a definite commitment: the program was assured, although the amount and the time of delivery might have to be adjusted according to manifold unpredictable wartime pressures. But General Giraud, with his uncomplicated faith in American productive capacities, seemed to believe that the President need only clap his hands to bring tons of planes and tanks down like manna on the North African shores. He apparently believed that a major effort, even at the expense of equipping American forces in North Africa, was to be made to arm his own troops and to get them into the fighting with the shortest delay. He therefore found it impossible to believe Béthouart's report that months might pass before the first deliveries could be unloaded at Casablanca or Algiers. Giraud sensed a conspiracy to deprive him of his matériel. Less than a month after the Anfa Agreement had been signed, General Giraud was not only complaining about lack of co-operation on the part of Americans but actually insinuating that the President had gone back on his word. To American representatives in the theater, the import and consequences of Giraud's complaints were keenly appreciated. Murphy could see the imminent collapse of the entire North African policy if Giraud would have to continue his negotiations with De Gaulle without appreciable improvements in his military forces.

Eisenhower was no less concerned than Murphy about Giraud's accusations. The spirit of the Clark-Darlan Agreement, under which he was operating in North Africa, required that the French would operate as allies, take care of all problems of civil administration, and co-operate in providing the services and transportation facilities necessary for the Allied campaign. If the French became disaffected, any number of administrative difficulties could develop which would divert Eisenhower from his major preoccupation. Not least of all, General Giraud threatened to resign, and at the time it appeared that such an action would have provoked another political crisis with which the Allied Commander was not anxious to contend. Eisenhower thus seconded Murphy in an appeal to Washington that something be done to reassure the French. In due course the complaints from the theater reached the President, who bristled before the double insinuation that he had overplayed his hand at Casablanca and now had to make good. He was nettled that his decision at Anfa had not closed the matter, and he pointed out in his defense that while he had approved the principle of arming the French, he had not committed himself to any specific date. With Rooseveltian urbanity he admonished Murphy and Giraud, like a schoolteacher with two overanxious students, that they must be patient. He wrote Murphy:

> Tell your good friends in North Africa that they ought not to act like children. They must take prompt steps to deny the silly rumors that they have been let down in equipping an expeditionary force to go into France or that slowness in supplying armament is delaying political progress. . . . They must remain calm and sensible.[33]

The Roosevelt magic could not produce solutions to every difficulty, however. Powerful forces did oppose the implementation of the Anfa program, and Giraud was not entirely naïve when he suspected that some elements were operating in Washington or London to deprive him of his equipment.

The Anfa program arrived in priority-minded Washington with the popularity of a sea lion who tries to force his unwelcome bulk on to an overcrowded rock. Every agency was already overtaxed to handle orders for which commitments had been made. The Combined Munitions Assignments Board (CMAB) administered a program of military allocations which strained to their utmost the extensive but not unlimited resources of American production and shipping. Convoys staggering through U-boat lanes to Russia, England, and North Africa could not, early in 1943 when the Battle of the Atlantic was still touch and go, guarantee the minimal supplies to forces already committed to battle. In spite of these pressures, the CMAB had toyed with the possibility, before Casablanca, of sparing enough tonnage—perhaps 25,000 a month —to equip several French regiments. Now, suddenly, as a result of the Anfa memorandum, the regiments had jumped to divisions, and the tonnage required to complete the program by the end of the year—over 100,000 tons a month—could be provided only at the expense of some previous allocation.

To the British the logic of this situation was as clear as it was repre-

---

[33] 20 Feb. 1943. Cited in Vigneras, *Rearming the French*, 43.

hensible: the share which the French received would of necessity come from matériel already designated to other Allies. But the ax was double bitted: not only would shipments to the United Kingdom be reduced, but the forces of General de Gaulle, now benefiting from Lend-Lease agreements, would suffer at the expense of the build-up of Giraud's eleven divisions.

According to the British view, the Anglo-American war effort should be co-ordinated and directed toward the common goal of winning the war. The instrument for administering the military coalition was the Combined Chiefs of Staff; therefore, any collaboration with the French and any supply program to implement this collaboration should be under the cognizance of the CCS. The logic of this view was irrefutable providing one accepted a basic assumption: that the decision on French rearmament had been a military and not a political decision. If the latter, it became a question to be decided not by the Chiefs of Staff but by the chiefs of state.

The Americans took the positon that since the decision had been political and had been accepted at Anfa, it was now out of their hands; all the Combined Chiefs could do was to make recommendations to the CMAB concerning the most effective way to carry out the program. To this interpretation the British Chiefs took definite exception, and they pointed out, with complete justification, that Churchill and Roosevelt had not reached an agreement on French rearmament. The Americans, if initially skeptical, found themselves defending the President's action with vehemence. To Admiral Leahy the Giraud program coincided with his own anti-Gaullist conceptions and with his convictions in regard to continuing aid to French military leaders who proved themselves anti-German even though previously associated with Vichy. General Marshall defended rearmament of the French from the point of view of saving American lives and of liberating the shipping required to transport 250,000 American soldiers to North Africa.

In meeting after meeting, throughout the latter part of February and early March, the Combined Chiefs wrestled with the problem; but as the days turned into weeks they came no closer to a decision.[34] It was

[34] The Combined Chiefs of Staff discussed French rearmament on 26 Feb. and 5, 11, 12 Mar. 1943 (*ibid.*, 49-54).

this stalemate which, giving rise to rumors that the program was to be abandoned, caused Giraud to despair and Eisenhower and Murphy to become apprehensive about the future of the North African policy. Their apprehension was duplicated in Washington where the American Joint Chiefs of Staff accepted the responsibility of supporting Giraud. If British argumentation during the sessions of the Combined Chiefs succeeded in postponing effective aid to Giraud for several months, American prestige in North Africa might diminish to the point where the whole approach in North Africa might have to be abandoned. De Gaulle might be able to introduce himself at Algiers on his own terms.

To extricate themselves from their dilemma, the American Chiefs sought some way of providing Giraud with a token of American good faith—a speedy delivery of enough equipment to demonstrate that even though an Anglo-American agreement had not yet been reached, the President had not gone back on his word. Since it was deemed impossible for Eisenhower to surrender matériel earmarked for his own operations in the North African theater, the only solution seemed to be a special convoy that would be organized and dispatched as soon as possible. Somervell was sounded out and by February 19 had concluded that it would be possible to assign some fifteen ships to a special convoy which could be loaded and dispatched within a month. Such a convoy would provide 125,000 tons of matériel—enough for two divisions and, if not all that Giraud expected, all that French facilities could handle for the moment. Somervell estimated that the convoy could be expected to discharge its cargo at Algiers before the middle of April.

When this emergency move was proposed to British representatives late in February, they realized that they faced a unilateral decision they were powerless to annul. They argued that the amounts and times of delivery should be controlled by the Combined Chiefs, and they pointed out that no strategic decision so far made envisaged the need for eleven French divisions; but they argued in vain, faced by the dour and indefatigable Leahy who insisted that the special convoy, designated UGS–6½, be dispatched as planned. Realizing that the convoy would leave whether they acquiesced or not, the British members of the Combined Chiefs approved the special convoy on March 12.

Approval of this temporary emergency measure did not mean that the British acquiesced to the principle of sending General Giraud the equipment for eleven divisions and 450 planes. By March 12 it had become clear that the deadlock was so complete that further discussion would serve merely to ravel further the frayed tempers of the overworked Chiefs of Staff. It had become increasingly clear in any case that political rather than military aspects of the problem were paramount and that the Chiefs would be best advised to wait for an understanding between Roosevelt and Churchill. Since Anthony Eden was scheduled to come to Washington in mid-March, it seemed appropriate and sagacious to let him carry the burden of the British position. Accordingly, the Combined Chiefs of Staff turned their attention to other matters and left the French affair without having adopted any basic policy in connection with French rearmament.

▶ 3. The French Committee of National Liberation Is Formed

British and American Attitudes toward the Fighting French

By REVISING the Anfa memorandum, and by slowing down the re-armament program discussions in the Combined Chiefs of Staff, the British had prevented American support of Giraud from bringing about a complete elimination of De Gaulle as a possible contender for influence in North Africa. But they had done very little to build up De Gaulle so that he would be a more acceptable figure in Washington's suspicious eyes. In the spring of 1943, during his negotiations with Giraud following Casablanca, when he could use all the support he could possibly find, De Gaulle seemed, in fact, to be losing prestige in both England and the United States.

Shortly after the Casablanca Conference it looked as if De Gaulle might visit North Africa to confer with Eisenhower. On February 21, General Leclerc's Free French armored division, which had struggled across two thousand miles of desert to reach Tripoli, had joined the British Eighth Army, and a Gaullist detachment had joined forces with Giraud's troops in southern Tunisia. The end of the Tunisian campaign was in sight. But although Fighting French forces would not be oper-ating in areas where American command predominated, no over-all arrangement in regard to collaboration had been made. Toward the end of February, Eisenhower and De Gaulle exchanged communications, with a view toward conferring in North Africa. Before the French General had an opportunity to complete his plans, however, the British government announced that it would not provide the clearance or means of transportation whereby De Gaulle, who planned also to make a tour of Free French installations in the Near East and Africa, could leave London. Churchill may have feared that the Fighting French chief would stir up the Middle East, but rumors were also current that De Gaulle intended to visit Moscow and Washington. More likely Churchill simply wanted a clearer understanding between his government and Washington before he permitted De Gaulle to move into North Africa. He undoubtedly was kept well informed by Macmillan of political developments in Algiers, and he may have hoped that by sending Anthony Eden to Washington some of the major misunderstandings could be ironed out. As a result of the British action, the tension between De Gaulle and Churchill reached a dangerous point; for almost the entire first week of March, De Gaulle refused to carry on any normal business.

At the same time that this crisis took place in London, another disturbing incident had occurred in New York. As a result of Giraud's agreement with President Roosevelt, arrangements had been made to bring the battleship *Richelieu,* the cruiser *Montcalm,* and two destroyers from Dakar to the United States for reconditioning. The ships had been idle for two years, and the crews—their uniforms shabby, their morale low, and their diet inadequate—exhibited dissatisfaction with the role they had thus far played in the war. February 23, the day the ships arrived in America, was declared "Freedom for France Day," and an enthusiastic crowd, which did not entirely grasp the subtle distinctions and enmities between Gaullist and Giraudist French, cheered the French sailors marching up Broadway. Within a week it was learned that a number of seamen had deserted from the ships, enlisted with the Fighting French, and were on their way to England via Canada. The deserters reported that the *Richelieu's* captain had called Churchill a babbler (*barbouilleur*), Roosevelt a blackguard (*voyou*), and Pétain the only chief. Most of the volunteers hoped they would see action quicker by rallying to De Gaulle, and they scoffed at the accusation that they had been bribed. All together about three hundred Frenchmen (about fifty from the *Richelieu*) out of a total of three thousand seamen in the French fleet in America were involved.[1]

[1] *Les documents,* Vol. XXXIX (1 Apr. 1943), 48–50; Ben L. Burman in *N. Y. Herald Tribune,* 10, 11 Mar. 1943; Helen Kirkpatrick in *Daily News,* 10 Apr. 1943; Leahy, *I Was There,* 145–46.

After remonstrations by the chief of Giraud's Naval Mission, Admiral Fenard, who protested personally to President Roosevelt, official pro-Giraudist Washington was stirred to indignation. Secretary of the Navy Knox went into action. On March 11 immigration authorities and military police rounded up twelve French sailors, all of them under twenty-five years of age, and interned them on Ellis Island, where they remained until they were released on bond on April 2. Knox made a public statement about the damage to the war effort, and to Leahy and Hull it appeared that the irresponsibility of De Gaulle had once again been demonstrated. The incident had not been engineered personally by De Gaulle, but it added one more footnote to the Washington indictment against the Fighting French.

Another incident occurred about the same time which emphasized the unreasonable prejudice held against the Gaullists by Washington. On March 16 a popular demonstration against the Vichy governor of French Guiana, René Weber, forced his retreat from the colony. Separate messages from the demonstrators went via Washington to General Giraud at Algiers and to General de Gaulle at London, requesting the appointment of a governor. Both chiefs responded in an identical manner, designating their military attachés at Washington to go to Guiana until the permanent appointee could arrive. In this race to rally Guiana, the Gaullists were left far behind. The Free French representative, Colonel de Chévigny, was refused transportation, while Colonel Lebel, of Giraud's Mission, was given an immediate priority, and a few days later the permanent Giraudist governor, Jean Rapenne, was flown in from North Africa. Meanwhile the Gaullist appointee, Maurice Bertaut, who with British assistance had traveled from the Cameroons to Trinidad, was unable to proceed farther, for reasons lucidly exposed by Admiral Leahy:

> The next irritant was the action of the British in providing transportation to Trinidad for a M. Bertaut who had been named Governor of French Guiana by de Gaulle. It was a pleasure to fulfill a request of Under Secretary of State Welles (April 6) that our Navy not give M. Bertaut transportation from Trinidad to French Guiana. The British Government seemed at this time determined to exploit de Gaulle at our expense.[2]

[2] *I Was There,* 146. See also De Gaulle, *Mémoires,* II, 455–56.

The British government may have wished to exploit the Fighting French, but they had demonstrated no great eagerness to support De Gaulle himself in his wish to make an extended tour in Africa. Leahy seems to oversimplify British motives and actions, for Churchill definitely appeared reluctant to permit De Gaulle to move in the direction of Algiers until he had heard from Giraud.

But if his position relative to the British and American governments was far from satisfactory, De Gaulle could nevertheless draw some reassurance from the fact that his relations with France were steadily improving. The Gaullist position became stronger as more and more Resistance groups adhered to De Gaulle and as several important Frenchmen escaped from France and brought their allegiance to the London group. René Massigli, a distinguished career diplomat and former head of the League of Nations section at the Quai d'Orsay, had become convinced after the North African landings that he could help France in the war by affiliating with De Gaulle, who appointed him his commissioner for foreign affairs. Tall dignified, and personable, Massigli joined forces with the "moderates" in the French Committee and represented De Gaulle with a balance and good judgment that increased the prestige of Fighting France in diplomatic circles. Two parliamentarians also came over to De Gaulle early in 1943—André Maroselli, mayor of Luxeuil-les-Bains and the first senator to join the movement, and Fernand Grenier, Communist deputy from Saint Denis. Overt proof that the far left had thrown its support behind De Gaulle provided unmistakable evidence that the Fighting French now commanded the allegiance of all the major political groups opposing the Vichy regime.

By the early spring of 1943 there could no longer be any question but that the major Resistance movements had rallied solidly behind De Gaulle. It is true that the French Army secret service with headquarters at Algiers was still controlling hundreds of operatives in France, but members of the "political" underground, the French civilians who formed *Libération, Combat,* the *Franc-Tireur,* the Committee for Socialist Action, and the *Mouvement Ouvrier Français* had all bound themselves to collaborate with Fighting France. Not only were the political networks now bound to De Gaulle, but a "Secret Army Command" was being clandestinely maintained, which by March claimed it could raise 150,000 men. Two months later, on May 27, Jean Moulin succeeded in achieving the unification of all major underground elements, labor unions, resistance movements, and the political parties in the National Resistance Council. The guiding committee of this council, headed, after Moulin was arrested in June, by Georges Bidault, became the central moving force in the underground in France, and its co-operation with the Gaullist liaison network, the BCRA, demonstrated the strength of De Gaulle's ties with the *métropole*.

None of these facts, however, even though they were reported to Washington,[3] seemed to persuade the administration that American support should be shifted from Giraud to De Gaulle.

Washington Persuades Giraud to Embrace Democracy

It was a proposal of Harry Hopkins which initiated a new phase of American policy in North Africa. Hopkins had become convinced while at Casablanca that Giraud would be well served by the counsel of Jean Monnet, the dynamic French Cognac manufacturer who at the time was working on Hopkins' Munitions Assignment Board. Hopkins had persuaded the President, who in turn had convinced Giraud, that Monnet should be invited to provide the French Commissioner with the sort of advice he needed in civilian matters. Arriving at Algiers in February, Monnet quietly put himself to the task of persuading Giraud that he must be more receptive to democratic concepts. Monnet's position was at first rather ambiguous; it was not clear whether he represented the United States or whether he acted as a French citizen. There was even some talk of providing him with offices at Allied headquarters. In actual fact, Monnet had come to North Africa in a largely French capacity, but he still represented the CMAB, and, having talked with the President before leaving Washington, he had obtained a very clear idea of the disiderata of American policy. In Hopkins and in Assistant Secretary of War John McCloy he possessed influential friends who believed that his abilities would provide the sort of guidance that Giraud re-

---

[3] COMNAVEU Documents, III, 34–39. A joint British–Free French mission of Wing Commander Yeo-Thomas and Colonel Passy brought back firsthand information from France on 16 Apr. 1943 (Bruce Marshall, *The White Rabbit*, 20–44; Passy, *Missions secrètes*, 67–184, 321–26).

quired. Some American officials in North Africa saw in Monnet a Gaullist and Foreign Office instrument who sold out Giraud when the Fighting French came to Algiers in June, and they argued that Monnet thus counteracted the basic American policy of supporting Giraud and should have been recalled. They believed that Monnet went too far in threatening Giraud that the arms program would be curtailed unless he moved in the direction of republicanism, but it is not unlikely that such a threat, which Robert Murphy had failed to make, was considered in the White House as the only means of arousing Giraud into action.

In any case, Jean Monnet soon convinced Giraud that his counsel must be accepted if the arms program was to be approved, and he gradually edged Lemaigre-Dubreuil out of the General's inner circle of advisers on American affairs. As rapidly as he could, he persuaded Giraud that only a major policy statement affirming his democratic tendencies and his intention of returning to republican laws would permit a reaction favorable enough in Washington to guarantee the continued delivery of arms. It took Monnet just six weeks to persuade the General, and by the beginning of March, Giraud had finally conceded that if Paris was worth a mass, armament was worth a speech.

Monnet put his inventive capacities to work to formulate for Giraud the sort of remarks which would be most likely to enhance his position among the Allies and to counter the claims of the Fighting French that they were the unique representatives of France. The speech would have to take into account the De Gaulle-Giraud negotiations which had continued since Casablanca and in which Monnet, since his arrival in North Africa, had participated; it would have to find arguments to counterbalance the ever increasing influence of the Gaullists in France and England; and, if possible, it should demonstrate to the world that Giraud was a leader of such stature, magnanimity, and tolerance that he rose above the petty machinations of politics. The rapidity with which Monnet drafted the speech, once the General had consented to deliver it, partially explains Giraud's tactical error in failing to prepare his army, his administrators, and his governors for the impact with which his unexpected and unprecedented reversal of policy would strike them. Even Bergeret, Boisson, and Peyrouton, who had been meeting in Algiers as the Committee of War since March 8, did not know the final text until the evening before the speech was to be delivered. When, on their behalf, André Poniatowski asked Giraud for a copy, the General remarked absently, "Oh, that interests them?"[4]

It interested them to the extent that they worked until midnight to revise sections of the speech. Poniatowski submitted the revisions to Giraud early next morning but learned that he would have to clear them with Monnet. Although Murphy and Macmillan had already wired the text to their respective governments, some practical changes were incorporated at the last minute, but they did not alter the tenor of the speech. The principal passages of this extraordinary allocution, delivered on March 14, are worth examining.

General Giraud's address commenced with a tribute to the French people who had so courageously stood up against German aggression. He generously praised De Gaulle's forces, as well as his own, for their part in the struggle, and he made a felicitous reference (clearly not for the benefit of his French audience) to Abraham Lincoln. He referred to the arms which had been promised by the United States and even gracefully mentioned that some had already appeared, although in fact the special convoy, UGS–6½, had not yet arrived and thus far only token transfers had been made. In the latter part of his remarks he guaranteed a return to the Third Republic, and he assured his audience that the right of self-government remained with the French people. He declared Vichy legislation null and void, although, accepting the advice of his administrators, he admitted that all the reforms were not to be accomplished overnight.[5] He ended on an appeal for the unity of all

4 Details of the speech's preparation were told the writer by André Poniatowski.

5 Vichy legislation filled four columns of one thousand pages. Shortly after, Giraud modified his statement by ordering that Vichy laws which were not specifically repealed in three months would remain in effect. Not until 26 June 1944 did De Gaulle's provisional government formally annul Vichy legislation in France, but Article 9 of the ordinance gave temporary validity to Vichy administrative acts which would be examined later. Many Vichy laws were still in effect ten years after the war. Also in his speech, Giraud excepted the act annulling the Crémieux Decree. This decree, promulgated on 24 Oct. 1870, bestowed French citizenship on Algerian Jews but not on Moslems. Jews lost their citizenship when Vichy abrogated the decree on 18 Feb. 1942. What Giraud had done was to declare all Vichy legislation null and void except the law abrogating the Crémieux Decree. It could only be wondered by what authority Giraud abrogated a law honored by the Third Republic. In any event, Giraud's decision was not implemented, and on 21 Oct. 1943 his decision was overruled by the French Committee of National Liberation. To give Giraud his due, however, it must be noted that by 17 Mar. 1943 no less than sixty-two anti-Jewish laws had been repealed.

French forces in what amounted to a sincere invitation for the Gaullist forces to enter into an arrangement whereby both could contribute to the fight.

The speech was generally well received, even by the press in the United States which had been critical of Giraud and his administration. Secretary Hull gave it his enthusiastic blessing, and even Winston Churchill made a comment in Commons, approved ahead of time by Washington, which stated that "in view of Giraud's speech and the National Committee's memorandum, it now appears that no question of principle divides these two bodies of Frenchmen." George Bernard Shaw could not restrain himself in his admiration: "It was a staggering performance," he wrote, "for it was at once evident that General Giraud could not have composed it himself. If he had he would have made his mark as a famous orator long before. . . . No soldier short of another Caesar, Cromwell, or Wellington could have achieved such a feat."[6]

Some spectacular changes in personnel, which revealed the influence of Monnet in North African civil affairs, followed immediately. General Bergeret resigned the day after the speech was delivered; he was transferred to a military command in West Africa. On the same day Jean Rigault voluntarily relinquished his important post of secretary of interior affairs. Bergeret and Rigault were replaced by Maurice Couve de Murville, who had recently come to North Africa from France,[7] and by Dr. Jules Abadie, a North African Jew with Gaullist sympathies. A friend of Monnet's, René Mayer, also Jewish, former administrator of the French National Railways and later chairman of the Inter-Allied Executive Committee on Armaments and Raw Materials, was appointed secretary of communications on March 27. Monnet himself replaced Lemaigre-Dubreuil as the delegate on inter-Allied relations who would deal principally with rearmament questions.

Even though the Governors General Peyrouton, Boisson, and Noguès

---

[6] *New Leader* (6 Apr. 1943).

[7] An official in the Vichy Finance Ministry, Couve de Murville had been chairman of the Finance Subcommittee in the French Armistice Delegation at Wiesbaden. From 1940 to 1943 he participated in innumerable altercations with the Germans over French payments, and after 5 Mar. 1943 made his way to North Africa. En route he wired De Gaulle his belief that France should be united behind De Gaulle (De Gaulle, *Mémoires*, II, 457).

retained their offices for two months longer, the passing of Bergeret, Lemaigre-Dubreuil, and Rigault marked the end of an era in Giraud's relations with Washington. Their influence had gradually waned since Casablanca, and by the end of March not only had Giraud repudiated Lemaigre-Dubreuil by his acceptance of Monnet, but the final form of the revised Anfa memorandum, lacking all teeth whatsoever, had been approved in Washington. Lemaigre-Dubreuil could only address to Giraud a long letter protesting that the General had abandoned his original policy in favor of General de Gaulle and the Foreign Office; he was unable thereafter to exert influence on the course of events.[8]

In spite of the portentous tone of Giraud's discourse of March 14, North Africa did not overnight wrap itself in the protective cloak of democracy and republicanism. Robert Aron, who worked in Rigault's Secretariat of the Interior, paints a vivid picture of the Algerian administrators fumbling to obtain information about "this mysterious regime, rediscovered by the grand chief."[9] When General Prioux, Giraud's chief of staff, objected that there would be much unrest generated among army officers as a result of the new policy, he was told by Giraud to inform them that he was not attacking Pétain, that if some Vichy legislation proved good, it would be retained, and that he would brook no party allegiances in the army. These sentiments were exposed by Prioux to officers at Dakar, and General Mendigal made similar comments at Biskra on April 5:

> The need for the present bluffing is because for the time being the French find themselves Allies of the democracies. These powers get their people into action by talking to them of democratic ideals and liberty. It would not do to give the impression that this ideal is despised by many Frenchmen. It would not be politic, for Americans have not understood our subtle game of 1942. They remember only French actions directed

[8] Crusoe, *Vicissitudes d'une victoire*, 152–54. In June, 1944, Lemaigre-Dubreuil, in danger of arrest, left North Africa via Spanish Morocco for Lisbon. Returning to France in Dec., 1944, he was arrested and held for five months on charges of treason. The charges were later dropped for lack of evidence. During the Moroccan crisis ten years later, Lemaigre-Dubreuil, who had since obtained a controlling interest in *Maroc-Presse*, attempted to mediate the quarrel between Moroccan nationalists and the French government. As he was leaving his Casablanca office on 11 June 1955, he was assassinated.

[9] *Le piège où nous a pris l'histoire*, 249.

against Anglo-Saxons—and it must be admitted there have been some. Also the government of Algiers has been obliged to revise laws and decrees of Vichy or at least to simulate such revision . . . . Basically what is there for you to worry about, Gentlemen, if the words liberty, equality and fraternity are written anew on the front of mayoral halls in place of other words? Nothing at all. And this is an illustration which enables you to understand what General Giraud is doing. He has taken the old writing and restored it for the benefit of strangers. That is all. Nothing is changed for us. We change only the face.[10]

When reports such as these reached the press in England and the United States, they did not bring reassurance to those who had hoped for a real change of heart on the part of Giraud and a major turning point in North African administration.

Effects of North African Developments on Anglo-American Policy

Once General Giraud, the willing bridegroom, publicly expressed his adherence to democratic ideals, it only remained for Washington to capitalize on his new position by doing what it could to effect a union of the two French groups under Giraudist leadership. A major accomplishment, from the American point of view, would be achieved if De Gaulle could be persuaded to leave for Algiers as soon as possible and align himself with Giraud without attempting to subordinate the Giraudist group under the banner of Fighting France. It was not impossible, Roosevelt believed, that this could be accomplished in March, at the same time that Anthony Eden was scheduled to come to Washington for general talks on over-all strategy.

At this time, Francis Spellman, the Archbishop of New York, was touring North Africa. He had seen President Roosevelt shortly after the Casablanca Conference, and he had agreed to talk to the two French leaders in an effort to bring about some sort of union between them. After a short stay in North Africa, where he met General Giraud and the Allied leaders, the Archbishop proceeded to London. He met De

[10] *Free France* (1 June 1943), 361.

Gaulle at Ambassador Biddle's on March 22 and later had two long talks with him. Anxious as he was to go to Algiers, De Gaulle would not agree to go there under what he considered to be the humiliating condition of subordinating himself and his movement to General Giraud. He reluctantly but firmly rejected the Archbishop's suggestions.[11]

While Archbishop Spellman was talking with De Gaulle in London, and while Giraud was cleaning house in Algiers, Anthony Eden was discussing Anglo-American policy with Roosevelt, Hopkins, Hull, Welles, and others. It must not be thought that the major purpose of his visit was to clarify the French situation; actually he came to talk over a wide range of topics pertaining mostly to postwar organization. In the notes which Harry Hopkins made of his conversation with the President on March 14, the day of Giraud's speech, reference was made to Russia, Poland, Finland, Germany, India, and other countries, but France was not even mentioned. Hull summarized in some detail in his memoirs his discussion with Eden on the French question, which he obviously felt to be extremely important; but Eden later told Hopkins that he found Hull "a little difficult to talk to and obsessed with the problems of the Free French." After Eden had left, the President told correspondents that he and the British were "about ninety-five percent together." Sherwood asked Hopkins at the time "what the other five per cent consisted of, and he replied, 'mostly France.' "[12]

Confronted with the unreasonable hostility toward De Gaulle that dominated the State Department, Eden tried to approach the problem with simple logic. First of all, did the United States oppose the two factions' getting together? When this question was answered in the negative, he posed the second: what sort of agency would be acceptable to the United States in case they did join forces? Hull could only say that he had no objection to a joint committee so long as there was no effort to form what might be considered a provisional government which would attempt to force itself upon the French people after the war. Since the British were equally disposed to refrain from committing themselves on De Gaulle's status, it would seem that there was no outstanding difference between the British and the American view. In

[11] De Gaulle, *Mémoires,* II, 95, 457; Francis J. Spellman, *Action This Day,* 69, 78.
[12] Hull, *Memoirs,* II, 1216; Sherwood, *Roosevelt and Hopkins,* 719–21.

actual fact, there were very basic differences which stood solidly in the way of complete understanding.

The British position required a strong, well-armed, independent France, which by association with England would help serve as a balance to a potential Russian hegemony in central Europe; the American (i.e., Roosevelt-Hull) concept dealt in terms of a collective-security arrangement which would permit the major powers to deal individually with potential danger spots. The purely military arrangement with Giraud served this American concept ideally, but the Americans feared that an enlarged National Committee would work toward the Anglo-Gaullist scheme which they were disposed to thwart. On the other hand, since no responsible American official was willing to express himself as opposing a De Gaulle–Giraud *rapprochement,* the best policy (if De Gaulle refused to subordinate himself to Giraud) seemed to be to delay their meeting if possible until Giraud's "democratic" attitude should develop for him a stronger position in regard to any proposed French body.

Winston Churchill appreciated the subtlety and complexity of this situation. If De Gaulle should go to Algiers too soon, before an adequate Giraudist team was available to balance him, he would soon dominate the entire French Resistance movement. This could have several consequences: first, it could antagonize those Americans (i.e., Hull, Leahy, and possibly the President) who would feel that this had been accomplished as the result of an Anglo-Gaullist conspiracy; or second, though not so probable, De Gaulle in North Africa might operate so sagaciously as to obtain American (or Russian) support and therefore be in a position to reorient his policy counter to that of Great Britain. What Churchill meant to do was to insure that the enlarged provisional committee would be representative enough and strong enough to prevent De Gaulle from dominating it. As of the end of March, he was not sure that this could be done.[13]

One plan that Churchill had counted upon, that of spiriting important figures out of France, had not matured effectively. None of the prewar non-Vichy statesmen seemed to be available. In March he concentrated on an effort to get an old friend out of France: General Alphonse

[13] Churchill, *Hinge of Fate,* 803; Churchill, *Closing the Ring* (vol. V of *The Second World War*), 177–79.

Wide World Photos

A Franco-American affairs discussion was imperative for Roosevelt and De Gaulle in 1944. De Gaulle arrived for the talks on July 6; Henri Hoppenot, chief of the French Mission to the United States, is at his right in the picture.

Even though their welcome was cordial, these two Americans were influential in delaying recognition of De Gaulle's government: Secretary
of State Cordell Hull, left, and President Franklin D. Roosevelt, center,
greeted De Gaulle at the White House on July 6. At rear is Mrs. Anna
Boettiger, the President's daughter.

Georges, the sixty-eight-year-old former commander of the French Northern Army who had nearly received Weygand's command in the anxious days of June, 1940. It was Georges (as Churchill later told Emmanuel d'Astier[14]) who had advised the Prime Minister that Weygand intended to negotiate for an armistice and that the twenty-five squadrons of British pursuit planes which Weygand had requested would be better saved for the impending Battle of Britain. Unfortunately for Churchill's hopes of building up a well-balanced committee, General Georges had neither the personality nor the political capacity to oppose the intense, competent, young politicians that surrounded De Gaulle; and furthermore, although he had received Churchill's message through the underground in March, Georges sent word back to the Prime Minister that he would not be able to leave before April.[15]

When Eden left Washington on March 29, he had not reached a firm agreement with the United States on French affairs. It was perfectly clear that the Americans were going ahead unilaterally with the rearmament program—Convoy UGS–6½ was then halfway to North Africa —and that while they would express no open objections to a unification of the two French groups, they still hoped to sustain Giraud against De Gaulle and to negotiate local arrangements in French colonial areas without postwar commitments. If agreement was to be reached on the French question, it would have to be at a level higher than that of the foreign ministers.

The conflicting attitudes prevailing in London and Washington toward the question of De Gaulle's immediate departure for Algiers were mirrored also in French circles. While Eden was in the United States, General Catroux had flown to Algiers to discuss with Jean Monnet, whom Giraud had authorized to represent him, the possibility of De Gaulle's arrival in North Africa. Both Catroux and Monnet held the opinion that the political climate was unfavorable; they believed that the antagonism generated in the army over the speech of March 14, the tension which had developed over administrative replacements, and the animosity promoted by desertions of Giraud's men to the Free French

---

14 D'Astier, *Les dieux et les hommes*, 41.
15 Pierre Nord, *La préparation du débarquement* (vol. III of *Mes camarades sont morts*), 103–104.

created a critical mixture which the catalyst of De Gaulle's arrival might transform into an unstable and dangerous ferment. If De Gaulle could be persuaded to postpone his visit, it was likely that time would prevent or at least mitigate the possibility of political outbursts in the Algerian capital. In recommending a compromise with Giraud, Catroux incidentally incurred the wrath of De Gaulle, who believed his representative was wavering in his devotion to Fighting French ideals.

Back in London there was a feeling on the part of Soustelle and Diethelm, and others who shared their views, that the time was ripe for an immediate departure for Algiers. They believed, apparently, that time favored Giraud, who as the weeks passed would have more and better-equipped troops at his disposal. By March 30, De Gaulle had reached the decision, which was shared by a majority on the Committee, that in spite of General Catroux' advice, it would be best to fly immediately to Algiers in the *Liberator* which the British government had been persuaded to place at his disposition. When De Gaulle let the British authorities know of his intention to leave as soon as possible, he learned that one of the plane's engines required repairs which would delay the departure for several days. Churchill took advantage of the postponement to invite De Gaulle to see him. The conversation of the two men, on April 2, marked the first time they had met since De Gaulle's behavior in connection with the Casablanca Conference three months previously had so outraged the British Premier. Churchill suggested that De Gaulle postpone his departure until April 5 or 6, which would provide him with the opportunity of consulting with the Foreign Minister, then on his way back from Washington. De Gaulle agreed to the delay.

Meanwhile, the Foreign Office requested Harold Macmillan in Algiers to find out from Eisenhower whether or not, on the eve of the last phase of the Tunisian campaign, it would in fact be expeditious for De Gaulle to come to North Africa. Although at the time Eisenhower was absent from Algiers, Allied headquarters rendered the opinion that if De Gaulle's arrival provoked a crisis, it would certainly endanger Allied communications at a crucial moment. Macmillan forwarded this opinion to the Foreign Office, which in turn relayed it to De Gaulle on April 4 in a phrasing so couched that it appeared to be a message from Eisenhower to De Gaulle. Accompanying the message was a British request with which De Gaulle had no alternative but to comply, that he postpone his departure indefinitely in order not to embarrass Eisenhower.[16]

De Gaulle's indignation, intensified by the impotency of the French position, was denied adequate avenues of expression. To comprehend the violence of De Gaulle's reaction it must be remembered that a proposed visit to Washington in June, 1942, had been vetoed by the British government; that his flight to the United States in December, 1942, had been canceled by the Darlan assassination; and that in February, 1943, he had been compelled to refuse an invitation to visit Eisenhower because the British had intervened. In a rage he penned a savage and vituperative message to Eisenhower. Massigli, in an attempt to shroud De Gaulle's indignation in the wrappings of diplomacy, threatened to resign if the message went through. Admiral Stark refused to permit the facilities he controlled to be used for its transmission. London, Washington, and Algiers waited tensely to learn if the Gaullist tempest would abate or whether it presaged a break in the negotiations which had thus far hopefully led to the possibility of French unification.

In his exasperation at being excluded from North Africa, De Gaulle had difficulty in comprehending why Eisenhower should want to forbid his journey. He immediately wired Eisenhower and learned that the controversial message had not originated directly from the Allied commander. On April 7, Eisenhower published a communiqué expressing "surprise" at the Fighting French press release which referred to General de Gaulle's regret at the delay, which, according to Carlton Gardens, could not be "prolonged without serious disadvantage." On April 8, Eisenhower's headquarters admitted their message had been "advisory" and not "mandatory." President Roosevelt and Secretary Hull were taken completely off guard and found themselves forced to tell correspondents that they knew of Eisenhower's request only through the newspapers. With De Gaulle's certain knowledge that Eisenhower's "request" had in reality been brought about at British instigation, it was no wonder that the discussions between Churchill, Eden, and De Gaulle on April 5 and 6 were tempestuous. One report asserted that the Gaullist com-

[16] Interview of the writer with General de Gaulle; *N. Y. Herald Tribune*, 6 Apr. 1943; Wallace Carroll, *Persuade or Perish*, 96–98; De Gaulle, *Mémoires*, II, 96–97.

muniqué had "brought forth from No. 10 Downing Street the sharpest rebuke that has ever been directed against General de Gaulle and his movement by a member of the British Government."

It required all the tact and persuasiveness of Massigli and Catroux (who returned from Algiers on April 10) to calm De Gaulle and to urge him to reconsider the prospects of further negotiation. De Gaulle ultimately submitted to their insistence and authorized a graceful letter to Eisenhower which extended to him "the ardent good wishes of the French people." This curious incident obviously did little to repair the strains between Washington and London. All the interested parties seemed to be working at cross-purposes—Roosevelt attempting (through Archbishop Spellman) to persuade De Gaulle to leave London, and Eisenhower apparently opposing his departure; Catroux and Monnet seeking a delay, with Diethelm and Soustelle pressing for an immediate trip to North Africa; and Churchill wishing to wait until General Georges or other Frenchmen could make themselves available, yet not wishing to antagonize Roosevelt over the relatively minor French problem. Little wonder that Churchill was anxious to have face-to-face conversations with the President as soon as possible!

For the moment, during the last weeks of April, concern with the De Gaulle–Giraud problem was relegated to the background while Washington and London occupied themselves with the closing stages of the North African operations. In May the victory of British, French, and American troops over Rommel and the liberation of Tunisia ended an important phase of the war. Although the decision for the next operation, the invasion of Sicily, had been reached at Casablanca, no definite commitments had yet been made about whether a Mediterranean operation or a cross-Channel attack should occupy the Allied forces thereafter. In either case North Africa would gradually shift from being the center of an active campaign to a staging area which the course of the war would leave more and more in the background.

The victory clearly demonstrated the supremacy of Allied arms, and the doubts entertained by some Frenchmen concerning the ultimate outcome of the war were now largely dissipated. Admiral Godefroy, whose fleet of warships had been immobilized at Alexandria since 1940, and

Admiral Robert, whose ships stood idle at Martinique, found that Great Britain and the United States were no longer disposed to erect their policy on the fear that Vichy or Germany might make use of North Africa and the West Indies. Since February, 1943, when an economic boycott was imposed by the British, Admiral Godefroy had begun to plot his course toward the Giraud haven, and he promised to align his ships behind Giraud as soon as the North African situation was stabilized—in other words, when it became clear that the Germans could no longer hope to obtain hegemony on the southern Mediterranean shore. Five days after the fall of Tunis, Godefroy agreed to conduct his ships to Dakar.

The United States had begun to exert comparable pressure on Admiral Robert, who realized that it would not be long until he would have to resign or shift his allegiance to De Gaulle or Giraud. On April 26, Washington abruptly informed Robert that the agreement with him was no longer valid and that supplies to Martinique would be stopped. In spite of the boycott, however, Robert was able to negotiate and procrastinate for several more months before he had to give up.

The victory in Tunisia also influenced American and British attitudes toward French rearmament. If French troops were to be used in future campaigns, there would be justification for continuing the Anfa program, but if, as Eisenhower recommended, French forces were to be employed mostly as occupation and service troops, a complete reappraisal of the program might be necessary. It was not clear in May, 1943, whether the French question could be decided purely on military grounds or whether the resolution of the Giraud–De Gaulle negotiations, which had political overtones, would govern the determination of future policy. It will be recalled that the Combined Chiefs of Staff had abandoned the rearmament problem in the middle of March with the hope that some solution would emerge from Eden's visit to Washington. Since nothing definite had developed from the Eden-Hull conversations, it became even more imperative that the question be resolved when Churchill next came to Washington for high-strategy discussions. Meanwhile, in addition to the special convoy which had arrived on April 14, about 15 per cent of each American convoy to North Africa was allocated to the French. At this rate about three divisions would be

armed by the middle of August, but this rearmament, unilaterally conceived and implemented by the Americans, had not yet been sanctioned
by the Combined Chiefs of Staff.

As Winston Churchill prepared to see the President during the latter
part of May, his policy toward the Free French was complicated, as
usual, by De Gaulle's tactless and stubborn demeanor and by American
touchiness in regard to Giraud. Churchill believed in the desirability of
a central French authority, just as he believed in the desirability of Belgian, Czech, and Polish governments-in-exile; and he hoped that a
French provisional regime would in time orient postwar France toward
a policy which would strengthen the British position in Europe. He had
no objection if this authority should work for the preservation of the
French Empire, so long as the declaration for the independence of
Syria and Lebanon, already made, was not abandoned. On the other
hand, he feared that De Gaulle's personal qualities, coupled with the
influences of leftist elements within the FNC, endangered the evolution
of the Gaullist Committee into an acceptable provisional government.
Churchill was not so naïve, as those in Washington seemed to be, as to
under-assess De Gaulle's personal prestige, and he feared that cutting the
ground from beneath him might force De Gaulle to seek backing from
the Soviet Union. What could have happened in France did happen in
Poland, and Churchill possessed the political imagination to foretell
what shape the postwar world might take if De Gaulle, with Socialist,
Communist, and Russian support, headed an agency that was opposed
only by the politically incompetent Giraud.

Churchill had never abandoned the plan, formulated at the beginning of the year, to broaden the French Committee in such a way that
De Gaulle's personal domination would be reduced. He was far from
convinced that the men around Giraud, with the possible exception of
Jean Monnet, carried sufficient prestige and influence to counteract
the capabilities of the advisers that De Gaulle would bring with him
to Algiers. The Prime Minister still had confidence that General Georges,
the only person he had succeeded in persuading to come out of France,
would do a great deal to strengthen Giraud's team. But the efforts to
fly Georges to England had been plagued by difficulties; illness and bad
weather had delayed the flight week after week, until Churchill was

finally forced to sail for America before conferring with the French General. Toward the end of May, Georges was finally flown from France directly to North Africa.[17]

In Washington the most frenetic voice raised in criticism of De Gaulle remained that of the Secretary of State, whose monomania was constantly irritated by the propaganda onslaught which Fighting French publicists regularly unleashed against American policy. Knowing the extent to which De Gaulle was supported by British funds, Mr. Hull could not escape the conclusion that the attacks were not only sub- sidized but secretly approved by the British. François Quilici, who edi- ted the Gaullist *Marseillaise* in London, directed a campaign of abuse with enthusiastic skill, and Jacques Soustelle's information service made available an array of pro-Gaullist press releases that could not be matched by the Giraudist service headed by General Chambe.

In anticipation of Churchill's visit, Hull drew up a memorandum for the President to use as a basis for his conversations. Toward the close of his suggestions, he recommended that an agreement on France's future should be reached; if this were impossible, the President should then tell Churchill:

> Since General Giraud is fully co-operating and contributing to the military purposes we had in view, and his military aid in North Africa is an essential to our war effort, we intend to support him in every way as military head of the French Allied forces whose collaboration is not only essential to the British and Americans, but to the cause of the United Nations as well.

According to Hull, the President said he agreed with his points and he promised to take them up with the Prime Minister.[18]

It is not likely that Roosevelt had radically changed his thinking about Giraud and De Gaulle since Casablanca, and he seemed at this time agreeable to letting events take their course. He doubted whether the people of France, who did not know De Gaulle's traits, would really support him when they learned the differences between Free French

---

[17] Nord, *La préparation du débarquement*, 104–105.
[18] Hull, *Memoirs*, II, 1217–18.

objectives and De Gaulle's personal ambition. Roosevelt had become more and more disturbed by the continued machinations of De Gaulle, and he was inclined to think that after liberation France would have to be controlled like an occupied country, in which, although most administration would be in local hands, top decisions would have to be made by American and British administrators. Believing that the old form of government would not work, Roosevelt anticipated that six months or a year of this military government would be necessary before elections could be held and a new type of government established. In anticipation of talks with Churchill, the President even toyed with the idea that an entirely new French committee, of which De Gaulle would be a member but not chairman, should be formed.[19] Yet Roosevelt did not appear inclined to interfere with the Combined Chiefs' argument over French rearmament, and apparently he was willing to let them proceed with their discussions before he made any move. The President found himself greatly occupied at this time with other matters: not only had a serious coal strike recently taken up much of his attention, but the Trident Conference, which had brought Generals Stilwell, Chennault, and Wavell to Washington for consultations on Asian strategy, called for intensive preparation.

From May 12 to May 25, during Trident, British and American officials discussed policy and strategy. Because Roosevelt had made little headway with Churchill on the French problem, Hull was invited to confer personally with the Prime Minister on May 13. Hull gave vent to his grievances against De Gaulle and his propagandists, but although Churchill admitted that he was "disgusted" with De Gaulle, he did not promise to stop British aid. Churchill did, however, take note of Hull's annoyance, and gaining from his visit an appreciation of the influence of the Secretary of State in Congress and upon Roosevelt, made mental calculations on the degree to which British support of De Gaulle could go without causing a powerful reaction in the State Department. Churchill's subsequent public utterances about De Gaulle's unreliability, made for American consumption, may have stemmed from this conversation with Hull.

Most of the discussions during Trident were devoted to the Burma

19 *Ibid.*, 1216–17.

campaign and to "Overlord," the cross-Channel attack, and the Combined Chiefs of Staff did not reach the question of French rearmament until May 18. With Eisenhower's recommendation that French troops would be largely of value in the future to garrison North Africa, and with no specific directive from the President, the Chiefs failed to work out a clear-cut program on further armament beyond that which had already been allotted. They finally agreed on a formula whereby arming the French would proceed "as rapidly as the availability of shipping and equipping will allow, but as a secondary commitment to the requirements of British and United States forces in the various theaters." They also agreed to consider seriously the possibility of adding a French division to the attacking forces that should land in France.[20]

These decisions were inconclusive, and the Conference ended on May 25 without the French having received any firm commitments. Two days later, however, President Roosevelt issued an invitation for General Giraud to come to see him.

French Negotiations Leading to the Formation of the Committee

While Roosevelt, Churchill, and their advisers were trying to come to effective grips with the French problem, the French themselves were making erratic strides toward unity. During April the negotiations, handled largely by Catroux and Monnet, made encouraging progress, but in the following month, with the Tunisian campaign entering its final phase, a situation developed which threatened to end all possibility of an agreement between the generals.

Expressed in simplest terms, this situation constituted a spread of Gaullism in North Africa. It revealed itself by the enthusiastic reception of the Gaullist periodical *Combat* and by the steadily increasing frequency with which "Vive De Gaulle" was heard in the streets of North Africa. Toward the end of April, as the Fighting French troops of General Leclerc and General de Larminat came into contact with those of General Giraud in Tunisia, groups of soldiers began to desert from the regular army forces to join the Cross of Lorraine. Roadblocks, special guards, and threats of court martial failed to deter the emigra-

[20] Vigneras, *Rearming the French,* 57.

tion of enlisted men—attracted by the morale, equipment, and recruiting promises of the Fighting French—to the corps whose epic-like ex-
ploits had made them celebrated throughout the French-speaking world.
Some Frenchmen were not unreceptive to the thought of promotion, for
many of De Gaulle's men, particularly officers, had obtained higher rank
than they would have held in the regular French Army.

With this Gaullist excitement in the air and with knowledge of
plans for a mammoth reception for General de Gaulle upon his arrival at
Algiers, Giraud and his advisers, with Catroux' agreement, concluded
that some locality other than Algiers would be preferable for Giraud's
and De Gaulle's preliminary discussions. General Giraud therefore suggested that they meet sometime after May 5 at Marrakech or Biskra and
return to Algiers when a firm agreement had been reached. For precisely the reason that Giraud wished to avoid an encounter at Algiers,
De Gaulle insisted that Algiers provided the only possible locality for
a meeting. In his reply to Giraud, he was so adamant on this point that
Catroux refused to transmit so undiplomatic a response. The final blow
of De Gaulle's petulance was added on May 4, when he delivered a
speech at Grosvenor House in which he ridiculed Giraud's regime in
deprecating tones. The speech could have meant the end of all further
negotiations. When Massigli encountered Soustelle on the sidewalk outside Grosvenor House, he expostulated: "Well, you're happy! Now it's
done for." Churchill was reported to be ready at last to wash his hands
completely of De Gaulle, and Giraud was advised to break off negotiations and go his own way.[21]

Catroux and Massigli were both on the verge of repudiating De
Gaulle. Catroux wrote De Gaulle that there was no hope for the future
unless some sort of conciliatory reply were produced which would placate
the grievances Giraud felt. De Gaulle may have believed he had gone too
far. Not insensible to Catroux' advice, he did in fact write Giraud on
May 6 a courteous explanation of his reasons for insisting on an encounter at Algiers.

But he refused to go further in an effort to make his presence acceptable in Algiers. He sent Catroux a long communication expressing the
greatest distrust of American policy, which he asserted opposed French

[21] Soustelle, *Envers et contre tout*, II, 241; Giraud, *Un seul but, la victoire*, 160.

unity and a strong France. Catroux had by this time become so exasperated at De Gaulle's stubbornness that he showed the message to Robert Murphy and recommended that the Allies take a definite stand against De Gaulle's personal drive for power. The note was forwarded by Murphy to Hull and to Roosevelt, who received it on May 19 in the midst of his discussions with Churchill at Washington.[22]

Although General Giraud could count many reasons why he should refuse further communication with De Gaulle, there was one overwhelming consideration that made it impossible for him to break off relations: the hope of achieving unity of command. To his purely military way of thinking, the maintenance of two forces fighting for the same objective yet with separate commanders, with internal disputes and rivalries, and not subject to a common discipline, verged on the ridiculous. On May 17 he suddenly wrote De Gaulle:

> . . . the hour of action and of our common responsibilities has come. Time presses and, among other questions, the rapid fusion of all the French forces in a single army of victory is urgent.
>
> I propose that we should pass to action and immediately bring about our union.

In his proposal, Giraud agreed to the idea of a cochairmanship and suggested that De Gaulle and he name two committee members each, after which the committee as a whole would decide on additional members. The letter proposed that the committee "will discuss all the other questions that have been the subject of our exchange of views based on the notes that we have exchanged." Thus De Gaulle was being invited to Algiers without any firm commitment on either side about the dismissal of Boisson, Noguès, and Peyrouton or about the relationship of the commander in chief with the committee. In a note of April 15, De Gaulle had stated that the commander in chief "must be subordinated to the central authority and should not participate in it." When Giraud replied on April 27, he wrote that he "recognizes that it is in accordance with the tradition of France to subordinate the commander in chief to the central power. However, the present exceptional circumstances jus-

22 Hull, *Memoirs,* II, 1219–20.

tify and make necessary the participation in the council of the commander in chief." On this matter there had been no further clarification. Nothing would persuade Giraud to surrender the supreme command over the French armies, but if he gave up his post in the new committee, he would have made such a concession, as Monnet and Murphy undoubtedly warned him, that the United States might lose interest in continuing the arms program.

In spite of the vagueness of the engagements that had been reached, De Gaulle immediately accepted the new offer when Catroux brought it personally to London on May 22. The National Committee officially dissolved itself three days later, and Catroux returned to Algiers on May 27 with word that De Gaulle and his two nominees for the new committee would soon follow. For the members to accompany him, De Gaulle had the sagacity to include one "moderate" as well as an "extremist": René Massigli and André Philip. It is interesting to note that neither of these men, both of whom had come to London within a year, were supporters from the first days of Free France; on the other hand, they had "legitimate" ties with permanent French institutions—Massigli with the diplomatic corps, and Philip with French labor movements and the Socialist party. This time no impediments were placed in the way, and on May 30, De Gaulle, Massigli, and Philip, with a small staff, landed at Boufarik near Algiers for the long-anticipated union with Giraud.

The French Committee of National Liberation

The day before De Gaulle arrived, Winston Churchill, with General Marshall, Sir Alan Brooke, and other British military chiefs, landed in Algiers after a flight directly from New Brunswick. The Prime Minister, ever since Eden's visit to Washington, had tried to organize a full-dress conference at Algiers, where the various military commanders from the Mediterranean theater could be readily convoked and where an atmosphere favorable to his "soft underbelly" strategy might be found. He had asked Marshall to accompany him undoubtedly to have an opportunity to persuade the American Chief of Staff that his obdurate insistence on a cross-Channel invasion should not prejudice him against the possibility of exploiting the Mediterranean. While considerations of high military strategy may have been uppermost in Churchill's mind, he was not blind to the influence his presence might have at the very moment the embryonic French committee was to be born.

What Churchill could do in Algiers was not entirely clear. He was able to confer with his friend General Georges, and he registered satisfaction with Giraud's choice of Georges and Jean Monnet as his nominees. Georges would represent a conservative, military, and possibly pro-British point of view, while Monnet, although unpredictable, would provide intelligence and a capacity for locating solutions to the tangles which would inevitably develop. In the French matter there was nothing to do but wait to see whether De Gaulle would make some overt move to eject Giraud from the committee, on which Churchill and Eisenhower were agreed he should remain. In the event of unanticipated development, British policy would have to improvise and do what it could to maintain the delicate balance between the Americans and the French. Since Churchill had taken steps to bring Eden down from London, it could be hoped that his presence would double the weight of British influence. In case an important move became necessary, Eden would be able to guarantee that the Foreign Office would concur and thus diminish some of the friction that occasionally developed when the Prime Minister plotted his course in accordance with the wind that blew from Washington.

It had been arranged by Catroux and Monnet that preliminary discussions for forming the new organ would take place on May 31. Throughout most of the day the seven French representatives argued. De Gaulle and Philip insisted on the immediate dismissal of Peyrouton, Boisson, Noguès, Bergeret, Mendigal, and Admiral Michelier, all of whom Giraud and Georges vigorously defended. Catroux, Massigli, and Monnet tried to persuade the Generals to establish the committee first and discuss administrative changes afterward, but they could not make their voices heard. The most unresolvable difference, however, pertained to control of the army. Giraud insisted on retaining the cochairmanship and the post of commander in chief for himself, and he proposed to install General Georges as commissioner of defense. De Gaulle, on the other hand, demanded that the supreme command be subordinated to the committee; or at the least that the commander in chief should control only French expeditionary forces while the committee dealt with the remaining military questions, such as training, supply, and rearmament. Since Giraud was unwilling to lose control of armament, he and De Gaulle reached a deadlock which induced the latter to close his briefcase, rise from the table, and stalk from the room, slamming the door behind him.[23]

The next two days saw unbelievable tension and confusion in Algiers. It had been reported that two or three thousand men of De Larminat's force, which, conforming to De Gaulle's instructions, remained in Tunisia, had filtered into Algiers on leave and would be available to support De Gaulle in whatever overt move he might make. Giraud, on his part, appointed Admiral Muselier, who had offered his services to General Giraud, to be head of all police agencies and gave him instructions to maintain security within a radius of fifty miles around Algiers. There were rumors that the Gaullists planned a *Putsch,* and it was reported that Muselier had a warrant for De Gaulle's arrest.

Much of this turmoil had been generated by Marcel Peyrouton when, on June 1, erroneously assuming that De Gaulle and Giraud jointly acted as chairmen of a central authority in North Africa, he sent identical letters of resignation to them both. Since the committee had not yet been established, it cannot be alleged that De Gaulle possessed at this time any legal jurisdiction over Peyrouton. In spite of that fact, De Gaulle called a press conference around midnight to publicize what Peyrouton had done, only to have the news censored when Giraud's new information officer, the anti-Gaullist André Labarthe, learned what had happened. The tension became acute. De Gaulle feared he would be unable to remain in Algiers. He wired Pleven and Soustelle in London:

> I have more and more the impression that an ambush is being prepared. Giraud has brought in Goumiers from Morocco and has given orders to arrest Fighting French soldiers on leave.
>
> He has just sent me a letter calling on me to declare publicly that I undertake not to establish a fascist régime in France.

[23] Catroux, *Dans la bataille de Méditerranée,* 364–65; Giraud, *Un seul but, la victoire,* 162–69; De Gaulle, *Mémoires,* II, 105–106.

Catroux and De Gaulle had a sharp argument in which the former denounced De Gaulle's action in usurping Giraud's rights in the Peyrouton affair. "Giraud has no rights here!" shouted De Gaulle. Catroux had stood enough. "I can't follow you," he said. "We made an agreement with Giraud. I am leaving, and because the other day you showed me the way to break off a discussion, I am doing the same." And he left the room, slamming the door. His letter of resignation followed.[24]

The presence of Churchill, Eden, Eisenhower, and Marshall in Algiers permitted the full weight of Allied authority to be brought to bear on the French generals. On June 2 some of the tension subsided, and possibly as a result of the pressure which the Allied leaders were able to apply,[25] De Gaulle and Giraud were persuaded to accept the "moderates'" proposal of forming the committee first and subsequently working out the details of administration. The program which Monnet and Catroux had planned for May 31 was accordingly adopted on June 3, and the French Committee of National Liberation was officially established on the following basis:

> The Committee is the central French power which ensures the conduct of the French effort in the war. It exercises French sovereignty over all territories outside the control either of the French National Committee or of the Civil and Military Command.
>
> It shall continue to exercise its functions until the liberation of French territory shall permit the formation in conformity with the laws of the Republic of the Provisional Government to which it shall hand over its powers. This shall be done at the latest upon the total liberation of French territory.

De Gaulle and Giraud were designated cochairmen, to preside alternately over the sessions. As cochairmen, both had to sign decrees of the Committee before they could be officially promulgated. Thus, each pos-

---

[24] Soustelle, *Envers et contre tout*, II, 249–51; Butcher, *My Three Years with Eisenhower*, 320; Catroux, *Dans la bataille de Méditerranée*, 366–69; Marcel Peyrouton, *Du service public à la prison commune*, 231–34; De Gaulle, *Mémoires*, II, 488.

[25] Such pressure, conscious or unconscious, is implied by Butcher (*My Three Years with Eisenhower*, 321–23) but was denied by Churchill in Commons on 8 June (*Debates*, Vol. CCCXC, Col. 568).

sessed a veto over the Committee's decisions. To the charter members the following responsibilities were allocated:

René Massigli—Foreign Affairs
André Philip—Interior
Jean Monnet—Armament
General Georges—Commissioner of State without portfolio

It was also agreed that General Catroux, who participated in the first session in spite of his letter of resignation, should become a member of the Committee as commissioner of state and co-ordinator of Moslem affairs. Catroux was also appointed governor general of Algeria, replacing Peyrouton. The addition of Catroux actually provided De Gaulle with a four-to-three majority, but the recent differences between De Gaulle and Catroux undoubtedly gave Giraud confidence that Catroux' votes would be anything but blindly and devotedly Gaullist. It was generally believed that Catroux, Massigli, and Monnet would provide a "moderate" base which would prevent too much movement toward extremes in either direction. Churchill assumed that these three might align themselves with Giraud and Georges, and he thus reassured Roosevelt: "If de Gaulle should prove violent or unreasonable, he will be in a minority of five to two, and possibly completely isolated. The Committee is therefore a body with collective authority with which in my opinion we can safely work."[26]

Roosevelt and Hull agreed to accept the formation of the FCNL, but with reservations. Roosevelt "hesitated to make any statement" on the possibility of accepting the new French body as one of the United Nations, and he was quite firm on the idea that Boisson and French West Africa should not be subjected to a Gaullist invasion. "North Africa," he wrote the Prime Minister on June 4, "is in the last analysis under British-American military rule, and for this reason Eisenhower can be used on what you and I want. The bride evidently forgets that there is still a war in progress over here."[27]

[26] Churchill to Roosevelt, 6 June 1943 (*Closing the Ring*, 174).
[27] Roosevelt to Churchill, 4 June 1943 (*Closing the Ring*, 173–74); Hull, *Memoirs*, II, 1220–21.

Jules Jeanneney was acting head of the French government during De Gaulle's visit to the United States. Here, he greets the General at Orly Field, Paris, after his return on August 30.

A guard of honor was in store for Prime Minister Winston Churchill, left, and British Foreign Minister Anthony Eden, rear center, on their arrival in Paris on November 10, 1944. General de Gaulle and Jules Jean-neney, far right, escorted the British leaders through the ranks.

The French Committee of National Liberation Is Formed

The Crisis over Command of French Troops

For the first few days of its existence the Committee seemed to function smoothly. After the first official sessions both De Gaulle and Giraud spoke over Radio Algier, and Giraud made some graceful allusions to democracy, Jefferson, and Lincoln. He also acquiesced to some basic personnel reforms, permitting Noguès to be replaced by General Puaux as governor general of Morocco and permitting General Mendigal, who had made such a fanatically Pétainist speech on April 5, to be succeeded by General Bouscat as commander in chief of the Air Force. Giraud stood fast, however, on the question of Boisson, and for the time being, De Gaulle did not press the matter. It was later reported to Roosevelt that when Giraud argued that the President was satisfied with Boisson's co-operation, De Gaulle dismissed the argument with contempt.[28]

On June 7 the first step to enlarge the Committee was accomplished with care to make sure that the balance appeared equal. This action was not known, even to Murphy, until June 14, when it was publicly announced in the *Journal Officiel*. Several Committee members had assured Murphy between June 7 and 14 that no changes were contemplated. The following men were chosen:

Gaullist:
René Pleven—Colonies
André Diethelm—Economic Affairs and Production
Adrien Tixier—Labor and Social Welfare

Giraudist:
René Mayer—Transportation and Merchant Marine
Jules Abadie—Justice, Education, and Public Health
Maurice Couve de Murville—Finances

With these six additions the Committee still contained an odd number —thirteen—and General Catroux placed the balance on the Gaullist side. For the fourteenth place, Public Information, Giraud proposed Labarthe, a nominee absolutely unacceptable to De Gaulle, who wished Soustelle

[28] Murphy to State Department, Dispatch No. 1069 of 9 June 1943, 851.01/2238; Leahy, *I Was There*, 168; Catroux, *Dans la bataille de Méditerranée*, 370–71.

to hold the post. A compromise was reached in the appointment of Henri Bonnet, for many years director of the International Institute for Intellectual Co-operation, and at the time teaching in New York. It was assumed that Bonnet would affiliate himself with the moderate elements, since he had not demonstrated any strong leanings toward De Gaulle; it turned out, however, that his sympathies inclined much more toward Fighting French concepts than toward Giraudist. Although it was not apparent simply through the names of the Committee members, De Gaulle did in fact possess a considerable advantage, for in Philip, Pleven, Diethelm, and Tixier he possessed a solid bloc of able politicians who knew what they wanted and where they were going; Giraud had no comparable unity or loyalty among his "appointees," who would be inclined to vote not out of loyalty to Giraud but according to what they considered to be the best interests of the cause they were serving.

It might be thought that De Gaulle would now rest before pushing on to the next objective—control of the army. Had he waited three or four weeks, he would have been able to count on the support of a Gaullist movement which was certain to develop rapidly in North Africa, and he would have had the backing of his London associates, who would by that time have arrived at Algiers. That he refused to postpone the offensive emphasizes that singleness of purpose which so characterized De Gaulle; it was the quality that made him the unique advocate of mobility in warfare when the French high command emphasized defense—the quality that brought him to England when no other leader was prepared to make a stand. It is difficult to understand the aims and methods that motivated De Gaulle and pushed him into so many apparently avoidable conflicts—unless one comprehends something of the cold, direct, humorless passion which, sustained by his great ambition to restore the historical glory and grandeur of France, drove him with the inevitability and relentlessness of a rising tide. De Gaulle once told the British ambassador, Duff Cooper, that for a few minutes each day he paused to contemplate how his decisions and actions would look in the light of history. The detachment which permitted De Gaulle to regard himself searching for his historical niche explains in part the determination which forced him to construct an ideal and act in accordance with it. In his own judgment, the least backsliding would be followed by the destruction of himself and the crumbling of his movement.

To his direct way of thinking, with the Committee formed, the next problem to arrange was the relationship of the commander in chief to the Committee. It did not matter that a showdown with Giraud was sure to promote a crisis with the Allied command. Perhaps, as in the Saint Pierre–Miquelon affair, De Gaulle wanted to hurl another stone into the frog pond to see how loudly the frogs would croak. It did not matter that a flank attack, delayed several weeks, might have better chances of success; or that with no military operations for French troops envisaged in the immediate future, the relationship of the commander in chief with the Committee was not at the moment crucial. The problem was there; it must be attacked.

At the FCNL meeting on June 8, De Gaulle launched his offensive, demanding of Giraud that he surrender either his position as cochairman or as commander in chief. During the brisk argumentation that followed it became clear that De Gaulle insisted on filling the thus-far-vacant post as commissioner of defense himself, while Giraud demanded it with equal firmness for General Georges. Although Giraud was stubborn and obtuse, he comprehended that his relinquishment of authority within the Committee would provide a civilian group with control over rearmament and appointments in an army which he felt had been his own creation. Giraud told Murphy he was determined to retire if he was outvoted, and he asked Murphy, in the event of his resignation, to inform the British and American governments and the French people of the injustice caused by De Gaulle's ambition.[29] De Gaulle had also reached the conclusion that it was useless for him to continue to co-operate under the conditions imposed by Giraud. On June 9 he sent the Committee a written communication to the effect that he would not participate in further sessions of the FCNL unless his basic recommendations were accepted. He pointed out that the present structure of the Committee:

> . . . does not conform to the responsibilities which I believe I must carry in this war *vis à vis* the country, by virtue of the confidence of a very large number of Frenchmen.

[29] Roosevelt to Churchill, 10 June 1943 (Leahy, *I Was There,* 167–68). Cf. Churchill, *Closing the Ring,* 175.

I would not fulfil my obligations if I associated myself any longer with the French Committee of National Liberation in the conditions under which it functions, and I ask you, consequently, to consider me no longer as member nor as chairman.[30]

This letter did not, as widely alleged, have the form of a "resignation"; it could better be termed an ultimatum which stated in effect that he would abstain from meeting with the Committee until Giraud agreed to accept his propositions.

The terms of this ultimatum were promptly forwarded by Macmillan to London and by Murphy to Washington. On June 8, Churchill had somewhat prematurely delivered a speech in the House of Commons in which he had praised the Committee and the high personal qualities of its members; but he had not committed himself on the question of the degree of recognition to give the new Committee. When London learned of the crisis, there was not much that could be done except to keep the London Gaullists from going to Algiers and to suspend all financial arrangements with Fighting France until it could be learned what De Gaulle would do. On June 11, Churchill wrote Macmillan:

> There can be no question of our giving recognition until we know what it is we have to recognize. See St. Matthew, Chapter VII, Verse 16. ["Beware of false prophets which come to you in sheep's clothing, but inwardly are ravening wolves. By their fruits ye shall know them . . . .] Indeed, the whole chapter is instructive.
>
> You are quite right to play for time and let de Gaulle have every chance to come to his senses and realize the forces around him. We play fair with him if he plays fair with us and with France.[31]

President Roosevelt's reaction to the developments that were reported to him was vigorous and his action decisive; he reaffirmed immediately his contention that North Africa was an American military appanage. His distrust of De Gaulle is reflected in the instructions he transmitted to Eisenhower on June 10:

[30] De Gaulle, *Mémoires*, II, 493–94.

[31] Churchill, *Closing the Ring*, 175. Macmillan wired back: "Doing my best. See Revelations, II, verses 2–5" [I know thy works and thy toil and patience, and that thou canst not bear evil men. . . . But I have this against thee, that thou didst leave thy first love.] (Pendar, *Adventure in Diplomacy*, 177).

Possible de Gaulle domination of Dakar cannot be considered. Neither of us know where he will end up. If de Gaulle should attempt to move in on French West Africa I will be impelled to consider sending Naval and ground forces to Dakar. Giraud must have complete control of the French Army. I would be concerned about the safety of British and American lines of supply and the territory behind the British and American lines should control pass to de Gaulle.[32]

The President also sent instructions that Giraud was to keep the post of commander in chief. These steps by the President, together with his dispatch of Admiral Glassford to Dakar, marked a degree of irritation concerning De Gaulle's ambitions that revealed more strongly than ever before how much he mistrusted the Fighting French. It demonstrated the fact (which Churchill was not slow to notice) that American disapprobation of De Gaulle was concentrated not simply in Secretary Hull and the State Department but in the White House as well. So long as De Gaulle's actions had been limited to propaganda attacks directed largely at Mr. Hull, the President had rather enjoyed the game; but when De Gaulle impinged on interests which Roosevelt considered vital to the United States, he did not hesitate to intervene, quickly and decisively.

Eisenhower was much more reluctant to participate in French political matters than Roosevelt. He turned the President's letters over to Robert Murphy to have him reveal their contents to the French. De Gaulle reacted with an hour-and-a-quarter denunciation of the American policy of intervention and a staunch defense of the Committee's sovereign rights in West Africa; but while he agreed to take up the President's wishes with the Committee, he showed no inclination to accept them. But the Committee failed to reconvene, and each day, as the deadlock continued, observers became more and more discouraged at the possibility of finding a way out of the impasse. During the crisis, Catroux, Massigli, and Monnet proposed a variety of compromises, none of which proved acceptable. Monnet was especially inventive in attempting to find an adequate solution, but even he seemed unable to produce a plan acceptable to both sides. Monnet did not want to see De Gaulle obtain

[32] Leahy, *I Was There,* 168; Butcher, *My Three Years with Eisenhower,* 330–31.

control of the armed forces, but he feared that Giraud would prove inadequate to the task of revitalizing the French Army. If De Gaulle continued to boycott the Committee, it would be only a matter of months, Monnet believed, before Giraud would be swept aside before a widespread public clamor for De Gaulle.

By June 13 all of the newly appointed Committee members, except Bonnet, had arrived in Algiers. His confidence restored, De Gaulle chose to ignore his "resignation" and proposed to Giraud that the full Committee meet together on June 15. When Murphy learned of the new appointments (made public for the first time on June 14) and of De Gaulle's latest tactics, he became quite apprehensive that De Gaulle might achieve military command before the United States became aware of what had happened. Murphy realized that Eisenhower alone possessed sufficient authority and prestige to restrain De Gaulle, yet Eisenhower was unfortunately absent from Algiers at the time. Faced with a crisis, Murphy obtained a postponement of the Committee meeting and urgently telegraphed the President for support, suggesting that Eisenhower not only explain American requirements to the French, but also that he be empowered to threaten them, if necessary, with a cessation of military aid. It is very possible that the moderate group in the FCNL would have restrained De Gaulle from gaining control of the army, but Murphy did not apparently have faith in their capacity to cope with the Fighting French elements.

The President responded with alacrity to Murphy's insistent appeal and on June 17 decided to transmit to Eisenhower instructions which would permit no ambiguity concerning his attitude. The order was drawn up by Admiral Leahy and Harry Hopkins, and since it expressed so clearly White House thinking at this time, it is worth reading with care:

> The position of this Government is that during our military occupation of North Africa we will not tolerate the control of the French Army by any agency which is not subject to the Allied Supreme Commander's direction. We must have someone whom we completely and wholly trust. We would under no circumstances continue the arming of a force without being completely confident in their willingness to co-operate in our military operations; we are not interested moreover in the formation of any Government or Committee which presumes in any way to indicate

that, until such time as the French people select a Government for themselves, it will govern in France. When we get into France, the Allies
will have a civil government plan that is completely in consonance with
French sovereignty. Lastly, it must be absolutely clear that in North and
West Africa we have a military occupation, and therefore without your
full approval no independent civil decision can be made. We want our
policy of encouraging local officials to run their own affairs to be extended,
but this policy must not be allowed to so endanger our military situation
that it might make it necessary to keep more troops in North Africa than
now is planned.

At this time we are not going to allow de Gaulle personally or through
his partisans to control the French Army in Africa. You know you are
authorized to take any action you think best in behalf of the United
States Government.[33]

Churchill immediately agreed that his government would associate
themselves with the President's policy. Churchill, in fact, was beginning
to develop fears that De Gaulle's arrival in Algiers was producing what
he had long anticipated, a rift between Britain and the United States.
With De Gaulle's behavior producing a protracted crisis in Algiers, an
understandable reaction would develop in Washington to the effect that
the British stood behind De Gaulle's conniving to obtain control of the
French armies. As the Prime Minister took cognizance of Roosevelt's
increasingly impatient communications, he cast about him for means of
reducing the pro-Gaullist sentiment that prevailed in Britain. To help
accomplish his aim, he drew up a confidential memorandum for the
guidance of the press, enumerating De Gaulle's faults and errors. The
principal points made by the Prime Minister were that De Gaulle had
left a trail of Anglophobia behind him, that he had tried to play
Britain against the Soviet Union, that he had created friction in Syria,
that he had Fascist and dictatorial tendencies, and that he had switched
from an anti-Communist position to the enjoyment of Communist
support. The memorandum pointed out that Great Britain had treated
De Gaulle fairly and hoped for his co-operation in the FCNL, but did
not wish, particularly considering Roosevelt's strong views, that De
Gaulle interfere with British-American relations. The principal ele-

[33] Leahy, *I Was There*, 168; Churchill, *Closing the Ring*, 175–76.

ments of this paper were discussed with British and American correspondents by British Minister of Information Brendan Bracken, but Bracken's comments did not have much influence on the British press. The text of the memorandum was also immediately given to Murphy for transmittal to the State Department (Hull received it on June 17), from which it was later permitted to "leak" to the columnist Ernest Lindley, who printed it on July 12, at the time of Giraud's visit to the United States. Churchill would probably have been inclined to let the French matter work itself out, but he could not risk alienating the President at a time when world-wide interests demanded the closest cooperation between Great Britain and the United States.[34]

Eisenhower, who had been absent from Algiers, received the President's instructions when he returned on the evening of June 18. He found himself thus faced with the sort of political role for which he had no enthusiasm. From a military point of view, it was immaterial who controlled the French Army so long as its commanders proved themselves competent and loyal; the choice of Giraud rather than De Gaulle had been reached on political and not military grounds and was outside of Eisenhower's sphere of direct responsibility. It should be remembered that no French units at this time were scheduled to participate in any Allied action, and the intervention of the Allied Force commander could hardly be justified on the basis of tactical requirements. Eisenhower had no stomach for involving himself in French family squabbles; nevertheless he had no alternative but to carry out the President's directive. The incident provides an outstanding example of the way in which the President occasionally intervened in military affairs when political issues were at stake; the field commander in this case was disregarded in policy formulation but was required to implement a politico-military decision for which he did not actually bear the responsibility.

With no solution or agreement apparently emerging from the inert

[34] Washington *Post*, 12 July 1943; Hull, *Memoirs*, II, 1223; Soustelle, *Envers et contre tout*, II, 258. A member of Parliament, Mr. Boothby, questioned the Prime Minister about this memorandum, which seemed to differ from official statements of policy. Churchill replied on July 21: "I take full responsibility for this document, the text of which was drafted personally by me. It is a confidential document. I am not prepared to discuss it otherwise than in secret session" (*Debates*, Vol. CCCXCI, Col. 891).

FCNL, Eisenhower decided to explain President Roosevelt's policy frankly and directly to the two generals. He invited them to his villa on the morning of June 19 to acquaint them with the President's requirements. Before Eisenhower could begin, De Gaulle endeavored to clarify his position, pointing out that he came as head of the French government and that he would be willing to entertain only such requests as were compatible with the interests he represented. De Gaulle did not, in fact, claim publicly to represent the French government until several months later. If at this time he opened his discussion with Eisenhower on these unequivocal terms, giving no heed to General Giraud's equal position as cochairman of the Committee of Liberation, he took a position unknown to many Frenchmen and certainly not calculated to endear himself to the Americans with whom he would necessarily be in much closer contact than ever before.

Eisenhower then proceeded to set forth the President's stipulations: that Giraud should remain as commander in chief, that no change should be made in command relationships, and that if these terms were not accepted, further arms deliveries would be terminated. For an hour De Gaulle protested that the designation of French commander in chief was a purely French affair and that Allied intervention in the matter constituted a flagrant and unwarranted violation of French sovereignty. It was clear, of course, that so long as the President insisted that North Africa was "occupied territory," and so long as the President controlled the future of French armament, De Gaulle could do no more than envelop himself, as he had since June, 1940, in his pride and his firmness in upholding what he considered to be France's prerogatives. De Gaulle refused to make a concession. He asked Eisenhower to draw up the American policy in writing for submission to the Committee; then as Giraud began to point out that the embryonic French Army could exist only within an Allied framework, he stood up, courteously excused himself, and walked out.[35]

As his tall figure retreated down the path from Eisenhower's villa, with him, it seemed, went the last chance of achieving that solidarity which alone could restore the prestige of stricken France; and the un-

[35] De Gaulle, *Mémoires,* II, 115–16, 500–501; Butcher, *My Three Years with Eisenhower,* 335–36.

happy Committee of National Liberation, conceived in hope and in the imperative need for French unity, remained stillborn.

In the crisis precipitated by the French command relationships, De Gaulle decided finally to refer the matter to the thirteen members of the Committee of National Liberation; but he felt that if the Committee acted in accordance with Eisenhower's demands, which in his view encroached upon French sovereignty, he might be obliged immediately to retire. Late into the night of June 21 the FCNL deliberated over the consequences of the alternatives facing them, before they reached agreement on a compromise engineered by Jean Monnet which amounted to no more than a postponement of the issue. For the time being there would be two commanders in chief, each with his complete staff: Giraud for North and West Africa, De Gaulle for the rest of the Empire. The alternating chairmanships would continue. No commissioner of defense would be appointed, but a Permanent Military Committee, to consist of Giraud and De Gaulle with their chiefs of staff, Juin and De Larminat, would consult together in an effort to work out plans for military fusion.

The scheme, which was announced on June 22, received the support of Giraud and the assent of De Gaulle, but it persuaded no one to the belief that it could be anything but a temporary measure. It solved nothing, but it avoided a catastrophe. It served to hold the Committee together until a better solution could be found, and it produced an appearance of unity during Giraud's voyage to Washington. It is difficult to give De Gaulle credit for much magnanimity in agreeing to accept the compromise. To the majority of members of the FCNL it was obvious that with De Gaulle's prestige, with the swing of the population behind him, with the well-organized governmental services he had built up, and with his competent propaganda enterprises, he would in any event gradually dominate the political and administrative elements of the new governmental machinery. Once having achieved domination he could gradually have brought pressure to bear on Giraud and the army. No immediate benefit derived from control of the military organization. No plans existed for the use of the French Army in any future campaign, and the entire strength of the potential French Army resided in its capacity to tap the American arsenal, for which Giraud, at the moment, alone possessed the key. If De Gaulle had accepted Giraud's dual prerogatives on June 4, he would have avoided the crisis of June 18 and would have placed himself in an advantageous position from which to achieve his ultimate objectives. On the contrary, by insisting on his claims to represent France, he so tactlessly increased the apprehension of the White House that Roosevelt became increasingly determined that De Gaulle should not control any part of the re-equipped French armies. De Gaulle believed that by acting as the "inflexible champion" of France he would obtain "respect and consideration" from foreigners; "it was necessary for me," he insisted, "to achieve the summit and never descend from it." He never understood that one could be firm and yet tactful or that all compromise is not appeasement.

While for the time being the compromise of June 22 saved the FCNL, it did little to reduce the number of desertions of regular army personnel to Fighting French units. Although De Gaulle on June 8 had signed an order to prevent transfers from Giraudist companies and had acquiesced to De Larminat's transfer to Tunisia, the recruiting continued, and by the end of June, Giraud acknowledged that some 2,750 transfers had occurred in Algeria alone. Other estimates placed the figure much higher, asserting, for example, that more than 10,000 men and officers had rallied to Leclerc by July. It would take more than unity of command, under such circumstances, to weld the French Army into a single effective weapon.

One branch of the army, the intelligence services, suffered especially from the dyarchic arrangement of June 22. If the establishment of two commanders in chief, two staffs, and two armies meant the maintenance of two *Deuxièmes Bureaux,* the arrangement would be patently absurd. Armies could be stationed in separate areas, but there was no limit to the localities in which intelligence agents would operate. To employ two separate operatives to gather identical data doubled the risk and the expense, and it enormously decreased the security of the tasks undertaken. This problem was especially important to the Allied governments because of the necessity for their own intelligence services to work efficiently with the French. It affected the United States because OSS and G–2 personnel had long since made contacts with General Giraud's operatives and were inclined to trust them more than the "amateur" agents working for Fighting France.

Parallel activity on the part of the French already existed. The Gaullist BCRA, operating out of London, supervised the Gaullist underground networks and kept in touch with the Resistance. Although the BCRA, under the guidance of Colonel Passy (André de Wavrin), fulfilled some of the functions of traditional military intelligence, such as obtaining information, it had assumed many other responsibilities, namely, sending arms to the underground, fabricating false papers, organizing sabotage, developing escape networks, and disseminating propaganda— tasks which had been forced upon it by the German occupation. Giraud's intelligence services were patterned along more classic lines, for they included the intelligence and counterespionage services of the regular French Army which had operated clandestinely during the occupation. Shortly after the North African landing, Colonel Rivet, head of military information (SR, *Services de Renseignement*), and Commandant Paillole, the counterespionage expert who had continued to operate in France through the clandestine TR (*Travaux Ruraux*), had reported to North Africa where under General Ronin they continued to maintain contacts with agents in France.

The intelligence services problem stood at the heart of the Gaullist-Giraudist controversy, because whoever controlled the networks controlled the co-ordination with the Resistance in France. If the BCRA was absorbed by Giraud's Intelligence, and if Giraud became commander in chief of all French armies, it could mean that the Gaullists would lose contact with the very groups on which depended much of their strength and that the Resistance, organized on a regular army framework, would develop along traditional military lines. To the Gaullists who had worked for three years to build up their clandestine organization, it was unthinkable that they should now subordinate themselves to an army command which they mistrusted for its pro-Pétainism. For the remainder of the year, although the Gaullist and Giraudist armies became technically fused in August, BCRA and French Army Intelligence continued their parallel and mutually suspect activities; ultimately their differences were to promote one of the gravest crises which the Committee of National Liberation was destined to undergo.

Giraud Comes to America

Once the compromise of June 22 had been effected, both Giraud and De Gaulle sought, in their own ways, to strengthen their positions. Incapable of estimating the problem in any but military terms, Giraud thought only of surrounding himself with a sympathetic staff and a strong army. He believed that once his regular North African army received the equipment promised by Roosevelt at Casablanca, it would achieve such power and importance that not only would "desertions" cease but his own value as commander in chief would be indisputable. He was far from right. One can understand how the forthright, simple soldier Giraud could badly misjudge the political strength and attraction of the Gaullist *mystique,* but it is more difficult to pardon the general Giraud his miscalculations concerning the French Army's possibilities. Admitting that his army lacked European specialists, he refused to accept the fact that scarcely enough were available for an army two-thirds the size of the one he hoped to build; and he failed to anticipate that with the Anglo-Americans employing most of the port facilities in North Africa for the Sicilian campaign build-up, confusion would follow inevitably if the French were incapable of unloading, assembling, storing, and distributing the equipment as it arrived.

By June space in the harbors at Casablanca, Oran, and Algiers was so limited that Eisenhower began to entertain serious misgivings about extending allocations to the French. Forced to give priority to ships with his own equipment, he had occasionally found it necessary to order vessels with French matériel to stand by at Gibraltar until facilities opened up in North Africa. With the Sicilian campaign scheduled for July, and with a possible follow-up in Italy, Eisenhower did not believe that the situation would ameliorate before November. He was in any case unenthusiastic about adding French forces to the British and American troops already under his command. Coalition warfare is always difficult, and Eisenhower believed that his responsibilities and difficulties as a theater commander would be eased by the employment of only American and British forces in combat; but he was willing to accept direction from Washington if, for the benefit of the over-all war effort, it was believed there that mounting a French expeditionary force was desirable. The War Department and the Combined Chiefs of Staff, on the other hand, did not wish to burden the theater commander with a program that would tie his hands and reduce the efficiency of his offensive operations. Even President Roosevelt, although he supported Giraud for political reasons, was now disinclined to push French rearmament against the firm opposition of the field commander. If there was not precisely opposition on the subject between Allied headquarters in Algiers and Washington, there was at least a hesitancy on the part of each to take the responsibility; Eisenhower sought a firm directive from the Combined Chiefs, whereas Marshall looked for a firm recommendation from North Africa. It was this ambiguity concerning responsibility, and the lack of enthusiasm at Eisenhower's headquarters, that convinced Giraud to accept the offer, sent to him on May 27 (before De Gaulle had reached Algiers) to visit President Roosevelt. Although his absence would leave De Gaulle to handle affairs by himself at Algiers for three weeks, Giraud believed that the rearming of the French Army took precedence over all other considerations.

It will be recalled that in May the Combined Chiefs of Staff had approved the continuation of arms shipments but had not committed themselves to any specific schedule of deliveries. Giraud was alarmed at rumors that Washington might curtail the entire program because of De Gaulle's arrogant behavior, and he feared that the program might come to be administered through the FCNL rather than through the commander in chief. By placing his case directly before the American authorities in Washington, Giraud hoped to convince them of the value of a French expeditionary force, to find support for himself as commander in chief, and to obtain another special convoy which would bring 200,000 tons of matériel—enough for two armored divisions—to North Africa in July.

From the point of view of Giraud and American policy makers, the visit, from July 7 to July 16, was a great success. Washington outdid itself to make an impressive affair out of the General's tour. There were banquets of state; personal receptions by the President; visits to Fort Benning, West Point, and Detroit; a suite at the Waldorf Astoria in New York (where three floors were reserved, one for the General and two for the FBI), and meetings with Marshall, Leahy, Hull, McCloy,

Somervell, and many lesser dignitaries. Giraud was visibly impressed, and like a small boy at the circus for the first time, enjoyed himself enormously. No pains were spared to increase the appearance of the General's prestige at the expense of De Gaulle. During Giraud's visit, Churchill's anti-Gaullist "advice to the press" made its appearance in Ernest Lindley's syndicated column, and data on a Fighting French personal oath to De Gaulle were released to the press.[36] On July 11, President Roosevelt, speaking on the Sicily landings, referred to Giraud's visit as a symbol which presaged the march toward the freedom and unity of France. He did not mention De Gaulle.

After one of the formal dinners at the White House, Giraud had a personal conversation with the President which lasted for over an hour. In Giraud's words:

> In regard to General de Gaulle, [Roosevelt] distrusted his ambition and pride. The men which de Gaulle had sent to America, Philip, Pleven, Tixier, had not been good ambassadors. He feared, as democratic President of the most democratic state there is, that he might see installed in France, through Gaullism, a new totalitarian state, leaning much more toward fascism than toward true democracy.
>
> He also feared the Franco-Russian flirtation pushed too far, and Bolshevism making rapid progress in Western Europe, with the more or less sincere complicity, if not of General de Gaulle, at least of his entourage.
>
> I repeated to him the reasons, without however emphasizing his own friendly insistence, which influenced me to have General de Gaulle come to Algiers. . . . I believed sincerely that I would continue to exercise in

---

[36] The essential portion of this oath, which had been revealed by General Eon, was printed in *The Scotsman* on 5 Apr. 1943. Its text was: "I swear to recognize General de Gaulle as the sole legitimate leader of the French and to use my efforts to cause him to be so recognized, if necessary, by utilizing the methods employed against the Germans." Fighting French headquarters denied any knowledge of such an oath. American officials obtained copies of this oath from what was believed to be a valid source, and it was forwarded to Washington on May 25 (Butcher, *My Three Years with Eisenhower*, 310–11). A convincing explanation of the oath is given in Barlone (*La route des sommets*, 178): "The document exists; it is not false. In France we have volunteers for the Secret Army sign the same enlistment papers as in London, where there is no question of General de Gaulle personally. But an over-zealous section chief added, unknown to us, a formula of allegiance, a sort of personal oath to the General, which he had several hundred enlistees sign." It is interesting to note that although the document had appeared in the British press in April and was available to official Washington late in May, it was not released in the American press until July 8, the day General Giraud arrived in Washington.

complete independence the command of the army, and that this army, re-equipped by the United States, would be the surest guarantee of the future tranquility of France. I insisted then, to the President, that rearmament should enter into a more active phase, and that he should use his personal influence to enable France to obtain a favorable chance in the allocations of material and of transportation. . . .

The conversation, often animated, remained on most friendly ground. We did not part before one a.m., the President making me promise to write him anytime I needed to let him personally know my thoughts.[37]

Admiral Leahy and General Marshall took up the burden of the General's cause before the Combined Chiefs of Staff, whom Giraud met on July 8. Marshall appeared to believe much more strongly than Eisenhower in the argument that the rearmament program would save American lives. If it were true that 250,000 French soldiers, already in North Africa, could be brought into the Italian or French campaigns by the end of the year, it stood to reason that 250,000 fewer American soldiers would have to be transported to Europe. While the British members of the Combined Chiefs remained cool to General Giraud's proposals, their opposition, now that De Gaulle had installed himself in North Africa, seemed to have diminished. Ultimately the question was not resolved by the CCS but by the problem of shipping and port facilities, which had to be solved by Somervell in the United States and by Eisenhower in North Africa. Before Giraud left the United States, Marshall and Somervell, aware of the importance the President and Leahy placed on the program's continuance, had arranged that twenty-seven vessels in three convoys during August and September would transport enough matériel to complete the second third of the Anfa commitment of eleven divisions. The deliveries would, of course, be subject to Eisenhower's clearance on unloading in the theater. With 75,000 men already armed, this would mean that by the end of September, Giraud could count on over six modern rearmed divisions to De Gaulle's two. Content that his voyage to Washington had accomplished most of what he had hoped for, Giraud continued his triumphal tour through Canada and England,

[37] *Un seul but, la victoire,* 199–200.
[38] Vigneras, *Rearming the French,* 82–86.

where his reception was cordial if somewhat less enthusiastic than in Washington, and on July 25 returned once more to Algiers.[38]

Soon after he arrived in North Africa, Giraud learned that his voyage had not confirmed his position as solidly as he could have wished. In his absence Eisenhower had become increasingly convinced that he needed more authority over French forces and rearmament to keep the program from effecting division rather than fusion of the Gaullist and Giraudist armies. It seemed neither logical nor efficient to arm eleven "Giraudist" divisions with American equipment, when two Gaullist divisions, with British matériel, were to be incorporated into the same army. This was especially true since the Gaullist troops needed additional arms, there was a shortage of technicians and specialists, and several Giraudist divisions were still in the formative stage. Common sense dictated that all of the French divisions should have one standard type of equipment and that the two Fighting French divisions (Leclerc's armored division and Brosset's [formerly Koenig's] First Free French) be included among the eleven divisions of the Anfa program. The Combined Chiefs of Staff deliberated on this matter the same week that Giraud returned to North Africa, and on July 30 they agreed that all French forces should be controlled through Eisenhower's headquarters and that Giraud should include the Gaullist troops in his eleven-division program. Giraud seemed to be losing ground as rapidly as he gained it.

Developments in North Africa

During the weeks that Giraud spent away from North Africa, General de Gaulle and his adherents labored to improve their own status and to resolve the compromise arrangement of June 22. Throughout North Africa, De Gaulle's supporters became increasingly demonstrative, and as the trend was sensed by the indecisive who were swayed by whichever way the political wind blew, the majority of the population gave vent to their approval of De Gaulle. His reception in Tunisia toward the end of June provoked vastly more enthusiasm than Giraud had inspired there six weeks earlier. As Gaullists began arriving from London, they began to infilter the administrative agencies in which, though a minority, by their singleness of purpose and dedication to a doctrine, they exerted a considerable influence. With their control of Interior, Colonies, and Information, the Gaullists were in a position to carry out measures and employ propaganda in areas that were extremely significant in building popular opinion. Fighting French organizations, the newspapers *Combat* and later the *Marseillaise* (transplanted from London), and Gaullist propaganda agencies worked steadily and efficiently to build up De Gaulle and deprecate the work of Giraud and his entourage. Even by the end of June a poll showed that although about 70 per cent of United States newspapers had previously backed Giraud, 40 per cent now supported De Gaulle and 34 per cent supported Giraud.[39]

By July 31 a new compromise had been reached. Instead of alternating as presiding officers of the FCNL, henceforward General Giraud would direct the discussions and follow the execution of the Committee's decisions in affairs concerning national defense, while General de Gaulle would preside over all other affairs and over general policies. Giraud was furthermore appointed commander in chief of all French forces and was put in charge of organization, planning, training, and distribution of armament. There were, however, some very important reservations to Giraud's appointment. First, the FCNL retained the responsibility for the general conduct of the war and for the disposition of all land, naval, and air forces. Secondly, a Committee of National Defense, with De Gaulle as chairman, was created to carry out the FCNL's directives and to bring about the fusion of the armed forces. If the Allies recognized the FCNL, it would be possible to argue that all military discussions with the Allies above the field level should be conducted by the Commissioner of National Defense rather than by the Commander in Chief. Finally, an interesting clause in the decree of July 31 provided that whenever General Giraud exercised "an effective operational command he will cease to exercise the functions of chairman of the National Committee of Liberation." In other words, if French forces would be used in the field, in Italy or in the liberation of France, and Giraud commanded those troops directly (which type of command he was best qualified for), he would automatically relinquish the cochairmanship. It was not clear, however, whether under these circumstances he still retained a seat in the FCNL.

[39] *News Chronicle,* 2 July 1943.

For the moment it appeared as if the Committee had come to its senses. De Gaulle had magnanimously turned over all French troops to Giraud and had apparently bowed to the consensus of opinion within the civilian dominated Committee. He wrote to Giraud in the most amiable terms:

> I am sure that these men [the Free French forces] will follow you with the confidence and loyalty that such a great soldier and fine leader deserves. Tomorrow, with God's help, you will lead them into the decisive battle which will liberate our homeland.[40]

Under these circumstances there seemed to be no reason why the FCNL could not expect early recognition by the Allies.

With the fusion of the Gaullist and Giraudist forces announced officially on August 4, General Giraud and his staff were immediately confronted with the problem of incorporating Free French units into the rearmament program. In spite of the shortage of Frenchmen to carry out service functions, General Giraud ignored the dangers of the situation and instead endeavored to increase the size of the program so that he would lose no divisions by the inclusion of Gaullist elements. After a thoroughgoing re-evaluation of the needs of the French Army, he proposed that the larger of the two Free French units should retain its British equipment and that only the smaller, the 3,000-man Leclerc division, should be included in the eleven-division program already authorized. This arrangement was accepted for the time being at Eisenhower's headquarters (it came to be known as the "August 15 Plan"), but the rapidity with which it could be implemented required a decision by an authority higher than Allied headquarters. At this time the Combined Chiefs of Staff were meeting at Quebec, where Roosevelt and Churchill had come together for the "Quadrant" Conference, and it was believed that from their deliberations some firm commitment would emerge. A favorable decision on the program was believed to be especially possible if, as most observers anticipated, one of the outcomes of the Quebec Conference happened to be recognition of the Committee of National Liberation.

[40] Letter of 2 Aug. 1943 (De Gaulle, *Mémoires*, II, 519).

▶ 4. The Committee Is "Recognized"

The Question of Recognition

ALMOST THE first collective act of the FCNL had been to request the United Nations to recognize it as the "body qualified to ensure the conduct of the French effort in the war, within the framework of inter-Allied co-operation" and as "the body qualified to ensure the administration and defense of all French interests." The new Committee possessed wide powers of administration and authority over French forces, but it could not play an important role in the military liberation of France unless it was accepted, particularly by the United States and Great Britain, as qualified to fulfill the function which it considered proper. Recognition meant that the Committee would have to be consulted in regard to any question pertaining to France and her empire, of which all elements except Indochina now accepted the authority of the FCNL. (Martinique, the last area that had remained loyal to Pétain, had accepted the Committee's authority in July.) If the United States recognized the FCNL's authority, it would mean that Washington was prepared to abandon the policy of making local arrangements with individual French governors.

Recognition meant, furthermore, that although the FCNL was not accepted as a provisional government, it could justify in Allied eyes the assumption of the prerogatives of a French administrative body according to the traditions of the Third Republic. One of these traditions, imbedded in republican thinking since the Dreyfus Affair, required the subordination of the military command to the civil authority; thus, if Washington recognized the FCNL, American officials would have difficulty in explaining why they insisted on negotiating not with the Committee but with the Commander in Chief. More important, recognition

148

would open the way for representatives of the FCNL to participate in Allied committees, planning organizations and possibly in the strategic deliberations concerning future campaigns. It would be difficult for the Allies to plan the invasion of France and yet exclude delegates from the body which had been recognized as representing France. In July and August, as the Allies commenced their secret negotiations with Badoglio, De Gaulle became very sensitive about his being excluded from the discussions, not only because the Badoglio deal resembled the deal with Darlan, but because France, having been attacked and occupied by Mussolini, felt herself to be fundamentally concerned in any arrangement made with Italy. Recognition would presumably permit the FCNL to have a voice in the Italian settlement.

All of the financial and economic arrangements already made between De Gaulle, Giraud, and the Allies, and future arrangements, would be facilitated by recognition. With both De Gaulle and Giraud having received Lend-Lease aid, and arms, equipment, and financial support from the Allies, the continuation of separate contracts was obviously absurd. A much larger question was also opened up by the formation of the French Committee: would recognition of the Committee permit its access to French credits held in the United States? It was estimated that over $1,000,000,000 worth of gold and credit was held in the custody of the United States Treasury. Included in this amount was $64,000,000 claimed by Belgium and $228,000,000 claimed by Poland, but the remainder, if turned over to the FCNL, would provide an amount that could liquidate the obligations of De Gaulle and Giraud to the Allies and permit considerable latitude and independence to the Committee. If French money was turned over to the FCNL, the transaction would be tantamount to *de facto* recognition as a provisional government; on the other hand, recognition of the FCNL would justify claims by the Committee that it should receive the credits.

Another consideration uppermost in the minds of the French pertained to questions of sovereignty in North Africa and, after the liberation, in France. The Clark-Darlan Agreement was justified as a military arrangement made, not with a government, but with a military commander in an area where no recognized government functioned. Recognition of the FCNL could pave the way to a modification of the

Clark-Darlan Agreement, and it would require the Allied Commander to work through the Committee. More important was the question of France. Would the Allied Commander, after the landings, sign another Clark-Darlan accord with some Pétainist official or with Pétain himself? Would the Allies develop an AMGOT (Allied Military Government for Occupied Territories) and administer the area without consultation with French representatives? Would the Allies ignore the Resistance, or would they by-pass the FCNL in trying to co-operate with the underground directly? These questions could possibly be resolved if some sort of recognition were accorded before the landings in France actually took place.

Anglo-American Attempts to Agree on a Recognition Formula

Winston Churchill appreciated fully the importance of rapid recognition of the Committee, but he had no illusions about the difficulties he might encounter in Washington. He wrote Roosevelt on July 21:

What does recognition mean? One can recognise a man as an Emperor or as a grocer. Recognition is meaningless, without a defining formula. Until de Gaulle went to Northwest Africa and the new Committee was formed, all our relations were with him and his Committee. I stated to Parliament on June 8 that "The formation of the Committee with its collective responsibility supersedes the situation created by the correspondence between General de Gaulle and myself in 1940. Our dealings, financial and otherwise, will henceforward be with the Committee as a whole." I was glad to do this because I would rather deal with the Committee collectively than de Gaulle alone. I had in fact for many months been working to induce or compel de Gaulle to "put himself in commission". This seems to be largely achieved by the new arrangement. Macmillan tells us repeatedly that the Committee is acquiring a collective authority and that de Gaulle is by no means its master. He tells us further that if the Committee breaks down, as it may do if left utterly without support, de Gaulle will become once again the sole personality in control of everything except the powers exercised by Giraud under the armed force of the United States in Northwest Africa and Dakar. He strongly recommends a measure of recognition. He reports that Eisenhower and Murphy both agree with this. . . .

In his memoirs Churchill published a very interesting paper, which he wrote on July 13 establishing the lines he believed British policy should follow. He revealed himself to be deeply concerned with the way De Gaulle's conduct had alienated the Americans, and he noted that "not only Mr. Hull but the President have become bitterly antagonized thereby." He believed the solution would be to submerge De Gaulle in the Committee and to permit the civilian element an opportunity to demonstrate its value. Although it would be necessary to act with the FCNL as a *de facto* authority, he believed that any efforts to accord *de jure* recognition, or even any use of the word "recognition," would give offense at Washington. Churchill then commented on the elements which were steadfastly the basis of his policy. He hoped for a strong postwar France:

> I have repeatedly stated that it is in the major interests of Great Britain to have a strong France after the war, and I should not hesitate to sustain this view. I am afraid lest the anti-de Gaullism of the Washington Government may harden into a definite anti-France feeling.

He feared equally that if the French Committee were held at arm's length by the Western Allies, it would nevertheless be recognized by the Soviet Union and would orient its policy toward Russia. This Churchill would go to great lengths to prevent, but never far enough to cause a break with the United States; even if the U.S.S.R. did recognize De Gaulle, he said, "we should still wish to measure our course by that of the United States."[1]

Churchill had correctly estimated that opposition would develop to steps calculated to bring a degree of recognition from Washington. Secretary of State Hull regarded the moves of the new Committee with a suspicion which matched that of the President, who, considering the crisis in the State Department over Hull's differences with Sumner Welles, was little inclined at this time to annoy Mr. Hull any more than necessary. Since the matter of recognition involved a political approach, Roosevelt could scarcely by-pass the State Department on grounds that North African policy involved essentially military considerations. Hull

[1] Churchill, *Closing the Ring*, 177–79.

believed firmly that recognition of the French Committee should be postponed until it gave better evidence of co-operation in the war effort. On June 25, in anticipation of Churchill's visit, the Secretary of State drew up a list of prerequisites which he believed the FCNL should meet before recognition could be considered. These conditions were the following:[2]

1) Necessary facilities for the prosecution of the war to be granted as needed to the Allies.

2) Necessary facilities in the economic area for the prosecution of the war to be granted as needed.

3) All previous agreements shall remain in force.

4) All political, economic, and relief decisions shall rest with the Allied Commander-in-Chief until the military situation eases.

5) In the Western hemisphere (except for St.-Pierre and Miquelon) and in all theaters where Americans exercise the Allied command, General Giraud will make political, economic, and military decisions.

6) The French Committee of National Liberation shall not encourage those hostile to the United Nations.

7) The French Committee of National Liberation should promptly inform the Government of the United States of any commitments it may make.

8) The Committee should reaffirm the Treaty of 1924 on American rights; reaffirm the guarantee of independence to Syria and the Lebanon; and transfer power to local governments.

It was clear from the foregoing that Churchill and the Foreign Office would encounter difficulties in bringing the United States to anything approaching the formula which the British would like to apply.

The first British overture to obtain American collaboration in a recognition formula coincided with Giraud's visit to Washington. The British suggested that the FCNL be recognized according to the terms the French themselves had suggested early in June, although in the British text recognition as "the body administering all French interests" was modified to "the body administering those parts of the Empire which recognize their authority." His Majesty's government further-

[2] State Department, DCK File.

more made it explicit that they "count on the Committee to afford such facilities . . . as may be required . . . for the prosecution of the war." The British formula was discussed by Roosevelt, Hull, and Leahy, who agreed that a counterproposition should be drawn up which would make it clear "that the United States was reluctant to permit the Committee to interfere with the Allied war effort"; but they were in no hurry to take action, at least until Giraud's visit was ended.[3] Churchill found himself subjected to a good deal of pressure in England, particularly since pro-French elements felt that Bastille Day, July 14, should be marked by some overt demonstration of support. In a speech delivered on that day, René Massigli, who was in London to promote the possibility of early recognition, emphasized the fact that the FCNL did not pretend to become a provisional government but would turn over its responsibilities to such a government once the liberation of France was accomplished. Foreign Secretary Eden, questioned in Commons, could however report no favorable developments in the matter of recognition and explained Massigli's presence in London as pertaining only to French affairs in England and Syria.[4] Churchill began to become apprehensive that if some action were not soon taken, Russia would proceed on her own—to the detriment of Anglo-American prestige—and recognize the Committee. On July 21 he wrote the President:

I do hope therefore that you will let me know (a) whether you could subscribe to our formula or something like it, or (b) whether you would mind if His Majesty's Government took that step separately themselves. There is no doubt whatever in my mind that the former would be far the better. There are a lot of good men on the Committee—Catroux, Massigli, Monnet, Georges, and of course Giraud, who arrived here yesterday. He will certainly raise all this and bring it to a head.[5]

[3] Hull, *Memoirs*, II, 1225; Leahy, *I Was There*, 169–70. Although Washington demurred at recognition, the opposite was true of officers in the field. On 17 July, Murphy strongly recommended recognition and added that Eisenhower concurred (Murphy to State Dept., 17 July 1943, 851.01/2492). Some elements in the State Department's European division favored much more co-operation with the FCNL, but their voices were not heeded at top policy levels. According to Carroll (*Persuade or Perish*, 107–108), Winant also advocated such co-operation.

[4] *Debates*, Vol. CCCXCI, Col. 171.

[5] Churchill, *Closing the Ring*, 180.

By this time the State Department had produced a formula to express the American point of view. It read as follows:

The Governments of the United States and Great Britain desire again to make clear their purpose of co-operating with all patriotic Frenchmen looking to the liberation of the French people and territories from the oppression of the enemy.

Arrangements have been made with the French Commander-in-Chief in North and West Africa for continuing the co-operation of the French armed forces under his control. The two Governments will co-operate with the French Committee of National Liberation on other matters of mutual interest on the understanding that the Committee was conceived and will function on the principle of collective responsibility of all members of the Committee, for the prosecution of the war and not for the promotion of factional movements.

They desire to make clear, however, the following two conditions:

(1) that the constitution and government to be established in France must be determined by the French people after they shall have been afforded an opportunity freely to express themselves;

(2) that the relationship with the Committee will be subject to the military requirements of the Allied commanders in the prosecution of the war.[6]

This draft was sent to Churchill on July 22, along with a personal letter from the President which amplified his point of view. He emphasized the thought that military requirements were paramount to all civil matters and that more evidence was required concerning unity within the Committee. It was understood, said Roosevelt, that "as to matters of a military character the two Governments will deal directly with the French Commander-in-Chief of the French Forces. French political questions must be left to solution by the people of France . . . ."

The President continued:

I do not think that we should at any time use the word "recognition", because this would be distorted to imply that we recognise the Committee as the Government of France as soon as we land on French soil. Perhaps the word "acceptance" of the Committee's local civil authority in various

[6] State Dept., 851.01/2607a.

154

colonies on a temporary basis comes nearer to expressing my thought. We must however retain the right and continue the present practice of dealing directly with local French officials in the colonies whenever military advantage to the Allied causes so dictates. Martinique is an illustrative example.[7]

Churchill felt that the American formula was "rather chilling," but before the Foreign Office could draft a revision, the overthrow of Mussolini, the prospect of a deal with Badoglio, and the eventuality of an Italian surrender persuaded the Prime Minister that a thorough Anglo-American discussion of strategy would be in order before final commitments to the cross-Channel enterprise. Since Roosevelt was in accord with Churchill's proposal, plans went forward for a conference, with foreign ministers as well as military chiefs, to be held at Quebec in the middle of August. If no agreement could be reached on the recognition formula, it could be discussed then. Churchill also felt that the new command relationships, worked out by the FCNL on July 31, "seem more satisfactory." (Hull considered the new arrangement an effort by De Gaulle to take over Giraud's position as commander in chief.)[8]

The new British formula, received in Washington on August 3, toned down some of the abruptness of the American draft but insisted on recognizing the Committee as qualified to insure the conduct of the French effort in the war. It also invented a more gentle way of expressing the relationship of the Allies to the claim of the FCNL to represent all French interests: ". . . they take note with sympathy of the desire of the Committee to be recognized." In regard to military relationships, the British draft suggested: "The Committee will of course afford whatever military and economic facilities and securities in the territories under its administration as required by the United States and the United Kingdom for the procesution of the war." In his accompanying letter, Churchill placed emphasis on the inclusion of the word *securities*. "This gives us complete power," he wrote, "to override or break with them in the event of bad faith."

Although Roosevelt believed the whole question could be better post-

---

[7] Churchill, *Closing the Ring*, 181–82.
[8] *Ibid.*, 182; Hull, *Memoirs*, II, 1226.

poned until he and Churchill could talk it over together at Quebec, the State Department proceeded with another draft on August 5 to be used as a basis for discussions. This draft retained the first two paragraphs of the British formula (which were kept also in the final versions), but it proposed a new statement to delineate the nature of the military relationship: "In view of the paramount importance of the common war effort, the relationship of the two Governments with the French Committee of National Liberation must continue to be subject to the military requirements of the Allied Commanders." The remainder of the draft corresponded closely with the British suggestions, except that the expression *recognize* was replaced with *will deal*. In a memorandum accompanying the draft Hull avoided diplomatic jargon in urging the President to remember that rearmament of the French had been "predicated on the understanding that General Giraud would have the final word with respect to the French forces which we are arming, and that in military matters General Giraud would be the sole responsible French authority with whom the two Governments would deal with respect to the French armed forces."[9]

With this exchange of ideas having been effected, British and American representatives prepared to meet at Quebec on August 14. By this time the two formulas did not vary greatly, except in the phrasing which related to powers of the Allied military commander vis-à-vis the FCNL and in the use of the word *recognition*. These two small points, however, would reveal to the world that De Gaulle had, in fact, placed a wedge between the two Western powers. The presence of this wedge would not go unnoticed at Moscow.

The Quebec Conference

Although questions of world-wide strategy and discussion of novel possibilities opened up by the Italian surrender negotiations preoccupied the British and American leaders who assembled at Quebec in mid-August, 1943, French problems demanded a certain amount of Roosevelt's and Churchill's attention. Actually, since the major war theaters had moved away from Tunisia, the importance of North Africa and the

[9] Churchill, *Closing the Ring*, 182; Hull, *Memoirs*, II, 1226; State Dept. 851.01/2252a.

imbroglios there had diminished. Later, with plans to attack France becoming more definite, the problem of French participation and of collaboration with the Resistance would have to be faced; but in August the invasion of France was far distant, and Churchill had not yet abandoned the hope of diverting the majority of Anglo-American forces from a cross-Channel attack to a venture in the eastern Mediterranean. He failed to dissuade Roosevelt and the Joint Chiefs, however, and during the Quebec Conference not only were no changes made in regard to "Overlord," the Normandy invasion, but plans were started for "Anvil," a landing in southern France. In spite of the fact that France remained the focal point of Anglo-American strategy, no enthusiasm was expressed concerning the use of French troops in either of these operations.

These questions were debated at length by the Combined Chiefs of Staff, who were unwilling even to consider whether Frenchmen in the mother country should be armed and trained in addition to the North African forces for which commitments had already been made. Although the British members of the CCS repeated their protests that the French program was interfering with other commitments, they reluctantly approved the "August 15 Plan," to the degree that it did not interfere with other scheduled operations. They also agreed that French troops, when equipped and fit for war, would be used for offensive operations in the Mediterranean. At the time, although the Sicilian campaign was closing, it was not clear whether a campaign in Italy would follow or what specific theaters would be open for the employment of French troops. Neither did the Combined Chiefs provide any hint about the rapidity with which the program would be effected; on the other hand, American deliveries were continuing in accordance with the promises made to Giraud in July, and even these amounts provided more material than the facilities in North Africa could adequately receive and store.

It was equally difficult to arrive at specific commitments on the political plane. Cordell Hull arrived at Quebec on August 20, several days after the Conference had started, and settled down with Anthony Eden to draw up a joint statement of recognition of the French Committee. Having been kept on the side lines during much of the deliberations on French policy, Hull was determined to re-enter the arena in a manner that would make his influence—and his anti-Gaullist bias—thoroughly felt. At the end of the meeting Churchill wrote to Attlee about French recognition: "On this last we all had an awful time with Hull, who has at last gone off in a pretty sulky mood, especially with the Foreign Secretary who bore the brunt." This comment is worth comparing with one of Hull's: "After the conference was over the President said he thought he could have made much further headway with Churchill on the matter of recognition if it had not been for Eden."[10] It is probably true that Hull disliked and distrusted De Gaulle more than did the President, and Eden was less inclined to compromise support of the French Committee for the sake of insuring American co-operation than Churchill; and it is not unlikely that Churchill and Roosevelt together could have achieved a joint communiqué where Eden and Hull could not. For five days Hull and his advisers, Atherton and Dunn, worked with Eden and Cadogan to hammer out a compromise formula that would express both the American and British positions. The differences were not great and mostly revolved around the use of the word *recognition*. Hull was so adamant that at the end of their first conversations Eden suggested that it might be necessary for the two governments, in spite of the obvious acknowledgment of a divergence of views, to make separate announcements. Much as he regretted such an acknowledgment, Hull retorted promptly: "If you can stand it, we can too."[11]

Even when the problem was turned over to the chiefs of state, no real progress was made, although at one point the President undertook to draft the statement himself. But in the end, with Roosevelt insisting that he wanted "a sheet anchor out against the machinations of de Gaulle" and that he would not "give de Gaulle a white horse on which he could ride into France and make himself master of a government there," the two governments acknowledged the necessity of issuing separate formulas. Thus, official confirmation was finally accorded to the constant rumors in the press that American policy toward the French diverged seriously from that of the British.

10 Churchill, *Closing the Ring,* 93; Hull, *Memoirs,* II, 1241.

11 *Ibid.,* 1232–33. State Dept. Memos. of Conversations, 20 Aug. 1943, 851.01/8–2048; 21 Aug. 1943, 740.0011 EW/8–2143; 22 Aug. 1943, 740.0011EW/8–2243.

As a matter of fact, the similarities in the two statements, as they were finally issued on August 26, are more striking than the differences, which, except for the use of the word *recognition,* turned on matters of phraseology and innuendo. It will be worth while to examine the American communiqué and to point out its relationship to the British text.[12] The first two paragraphs of the American message, which follows, were almost identical to those of the British:

> The Government of the United States desires again to make clear its purpose of co-operating with all patriotic Frenchmen, looking to the liberation of the French people and French territories from the oppressions of the enemy.
>
> The Government of the United States, accordingly, welcomes the establishment of the French Committee of National Liberation. It is our expectation that the Committee will function on the principle of collective responsibility of all its members for the active prosecution of the war.

The British version differed only in the unimportant substitution, in the last sentence, of: "It is their *understanding* that the Committee *has been conceived* and will function . . . . [Italics mine.]" The American text thus formulated the snide implication that up until then the Committee had not functioned according to the principle of collective responsibility— that, in other words, De Gaulle had run the FCNL in dictatorial fashion. The expression in both texts, "all patriotic Frenchmen," seemed to imply that the door was open for the Allies to co-operate with other French resistance groups directly, not necessarily by means of the Committee of National Liberation.

The American statement continues:

> In view of the paramount importance of the common war effort, the relationship with the French Committee of National Liberation must continue to be subject to the military requirements of the Allied Commanders.

This paragraph served notice that North Africa was still occupied territory and that Eisenhower could still be justified in intervening, as he had done on June 19, in the internal affairs of the Committee. It did

[12] Goodrich and Carroll, eds., *Documents on American Foreign Relations,* VI, 668–70.

not hold out much hope for a rapid revision of the Clark-Darlan Agreement. The British statement included (paragraph 7) a similar military veto, which meant the same thing but was couched in more polite terms: "During the war military needs are paramount and all controls necessary for operational purposes are in consequence reserved to the supreme commander." The statement then continued to point out that this problem had come up before between His Majesty's government and the London Committee and had been resolved by agreements which Great Britain assumed were accepted by the new Committee.

The fourth paragraph of the American statement asserted:

> The Government of the United States takes note with sympathy of the desire of the Committee to be regarded as the body qualified to insure the administration and defense of French interests. The extent to which it may be possible to give effect to this desire must however be reserved for consideration in each case as it arises.

The comparable British paragraph (5) made essentially the same point (although "all French interests" was substituted for "French interests"), and it also reserved the right to consider how the principle should be applied in particular cases. The British government was willing to go further, however, by affirming that they intended "to give effect to this request as far as possible" and that they would consider practical applications "in consultation with the committee."

The next paragraph stated:

> On these understandings the Government of the United States recognizes the French Committee of National Liberation as administering those French overseas territories which acknowledge its authority.

This statement was duplicated in the British text (paragraph 4), which in addition recognized that the FCNL succeeded to the functions which the London Committee maintained in the Levant states. It was thus implied that the Free French declaration of independence to Syria and Lebanon was accepted by the new Committee.

The greatest divergence between the two communiqués existed in the American sixth and seventh paragraphs, which took quite a different form from the British counterparts:

> This statement does not constitute recognition of a government of France or of the French Empire by the Government of the United States.
>
> It does constitute recognition of the French Committee of National Liberation as functioning within specific limitations during the war. Later on the people of France, in a free and untrammeled manner, will proceed in due course to select their own government and their own officials to administer it.

Although the British also expressed a hope that "the French people themselves" would "establish their own government" (paragraph 3), they came out firmly in the controversial passage which the FCNL had itself composed, to the effect that they "recognize the committee as a body qualified to ensure the conduct of the French effort in the war within the framework of inter-Allied co-operation" (second half of paragraph 4). The inclusion of the words *French Empire* in the American statement was interesting, since for the first time it gave public utterance to an Amreican colonial policy that might have the intention of separating France and its empire. The phrasing implied perhaps that the United States would deal separately with Indochina, the only area not under the FCNL, in the future event of its liberation. It should be borne in mind that Hull was ardently pursuing the anti-imperial idea, which had been formulated in the State Department in March and which he would bring up again in Moscow in October. At Quebec he attempted to get Eden's support in this matter, but ran headlong into difficulties with the Foreign Minister, who admitted, in a masterpiece of understatement, that he did not like the American draft very much.[13]

The American statement ended with the following words:

> The Government of the United States welcomes the Committee's expressed determination to continue the common struggle in close co-operation with all the Allies until French soil is freed from its invaders and until victory is complete over all enemy powers.
>
> May the restoration of France come with the utmost speed.

13 Hull, *Memoirs*, II, 1237.

The British sixth paragraph included the same wording, although the ungracious "expressed" is omitted. It would seem that the State Department wished to imply that French actions were not up to French words or that the French had no real intention of fighting. One other small alteration in the British text is interesting. Where the American version spoke of co-operation "until French soil is freed," the British spoke of co-operation "until French and Allied territories are completely liberated." This would mean that Great Britain envisaged France as an ally moving into Belgium, Holland, Czechoslovakia, Denmark, and possibly Indochina, whereas the United States did not commit itself to work with the FCNL except for the liberation of France.

The fine phrasing and subtle innuendos in the British and American formulas contrasted markedly with the brief and unambiguous Russian statement, which had been withheld so that the three powers could issue their declarations simultaneously.

Press reaction to the American government's action at Quebec was generally favorable, but many papers commented on the ambiguous and curt way in which the statement was formulated. The Washington *Post* castigated the announcement as "no recognition at all." "It is couched in such ungenerous and ungracious terms," the editorial continued, "as to constitute an insult to France and an affront to our Allies." The New York *Herald Tribune* was even less flattering:

> A diplomatic vacuum of peculiar idiocy has at last been filled, after a fashion—or rather after several fashions. . . . The grudging air of the American statement is very unfortunate. . . . In particular the question of the procedure to be adopted when the invasion of metropolitan France begins is left unanswered. . . . In comparison with the broad and simple formula which the Soviet Union has adopted . . . the elaborate qualifications deemed necessary by the Western Allies would benefit by a tone of cordiality. This tone, unfortunately, the State Department did not see fit to adopt.

Churchill was understandably concerned lest the brusqueness of the American statement would bring offense at Algiers and aggravate the delicate situation by causing outbursts which could only postpone a more favorable form of recognition by the United States. He advised Macmillan:

> You should tell my friends on the Committee that I am sure the right course for them is to welcome the American declaration in most cordial terms, and not to draw invidious distinctions between any of the forms in which recognition is accorded. On the contrary, the more pleasure they show at the American declaration the more value it will have for them. This is a moment when a friendly attitude towards the United States would be singularly helpful to the interests of France. If, on the other hand, newspaper or radio polemics and reproaches are indulged in, the only effect will be to rouse new flames of resentment in the State Department.[14]

Fortunately the press in Algiers received the recognition notices with restraint and generally took the position that their importance would be judged by whatever gains were achieved as a result of them. The next step, it seemed, would be to find out what benefits would now accrue for France and the French Committee of National Liberation.

The Meaning of Recognition: The Civil Administration Question

After the Quebec Conference was concluded, the question was not so much what sort of formula had been promulgated, but what attitudes the Great Powers would assume in the following months. At first it appeared that the Quebec statements would mean a real and cordial improvement of relations with the French Committee, which would lead to firmer and more favorable understanding with the Allies. There were significant indications that the United States was prepared to accord the Committee more important responsibilities than previously.

One of the first indications of this new attitude related to a broadening of Lend-Lease undertakings. Since a variety of Lend-Lease agreements had been negotiated by the United States with the London Committee and with Giraud, it was necessary to bring all the loose ends together into one central and over-all agreement. This task was carried out at Algiers by Robert Murphy, together with René Massigli,

[14] Churchill, *Closing the Ring*, 182–83.

commissioner of foreign affairs, and Jean Monnet, commissioner of rearmament, relief, and rehabilitation, and was concluded on September 25, when the first formal agreement was signed between the United States and the FCNL. Although no new commitments were involved in the negotiations, the agreement was hailed in the press at Algiers and Washington as an indication of the improved stature of the Committee and as a step toward its acceptance as one of the United Nations.

The negotiations for the Committee's adherence to the United Nations Declaration served to dampen the enthusiasm of those who saw the FCNL on its way to play a significant role among the Allies. Upon his return to Washington from Quebec, Hull took steps to obtain clearance from Britain, Russia, and China for the Committee's adherence. Since his pro-French moves had received favorable publicity, Hull, so long the target of Gaullist denunciation, was hailed by *L'Echo d'Alger* as the benefactor of France: "The warmth and cordiality of the terms employed by the American Secretary of State will touch our country to the bottom of its heart." However, they did not quite touch De Gaulle. Murphy cabled Hull saying that the Committee wanted to know if adherence to the declaration would make it a member of the United Nations. Hull's negative response revealed to those who cared to take notice that the FCNL had a long way to travel; it would be fifteen months before the Committee, by that time the Provisional government of France, would finally adhere to the Declaration.

General Giraud looked to the "recognition" statements as evidence that the United States was prepared to implement rapidly the provisions of the "August 15 Plan." On August 27 he wrote to General Marshall, asking for an assurance that the program would be completed before the end of the year. The fact that Marshall did not reply to Giraud's appeal for almost six weeks provides evidence enough that the United States saw few advantages in giving rearmament the highest of priorities. As the year drew to a close, Giraud was to find himself completely lacking in assurances from Washington concerning rearmament and also partially abandoned by the Americans, on whom he relied for his greatest and surest support.[15]

It was in the area of political arrangements, however, that the FCNL

[15] Vigneras, *Rearming the French,* 97.

found itself principally by-passed and mistrusted, and in this field it
became soon apparent that the Quebec recognition formulas were essentially meaningless. One of the fundamental tasks to which the Committee had set itself was a working out of the arrangements whereby the FCNL would function in France after portions of the country were liberated. This was a problem closely affecting the United States and Great Britain because, once a cross-Channel attack had been successfully launched, some kind of arrangement for civil administration would have to be worked out by the military authorities. Co-operation with a French group was obviously going to be required, and if the Quebec recognition meant anything at all, it seemed perfectly clear that this group would be the French Committee of National Liberation.

Meanwhile the Algiers group was going ahead with its own plans for civil administration. The problem was greatly complicated because it involved so many questions to which the answers were unknown. The Committee did not know, for example, when or where France would be attacked; they did not know if French troops would be able to participate in that attack or whether the Allies would co-operate with French underground troops; they did not know whether secret negotiations were going on with Pétain as they had with Badoglio after the fall of Mussolini; nor—and this was extremely objectionable to them—did they know whether the Allies planned some sort of AMGOT which would violate French sovereignty more arrantly than the Clark-Darlan Agreement. It appeared reasonable and logical to the Committee that
they should draw up a plan which would provide for an orderly control of civil administration behind the Allied lines and then insure that the Allied governments and the Allied commander in chief co-operated with the Committee. The effectiveness of such an arrangement seemed self-evident to the FCNL, but its harmonious application hinged on one decisive point—effective recognition of the Committee by the Allies as the agency through which civil government should be handled.

The Fighting French in London had for many months been studying the administrative problems which the liberation would produce. As early as June, 1942, Professor Pierre Tissier was preparing decrees for administration in France after the landings; later, Henri Queuille, the Radical Socialist senator who had rallied to De Gaulle shortly before the move to Algiers, had been appointed chairman of a *Commission de Débarquement,* the functions of which included the study of problems connected with landings in France and the preparation of proposals to be examined in turn by the FCNL. Three separate but related problems had to be studied: (1) the relationship of the French military command with the Allied supreme commander, (2) the means whereby a new government in France would be established, and (3) the temporary civil administration to be placed in operation immediately after the landings. Since the supreme Allied commander had not yet been designated and since the second problem would have to be debated at length in the proposed Consultative Assembly scheduled to convene in November, the third problem appeared to be the principal one which could be solved at once by direct discussion between the FCNL and the two Western governments.

Early in September, 1943, André Philip, commissioner of the interior, was charged with responsibility of establishing closer relations with the Resistance and formulating plans on civil administration. By September 7, under his auspices, the civil arrangements which had been under discussion for some time were finally drafted.

According to the proposed agreement, the FCNL intended to divide France into three areas: (1) the combat zone; (2) militarized zones, such as harbors, training camps, and supply depots; and (3) a zone of the interior. Determination of the zones would be fixed by common accord between the Allied supreme command, the French commander in chief, and a delegate of the FCNL. Although the Allies were to control the two military zones, all·decisions in the interior zone were to be made by a competent French authority, who would, however, accept Allied proposals concerning measures considered to be essential. The FCNL's principal agent was to be a delegate appointed by the Committee. He was granted broad powers and charged with centralizing and facilitating the relations between the Allied military command and the French authorities. The French proposal envisaged important liaison functions to be developed by means of liaison officers or agents who would be detailed to different Allied units for the purpose of maintaining communication between these units and the French authorities.

Included with the draft proposal were annexes which attempted

166

to improve on some of the more debatable aspects of the Clark-Darlan Agreement. Annex A dealt in detail with requisitioning, which was to be permitted but was to require (except in the combat zone) a visa from French authorities. Annex B established regulations for passive defense and fire fighting, and Annex C was concerned with police measures and military courts. Except for the combat zone, general police measures were to pertain to the French authorities, although the Allied Command would retain rights over its own forces and would try military personnel in its own courts. The Allied command would be able to make recommendations on police measures via the the Liaison Mission. Annex D, on reparations for damages, asserted that compensation should be made in terms of French law or before a commission on reparations.[16]

Several provisions in this plan were certain to run counter to the thinking of Roosevelt and many officials in Washington. First of all, it gave all authority in liberated areas to the FCNL's delegate rather than to the French commander in chief. If, as was likely, the appointment of a Gaullist were made, it would give De Gaulle rather than Giraud almost dictatorial powers in liberated areas. Secondly, military liaison with the Allied supreme commander would become the responsibility of the delegate appointed by the FCNL rather than of an officer appointed by Giraud. Third, it appeared that the delegate, rather than the French commander in chief or the Allied commander, would give orders to the French underground. Since the resistance was by this time largely Gaullist it was unthinkable to De Gaulle and his associates that Giraud should in any way exercise control over clandestine forces. Finally, the draft gave to the FCNL's delegate complete control over rear-zone civil administration, exclusive of any control by the Allied commander. In other words, liaison and co-operation with the Allied commander was expected to develop, but authority would derive not from him but from the FCNL.

The French scheme was discussed with Robert Murphy and Harold Macmillan early in September and sent to London and Washington

---

[16] French "Projet d'Accord" of 7 Sept. 1943, transmitted to State Dept. by Murphy in dispatch No. 292 of 12 Sept. 1943 (851.01 AMG/5). Letter of transmission but not text in De Gaulle, *Mémoires*, II, 524.

to serve as a basis for discussion. André Philip, who went to London in October, and Henri Hoppenot, who became the FCNL's representative in the United States at the end of September, discussed the draft proposal with British and American authorities. But the note was never answered. Month after month passed, and by March, 1944, with the Normandy landings less than three months distant, the FCNL had still received no official communication in response to its proposal and no advice pertaining to any alternate arrangements which the Allies themselves planned to introduce. The French then went ahead with their own plans, but when the first waves of Allied troops landed on French soil on D-Day, no reply had yet been received in Algiers.

If the Allied governments ignored the French proposals, it was not because they deprecated the importance of means for handling civil administration problems. In London, the Anglo-American staff, COSSAC, which was making preliminary plans for the Normandy attack, appreciated the necessity of such a scheme, and its deputy chief, General R. W. Barker, discussed the problem with Hull in August, 1943. The War Department was also interested in the question, and Secretary Stimson hoped to avoid such an artificial and improvised solution as the Clark-Darlan Agreement by concentrating civil authority as much as possible in the hands of the military commander. Stimson's aide, John J. McCloy, devoted a great deal of his attention to civil affairs, but he ultimately reached the conclusion that in France it would be extremely difficult—if not dangerous—to by-pass the French Committee. Both State Department and War Department planners worked on various schemes, and on October 5, Roosevelt approved a draft brought to him by Hull, who planned to use it as a basis for discussions at Moscow. It is interesting to compare this with the French project:

> [The United States and Great Britain] agree that the ultimate aim of the Allies shall be the free and untrammeled choice by the French people of the form of government under which they wish to live. Until that stage is reached, the largest measure of personal and political liberty compatible with military security shall be restored to the French; there shall be freedom of speech, of opinion, of the press and of correspondence; and the French flag shall be used on public buildings.

In all liberated areas the Supreme Allied Command will have supreme authority so long and so far as military necessity requires. The civil administration under the Supreme Allied Commander shall be conducted by French citizens as far as possible. The Director of Civil Affairs will be a French officer appointed by the Supreme Allied Commander from the French contingent or French Liaison Mission with the military operations in France.

Military control of civil affairs will be as short as practicable. If circumstances permit, the transfer of civil responsibility to French hands will be progressive.

The Supreme Allied Commander, in order to achieve the eventual aim of full freedom of choice by the French people of the form of government they wish, will do his best to hold the scales even between all French political groups sympathetic to the Allied cause. One of his first tasks will be to establish relations with resistance groups within France and to secure their co-operation in civil matters. He will have no dealings with the Vichy regime except to liquidate it. He will not employ anyone who has collaborated with the enemy.[17]

An arresting quality of this document is the way in which it completely avoids reference to the FCNL. It is also extremely ambiguous in regard to the manner in which powers were to be transferred to a French civil authority. All authority in France was given to the Allied commander, under whom French citizens would function as administrative officials; but the document did not say *which* French citizens, Vichyites or Resistance. The Allied commander would appoint a director of civil affairs (not accept a nominee from the FCNL), who, however, would not be a civilian but an army officer; and the instrument was not specific about whether this officer would be attached to the staff of the French commander in chief or the commissioner of defense of the FCNL. It would even appear that French elections would be conducted under the auspices of the Allied commander, for since no French civilian group was thought of as the temporary repository of

[17] Adapted from Hull, *Memoirs,* II, 1244. Cf. Forrest C. Pogue, *Supreme Command,* 142. A text published by De Gaulle (*Mémoires,* II, 591–92), dated Sept., 1943, is apparently an earlier draft of this document. It is noteworthy that this earlier draft, which grants considerable powers to the Allied commander in chief, is the one that had become available to the FCNL. De Gaulle does not state how the FCNL obtained the document.

powers which would permit the conduct of an election, no authority remained but that of the Allied military chief. Such an arrangement, which might possibly be acceptable for a former enemy or backward nation, would lead to universal opposition among Frenchmen who feared the insult of an AMGOT, and it would find vehement denunciation among members of the Resistance, whose pride and independence provided the very backbone of their movement.

In the course of the Moscow Conference, on October 26, Secretary Hull submitted, on behalf of the American and British governments, the draft which the president had approved; but it was decided to refer the proposal to the new European Advisory Commission, which, at Eden's suggestion, was to be established in London to deal with problems related to the occupation of liberated areas. The document, once filed in the dossiers of the EAC, never again saw the light of day.

The Meaning of Recognition: The Italian Question

The fall of Mussolini, the accession of Badoglio to power, and the Allied deal with Badoglio, so reminiscent of the one made with Darlan, brought in their wake the resentment of the French Committee, which felt itself to be tactlessly shunned and by-passed in an area of vital interest to France. On July 27, two days after Mussolini's sudden collapse, De Gaulle emphasized his interest in the Italian question by pointing out in a radio address that no general settlement concerning the Italian peninsula could be valid or durable without France. A few days later the FCNL sent a formal note to the United States, asserting that French interests included: (1) the use of Italian bases, (2) the liberation of French nationals held by Italy, (3) the return of French war matériel, and (4) the return of French property confiscated by Italy in 1940.[18]

Fearing a rebuff on the Italian question from the Western Allies, De Gaulle did not lose sight of the friendliness which had long been extended toward Fighting France from the direction of Moscow. Early in August, while making a tour of Morocco, he put out a very modest feeler during a press conference he held at Rabat. "At the present time,"

[18] FCNL to U.S. and U.K. governments, 2 Aug. 1943 (De Gaulle, *Mémoires*, II, 519–20).

he told the correspondents, "there does not exist any opposition between the French and the Russian peoples. I feel that after this war there will be a general and genuine *rapprochement* among the peoples, among the masses, and this will be a great advantage to the world." Although there was no part of De Gaulle's makeup that inclined him toward Communism, the General nevertheless appreciated keenly the importance of Russia as an element which France's foreign policy could not neglect. De Gaulle never forgot the traditional alignment of France with Russia that went back to the Dual Alliance of 1894 or the weakness of France when she faced Germany in 1940, surrounded by the hostile Axis and lacking allies to the East; his military perception readily grasped the geographical axiom that France, placed between the massive Western and Eastern powers, might become a satellite of one or the other unless she turned her position to advantage by effecting a skillful balance between East and West.

Making gestures toward the Soviet Union was not a novel experience for De Gaulle, who had long realized that the Kremlin saw advantages in cultivating the men of Carlton Gardens. But just as Churchill could not support the French Committee of Liberation too energetically without antagonizing a sensitive Washington, so De Gaulle could not lean too openly toward Moscow without endangering his relations with England, on whom, in spite of innumerable squabbles and irritations, he was, after all, dependent. Once in Algiers, however, and no longer a "prisoner of the English," De Gaulle achieved more freedom to maneuver the French Committee into directions he believed to be in the interests of France. A move in the direction of Russia could not be made—and De Gaulle was painfully aware of the fact—without encouraging the Communists, whose bustling activity in Algiers had already revealed their intentions of resuming the factional politics which Fighting France had so far largely escaped. If De Gaulle became increasingly friendly with the Soviet Union in the autumn of 1943, it was because he could not free himself of the impression that Britain and the United States were pursuing a policy deliberately aimed at diminishing the influence and prestige of the FCNL.

The Soviet Union had nothing at all to lose from a *rapprochement* with the FCNL. Since the Communist-dominated *Front National* and its military arm, the *Franc-Tireur et Partisan,* ostensibly accepted the guidance of De Gaulle and the BCRA, Russia would be well advised to support the FCNL as long as it promised an important place to the French Communist underground. Since there was no question of infiltrating the Vichy government, Communists aimed at achieving influence in the interior National Resistance Council and in the exterior French Committee of National Liberation, from either of which a future provisional government might emerge. It was easy for Moscow to believe that a grateful De Gaulle might become sympathetic to the idea of bringing Communists into the FCNL and might even go so far as to invite Maurice Thorez, then exiled in Russia, to North Africa or to France.

The Anglo-American negotiations with Badoglio for an Italian armistice, which were proceeding between August 19 and August 27 (while Churchill and Roosevelt deliberated at Quebec), revealed to the Russians and the French that they stood on common ground. While Stalin had an advantage over the French in that he had been informed of the prospective arrangement, he, like De Gaulle, realized that a major development in the war was being effected without Russian or French participation. The FCNL had already expressed the bases for their interest in the Italian settlement; and Stalin must have immediately grasped the fact that with Italy in Allied hands, Churchill would push for a Mediterranean operation, which he could not view but with a certain uneasiness. Both the French and Russians could make a common ideological cause in denouncing the materialistic and callous arrangement made with the Fascist butcher of Ethiopia, but fundamentally they were more irritated at the danger of being by-passed while a significant Mediterranean operation was in the process of development.

These considerations caused Stalin to propose that an inter-Allied commission be established in the Mediterranean to deal with questions such as the Italian peace feelers. When the armistice was announced on September 8, Russian insistence that such an agency be created became more pronounced; and a tentative agreement was reached between Roosevelt and Churchill, who had come to Washington after the Quebec Conference, that a political council of the sort requested by the Russians should be established.

When news of the Italian armistice reached Algiers, De Gaulle was outraged that the affair had been carried off without his having been notified. His indignation was especially marked because one week previously he had received a note from the Allied governments, which not only requested FCNL authorization for Eisenhower to carry on negotiations but implied that a French representative would be invited to sign the capitulation. Then suddenly, without further reports from the Allies, came the Italian surrender announcement; and when Massigli protested that the FCNL had been kept in the dark, Murphy and Macmillan told him that, to the best of their knowledge, Giraud had been kept informed. In an explosive session of the Committee on September 9, General Giraud denied that he had received any information and insisted that the text of the surrender document was unknown to him. Murphy and Macmillan apologized next day for being misinformed about the extent of Giraud's knowledge. While the evidence is incomplete in regard to the actual intelligence received by Giraud's staff, the entire handling of the negotiations was not conducive to an improvement of De Gaulle's feelings of good will toward the Western Allies.[19]

Whether because of De Gaulle's continuous protests or because of Russian urging, arrangements were concluded in September among the three major allies that on the new Mediterranean political commission there would be a seat for a representative from the French Committee. The sympathy with which Russia viewed De Gaulle was revealed on September 19 when the Soviet publication *War and the Working Class* carried an article advocating a permanent Anglo–Soviet–American committee to co-ordinate military and political actions with a representative of the FCNL. Two days later came the official announcement that the new commission would shortly be established. Russia demonstrated the importance with which she viewed the commission by appointing Andrei Vishinsky as her representative. Great Britain followed shortly by naming Harold Macmillan. It was expected that Robert Murphy would represent the United States, but no announcement was forthcoming and no official invitation was yet sent to the FCNL asking

[19] De Gaulle, *Mémoires*, II, 138–40, 524–29, 590–91. According to the French correspondent Pierre Sandahl, Georges Picot, director of Giraud's political cabinet, told a Gaullist that Giraud's staff had been kept informed about the Italian developments (*De Gaulle sans képi*, 53).

it to designate a member. It required no great gift of clairvoyance to surmise that Washington was unenthusiastic about the proposed commission and might delay its establishment until Hull would have an opportunity to discuss the matter with Eden and Molotov at Moscow late in October. On October 5, Hull did, in fact, discuss the new commission with the President, who told him that French representation "should be restricted to matters other than the military occupation of Italy and to matters on which Britain, Russia and the United States decided that France had a direct interest. The French were not to function as full members."[20]

From what he could see of events during September, De Gaulle could only reach the conclusion that French interests had been aided by Russia and impeded by the United States. On the occasion of a speech delivered at Ajaccio on October 8, after the conquest of Corsica, De Gaulle publicly announced that he was not indifferent to Russian assistance. He apostrophized the Mediterranean, the sea from which French civilization had come: ". . . this sea which binds us to the valiant Balkan people, this sea which is one of the roads toward our natural ally, dear and powerful Russia." This speech corresponded with the arrival at Algiers of Russian Ambassador Bogomolov, who had been accredited to the Gaullist Committee in London and who had been ordered by his government to fulfill a similar function with the FCNL. It had been expected that Bogomolov would be in Algiers long before October 9, the date he arrived, but his passage from London to Algiers had been held up by Allied headquarters since early July. When the Russians had urged recognition of the FCNL in June, Moscow had been urged to postpone action until the Giraud–De Gaulle crisis was resolved. Feeling that they had been poorly informed on North African matters, the Soviet government on June 26 had asked that Bogomolov be permitted to visit Algiers. This suggestion seemed not unreasonable to both British and Americans, but they hesitated to permit one more element, whose effect could not be anticipated, to be introduced into an already troublesome situation. Although active combat had by this time left the North African theater, the Foreign Office and the State Department preferred to treat the proposal as a matter of military secur-

[20] Hull, *Memoirs*, II, 1243–44.

174

ity, and Bogomolov was forced to cool his heels in London for three months.

Bogomolov's presence in Algiers, together with his large staff (of thirty members), permitted the Soviet Union to implement its policies in regard to the French Committee with increased facility. Should Vishinsky soon arrive to sit in the proposed Mediterranean commission, a powerful Soviet influence could be brought to bear on the FCNL, and the Communists in North Africa would receive incalculable assistance.

The fate of the Mediterranean politico-military committee was finally settled at the Moscow Conference of Foreign Ministers during the final two weeks of October. Cordell Hull, in spite of his age, undertook the long sea and air journey to Russia and benefited by an opportunity to pause at Algiers long enough on October 15 to enter into discussions with De Gaulle, Massigli, Eisenhower, and Murphy. It must have been a singular experience for Hull to meet finally the Frenchman whose vigorous defense of French interests had for so long irritated him. Yet De Gaulle's personal demeanor, if not overflowing with hail-fellow mannerisms, can be warm and cordial upon occasion. Hull found him "more friendly than I thought would be the case," but their conversation, while long and "reasonably frank," did not reach any conclusions. If the subject of French participation on the projected Mediterranean commission was raised, Hull could not commit himself until he had discussed the question with Molotov and Eden. There was no question, however, but that the commission would be given consideration at Moscow and that, if created, Murphy would sit on it as the American representative. Murphy's replacement had in fact already been named. Edwin C. Wilson, a refined career diplomat, had been mentioned as the choice for the new American representative, with rank of ambassador, to be accredited to the FCNL; but his appointment could not be confirmed until the status of the commission was clarified.

At Moscow the plan for a Mediterranean commission was modified by the formation of a body to be known as the Italian Advisory Commission. The title implied that the Commission would deal only with Italian matters and not with broad problems affecting general Mediterranean strategy. The meaning of the term *advisory* soon became clear, when the Anglo-American command announced the formation of an

Allied Control Commission for Italy, into which, as soon became evident, the real powers for determining Italian policy had been placed. Thus, although the appearance of Anglo-American acquiescence to Soviet desires had been maintained, Russia and the FCNL were excluded from any meaningful or effective participation in Mediterranean or even Italian affairs. The Russians obtained one small advantage in their ability to send Vishinsky and his large corps of observers to Algiers, where Russian influence began to be felt in ever-increasing degree. The FCNL obtained almost nothing at all, except the honor of having representation for the first time on an Allied commission. The appointment of René Massigli to the Italian Advisory Commission marked a real recognition, which the uselessness of the Commission only partly nullified.

If the graceful tactic of shunting the French and Russians away from meaningful observation of Italy served one purpose of British and American policy, it could not help but have the untoward consequence of pushing France and Russia closer together and of demonstrating that with a common grievance they could benefit by making common cause. What Winston Churchill had feared seemed to be coming to pass, but in the face of such dangers as the alienation of the United States or Communist domination of Italy, the Prime Minister was incapable of formulating a policy simultaneously attractive to himself, Roosevelt, De Gaulle, and Stalin. De Gaulle faced an equal difficulty in delineating either a policy that would bring him Russian and Resistance support without Communist dominance in the FCNL or one that would permit him to continue to receive United States military assistance without compromising his ideal of French independence. The results of the Moscow Conference were not calculated to persuade De Gaulle that his future must be inextricably entwined with that of the United States; but whether he must necessarily move farther to the left was a question that still remained unanswered.

▶ 5. Shifting Attitudes Toward the Committee

Aspects of American and Allied Policy

B Y THE summer of 1943 some of the issues faced by the Allies had clarified themselves by a natural process of evolution. As long as an active campaign continued in North Africa, it was only reasonable that military questions should have received maximum attention. No responsible Allied official was willing to give the French political situation priority over the necessity of ejecting Rommel from Tunisia. While the fighting continued, one Allied aim remained paramount: to establish and maintain, with a minimum of effort, an administration in North Africa that would permit maximum exploitation of military objectives. A policy of "temporary expedients" had accordingly been justified and had produced a longer perpetuation of the Darlan—and later the Giraud —regime than could reasonably be defended. To be sure, the policy had succeeded within its limited objectives. Darlan and Giraud had co-operated, and the understaffed French administration, whatever its political predilections, had continued to keep the ports, railroads, telephones, telegraphs, and police forces operating in basically loyal collaboration with the Allied forces. The Clark-Darlan Argeement provided essentially what the Anglo-American command required, and Allied headquarters was not interested in radical changes.

But temporary expedients, by nature, tend to restrain or disregard disquieting elements which sooner or later must be taken into account. A continued repression of the basic drives inherent to the *mystique* of Gaullism could result only in promoting a psychic unbalance, which one day, if left untreated, would produce political aberrations too complex for Allied control. The better part of wisdom called for an impartial diagnosis of the French illness, with a determination to locate an honest and reasonable cure before the symptoms became too exaggerated.

The Allies had to face certain realities. They had to recognize that the dissident French were in a position to administer not only Morocco, Algeria, and Tunisia but essentially the entire French Empire, except Indochina. Whether or not the millions of inhabitants in these areas could make a contribution to the war effort consistent with their numbers, the extent of these territories provided a tangible political reality that could not be overlooked. It was unreasonable, considering the French will to re-enter the war, for the Allies to insist on political division. By all laws of logic, and certainly by the traditions of French administrative structure, the French Empire should have been unified administratively behind a central French authority.

This authority had been established in the French Committee of National Liberation, but in spite of the formulas produced at Quebec, the new Committee had never obtained unqualified Anglo-American acceptance, and lack of recognition magnified the manifold problems facing both the French and the Allies. For both parties the problem now centered on two points: the French Army and French sovereignty. While rearmament had been a minor factor up until the summer of 1943, both French and Allies were looking toward the time when six or eight newly equipped French divisions would be trained and ready for combat. Presumably these divisions would fight in Italy and France; they would bring prestige and power to their commander; and, most important, they might be decisive in determining the outcome of a power contest in France after liberation. But how effective these new French troops would be depended on a series of unanswered questions: how soon would they be equipped; how efficient would they be; once equipped and trained, would they be available in time to participate in France's reconquest? Equally important in both French and Allied thinking was the question of control: would General Giraud as commander in chief exercise an effective military command once French troops were committed? Or would General de Gaulle and the FCNL's commissioner of defense determine military policies? The resolution of these questions was crucial, for if General Giraud controlled the army and the army's secret-service contacts with France, there was a possibility that the Gaullist networks and underground armies might lose so much power and influence that they would be unable to play a determining role in the post-liberation struggle for power. Such a split within French ranks might encourage the Communist FTP to break completely from Gaullist resistance groups, with the dismaying possibility of a three-cornered civil conflict during a period when all military and political energies would be needed against Germany.

If these questions perturbed the French, they produced similar apprehension in Washington. The White House seemed to be convinced that if De Gaulle and the Committee achieved control of the armies, there would be more chance of internecine conflict than if Giraud retained his command. Thus, while all parties agreed on the objective of producing a loyal, stable, disciplined France behind the combat zones, there were diametrically opposed concepts of how this might be achieved. De Gaulle was convinced that Giraudist influence could bring about a continuation of Pétainism and consequent wide civil disturbance; Roosevelt believed the same about the influence of Gaullism; but all appreciated the fact that the key to the matter resided in effective control of the embryonic French Army.

Equally controversial, and even more crucial, was the question of French sovereignty. With administrative control of the French Empire in its hands, with concrete evidence of support from the National Resistance Council in France, with qualified recognition from the major Allies, the French Committee of National Liberation concluded that it must legally take the title—which it already possessed *de facto*—of French Provisional government. Only by assuming that it would have governmental authority when France was liberated could the Commitee plan for its future administrative responsibilities. If it could not plan for this eventuality, it had no reason for existence. The Committee frequently reminded itself and the Allied governments that it already administered territories and populations greater than those of any government-in-exile.

But while the Allies, and particularly the United States (through its rearmament program), had been partially responsible for the French Committee's growing prestige, they appeared now to regard their creation with a certain apprehension. Had they been consistent, Britain and America would have regulated all matters relating to the French only through the FCNL; and with recognition of this sort, most administrative and military questions could have been resolved probably with a minimum of negotiation and friction. But London and Washington, largely because of the latter's reluctance, could not easily agree on ways to co-operate with the Committee in Algiers. The suspicions and fears which had long smoldered in the White House were not easily extinguished. The President continued to believe that De Gaulle would become a dictator, that he was Fascist (but had dealings with Communists), that he was impossible to work with, that he was not to be trusted, and that he would provoke civil war; all the old arguments had been woven into a pattern of anti-Gaullism that President Roosevelt could not be persuaded to discard.

Gaullist Differences with Giraud

As the French problem shifted during the final quarter of 1943 from preoccupation with behind-the-lines security for military operations to matters of rearmament and sovereignty, events moved rapidly. De Gaulle was not permitted the luxury of an inaction which would avoid friction with the great powers; even if he had wanted to pursue a policy of "wait and see," he could not escape the pressures—Giraudist, Communist, military, Resistance, colonial, economic, and even Gaullist—which were placed upon him. It was ironic that the policies followed by De Gaulle, logical as they may have been from his own point of view, served consistently to deepen the cleft between him and the Allies. In seeking to take power from General Giraud he antagonized the White House; yet in permitting Giraud to retain military control he alienated those officers in Allied headquarters who considered Giraud inefficient and unrealistically stubborn. In attempting to preserve the French Empire he ran counter not only to Hull's anti-colonial policy but to Churchill's ambitions to extend British hegemony in the Middle East.

Of all De Gaulle's problems, the one most likely to jeopardize his position in Washington related to his colleague on the Committee of Liberation, President Roosevelt's "willing bridegroom," General Giraud. It became increasingly apparent, through the summer and fall of 1943, that in spite of the support which Washington was inclined to tender its champion, Giraud must be eliminated from the main stream of military and political activity.

There seemed to be no possible manner in which De Gaulle could improve his position vis-à-vis General Giraud. The fundamental attitudes, methods of work, and ambitions of the two men served to hinder their co-operation. And Giraud, helping to pave the way for his own downfall, entangled himself with curious unconcern in situations that antagonized not only the FCNL and the general public but the Allies as well.

Strained thoughout the summer, the situation became acute in early September. In that month the FCNL initiated a program leading to a purge of individuals associated with Marshal Pétain's Vichy regime. All the members of the Committee agreed on a roster of names, headed by Pétain himself, against whom purge proceedings were to be started as soon as feasible. With his reluctant signing of the proscription list, Giraud symbolically condemned himself. It meant that he had abandoned his associates—Peyrouton, Bergeret, Boisson, and hundreds of lesser officers—to the pitiless vengeance of the underground; it meant that he had relinquished Pierre Pucheu, the Vichy minister whom Giraud had permitted to come to North Africa, to the Gaullists; it meant that he would lose authority and prestige from the only group, the French Army, to which he could look for support; and it meant that he would leave himself, and the FCNL, open to the criticism of the Allied governments, who had obliged themselves to the support of Boisson and Noguès. No one appreciated the danger of the Committee's decisions more than De Gaulle, who on August 7 had said that "nothing would be more deplorable for the future of France than to allow the purge to degenerate into an affair of personal bickering and local squabbling." Nevertheless, while advising moderation, he supported the Committee's actions and in the Pucheu affair engaged in ill-tempered and tempestuous altercations with General Giraud.

The differences between Giraud and De Gaulle had become so outrageous early in September that Robert Murphy was constrained to report to the State Department that "the controversy has reached a point where it is threatening the prosecution of the war."[1] On September 7,

[1] Vigneras, *Rearming the French,* 98.

President Roosevelt was so disturbed by advice from Algiers that he jotted down a note to accompany a report he planned to forward to Churchill:

> Please read and speak to me about this. I have very distinct feelings that we should not send further equipment or munitions to the French Army in North Africa if our prima donna is to seize control of it from the old gentleman.[2]

Although the note was not sent, it furnishes a suggestion of Roosevelt's frame of mind as De Gaulle moved inexorably in a direction which was aimed at relieving Giraud of his military authority.

More important in widening the breach between the Gaullists and Giraud was the French campaign in Corsica. With the surrender of Italy on September 8 the possibility of liberating Corsica became a reality. For months the Corsican underground had been storing arms, creating networks, and developing strategy for the day when an uprising might wipe out the German and Italian garrisons on the island. It was significant, however, that the Gaullist BCRA had failed to achieve control of the Corsican underground, which was controlled by the Communist-dominated *Front National* and which maintained contacts not with London but with Giraud's secret service at Algiers. Military plans for co-operation with the *Front National* had been drawn up in the utmost secrecy and were known only by Giraud, his staff, and the British and American secret services with whom he was collaborating; neither General de Gaulle nor the FCNL had been fully informed.

When word reached Corsica that the Italians had surrendered, a spontaneous popular rising took place in Ajaccio, whose prefect turned the administration over to the *Front National*. Giraud turned to Allied headquarters for transportation and air support, but learned that Eisenhower was too heavily committed by the landings in Italy to be able to spare many men or much matériel for the Corsican enterprise. Although the shortage of transportation facilities was certain to reduce the speed with which troops and equipment could be brought into action, Giraud ordered General Henri Martin to proceed with the operation and then

[2] E. Roosevelt, ed., *F.D.R.: His Personal Letters*, II, 1453.

notified De Gaulle of the decision he had taken. De Gaulle approved, and next day, September 10, the members of the FCNL were notified of the planned operation.[3]

Arguments were heated. The air had not yet been cleared since the stormy sessions of the previous week over civil administration and purge, the Committee was angry over its elimination from the Italian surrender negotiations, and now it found itself committed to an operation with serious political implications on which it had not been consulted. The FCNL could not forget that the United States had made, in its recognition formula of August 26, the caustic observation that it was their "expectation that the Committee will function on the principle of collective responsibility," an implication that De Gaulle would carry out some wild, unorthodox, and independent maneuver; and yet it now turned out that it was the American champion, Giraud, who, with American consent, flagrantly violated the principle of collective responsibility. The Committee as a whole felt that Giraud had overstepped his authority as commander in chief in planning an operation which involved an over-all deployment of forces and in collaborating with the *Front National*, a step which involved political as well as military decisions.

For over a week, while General Martin and elements of the Fourth Moroccan Mountain Division landed in Corsica, the FCNL debated the operation's chances of success, the responsibilities of the commander in chief, and the awkward dyarchy under which the Committee operated. By September 18, De Gaulle had reached a point where he could no longer tolerate the Committee's impotence. He suggested that the Committee elect a single chairman and separate the powers of the commander in chief from the power of the government.

On the following day, September 19, tension in the FCNL was so acute and arguments so fruitless that De Gaulle walked out and Giraud postponed further deliberation by flying to Corsica, where for three days he took over personal direction of the campaign. On his return to Algiers events drew rapidly to a climax. The commissioners were almost unanimous in their desire to see the FCNL reorganized under a single chairman and with a civilian commissioner of defense. Giraud ultimately

[3] De Gaulle, *Mémoires*, II, 141–45.

183

bowed to the solid opposition against him by acquiescing to a new decree designed to increase the FCNL's efficiency.[4]

The decree, promulgated on October 2 but not immediately placed in effect, called for the election of a single chairman. Since all ordinances and decrees had to be countersigned by the chairman, this arrangement would give De Gaulle (in the likely event that he was elected to the chairmanship) a veto power that would no longer be shared by Giraud.

Ironically, two days after the promulgation of the new decree, as the last of the German forces withdrew, the French seaport Bastia fell into French hands. Giraud had achieved the first French victory against Germany in World War II during a rapid-fire campaign accomplished entirely by French means. Instead of the "blood bath" his detractors had envisaged, Giraud had carried off the operation in less than a month and with negligible losses; he had demonstrated the efficiency of his secret services and the value of vigorous aggressive action in the face of apparent odds. Even his "deal" with the Communist Giovanni had not permitted the *Front National* to dominate the island, and the new prefect, Charles Luizet, appointed by the FCNL, was soon able to install regularly appointed prefects in place of the Resistance committees and to bring the civil administration under the supervision of Algiers. Yet at the very moment he achieved his greatest victory in World War II, General Giraud was stripped of his independence of military action and his effective power in the FCNL; without the veto power inherent in the office of chairman, he could be eliminated entirely by De Gaulle if it should be deemed necessary.

American Dissatisfaction with Giraud

If it was Giraud's vigorous activity that antagonized the Gaullists, it was, ironically, his indifference that disturbed Allied headquarters. In January, General Giraud had complained that American matériel had been made available to him in such small quantities that his troops were useless; by August such a mass of equipment had arrived that

[4] Catroux, *Dans la bataille de Méditerranée*, 379. De Gaulle does not mention this crisis of Sept. 18–19 in his memoirs.

Giraud's men were hard pressed to cope with what they received. It appeared that the French had overestimated their capabilities. The basic difficulty derived from the fact that Giraud's headquarters and Allied headquarters approached the rearmament program from an entirely different set of assumptions. The Americans assumed that their responsibility was fulfilled in providing the equipment and transporting it to North Africa; once unloaded, it should have been assembled, stored, distributed, and maintained by the French themselves. No large numbers of additional American forces had been assigned to carry out these functions on behalf of the French, and Eisenhower, especially after the Italian campaign began in September, could ill afford to spare many specialists from his quartermaster services to assist the French. Giraud thought of the rearmament program quite differently. He was driven by a passion to commit as many French troops as possible to combat, and he believed from his conversations with Marshall and Roosevelt that their views coincided with his.

To establish service units—supply, transportation, communication, repair, and medical—required the assignment of skilled, educated men (in other words, the white Frenchmen, of whom there was a limited supply, estimated at less than 150,000) rather than native North Africans. Thousands of Frenchmen in the North African army were young patriots who, after agonizing exertions, had labored across the Pyrenees, descended through Spain, and finally reported in North Africa to volunteer their services against the Nazis. They had not risked their lives to be given a clerk's job or to become a truck driver, and Giraud argued that to give them such assignments would demoralize his army.

Under these conditions, the French handling of the thousands of tons of trucks, tanks, guns, and ammunition which were now being unloaded every week at Casablanca and Oran was far from adequate. Although the assembling of vehicles was proceeding satisfactorily, distribution and storage provided examples of deplorable incompetence and inefficiency. Incapable of finding warehouses (many of which had been requisitioned by the Allies under the Clark-Darlan Agreement), the French were forced to line up hundreds and thousands of vehicles in open fields, where they either rusted or were pilfered. An inadequate stock of paper, cards, and stationery meant that no satisfactory paper records of invoices and transfers were maintained, with the result that few officials knew what had been ordered and what received. Inability to read English name plates, instruction books, and maintenance manuals resulted in improper installations and abuse of equipment. Matériel was distributed without requisitions and records, and in consequence some divisions received what they were not entitled to and others never were able to obtain what they needed. It is true that the fault did not lie entirely with the French. The American Army's accounting system was unduly cumbersome, and American tables of organization in many ways were inapplicable to French troops. The officers of a regiment of Goumiers could not see why, for example, when North African native soldiers habitually washed their own clothes, a laundry unit had to be accounted for and maintained. The lack of system became particularly evident in the handling of small items, such as tools, electronic equipment, and spare parts. Unless this type of matériel is stored in some orderly fashion with numbered receptacles or bins, it is impossible to find what is needed, deliver it promptly, or order its replacement; and yet storage facilities continued to be rudimentary, as thousands of crates came in and were piled here and there in helter-skelter fashion. Even by September, nine months after President Roosevelt had committed the United States to the program, no central French supply service had been established.

The problem of maintenance and bases provided similar difficulties. To American thinking, numerous repair centers should have been established and manned with personnel qualified to care for the complex machinery which was in so many ways unfamiliar to French soldiers. Yet by September only eleven out of thirty-one planned centers had been placed in commission.

More difficulties developed in September during discussions on the employment of French divisions in Italy. Giraud had consistently thought of his troops as seeing action primarily on French soil, where the need of self-sufficiency for French troops would be less than that of foreign forces. He thought in terms of permanent military installations already available in France or else assumed that the French would be able to use American bases. This concept he found to be diametrically opposed to the view current at Eisenhower's headquarters, which insisted that French troops form an expeditionary force which would be organized, equipped, and supplied exactly like American troops, with its own base of operations and separate supply and maintenance units. To provide such units would require a tremendous drain of Europeans from combat divisions and an inevitable reduction of the eleven-division program. For Giraud the problem was complicated by the fact that General de Gaulle began to insist that the Brosset (formerly Koenig) Free French division be among those scheduled to fight in Italy. It should be remembered that this division used British equipment, and Eisenhower's headquarters foresaw that great logistic difficulties would follow an attempt to incorporate them into a French Army operating from American bases. Giraud thus would have to surrender matériel planned for one of his own eleven divisions or request additional arms for the Gaullist forces. Since the former choice was impossible to him, Giraud was placed in the ridiculous position of asking for an augmentation of the Anfa program to twelve divisions at the very moment that Eisenhower was ready to recommend that it be reduced to eight.

When General Walter Bedell Smith returned to Washington early in October he reported personally on the North African situation to Marshall and to Roosevelt. Both the Chief of Staff and the President were committed to the belief that a field commander's recommendations should be honored as much as possible, and they had no reason to press the French program against the evidence that under General Giraud's command little had been accomplished to make effective use of the matériel sent. Eisenhower's staff had become acutely aware of the fact that many officers on the French war staff shared the American view that the number of divisions should be scaled down and that many of these officers were younger ones who were not members of Giraud's personal entourage. There was an inevitable tendency to accept the position that it was Giraud personally who refused to reorganize the French Army along modern lines, and that from the strictly military point of view, the views of the French war staff were more valid than those of the Commander in Chief.

The situation in North Africa posed a real difficulty for President Roosevelt, in view of his time-honored suspicions of De Gaulle. Roosevelt did not wish De Gaulle to obtain control of the French Army, and he did not wish De Gaulle's position in the FCNL to become so predominant that it would provide a springboard from which to achieve control of a postwar French government. On the other hand, he did not want to hinder rearmament if a rebuilt and revived French Army would help the war effort, nor, considering the outbursts that followed every American intervention in French affairs, did he wish to put himself into the position of having to exert any more pressure on the Committee than necessary. By October, Roosevelt had come to realize that Giraud's position as cochairman had accomplished very little in the way of decreasing De Gaulle's prestige and enhancing his own, but he could still rest on the comforting assurance that as long as Giraud controlled the army and was susceptible to direct military requests from Eisenhower, De Gaulle would at least be deprived of one important element in his campaign for personal power. Confronted with reports of Giraud's unreasonableness and inefficiency, Roosevelt began to see that no great case for Giraud's retention as commander in chief would be made by American headquarters or even by French officers, with whom Giraud's popularity had waned considerably since his denunciation of Pétain on September 3. Thus by October, 1943, the President had virtually abandoned support of Giraud as an instrument for promotion of the ends he hoped to achieve, and he cast about for other means of exerting pressure on De Gaulle.

There were not many means available. There was always direct intervention by Eisenhower, if the prosecution of the war seemed to justify it; but this was an extreme measure which had a way of producing adverse reactions and of sometimes not accomplishing what was expected of it. Ending the rearmament program would also place some pressure on the FCNL; but as long as Giraud continued to control the program, it would appear that such a move would tend to weaken Giraud more than De Gaulle. The only remaining device was nonrecognition, which would keep De Gaulle, no matter how much support he received from Great Britain and Russia, from playing an important role in Allied affairs as long as the war continued. Meanwhile, the President would wait and see. De Gaulle's moves to obtain power, his flirtation with Russia and Communists, the ever-increasing influence of civilians in the Committee, the convocation of the Consultative

Assembly, the chaotic condition of French Army supplies, administrative difficulties in the French Empire, and De Gaulle's irascible disposition could not help but produce strains which would soon reveal cracks in the structure of Gaullism which might be followed by De Gaulle's own collapse. In a memo to General Marshall dated October 13, the President referred to his feelings of the previous month, when he had considered canceling further arms to the French Army if the "prima donna was to seize control of it from the old gentleman." His memorandum stated:

> When I saw Beedle Smith the other day I raised the question of sending further equipment to fit out the new French divisions. Just as a matter of interest, I dictated the enclosed to the Prime Minister on September 7 last but did not send it.
>
> I think a showdown will come soon but it is a matter which, in a sense, relates a good deal more to Eisenhower than to Bob Murphy. . . .[5]

The President's comments reveal some significant points in regard to his attitude toward developments in North Africa. Roosevelt's acceptance of the idea that the problem related more to Eisenhower than to Murphy suggested that he had now been persuaded to place military considerations above political ones; it also suggested a modification in strategy, a willingness to permit De Gaulle to move along his own path with the assurance that sooner or later he would tumble into a pitfall of his own making.

In the midst of the heated exchanges on rearmament among French and American military authorities, the civilian expert on rearmament quietly bowed out of the dispute. Since June, Giraud's adviser Jean Monnet had filled the post of commissioner of rearmament, relief, and rehabilitation; but on October 18 he suddenly relinquished the word *rearmament* from the description of his office and announced that he would henceforth devote his attentions primarily to relief matters. Toward the end of September the draft of the UNRRA charter had been formulated, and Monnet went to the United States to attend the

[5] E. Roosevelt, ed., *F.D.R.: His Personal Letters*, II, 1453.

first UNRRA conference, which deliberated at Atlantic City in November. After November, 1943, Monnet spent most of his time on mission in the United States, where he concentrated primarily on relief and Lend-Lease matters, and his persuasive voice, so often raised in an effort to moderate the influence of extreme Gaullists, was lost to the FCNL. With Monnet's departure, it should be added, only General Georges, Abadie, and Mayer, of Giraud's appointments, remained in the Committee, whereas the appointment of De Menthon and Le Gentilhomme had given De Gaulle two additional supporters.

At the same time that Eisenhower received Giraud's incomprehensible request for twelve divisions, he learned that the Second Moroccan Infantry Division, the first French unit to embark for the Italian campaign, on the eve of its departure was short of clothing, spare parts, and 57-mm. guns. American authorities were exasperated at the apparently perverse unwillingness among the French to comply with hints, advice, threats, and directives that had been forthcoming for the preceding two months. Cognizant of the Giraud line of reasoning, they nevertheless insisted that as long as the United States provided the equipment and French troops functioned under Allied command, the French should conform to the pattern established by the power supplying the matériel. One of Eisenhower's difficulties—that under the terms of the Clark-Darlan Agreement, the French command operated independently—deprived the Allied Commander of means by which to force compliance with his instructions. Even after October 2, when the French Commander in Chief ostensibly became subordinated to the FCNL, Eisenhower could not formally and officially come to terms with the French Commissioner of War, because the FCNL had not been recognized and Eisenhower had thus far been authorized to deal only with the French Commander in Chief. It was clear that the time had come for a complete re-evaluation of the French rearmament program and that further deliveries should be withheld pending a satisfactory understanding on the matter. On October 27, Eisenhower personally wrote Giraud to inform him that French troops would not be supplied and serviced by United States units and that French expeditionary forces, including those to be used only in France, must have the correct complement of service elements, even if it meant that personnel would have to be transferred from other combat divisions. By November 3, Allied headquarters had definitely decided that the entire program must be revised, with the understanding that a self-sufficient French Army, completely manned and equipped with service units along American lines, should be developed. Washington was notified of this decision, and Giraud was told that he must take immediate steps to reduce the number of divisions by three or four if he wished to receive further deliveries of equipment.

The American ultimatum reached Giraud on the day that the Consultative Assembly met for the first time in Algiers. De Gaulle was now ready for a new move which would be calculated to broaden the FCNL and further reduce Giraud's influence. At the very time that Giraud needed American support to enable him to weather De Gaulle's anticipated action, he was confronted by concrete evidence that the Americans themselves wished to deprive him of the very divisions that Roosevelt had authorized. It would not be a mark of sagacity for General Giraud to count on the Americans in his quarrel with De Gaulle; whatever reassurance he may have obtained from Robert Murphy was more than negated by the coolness at Allied headquarters.

The Showdown with Giraud

Into overcrowded Algiers for the opening session, on November 3, of the Consultative Assembly, came the representatives who were to form the first French deliberative council since Pétain had dissolved the Parliament in 1940. Over half of the eighty-four delegates, representing Resistance movements and political parties, brought with them from France the vigor, ideals, and programs which they hoped to pour into the political melting pot of Algiers. Some of the celebrated names of the Resistance—Emmanuel d'Astier de la Vigerie, Jacques Médéric, Paul Giacobbi, Henri Frenay, Jean Bordier—swelled the list of members, while a cross section of the Resistance political parties was also represented: Louis Jacquinot, who had abandoned Flandin's *Alliance Démocratique* after Munich; Marc Rucart and Henri Queuille of the Radicals; Félix Gouin, Pierre Bloch, André le Trocquer of the Socialists; and from the Communist party, Fernand Grenier, who had joined

De Gaulle early in 1943, together with André Marty, Étienne Fajon, Henri Pourtalet, François Billoux, and others. The assembly provided the FCNL with the semblance of a democratic, representative body, which it was hoped would cement the relations of the Algiers Committee with France and impress foreign powers with the unity and forcefulness of French dissidence.

The convocation of the Consultative Assembly coincided with De Gaulle's conviction that he could no longer delay a broadening of the FCNL and a settlement of the question of dual chairmanship. Since early October the National Resistance Council had been insisting that representatives of the Radical Socialist, Socialist, and Communist parties and members of the Resistance movement be introduced into the Committee, which was overweighted with generals, bankers, and professional men. In the existing FCNL, only André Philip and François de Menthon could properly be considered representatives of the Resistance, and Philip had been out of France for over a year. The support of the Assembly would also make Giraud's retirement from the Committee feasible. Previous to the first session, five delegates representing the Resistance Council had demanded of Giraud that he make a public disavowal of his connections with Vichy. The General haughtily refused to make any such statement and later told the press: "The Resistance delegates are misinformed. Having no ties with Vichy and no reason to have them, I have nothing to disavow. I have abstained simply on principle, so as not to insult other Frenchmen." Standing on principle, however, did not benefit his reputation; and although the Assembly as a whole was not hostile, Giraud obtained no consolidated support from any influential group except the Communists, who, in their efforts to find allies to counterbalance De Gaulle, took up the burden of Giraud's defense.

During the FCNL's session of November 6, a decision was reached whereby all the commissioners agreed to resign in order to permit a new list of members to be drawn up. General Giraud voted for the measure, not realizing perhaps that the move was designed to separate military command from political power and that the new members would be designated by De Gaulle, assisted by a committee of three: René Pleven, Adrien Tixier, and René Mayer. In the course of the next

French Embassy Press & Information Division

In 1945 the funeral services of M. Paul Valéry were attended by a number of dignitaries: from left to right, M. Abrambrun, minister from Peru; M. Castello Bronco Clark, ambassador from Brazil; M. Guillaume, ambassador from Belgium; M. Duff Cooper, ambassador from Great Britain; Diethelm; Jacquinot; Mayer; M. Duhamel, secretary of the French Academy; M. Teitgen; M. Capitant; and General de Gaulle.

French Embassy Press & Information Division

The last meeting of the Council of Ministers before the 1945 elections that changed the constitution: from right to left are Messrs. Tanguy-Prigent, Bidault, de Gaulle, Teitgen, R. Mayer, Parodi, and around the circle, Thomas, Soustelle, Jeanneney, Tixier, and Jacquinot.

three days De Gaulle took decisive steps to broaden his cabinet by the entry of seven new members. Four parliamentarians were brought in representing the center, the radicals, and the Socialists: Jacquinot, Mendès-France, Queuille, and Le Trocquer. Mendès-France, who had been undersecretary of finance in Daladier's prewar cabinet, was at the time stationed in England as a member of the Fighting French air force. The portfolio of education was given to René Capitant, leader of the North African Gaullists. De Gaulle found difficulty in adding members from the Resistance and the Communist party. To Philip and De Menthon, De Gaulle wished to add Henri Frenay and Emmanuel d'Astier, and he offered Communist Fernand Grenier a post. The Communists, however, insisted that two party members who had been imprisoned in North Africa, Fajon and Midol, be brought into the Committee. D'Astier also insisted that a provisional government should be made up of Resistance leaders; that certain Vichy-tainted individuals in the existing FCNL be retired; and that Communists, whom D'Astier considered to make up 50 per cent of the Resistance, be included in the new Committee.[6] Although the Communists, stubbornly but vainly insisting on their conditions, were finally disregarded by De Gaulle, Emmanuel d'Astier agreed with some misgivings to accept the portfolio of interior, where he believed he could best co-ordinate the work of the Resistance with that of the Algiers Committee.

On November 9 the list of new members was announced. Not only was it discovered that three of Giraud's appointees, General Georges, Abadie, and Couve de Murville, had been dropped, but that the name of Giraud himself did not figure on the list. Only one Gaullist had been put aside, General Le Gentilhomme, whose post of commissioner of national defense was divided between the new civilian commissioners of war and air and of navy. On the following day De Gaulle invited representatives of the press to his office to explain to them what had been done. "A new General de Gaulle has been born," wrote Paul Brewster of the *Daily Mail,* "he showed a sense of absolute confidence . . . he completely dominated the conference." De Gaulle explained that the Committee was stronger, broader, and more sure of itself and would concentrate on purging collaborationists and on devising methods for

6 D'Astier, *Les dieux et les hommes,* 15.

the return of sovereignty to France. "Measures in France," he told the correspondents, "will be taken by the FCNL and only by it. No instructions given by any other authority will have any value—nor, I think, would be accepted in France." He pointed out that the Committee had under its authority all Frenchmen and all military forces, including their Chief.

Neither Giraud nor the Communists were inclined to accept De Gaulle's decision. On November 14 the Communists rallied ten thousand people at a meeting of protest, and two days later De Gaulle consented to grant portfolios of production and public health to Communists, on the condition that he choose the commissioners. These terms were refused by the Communists, who preferred to remain outside the FCNL rather than subject themselves to De Gaulle's dictatorship.

Giraud had no popular support behind him, and in his indignation at being removed from the Committee, he could do nothing but threaten to resign as commander in chief of the French Army. His resignation would undoubtedly have created severe repercussions in Washington which Robert Murphy was anxious to avoid, particularly since Roosevelt was at that moment en route to the Cairo Conference and would be in North Africa around November 20. Giraud engaged in countless discussions with the commissioner of war and air, Le Trocquer, and with Murphy to try to obtain a commitment that would not only confirm his military leadership but that would give him a free hand in directing war operations, a veto in purge trials of Army officers, and a right of approval over appointments of general rank. It was reported that between November 10 and 16, General Giraud threatened to resign six times, but that on November 15, Murphy persuaded him to postpone definite action for two weeks. It is not unlikely that Murphy anticipated the opportunity of being able to report directly to the President at Cairo and to ascertain from him what line the United States should take in connection with the long-expected clash between the two generals.

But President Roosevelt was unwilling to intervene directly on behalf of his champion. The eleven months between Casablanca and Cairo had diminished the President's confidence in Giraud as the sort of leader who could rally dissident French elements and shunt their energies into activities compatible with American interests. No matter how much

American support was given Giraud, it was now clear that he would never supersede De Gaulle—or even head an important parallel Resistance movement. The De Gaulle problem remained acute, but it demanded solutions different from those which Roosevelt had envisaged at the beginning of the year. North Africa was no longer the war's principal theater, and the President was looking toward problems of vaster import than one which concerned military command of a few units in North Africa. The fall of General Giraud added to President Roosevelt's list of complaints against De Gaulle, but he was unwilling to intervene as he had the previous June. Giraud remained commander in chief of the French armies but no longer cochairman of the French Committee of National Liberation.

American Preparation for Cairo and Teheran

The closing months of 1943 brought Roosevelt into personal contact with Stalin for the first time since the war began. It should be understood that at Teheran the problems of France, and of the French at Algiers, were not foremost among the difficult problems under consideration; the discussion nevertheless did touch on subjects related to the French and in which they had a keen interest. Any conversation or decision which affected Italy, French colonies such as Indochina, or the cross-Channel invasion obviously concerned the French. Yet at this crucial time De Gaulle's stock in Allied camps was probably at a lower point than at any time during the months since he came to North Africa.

Neither Churchill nor Roosevelt set foot in Algiers on their way to Cairo. The Prime Minister came extremely close to the Algerian capital when his warship anchored in the bay, but he deliberately snubbed De Gaulle by inviting no one except the deposed General Georges to come out to visit him. Roosevelt's plane flew directly over Algiers as it proceeded from Oran to Tunis, but the President also ignored the existence of the Frenchmen in Algiers.

During his voyage across the Atlantic on board the battleship *Iowa,* President Roosevelt had been able to reflect about De Gaulle's bid for control of the French Committee and about recent French moves in the Near East. Neither action was calculated to reinforce the President's faith in De Gaulle or his confidence that the French Committee of National Liberation wouuld achieve a stature permitting it to override De Gaulle's influence. On board the *Iowa* were Harry Hopkins, Leahy, Marshall, King, and Arnold, whose presence provided the President with the opportunity of consulting with them on all aspects of the political and military consequences of an altered attitude toward the French. The major reaction of the President involved a confirmation of his basic misgivings about De Gaulle's reliability. He was resigned to the fact that no American intervention could now weaken De Gaulle's position as chairman of the FCNL; but admission of De Gaulle's strength was not calculated to make the President recognize the necessity of dealing with him.

A recent Gaullist move in Lebanon had served to intensify Roosevelt's hostility and mistrust. Three months earlier—in August, 1943— the first independent elections in Lebanon had brought resounding victories to the nationalists. The pro-French candidate had been defeated, and Bechara Khoury was elected president with Riad Sohl as premier. National sentiments in the new assembly and French insistence on its privileged position inevitably came into conflict when, on October 25, Lebanon formally requested that the *Délégation Générale,* headed by Jean Helleu, convert itself into a diplomatic mission and surrender to the country all attributes of sovereignty. Considering such a decision too weighty to approach without consultation, Helleu requested a postponement on the decision and went to Algiers early in November to report to the FCNL. On November 5, the day before all the members of the FCNL resigned, he appeared before De Gaulle, Catroux, and Massigli to learn what policy to pursue in face of the Lebanese demands. Helleu was instructed that no amendment to the constitution could be permitted without FCNL approval and that any transfer of sovereignty must follow negotiations for a treaty determining the relations between France and Lebanon. During his trip back to Beirut, Helleu learned that the Assembly refused to await his return before debating the constitutional changes, and upon his arrival on November 9 (the day De Gaulle's action against Giraud was announced), he found that the constitution had been unilaterally amended. Acting on his own initiative, but possibly abetted by personal support from De Gaulle, Helleu decided to suspend the constitution and to arrest all the members of the government.

From the point of view of relations with Britain and the United States, a more ill-timed act could hardly be imagined. Not only was the *coup d'état* against Giraud calculated to increase American and British distrust, but the reappraisal of the armament program by the military authorities meant that the entire matter of sending equipment to the French was in question. Now, suddenly, came a savage act of reprisal which produced doubts concerning the FCNL's political sagacity and its good faith. The action, furthermore, was taken at the very moment that Churchill and Roosevelt were preparing to leave for their rendezvous at Cairo. On the eve of the President's departure Hull dispatched the following message to Murphy:

> Inform the FCNL that the United States Government has learned with surprise of the repressive actions taken by their authorities in Lebanon. It is difficult to understand how the French, whose country is now groaning under the heel of the invader, can be unmindful of the aspirations toward independence of another people. The French action in Lebanon must cast the gravest doubt upon the sincerity of the avowed declarations of all the United Nations. The United States Government can not permit itself to be associated in any way with such acts of repression.
>
> Unless the FCNL takes prompt steps to restore the duly elected Government of the Lebanese Republic and to implement the solemn promises of independence given to the Lebanese people in 1941 in the name of the French National Committee, the United States Government will be obliged publicly to announce its complete disapproval of the acts of the French authorities in the Lebanese Republic and to take such further steps as may appear appropriate. We will take such action with the utmost reluctance but we feel it would be less detrimental to the united war effort than for us by silence to appear to accept a situation which is contrary to the aims and principles for which the liberty-loving nations are fighting.[7]

After a conference with Massigli and Catroux, General de Gaulle agreed to send Catroux to Beirut, but he made no commitment about

[7] Paraphrased from Hull, *Memoirs*, II, 1544.

recalling Helleu or releasing the Lebanese officials. Arriving at Beirut on November 16, Catroux found that the danger of an uprising and the firm stand of the British, who on November 19 announced that they would declare martial law if a settlement was not reached in three days, counseled a policy of moderation; he advised the release of the ministers, the recall of Helleu, and the reconvocation of the Assembly. By November 21 the FCNL had approved of Catroux's settlement, and the danger of serious riots was temporarily averted.

Roosevelt's distrust of De Gaulle was also revealed by his attitude toward post-liberation France. The President was convinced that De Gaulle's control of the FCNL and his domination of Resistance networks was going to mean that Gaullists, crowding into France in the wake of the invading armies, would attempt to gain immediate possession of the administration. Why Roosevelt so greatly feared this eventuality can be explained only in terms of his imaginative projection of its consequences: civil war and a threat to American lines of communication. He believed that if the Germans withdrew prematurely from France, thus producing an unanticipated vacuum which the Gaullists would rush in to fill, there would be such domestic turmoil that Allied forces would be incapable of maintaining order. He therefore refused to accept this responsibility for American troops.[8] He also feared that if the United States accepted a southern occupation zone in Germany, it would be difficult and dangerous to administer if lines of communication stretched across France. (The President would engage in protracted argumentation with his Chiefs of Staff and the Prime Minister before he would be persuaded to accept the southern zone, but then only on the condition that the Bremen enclave would be available for supplying the zone directly by sea.)[9]

To reduce the danger of revolution and civic disorder, Roosevelt gradually leaned more and more toward Secretary of War Stimson's thesis that civil administration must be initially under military control. An extreme application of this idea would involve an AMGOT for France, the installation of which, as the President must have realized,

[8] This decision involved changes in "Rankin," the plan for an emergency occupation of Germany in the event of German withdrawal (Pogue, *Supreme Command,* 143).

[9] Churchill, *Closing the Ring,* 507–10.

would invite lively protests both in France and the United States; yet the firmness with which he held to his decision provides some measure of the certainty he entertained that introduction of the Gaullists into France would result in civil disorder. It is difficult to ascertain where or how the President obtained his conviction that the Pétainist administration still possessed enough moral or material backbone to provide a dangerous counterbalance to De Gaulle or the Resistance.

If no civil war occurred, and the Gaullists moved into control of the French government, Roosevelt would still object to co-operation with the FCNL, but for other reasons. In this eventuality it would seem that De Gaulle had been given his white horse on which to return to France; he could immediately establish himself as head of the French state. Roosevelt viewed this possibility without enthusiasm. He did not believe that France, which had been defeated in five weeks and had surrendered Indochina to Japan without a murmur, deserved a leadership which insisted on the grandeur and invincibility of France. Regardless of De Gaulle's magnificent work in rallying the French, it did not seem equitable that the man who in three years had rallied only two divisions of 14,000 men should inherit the power which had permitted 40,000,000 persons to accept defeat. Roosevelt's thoughts about De Gaulle were succinctly expressed a month after the Cairo Conference, on the occasion of the French Committee's placing an observer on the Allied Control Commission for Italy. Roosevelt wrote the Prime Minister:

> When you and I look back eleven months we realize that de Gaulle and his committee have most decidedly moved forward by the process of infiltration—in other words, here a little, there a little. . . .
>
> For the life of me I cannot see why France is entitled to anybody on the Allied Control Commission for Italy. His presence there will, we know from experience, cause controversy and more trouble with the French Committee. . . . I wish you and I could run this Italian business. We would not need any help or advice.[10]

One can only surmise whether, in the depths of the President's mind,

[10] 31 Dec. 1943 (E. Roosevelt, ed., *F.D.R.: His Personal Letters,* II, 1473–74). Cf. Hull, *Memoirs,* II, 1245–46; De Gaulle, *Mémoires,* II, 239, 606–607.

there lurked a similar paternalistic attitude toward France: "I wish I could run this French business—I would not need any help or advice."

Cairo and Teheran

At Cairo, where Roosevelt and Churchill conferred from November 22 until November 26, the presence of Chiang Kai-shek brought into discussion the eventual disposition of Indochina. The recent French inept handling of the Lebanon crisis was not forgotten: the President's sympathies lay entirely with the Lebanese ministers. On November 20 he had informed Hull that he thought "we should back up the British position in Lebanon and try to make it even more positive." De Gaulle's repressive measures in Lebanon, characteristic of the most unappetizing qualities of colonialism, did not persuade Roosevelt that Indochina should be turned over to Gaullists. The trusteeship solution was discussed in broad and informal fashion as the President talked about Asian problems with the Generalissimo. Roosevelt volunteered:

> The country is worse off than it was a hundred years ago. The white man's rule there is nothing to be proud of. The French have no right, after the war, simply to walk back into Indochina and reclaim that rich land for no reason other than it had once been their colony. The most the French should have is a trusteeship, looking toward eventual independence.[11]

Chiang assured the President that China did not want Indochina, and he registered his approval of trusteeships as a satisfactory approach. When Churchill was informed of Chiang's agreement with the President's ideas, he was so skeptical that Roosevelt obtained a second assurance from Chiang. Trusteeships, which Churchill gloomily suspected might be applied to parts of the British Empire, provided a conspicuous point of difference between the President and the Prime Minister. Roosevelt thoroughly enjoyed airing his grandiose views about the postwar

---

[11] Adapted from Edward R. Stettinius, Jr., *Roosevelt and the Russians*, 237–38; and E. Roosevelt, *As He Saw It*, 165. Although Elliott Roosevelt's testimony is sometimes untrustworthy, this appears to be a reasonable reconstruction of the President's position. See also Hull, *Memoirs*, II, 1596.

world in which neither balance of power nor imperialist conflict would threaten world harmony; but his expression of these ideas, which so discomforted Churchill, did not mean that he was formulating official United States policy. Roosevelt did make it explicit, however, that he looked to China as an ally in anti-imperialism, and, as Churchill was painfully aware, he would undoubtedly sound out Stalin on the same question when they conferred at Teheran on November 28. If Stalin concurred in the anti-colonial thesis, Churchill would find himself outnumbered on this essential point. There was little doubt in Churchill's or Roosevelt's mind that De Gaulle would align himself with England against Russia, China, and the United States in defense of the empire. Churchill would like to see De Gaulle's Committee recognized in order that a Franco-British front against the others could become effective, while the President continuously became more stubborn in his insistence that the FCNL should not be raised to the point where it could exert a government's influence.

The recent events at Algiers and Beirut, the discussions on civil affairs in France after the liberation, and his convictions on colonial matters led the President to the belief that any moves in regard to the French must be postponed. On November 27 he dispatched an important memorandum to Hull:

> I am convinced no final decisions or plans concerning civil affairs for France should be made at this time.
> The entire North African situation is complicated, but the Lebanon affair illustrates the general attitude of the committee and especially de Gaulle. The latter now claims the right to speak for all France and talks openly of plans to set up his Government in France as soon as the Allies get in.
> The thought that the occupation when it occurs should be wholly military is one to which I am increasingly inclined.
> I will discuss this informally with Stalin and Churchill, but I hope you can hold up the entire matter.[12]

The "plans concerning civil affairs" referred to the State–War Department proposal which had been turned over to the European Ad-

[12] Adapted from Hull, *Memoirs,* II, 1245.

visory Commission during the Moscow Conference, as well as to the FCNL proposal of September 7, which had been discussed in London late in October by André Philip and Anglo-American representatives. The President's action meant that during the next few months, while preparations for "Overlord," the cross-Channel invasion, went forward, no official conversations between Allied and French authorities took place in regard to administrative methods or powers to be introduced into France after the liberation began.

The inevitable move of De Gaulle to master the FCNL had combined in unpredictable fashion with bloodshed in Lebanon to produce an impression of ruthlessness which so repelled Roosevelt that it canceled out whatever favorable inclinations he might have had toward cooperation with the dissident French. The timing could not have been more unfortunate. No one realized how deeply the President felt on this matter or how much his personal attitude could affect the fate of the FCNL. But the President himself did not realize how much greater than his own power were the spirit and strength of De Gaulle as the symbol of French resistance.

From Cairo, President Roosevelt and Prime Minister Churchill flew to Teheran, where, on November 28, 1943, they met Marshal Stalin for top-level deliberations on the strategy to be pursued against Hitler. There were no outstanding matters concerning the FCNL to be decided among the Big Three because no common policy in regard to recognition or rearmament was desired or sought. On the other hand, with the invasion of France providing one of the major subjects for discussion, decisions were to be reached which, although De Gaulle was not a party to the deliberations, would have great interest and importance for the Committee which aspired to become the French Provisional government.

On the first day of the Conference, Roosevelt and Stalin, who had not previously met, sat down to informal discussions, during which they endeavored to learn something of each other's personality and aims. Roosevelt soon detected that Stalin would not prove too hostile to his own ideas about France, for Stalin, like Roosevelt, entertained powerful misgivings about the value of the French as allies. To Stalin the shuffling collaborationism of Vichy came closer to the real France than the fine-sounding but hollow defiance of De Gaulle, and the Soviet chief seemed to hold no illusions about France's future. Always impressed by military strength, Stalin inquired about the French divisions. Roosevelt told him that nine divisions would soon be ready, but, since no more than four divisions could be available for combat in the next few months and only two divisions had then been committed to the Italian theater, his estimate somewhat exaggerated French potentialities. (It is not unlikely that Stalin, whose representative Bogomolov had been at Algiers since October, possessed information about French rearmament almost as complete as Roosevelt's.) Nothing in Stalin's tone persuaded Roosevelt that the Soviet Union planned to press for early recognition of the FNCL or to join with the British in support of De Gaulle.

When Roosevelt raised the question of trusteeships, he found Stalin agreeably sympathetic to his idea of reducing imperial rivalries by international supervision. Stalin agreed that France had no special right to return to Indochina after the war. Roosevelt took away the impression that Stalin stood much closer to his own ideas of postwar collective security than he did to Churchill's pragmatic concern with balance of power and spheres of influence. While this may have been illusory on Roosevelt's part, it convinced the President that cultivation of Soviet good will was worth an enormous effort; he believed that with the United States, Russia, and China supporting a new Holy Alliance, Great Britain would be forced to co-operate in producing a peace which would "banish the scourge and terror of war for many generations." Convinced of the real possibility of eliminating power politics from the world, Roosevelt did not share Churchill's apprehension that handling De Gaulle roughly would push him and the FCNL into the Soviet sphere. As long as Russia remained committed to the formation of a United Nations organization which, by open discussion and the might of the Big Four, would keep peace, it did not matter greatly whether De Gaulle chose to face East or West.

To his disappointment, Churchill found Stalin seconded by Roosevelt in many of the areas of discussion at Teheran. In spite of the Prime Minister's vigorous and compelling arguments for extended operations in the Aegean, in the Adriatic, and in Italy, Russia and the United States refused to modify their insistence that the major Anglo-American military effort in 1944 should be across the English Channel; and before the

Conference broke up, a definite commitment to "Overlord" for May, 1944, was made. It was also agreed that a simultaneous diversionary landing ("Anvil") should be made in southern France.

For both Churchill and De Gaulle, the "Anvil" decision carried special significance. If "Anvil" developed into the principal enterprise in the Mediterranean during 1944, it would tie up so many men and landing craft that an expedition close to Churchill's heart—to puncture the soft underbelly—could not be realized. The Prime Minister had indeed acquiesced to the "Anvil" scheme, but he had not renounced making an effort to sidetrack it in behalf of more exciting enterprises farther to the east. The one consolation that Churchill extracted from Teheran was the Mediterranean command, for it had been agreed that Mediterranean operations would fall under a command separate from that of "Overlord." Since the Mediterranean commander would be British, the Prime Minister could at least draw satisfaction from the thought that British strategic concepts might be preponderant in Italy and the Aegean, regardless of commitments made elsewhere in the interests of over-all world strategy.

De Gaulle had a more immediate stake in "Anvil." It had not yet been decided what forces, or how many divisions, would disembark on the French coast, but preliminary discussions pointed to the desirability of employing French troops seasoned in Italy; and it was not beyond the realm of possibility that "Anvil" could become an exclusively French operation with a French commander in chief. With "Anvil" to be launched simultaneously with, or just prior to, "Overlord," it was possible that if German resistance in the south proved weaker than that in the north, a large portion of France might be liberated exclusively by French forces. What no Frenchman could tell, however, was the extent to which the FCNL would be invited to participate in Allied councils. An impartial observer might have anticipated that the door would not be opened very wide.

Although the British and American military chiefs, when they returned to Cairo, held further discussions—especially with a view to persuading Turkey to declare war—no basic alteration in decisions affecting the French was considered. The French at Algiers were, in fact, ignored as studiously now as they had been before the Conference. Eden stopped off at Algiers on his return to London, but Churchill, on the verge of pneumonia, was unable to travel further, and Roosevelt retraced his route without a gesture toward De Gaulle.

At Tunis, on his return trip, President Roosevelt notified Eisenhower of his selection as supreme commander for "Overlord." Eisenhower was to be relieved as Allied force commander by General Sir Henry Maitland Wilson at the end of December, when he would proceed to Washington for briefing and then assume command at SHAEF (Supreme Headquarters, Allied Expeditionary Force) in London before the end of January, 1944. "Overlord" was now only six months in the future, and not least among the tasks to be accomplished was an acceptable arrangement concerning the temporary government and administration for France. Inauspiciously for De Gaulle, nothing had occurred in the few weeks preceding Eisenhower's appointment to convince Roosevelt that De Gaulle and his Committee should be entrusted with the arrangements; on the contrary as a result of the Giraud dismissal and the Lebanon blunder, the President had become more suspicious than ever of the FCNL's qualifications.

A New Phase in American Relations with De Gaulle

With the Teheran and Cairo Conferences, one phase of American relations with the French Committee of National Liberation came to an end. Until this time two major themes had dominated those relations: would the Committee be recognized; to what extent would its armies be equipped with American supplies? By December, 1943, those questions had been answered with some clarity. It was obvious in Algiers that the FCNL had not been recognized, at least as an agency with which the western Allies would deal at governmental level or as an agency which would be included in military discussions on strategy. The Committee was considered as a body to be dealt with when it appeared useful but not as an entity in which resided the latent sovereign powers of France. If this attitude brought dismay to members of the Committee, they had to admit that the second concern, rearmament, had been conscientiously carried through by the United States. Although there had been problems and differences of opinion, the program had been implemented, and equipment for new French divisions had been delivered.

With the new year, 1944, the old themes remained, but their application was altered. While the question of recognizing the FCNL as an agency with which the Allies would deal continued, it became broader and more significant as those interests, came to deal specifically with France. As the date of liberation approached, the FCNL thought of itself more and more as the French Provisional government that would be responsible for civil administration in France once the Germans withdrew. Thus, the Committee became increasingly concerned about its inability to speak directly with London and Washington on governmental matters or even to deal directly with the new military organization, SHAEF, about problems associated with French liberation.

On the military side, the question of rearmament broadened into strategic and tactical matters: how would the re-equipped troops be employed; under what command would they fight; did the FCNL or the French commander in chief, General Giraud, control the disposition of these forces; would the Allied command deal with the Committee or only with Giraud; or would the Allied command deal with the FCNL secret-service agents in France or only with Giraud's intelligence service?

As De Gaulle reflected on these matters, he could see his way clearly enough. He must attempt to persuade Washington and London to grant true recognition to the Committee as the Provisional government of France. Once that was accomplished, all the other matters—including civil administration and employment of the French Army—would fall into place. It was obvious that whatever happened, the Committee of National Liberation must be strengthened so that it could truly speak on behalf of France to the Allies and so that, if not recognized, it would be in the best position to draw its strength from France itself.

In an address to the Consultative Assembly on November 25, De Gaulle made his ambitions for the Committee unmistakably clear. In the course of his remarks he said:

> You can estimate what a trial there has been for the Committee which, in the guise of its present title, knows and feels that it has the honor and

responsibility of being, in fact, in the most difficult period of our entire history, the Provisional Government of the French Republic.

From this date on, in his interventions and speeches to the Assembly, De Gaulle would consistently refer to the FCNL as "the government." This new pretension was regarded in the United States as a confirmation of Hull's and Leahy's certainty that De Gaulle planned to become dictator of France.[13]

The mistrust of De Gaulle which had for so long characterized the American capital seemed to be growing, curiously enough, in Algiers as well. Not only the Giraudists, but many other Frenchmen, regarded De Gaulle's unilateral pronouncements and actions as contrary to democratic conditions. Representatives of the Communist party, refusing to relinquish their political maneuvers for the sake of a unified front, provided a focal point for opponents to Gaullism. They began to collaborate (strange bedfellows!) with Giraudist elements, and they became the strongest adherents of General Giraud in his losing fight to retain control of the army. Following the Communist lead, Socialists also began to hold party congresses and in their formulation of programs began to submit the Committee of Liberation to a political pressure that it had not previously felt. As the second session of the Consultative Assembly began to gain momentum in January, 1944, many of the delegates became restless concerning their role in the "debating society," and they began to suspect that the FCNL's Chairman had summoned them simply to provide a springboard for his own ambitions.

Particularly active in their opposition to De Gaulle were the Communists. With their wide infiltration of the Resistance, with their support from Russia (whom De Gaulle did not wish to alienate, particularly since Vishinsky had arrived in Algiers for the opening session of the Italian Advisory Commission), and with their aggressive and effective political tactics, Communists maintained a formidable lobby, under whose steady barrage of criticism De Gaulle was forced to maneuver. The party's central committee was especially insistent on accelerating the purge of collaborators and continuously attacked the FCNL on

[13] Hull, however, did not seem to take notice of De Gaulle's use of the word *government* until 26 Mar. 1944 (*Memoirs*, II, 1427). Compare Leahy's reference to De Gaulle's claim under date of 6 July 1944 (*I Was There*, 244).

this point. The Communists accused the Committee of deliberately holding back its purge program. Although Pierre Pucheu had been arrested
in August and General Bergeret in October, General Boisson, Marcel
Peyrouton, and Pierre-Étienne Flandin, former Vichy foreign minister
then residing in North Africa, had not been subjected to the indignity
of arrest or trial.

With his sense of historical perspective De Gaulle realized the gravity
of subscribing to a Reign of Terror, and he was particularly sensitive
to the fact that the men in question had been supported by the Allies
when they first entered North Africa. Any action against them would
be sure to invoke strong protests from London and Washington at a
time when the definite preparations for "Overlord" demanded an effort
toward co-operation; but on December 21 the FCNL nevertheless authorized the arrest of Flandin, Peyrouton, and Boisson. The move did
not escape Roosevelt's notice. On the following day the President requested Eisenhower to direct the FCNL to take no action against the
three men at that time. The intervention of the President, and his use
of the word *direct* rather than *request,* is significant, especially when it
is recalled that he raised no finger on November 12 during the crisis
in which Giraud was dropped from the Committee.[14]

While the arrests of December 21 were not of great import in themselves, they enabled the President to mark down one more item in his
ledger of irritation and mistrust; and they came at a time when conversations of the greatest import for the future of the French armies
were in progress.

The rearmament and use of French armies, which involved such
complex relations between the United States and the French and between French factions, constituted a series of problems that were not
easily or rapidly solved. Eisenhower's personal concern with the matter,
however, had far-reaching consequences in that it led him ultimately
to a repudiation of Giraud and a *rapprochement* with De Gaulle.

With a complete restudy of the French rearmament program proceeding at Allied headquarters, Eisenhower warned Giraud on November 13, 1943, that if steps were not taken shortly by the French com-

[14] Vigneras, *Rearming the French,* 117–19; Duff Cooper, *Old Men Forget,* 318, 320;
Peyrouton, *Du service public à la prison commune,* 243–46.

After the war, honors were exchanged: above, on June 14, 1945, General
de Gaulle presents a sword made for Napolean Bonaparte to General of
the Army Dwight D. Eisenhower; below, on August 24, 1945, President
Harry S. Truman decorates General de Gaulle with the U. S. Legion of
Merit insignia.

Bastille Day, 1945, again exemplifies the defeat of absolutism, as General de Gaulle decorates Admiral Thierry d'Argenlieu, General Koenig, and several Tunisians.

mander in chief to provide adequate service forces, he would delay no longer a recommendation to the Combined Chiefs of Staff that the Anfa program be reduced from eleven to eight divisions. Giraud agreed that his staff should study the American proposals, but on November 29 he wrote Eisenhower that in his judgment the original eleven divisions, plus the Gaullist British-equipped division, would alone produce the type of army he required. "At the present time," he told Eisenhower, "the main consideration is to equip the divisions as originally planned for, for which cadre and fighting personnel are now complete. To delay their rearmament will be an error likely to have grave consequences." To Eisenhower, his staff, and the War Department it appeared that Giraud's thinking was so far from American policy that a modification in the program could no longer be delayed.[15] Before acting unilaterally, Eisenhower determined once more to try to reach an understanding through discussion with the French; but before he had an opportunity to initiate further conversations, an incident occurred which required examination of the entire question in a new light.

By early December two divisions, the Second Moroccan Infantry and the Third Algerian Infantry, had been sent to Italy, where they engaged in combat with the American Fifth Army under General Mark Clark. Giraud had been asked on November 18 to designate a third division to proceed to Italy and, in accordance with the understanding he had already reached with General de Gaulle, he issued orders to the Free French division (First DMI), still equipped with British matériel, to prepare for embarkation. When Fifth Army headquarters learned that the new French division would not have American equipment, they refused categorically to accept it. With the first two French divisions arriving in Italy short of equipment specified by American Army tables of organization, there had been strain enough on supply, maintenance, and repair facilities; to cope with repairs and replacements for British equipment within the framework of the Fifth Army would place more of a burden on United States supply services than General Clark wished to impose on them.

Faced with the alternative of a delay, estimated at two months, in

[15] Vigneras, *Rearming the French,* 109–17; Georges Marey, "Le réarmament français," *Revue politique et parlementaire* (Oct., Nov., 1947), 139–40).

re-equipping the Gaullist division or substituting one of his "own" divisions, Giraud chose the latter course and designated the Ninth Colonial Infantry (Ninth DIC) as the third French unit to proceed to Italy. His decision provoked a new crisis in the FCNL, for according to the reorganization plan of October 2, authority for the employment of units within the French Army had been relegated not to the Commander in Chief but to the committee of national defense. The incident demanded an immediate response because if Giraud's action passed unchallenged, it would mean that the long struggle to assert the superiority of the civilian FCNL over the Commander in Chief, presumably resolved on October 2, had not in fact been brought to a conclusive end. To permit Giraud the power of assigning divisions would be tantamount to recognizing that the Committee held only theoretical powers while the Commander in Chief, contrary to FCNL decrees, possessed the *de facto* authority. Although countermanding Giraud was sure to produce new repercussions in Washington, De Gaulle, still sensitive about Giraud's relinquishment of the cochairmanship, believed that the issue was too grave to be passed over. Not simply the employment of a Gaullist unit but the supremacy of the "state" over the military command was at stake.

On December 10 the FCNL countermanded Giraud's decision to send the Ninth Colonial Infantry to Italy. It was a classic example of a showdown between civil and military authority, but unlike the Dreyfus Affair or MacArthur's recall from Tokyo, it was resolved without fanfare and without reverberations in the press. Had Giraud insisted on defying the Committee, it would have meant a complete break in the French chain of authority and a warning that he chose to give his allegiance not to the Committee but to Allied headquarters. This he was incapable of doing. Giraud was too loyal a Frenchman to invoke such a solution, and he received no encouragement from the Americans; unfortunately for him, his popularity among Eisenhower's staff had been whittled away by his incompetent handling of the supply questions and his stubborn refusal to revise the armament program. Eisenhower's sympathies were undoubtedly not increased by Giraud's persistent attempts to by-pass Allied headquarters with direct appeals to Marshall (who as persistently referred matters back to the field commander).

Giraud had no alternative but to tell Eisenhower that the Gaullist division must after all be the one that should go to Italy.

Eisenhower's reactions were mixed. He was naturally provoked that the French division, expected and needed in Italy in December, would not be able to get there until February. The delay in arrival of this division might make a decisive difference in the Italian campaign. From this point of view it appeared that De Gaulle's insistence that the Free French division go to Italy injected a political maneuver into the war effort. On December 14, Eisenhower wrote Giraud that he would recommend discontinuation of the armament program unless the FCNL gave definite assurance that the use of French forces would be governed solely by military considerations. On the other hand, Eisenhower was irritated with Giraud because the French Commander had not anticipated the situation and resolved it in such a way that French forces could be used in the most efficient way possible. Finally, Eisenhower could not help but fume at his own impotence in being unable to issue direct orders to French forces operating with the American command. It was his understanding that, under the terms of the Anfa Agreement, French troops equipped by the United States would be at the disposition of the Allied commander in chief.

It was obvious to both French and Americans in North Africa that the French must first reach agreement among themselves in regard to the basic French military authority and then the Americans must deal with that authority. This was accomplished by a decree on December 16 which authorized the French National Defense Council to make all decisions concerning the military conduct of the war, the general program of rearmament, and relations with Allied bodies concerned with the war's prosecution. There should have been no question among the French but that disposition of troops and organization of rearmament came under the Defense Council and not under Giraud. It was nevertheless understood that Giraud should remain commander in chief.

By the end of 1943, however, Giraud's title had become rather meaningless, for proud as he was of his prerogatives, he could actually claim little authority. He did not exercise any real command in Italy, for General Juin controlled all French operations and maintained liaison with the Allied command. Then, in December, Giraud's personal command of French forces in North Africa was undermined by the arrival of one of France's great generals, De Lattre de Tassigny. Imprisoned in 1942 for attempting a military uprising at the time of the North African invasion, De Lattre had escaped from France in October, 1943, and after a short stay in London, had proceeded to North Africa. Young, vigorous, and confident, De Lattre was convinced that France stood solidly behind De Gaulle and the FCNL. He greatly impressed Admiral Stark, who wrote Eisenhower that De Lattre was "a great Frenchman and patriot, broad-gauged, tolerant, reasonable, no axe to grind, forceful." Six days after he reported in Algiers, De Lattre was given command of the Second French Army (Army B), which included all troops in North Africa. He was shocked to find how ill prepared and poorly cared for were the forces to come under his command, and he had the impression that much work would be required to improve morale, straighten out the supply situation, and prepare the divisions for battle. The decisive way in which De Lattre undertook his new responsibilities was calculated to usurp some of the attributes of command still remaining to the Commander in Chief. Even De Gaulle seemed somewhat apprehensive about the popularity and masterful personality of the new Army B commander.[16]

As soon as De Gaulle learned the contents of Eisenhower's letter demanding that the FCNL revise its position on use of French troops, he summoned the new American ambassador, Edwin C. Wilson, and Harold Macmillan to his headquarters. Pretending to the authority of chief of state, he announced that he would not negotiate directly with Eisenhower and insisted that his contacts remain at governmental level. In a long discussion with Wilson on December 16, De Gaulle admitted that Eisenhower's insistence on purely American-equipped divisions in Italy made sense, but, he pointed out, this feature of the problem had never been brought to his attention. In this way he emphasized the fact that Eisenhower still dealt directly with Giraud and not with the Committee. More important, De Gaulle argued that questions of armament should not be considered as a personal agreement between President

16 COMNAVEU Documents, LV, 10; Général de Lattre de Tassigny, *Histoire de la première Armée française*, 3–5. De Gaulle prevented De Lattre from accepting Churchill's invitation to come to see him at Marrakech in Jan., 1944 (Duff Cooper, *Old Men Forget*, 318).

Roosevelt and General Giraud but as a matter affecting the French government. Similarly, command of French units could not be surrendered to the Allies by reason of rearmament; an understanding on this question, he insisted, should be reached by the governments concerned.[17]

Next day, De Gaulle met both Wilson and Macmillan and agreed with them that an immediate preliminary conference on these vital questions should be held with General Eisenhower. December 23 was tentatively agreed upon. Before that date, however, the arrests of Peyrouton, Boisson, and Flandin almost caused a rupture in all negotiations between the Allies and the FCNL. After one postponement because of the new purge, the conference nevertheless took place on December 27.

In Eisenhower's absence, General Bedell Smith represented the Allied Commander. Others who attended, besides General de Gaulle, included General Giraud, René Massigli, Edwin Wilson, and Harold Macmillan. It was quickly agreed that the French proposals, envisaging participation in Allied strategic planning, should be referred by Wilson and Macmillan to their respective governments. Meanwhile, all representatives agreed that an interim practical plan should be worked out, and they accepted in principle the following points: that French forces should be employed in France; that there should be consultation between the French and Allied commands before French troops were committed; and that in case of disagreement, questions should be decided between the FCNL and the Allied governments. Undecided was the question of French forces to be engaged in "Overlord." The British wanted no native troops in England; yet the transport of armored divisions, the only ones with essentially all-French personnel, was rendered difficult by the shortage of ships. In the course of discussions the Americans outlined the decisions made at Cairo and Teheran which affected the French: the plan for invading southern France ("Anvil") and the intention of using French divisions which had received combat experience in Italy.

A few days later, in a letter to Macmillan and Wilson, Massigli forwarded a draft formula which included the stipulations agreed upon at the meeting. In his note he urged that the draft directive be forwarded for speedy approval by the Allied governments. On December 31, Wil-

[17] De Gaulle, *Mémoires*, II, 668–70.

son replied, saying that after consultation with Eisenhower he was authorized to accept the formula. This letter, of course, did not constitute approval by the British or American governments, but the French could not help but be pleased with the manner in which the negotiations seemed to be progressing.[18]

On December 30, shortly before he left Algiers, Eisenhower talked with De Gaulle, who proved himself to be extremely levelheaded in the matter of reorganizing French divisions. Unlike Giraud, he agreed with Eisenhower that the French Army should be thoroughly equipped with service units, and he said that De Lattre would see to it. He demonstrated such comprehension of over-all planning, a characteristic which Eisenhower had missed in Giraud, that the new chief of SHAEF feared he had underrated De Gaulle. In the course of the conversation Eisenhower emphasized that he would not enter Paris without French forces at his side and that he would find a way to overcome the transportation difficulties. At the conclusion of their talk, Eisenhower told De Gaulle:

> If I find the chance, I am prepared to make a statement expressing the confidence I have drawn from our contacts, recognizing the injustice I have done you, and adding that you have stated that you are ready, in matters concerning you, to assist me in my mission. For the approaching campaign in France, I will need your help, the co-operation of your officials, and the support of French opinion. I don't know what theoretical position my Government will insist that I take in my relations with you. But, along with principles, there are facts. I have to tell you that, in fact, I will not recognize any other authority in France than yours.

To this De Gaulle replied, with prescient insight into the role of historians:

> If we have experienced some difficulties in our relations, it is neither your fault nor mine. It has depended on conditions which were not in ourselves but which have resulted from the very complicated situation in which our countries find themselves relative to each other, since France

---

[18] *Ibid.*, 670–74; Pogue, *Supreme Command*, 151; De Lattre, *Histoire de la première Armée française*, 626.

no longer commands a position of power. But all this is merely momentary. When we have won the war, no trace of it will be left, except, naturally, for historians.

The mutual respect of the two men inspired Butcher to call their meeting a "love-fest," and indeed it did seem to augur what the press referred to hopefully as "a new era in United States–French relations." Eisenhower seems to have been convinced that further exclusive dealings with Giraud would be counter to Allied strategic interests. As he left for Washington, Eisenhower hoped to be able to persuade the White House that a clear, written agreement between SHAEF and the FCNL would be the only way to avoid the constant and recurrent arguments among Frenchmen which from time to time had hindered the war's prosecution.[19]

From the French point of view, the *rapprochement* with Eisenhower had been encouraging. It appeared that the Allied command, which had thus far communicated exclusively with Giraud as French commander in chief, now recognized the National Defense Council and in the future would deal with it. While this hope proved illusory, there is no question but that Eisenhower, Smith, and other members of the Allied staff were prepared to recognize the authority asserted by French civilian commissioners of war, navy, and air. The new tendency proved especially encouraging to De Gaulle, who, realizing that the Lebanon crisis and the purges had created ill feeling at Washington and London, needed all the support he could locate to avoid making further concessions to Communism. Much as he appreciated the work of Communists in the Resistance, he feared their independence and detested their revival of party politics at a time when Giraudist elements were finally coming into the fold of Gaullism. De Gaulle undoubtedly believed that he could withstand Communist pressure if he obtained a firm guarantee from the Allies that the French regular Army, controlled by the FCNL, would return to a France whose provisional civil administration would also be dominated by the French Committee. If the British and American governments would not permit a binding agreement with SHAEF concerning the Committee's authority in France, the FCNL would be

19 Butcher, *My Three Years with Eisenhower,* 473; De Gaulle, *Mémoires,* II, 674–76.

forced to strengthen its own position in France by controlling absolutely clandestine communications with France and the networks within the homeland. To do this without Communist co-operation would be difficult in the extreme, yet De Gaulle was not inclined to resort to a *rapprochement* with the Communists unless no other alternative was open. He preferred a "love-fest" with Eisenhower to one with Thorez.

After Eisenhower's departure, the French National Defense Council occupied itself with the task of bringing the French military program into line with American points of view. General Giraud continued to sulk and contented himself with vain appeals to General Marshall to intercede on his behalf. On January 7 the Council decided to cut the program by two divisions (Eighth Algerian and Tenth Colonial Infantry), but the Americans insisted that the program be further reduced. By January 23 agreement had been reached on an eight-division program (five infantry, three armored) with over two hundred supporting units. By this time most of the equipment for eight divisions had reached North Africa, but much of it still had to be accounted for and distributed, and many men would have to be instructed in its use before the French command would be able to report French divisions ready to participate in Operation "Anvil." This was the work that De Lattre set for himself.

The final decision of the National Defense Council on January 31 to officially approve the eight-division program was a major defeat for General Giraud. Once more he sought to influence his old friend, General Marshall, to save his eleven divisions by overruling the theater commander, and once more his appeal was rejected. The new program was placed in effect over Giraud's protests and without his formal approval. From then on, as commander in chief, Giraud had little work to do. With the National Defense Council handling the assignment of divisions and appointment of commands, with no tactical responsibility in Italy, and with De Lattre proceeding along his own vigorous lines, Giraud, denied participation in FCNL and Allied councils, could only hope for an army group command with the invasion of France. Yet he himself, by his refusal to build up supply units, had made it virtually impossible for the French Army to operate as a separate, self-contained unit. As winter gave way to the spring of 1944, Giraud's headquarters at the Palais d'Été, twelve months previously bustling with people and activity, was disturbed only by an occasional visitor and by the measured and monotonous pace of a Senegalese sentry.

SHAEF and the French: The President's Draft Directive

In Washington for conferences with the President and the Joint Chiefs of Staff early in January, Eisenhower did his best to persuade the men responsible for policy that a close understanding with the FCNL would be the only logical way of approaching some of the problems which the invasion of France was certain to produce. From the military point of view, the major questions to be solved included: (1) authorization for SHAEF to deal with the FCNL, (2) determination of command relations between SHAEF and the French Army, (3) determination of SHAEF's relationship to the Resistance and their military forces, and (4) arrangements for the civil administration in France after liberation. It will be recalled that all discussion with French representatives then in Washington—Henri Hoppenot, head of the Civil Mission, and Jean Monnet and Pierre Mendès-France, members of the FCNL—had been suspended since President Roosevelt's message of November 27 from Cairo, and since his return to Washington, the President had shown no inclination to lift his ban.

Eisenhower made some headway in the War Department, where Secretary Stimson, and especially John J. McCloy, became convinced that events now proved the necessity of working with the Committee, but by the time he left to take up his new command in London in the middle of January, the Supreme Commander had received no definite assurance that he would be permitted to negotiate with Gaullist representatives.

On January 22, shortly after his arrival in London, Eisenhower had a long conversation with General François d'Astier de la Vigerie, who one month earlier had been appointed by De Gaulle as military delegate under the FCNL's civil administration plan. General d'Astier's powers also included those of superior commander of French troops stationed in Britain, delegate to SHAEF on all questions of military administration in northern France, and territorial military commander in France. If the Allied governments accepted the French civil affairs plan and if Eisenhower was empowered to work out plans with a representative of the FCNL, D'Astier stood ready to make arrangements for French participation in planning and liaison. During their conversation, D'Astier pointed out some of the many areas in which close co-operation would be helpful: food and supplies to the civilian populations, use of the Resistance armies in place of parachutists, and the employment of a French unit in the liberation of Paris. To all this Eisenhower agreed, and he added that he hoped Washington and London would empower him to develop plans with the French. Only three days before his talk with D'Astier he had urged that the Combined Chiefs authorize General de Gaulle to designate individuals with whom SHAEF could enter into negotiations. Meanwhile he was powerless to make any firm commitments without a specific directive.

It was clear that any further evolution in the direction of an agreement between SHAEF and the French Committee would have to be initiated in Washington. Before he left Algiers, Eisenhower had realized this and had recommended that Ambassador Wilson and Brigadier General Julius Holmes, together with Massigli, should go to Washington to try to persuade the State Department that the French schemes were feasible. Although Massigli did not go, Wilson left shortly after De Gaulle's return from Marrakech and arrived in Washington on January 17. He had determined not to return to Algiers unless a satisfactory arrangement for dealing with the FCNL could be worked out.

In Washington the atmosphere seemed favorable for a move in favor of the French Committee. Wilson added the weight of his views to the arguments that Stimson and McCloy had pressed on Hull as a result of Eisenhower's visit. The conversion of Hull to belief that De Gaulle's Committee might be granted some sort of recognition was a major victory for the French cause, particularly in view of the fact that some elements in the State Department remained unconvinced. As recently as the beginning of January, a State Department memorandum had been drawn up as a guide for the President's use in drafting a basic policy letter for Ambassador Wilson. The memorandum emphasized two points: that military considerations were and must remain paramount and that since sovereignty should reside in the people and 90 per cent of the French people were not free, no individuals or groups would be recognized. In the memorandum many reasons for avoiding De Gaulle were expressed: he had engaged in "an unrelenting struggle for political power," he had used a propaganda campaign "to bring pressure against the U. S.," he had tried "to drive a wedge between the U. S. and Great Britain . . . and to play off the Anglo-Saxon powers against the Soviet Union," and he had observed that the "Committee knows and feels that it is the Government of the French Republic." Since Wilson did not return to Algiers and Hull came to modify his French policy, such a letter became unnecessary, and it was not given official form.[20]

All of the complex problems to be settled before D–Day—use of French troops, relations with the Resistance, civil administration, issue of currency, relief, and rehabilitation—could have been handled in either of two basic ways: by recognizing the FCNL as possessing governmental status and by direct negotiation between governments or by empowering Eisenhower as supreme Allied commander to deal with the French Committee. Although the British would undoubtedly have preferred the first solution, there was so much opposition to it in Washington that the second seemed to be the only alternative. Before any meaningful negotiations could take place on economic, legal, or administrative matters, or on the employment of French forces in "Overlord" and "Anvil," it would be necessary for Churchill and Roosevelt to agree on the terms of a directive to Eisenhower.

Such a draft directive, taking into account the British and French positions and the arguments of General Eisenhower and Ambassador Wilson, was drawn up in co-operation with State and War Department officials late in January and referred to the White House for approval.[21] Great expectations were current that some form of recognition of the FCNL would soon be reported. On February 8, Walter Lippmann wrote: "It seems to be settled that we shall treat with the FCNL . . . as the governing authority in France." Two days later, according to the *New York Times*, "a high government source revealed that recognition would come within the next few weeks. . . ." And it was hinted that the President had reserved Lincoln's Birthday, when a new de-

---

[20] State Dept. Memo. of 5 Jan. 1944 (711.51/341a); Duff Cooper, *Old Men Forget*, 325; Leahy, *I Was There*, 235–36; correspondence of the writer with Mr. Wilson.

[21] This draft has not been made public but is generally understood to have been couched in terms comparable to the sentiments expressed by Hull in his speech of 9 Apr. 1944. See Stimson and Bundy, *On Active Service*, 546.

stroyer escort, the *Sénégalais,* was to be turned over to the French, as the dramatic occasion on which to announce a new policy. During his press conference on the day preceding the ceremony, Roosevelt punctured some hopes when he said that "no revision of policy towards the French National Committee was under review"; but he did admit that "discussions were going on regarding government behind the lines when the Allied invasion armies landed in France, which is a different thing."

The French Naval Mission took pains to provide an appropriate atmosphere during the transfer ceremony of the *Sénégalais.* Very important people were flown in from North Africa for the occasion, which was to mark the first time that President Roosevelt had consented to attend personally a function involving the presentation of war matériel to a foreign power.

On February 12, at the Washington navy yard, French officials waited expectantly as the President, seated in his car, addressed the microphones that had been brought to him. "On behalf of the American people," he said, "I transfer to the Navy of France this warship. . . . This vessel . . . is a part of the growing strength of the French Navy. . . ." Calling on Admiral Fenard by name, the President then turned the *Sénégalais* over to him as representative of the French Navy. He did not so much as mention General De Gaulle, General Giraud, the French Committee of National Liberation, or any matter of military or political significance.[22]

President Roosevelt had, in fact, no liking for the proposal which lay on his desk, and he had not the slightest intention of signing it. He had become convinced that Eisenhower must have full authority not only over combat areas but over areas behind the lines, and he was reluctant to agree to any arrangement that would give De Gaulle exclusive privileges in liberated France. He seemed to believe that there was enough force left in Pétainism to promote civil war, and he may have wished to give Eisenhower freedom of action in making arrangements with Giraud or with a modified Pétain government. Some French-

[22] Rosenman, comp., *Public Papers and Addresses of F. D. Roosevelt, 1944-45,* 70-72. On the same day, Feb. 12, Eisenhower was issued a formal directive on SHAEF's mission, but in regard to liberated Allied territories, the directive said that instructions would be issued later (Pogue, *Supreme Command,* 55).

men believed that if Pétain would dismiss Laval and convoke the Parliament, he might be able to rehabilitate his regime to a point whereby it could achieve Allied acceptance. It is not likely that Roosevelt would have been willing to go this far, but it is possible that information which American intelligence officers obtained from Giraud's networks (rather than through the Gaullist BCRA) and from Colonel Malaise in Spain may have provided Washington with reports which tended to exaggerate the influence of Pétainism among the French people. On the other hand, nothing had occurred to diminish Roosevelt's mistrust of De Gaulle. The dismissal of Giraud, the handling of the Lebanon crisis, infiltration onto the Italian Advisory Commission, and claims to represent a "government" all added themselves to the fundamental uncertainty which the President had developed in regard to the Free French leader over the three previous years. No doubt Roosevelt was familiar as well with the contents of a personal dossier maintained by Churchill concerning De Gaulle's "misdeeds." According to Duff Cooper, who was shown the Prime Minister's file before he went to Algiers, the papers comprised "a grave indictment."[23]

It is revealing that Secretary of State Hull, who possessed no peer in Gaullist antipathy, should have been willing to bow to the evidence that American interests would now be served by coming to terms, while the President refused to be converted. Against him was ranged virtually the full weight of his cabinet, but he remained adamant. Once while John J. McCloy attempted to argue the case for recognition of De Gaulle during a meeting at the White House, Harry Hopkins scribbled on a scrap of paper that McCloy was going to have to leave town if he did not stop "sounding off about de Gaulle."[24] "Just give me a

[23] The Prime Minister's portfolio undoubtedly included complete details on the Dufour incident, a Gaullist blunder given considerable publicity late in 1943. Dufour, a Frenchman who had worked for the British Secret Service, was taken into custody by the Free French when he attempted to enlist under false papers. In the course of the investigation which followed, he had been beaten in May, 1942, by members of Col. Passy's BCRA in an effort to learn about his activities before he escaped to England. Dufour later escaped from the Free French and in Aug., 1943, brought suit in a British court against De Gaulle, Passy, and members of the BCRA. The case was not immediately tried. In Mar., 1944, the courts decided to proceed with the case, but upon De Gaulle's determination to publicize an instance of a Frenchman's death after he had been interrogated by British Intelligence, the matter was dropped.

[24] Mr. McCloy told the writer this note was found among Hopkins' papers by Robert Sherwood.

certificate," the President used to say, "that de Gaulle represents the French people, and I'll change my mind."[25]

In judging the President's procrastination in taking action on the Eisenhower directive, consideration must be given to the fact that Roosevelt's health was far below normal during the early months of 1944. Having become ill on his return from Teheran, he suffered from a nagging infection and overwork during the entire period that the subject was under discussion.

By the end of February no action had yet been taken on the directive to Eisenhower, and the press began to sense the truth—that the affair was being held up by the White House. Roosevelt had postponed taking action for an inordinately long time, but he finally dictated an alternative draft directive which gave extensive powers to Eisenhower. When Stimson went over the President's draft he was shocked to notice the bluntness with which he had phrased his ideas. The Secretary of War immediately attempted to round off some of the sharp corners and then asked the President for an opportunity to discuss the directive with him.

On March 3, 1944, Stimson went to see the President and later recorded the interview in these words:

> I . . . put up to him my revised draft of his own draft of a directive to Eisenhower in respect to the French Committee. This was a ticklish matter which I, after much reflection, decided to handle lightly and personally. I told him I had committed the great sin of attempting to revise one of his papers; that I had tried not to change the aim of his paper but merely to put it in a form which I thought would go down more easily with the French Committee and also not to lay too much burden of detail on Eisenhower. He was very nice about it. He said his paper was only a draft and he had dictated it in a hurry. We went over my draft together, I pointing out the changes. He said he thought that was all right and that he would approve the paper though he wanted to look it over more carefully that evening. I told him that I had shown it to Stettinius and that Stettinius had approved it, at which he expressed his approval.[26]

[25] Hull, *Memoirs*, II, 1431 (cabinet meeting of 20 May 1944).
[26] Stimson and Bundy, *On Active Service*, 547–48.

Roosevelt kept the new draft for over a week, making minor changes in it, and on March 15 authorized that it be sent to London for the Prime Minister's consideration. It must be emphasized that the document was not a directive to Eisenhower but a modified draft submitted to the British government as the basis for further discussion between the two governments. Since the document provides a detailed example of the President's thinking at this time, it is worth quoting:

1) The Supreme Commander will have supreme authority in order that the war against Germany may be prosecuted relentlessly with the full co-operation of the French people. As such Allied Commander you will have the ultimate determination as to where, when, and how the civil administration of France shall be exercised by French citizens, remembering always that the military situation must govern.

2) When and where you determine that there shall be set up a civil administration in any part of France, so far as possible there shall not be retained or employed in any office any person who has willfully collaborated with the enemy or who has acted in any manner inimical to the cause of the United States.

3) In order to secure the setting up of any such civilian administration locally in any part of France, you may consult with the French Committee of National Liberation and may authorize them in your discretion to select and install the personnel necessary for such administration. You are, however, not limited to dealing exclusively with the said Committee for such purpose in case at any time in your best judgment you determine that some other course or conferee is preferable.

4) Nothing that you do under the powers conferred in the preceding paragraph 3 in connection with the French Committee of National Liberation or with any other group or organization shall constitute a recognition of said Committee or group as the government of France even on a provisional basis.

5) In making your decision as to entering into such relations with the French Committee of National Liberation or other committees or persons for that purpose, you should as far as possible obtain from it the following restrictions upon its purposes:

(a) It has no intention of exercising indefinitely in France any powers of government, provisional or otherwise, except to assist in the establishment by the democratic methods above mentioned a government of France according to the free choice of the French people, and that when such government is established it will turn over thereto all such powers as it may have.

(b) It favors the re-establishment of all the historic French liberties and the destruction of any arbitrary regime or rule of personal government.

(c) It will take no action designed to entrench itself or any particular political group in power pending the selection of a constitutional government by the free choice of the French people.

6) In any area of liberated France, whether or not there has been set up local control of civil affairs as aforesaid, you will retain the right at any time to make such changes in whole or in part which in your discretion may seem necessary (a) for the effective prosecution of the war against Germany; (b) for the maintenance of law and order; and (c) for the maintenance of civil liberties.

7) As Supreme Commander you will seek such uniformity in the administration of civil affairs as seems advisable, issue policy directives applicable to British, French, and American commands, and review all plans.

8) You may at your discretion incorporate in your Civil Affairs Section members of the French Military Mission and other French officials.

9) You will have no talks or relations with the Vichy regime except for the purpose of terminating its administration *in toto.*

10) Instructions on economic, fiscal, and relief matters will be furnished you later by the Prime Minister, the President, or by the Combined Chiefs of Staff.[27]

It will be remarked that many of the features of this draft were similar to the document which the President had approved on October 6, 1943, and which Hull had referred to the European Advisory Commission during the Moscow Conference. One important feature was dropped, namely the appointment by the Allied Commander of a French officer who would be director of civil affairs. On the other hand, the directive gave Eisenhower wide powers of making what arrangements he thought best and of dealing with the FCNL at his own discretion. Since dealing with Vichy was specifically ruled out and there was no

[27] State Dept., 851.01/3645a. Cf. Pogue, *Supreme Command*, 144-45; Hull, *Memoirs*, II, 1427. A copy of the draft was later—on 8 Apr. 1944—sent to Stalin.

one else to consult with, it would seem that the document was perfectly satisfactory and would have permitted immediate negotiations to start between SHAEF and the FCNL. To make sure that no misunderstandings existed, the State Department made a public statement on March 21 denying any American sympathy with Vichy and affirming that "no loyal supporter of the Allied cause would make the ridiculous charge that the United States Government . . . would have any dealings or relations with the Vichy regime except for the purpose of abolishing it." At his press conference on March 20 the President told correspondents the general nature of the note he had sent, indicating that it was Eisenhower's business and that he could deal with the FCNL or not, depending on circumstances.

Ambassador Wilson, who had determined not to return to Algiers unless a satisfactory basis for relations with the FCNL could be worked out, concluded that under the draft directive SHAEF could develop adequate arrangements with the French before D–Day. He made reservations to leave for Algiers on a transport sailing from Norfolk on March 28, and on March 24 he discussed the French problem with the President. Roosevelt told Wilson to inform De Gaulle that if Eisenhower decided to deal with the FCNL, he might continue that relationship provided the Committee did a good job, refrained from extreme measures, kept good order, and co-operated with the military authorities.

It appeared to President Roosevelt that the matter was settled. He had finally made the magnanimous gesture of giving Eisenhower leeway to pursue the course he thought best; he had not recognized De Gaulle and the Commiteee, but he had at least not hindered the Supreme Commander from working with him.

But the difficulties had only begun. The British government took exception to the optional phrasing of the directive and insisted with such tenacity on changing the word "may" to "should" that negotiations over the directive were still proceeding when Allied troops waded ashore in Normandy. Two days after Wilson's talk with the President, Mrs. Wilson suddenly became ill and required an emergency operation. This resulted in a cancellation of the Ambassador's trip and the impossibility of his presenting De Gaulle personally with the President's message.[28]

[28] Correspondence of the writer with Mr. Wilson; Pogue, *Supreme Command*, 145. Pogue leaves the erroneous impression that Wilson returned to Algiers.

(Since publicity had been given Wilson's determination not to return without a satisfactory arrangement, his continued absence from Algiers was construed by some as indicating a deadlock in Washington.) Finally, although Eisenhower's carte blanche would help the situation, particularly on practical arrangements at the lower level, it left unsolved certain problems, which remained within the scope of the Combined Chiefs of Staff's authority or which could only be resolved at government level. Into this category fell the employment of French troops (requiring use of transportation facilities not under SHAEF's command) and the issuance of invasion currency. Furthermore, the directive seemed to duplicate the worst error of the North African invasion—shifting the political decision to a military commander who was less qualified than his government to accept it.

Instead of solving the problem of relations with the French, the hesitating and ambiguous American approach contributed to pushing the FCNL into the most severe crisis it had yet undergone. And the outcome would force Roosevelt to reconsider once again his attitude toward De Gaulle and the FCNL.

French Planning at Algiers

How long could De Gaulle wait? In January he had possessed good reason to believe that some form of Allied recognition would not be long in coming. But as the *Sénégalais* transfer passed by without an encouraging gesture and as reports came in from Washington that the Eisenhower directive was held up on Roosevelt's desk, De Gaulle became more and more discouraged at the prospects of favorable American action. Early in March he began to draw the reluctant conclusion that SHAEF would not be empowered to take cognizance of the FCNL in its planning. De Gaulle had to make a decision which was rendered almost impossibly difficult by the uncertain factors which had to enter into it. He did not know the date of D–Day, he did not know the exact terms of the SHAEF directive which was under study, he could not tell how long he could avert a crisis over the secret services or what the reaction would be if he strongly supported Soustelle, and he did not know how long he could hold Communists out of the FCNL without endangering his support in France. If he could obtain a clear understanding with SHAEF, the Combined Chiefs of Staff, or the Allied governments, he could dismiss local squabbles as inconsequential, but if he became certain that the Allies refused to take action, he would have to complete plans to impose the FCNL's authority in France regardless of what Great Britain and America chose to do.

All of the evidence at De Gaulle's disposal pointed to the fact that no satisfactory arrangements would be reached. The FCNL had been negotiating with Eisenhower's successor at Allied headquarters, General Maitland Wilson, to obtain a firm understanding in regard to the use of French troops in "Anvil." The belief was held at Algiers that since French forces would primarily be involved, General Giraud would be appointed Allied commander for the operation. The Committee was also insisting on the right to intervene with the British and American governments to insure that the allotment of French forces should take French interests into account as completely as possible. But on March 7 it was learned that an American officer would command "Anvil," and nothing that Giraud could do was able to bring about a reversal of that decision. Giraud was finally reaping the unpalatable reward of his own stubborn insistence that all his soldiers be front-line troops. The Americans insisted that since the administration of services, supplies, and maintenance would be in American hands, so should the over-all command. The decision virtually placed Giraud in the position of a figurehead.

Several days later the Combined Chiefs let General Wilson know that they refused to entertain the thought of the FCNL's discussing matters on the governmental level; and on March 14, Wilson forwarded De Gaulle a draft agreement to the effect that French forces, if used in Allied operations, would have to be placed at the disposal of the Combined Chiefs. On March 13, Duff Cooper, who had replaced Macmillan as ambassador accredited to the French Committee, wrote in his diary:

Apparently complete agreement was reached by all the authorities concerned on a procedure that would have satisfied the French, but at the last moment it was turned down by the President against the wishes of

Cordell Hull, the State Department, and ourselves. We are now leaving the Americans to fight it out with their President. It does seem intolerable that one obstinate old man should hold up everything in this way.[29]

Duff Cooper does not say whether he mentioned the state of negotiations to the French, but whether he did or not, sufficient evidence had by this time become available at Algiers to persuade De Gaulle that he would be ill advised to wait much longer for Allied favors.

De Gaulle's plan of action now involved preparation for the return to France based on an assumption that agreement with the Allies could not be reached, but it kept the door open for a *rapprochement* if the possibility developed. One of De Gaulle's first tasks was to complete plans for civil administration in France. It will be recalled that these plans had been made the previous September but, awaiting some Allied response to its proposals, the FCNL had not drawn them into definitive form or officially adopted them. The plan was put into its final shape early in March but, while adopted by the Committee on March 14, was not published in the *Journal Officiel* until two weeks later.

The new ordinance revealed an important departure from the September draft in its designation of two representatives of the FCNL: a (civil) delegate and a military delegate. Since the military delegate would be appointed by De Gaulle—not Giraud—his designation was calculated to by-pass the Commander in Chief and to make Roosevelt reluctant to authorize Eisenhower to deal with him.

Since the new ordinance granted wide powers to the Committee's delegates, it was reasonable to suppose that the Communists and their sympathizers, still unrepresented in the FCNL, would, when they learned of the edict, take violent exception to what they later called a "French AMGOT." De Gaulle planned to appoint his commissioner of war, the Socialist André le Trocquer, as delegate and to replace General François d'Astier with General Koenig as military delegate; but he refrained from taking action until he could see what developments the next few weeks would bring.

In an attempt to clear the air De Gaulle determined to deliver an important speech to the Consultative Assembly, whose members had

[29] Duff Cooper, *Old Men Forget*, 324.

become restive in their minor role as yes men to the FCNL. For several months the Assembly had subjected an FCNL proposal for re-establishing a legitimate government to criticism and debate. This plan (not to be confused with the civil administration plan adopted on March 14) envisaged methods whereby the Pétain regime would be replaced, a new constitution drawn up, and elections held.[30] The Assembly's complaints over ignorance of FCNL policy, particularly in regard to future economic and social measures, gave witness to growing pains which, if ignored, could inconvenience and embarrass the government.

On March 18, De Gaulle delivered his carefully prepared speech on general policy. He prepared his audience for drastic moves by opening his address with remarks about "cold and hard realities" on which action must be based. He warned the Allies that the French Forces of the Interior would take orders only from "the French Command, in accordance with the inter-allied plan of operations." He did not admit that the French command had been told very little about Allied plans, but he added that France had "the right to have a deliberative voice in the policies and strategy" of the Allies. A large section of his speech then made a bid for the wavering support of the left; he spoke of the necessities of purge; of supply, currency, and wage problems; of labor policies; of the future Constituent Assembly; and of the important part to be played by members of the Consultative Assembly. He made a direct appeal to the Communists. "The Government," he affirmed, "wishes to associate in its action and even in its membership men of all—I repeat, of all—origins and all tendencies."

If De Gaulle was precise in his invitation to Communists to join the FCNL, he made it also clear to the United States and particularly to Great Britain that he was not reorienting his policy for the time being in the direction of Moscow but, quite to the contrary, that he saw the possibility of a "Western bloc" which was shrewdly calculated to interest

[30] The "Organization of Public Powers in France after the Liberation" was adopted by the Assembly on 27 Mar., and put into the form of an ordinance by the FCNL on 21 Apr. 1944. In accordance with this plan, the FCNL would surrender its powers when elections had taken place in two-thirds of the departments and the Consultative Assembly had been enlarged into a Representative Assembly. Actually, two-thirds of France, including Paris, was liberated before the Assembly was able to return, and the Assembly had to be enlarged, long before elections could take place, by special ordinance.

the British Prime Minister. Then, having held out his hands to Communists and to the Allies, De Gaulle left no doubt in the minds of either that the FCNL was determined to control French administration after liberation. In decisive language he pointed out that "there cannot be any other public authority than that which proceeds from the responsible central power. Any attempt to maintain the Vichy organism, even partial or camouflaged, as well as any artificial formation of powers outside of the Government [e.g., AMGOT], would be intolerable and condemned beforehand." De Gaulle concluded with a final appeal for co-operation from the Allies. It was reported that his address was a bitter and despondent entreaty to Great Britain and the United States to reflect on the consequences of by-passing the French Committee of National Liberation before it was too late.

De Gaulle had made his bid. He received an immediate reply from François Billoux, one of the twenty-seven Communist deputies who had been released from prison by General Giraud in February, 1943. The Communists were prepared to resume discussions on the means whereby they would obtain seats in the French Committee. Moscow expressed immediate interest in General de Gaulle's speech. For a reply from Washington and London, De Gaulle was prepared to wait some time longer—but again, how long?

Meanwhile, the world wondered why the Allies and the French Committee of National Liberation had muddled their way to such an aggravating impasse. An editorial in the London *Daily Herald* on March 29 expressed with cogency what the world was thinking:

> Cannot the President realize, says the plain man, that it is not for him to decide from the White House how arrangements shall be made for the administration of freed France?
>
> Cannot General de Gaulle realize that it is not purely a matter for the Committee in Algiers?
>
> Why, above all, has this crucial question not been decided long since in sensible, businesslike talks?
>
> Why should it have been left to angry altercation at the eleventh hour?
>
> Why should French Notes go unanswered for six months?
>
> There is no end to the "whys."

The plain fact, the alarming fact, is that the machinery of political co-operation between the Allies is working badly.

Diplomacy is using bullock carts in the age of aeroplanes.

By this time the Normandy invasion was only two months distant. There were enormous and pressing problems that had to be resolved by both the French and the Allies. De Gaulle could ill afford to wait, and by the first of April events would have forced his decision.

De Gaulle's Reaction to Anglo-American Policy

No encouraging response to De Gaulle's speech of March 18 was received in Algiers from Washington or London. If Churchill or the Foreign Office were intrigued by De Gaulle's offer of participation in a "Western bloc," they made no sign. The Prime Minister, preoccupied with the Normandy embarkation, was undoubtedly disinclined to press French matters in the face of American hostility, when more important considerations demanded his attention. With a full-dress reappraisal of "Anvil" scheduled to take place on March 20, two days after De Gaulle's speech, Churchill must have realized that if he succeeded in getting "Anvil" postponed or canceled, he would be subjected to heavy recriminations on the part of the FCNL. In Churchill's judgment the immediate strategic exploitation of Mediterranean possibilities contained many more attractive elements than postwar blocs with France. An alliance with France could wait; an attack on Germany could not.

Nor were there encouraging signs from Washington that the United States had responded positively and sympathetically to De Gaulle's appeal of March 18. When, on March 20, President Roosevelt told correspondents about his draft directive for Eisenhower, which had been recently sent to Churchill, the French at Algiers could find no comfort in the President's comment that Eisenhower would be free to negotiate with any French agency he chose. Would Eisenhower be free to deal with Vichy? But on March 21 this was emphatically denied by the State Department. Then with whom? It would appear that the only remaining candidates must be General Giraud, as commander in chief, or the National Resistance Council in France. The logic of this situation impelled the Gaullists at Algiers to believe that they must not hesitate or delay in taking decisive steps to subordinate both the Communist-dominated NRC and the French command to the FCNL.

De Gaulle was troubled by the thought that another crisis was imminent and apparently unavoidable. During March the press reported that D'Astier, Bloch, and Mendès-France threatened to resign. The Communists, allying themselves with Giraud, attacked Commissioner of War Le Trocquer for attempting to subordinate the military to the civil authority. André Philip was attacked for his highhanded treatment of the Consultative Assembly, Massigli was criticized for his protection of the diplomatic corps, and De Menthon continued to be a target for vindictive leftists who claimed the purge was proceeding too slowly.

De Gaulle was not anxious to develop another dispute with Giraud, but the failure of the Allies to come forth with overtures, coupled with the impossible situation provided by the split in French intelligence services at the very moment that SHAEF established its Special Force Headquarters, proved that a decision could not much longer be postponed. As a result of information that Giraudist agents were working at counter-purposes to those of the Gaullists, Jacques Soustelle exerted constant pressure on De Gaulle to take a position in regard to Giraud's intelligence agencies. Also in March, SHAEF sent its first intelligence mission, under Lieutenant Colonel Dick White, to Algiers to start planning military security measures to be taken during the Normandy landing operations. Since White was most interested in working with Paillole, who headed the French Army's counterespionage and military security section, Soustelle was thoroughly disconcerted to note that SHAEF's first overtures seemed to reveal interest in Giraudist rather than Gaullist networks.

By the end of March, De Gaulle had finally made up his mind to embark on a firm and independent course. He gave Soustelle assurance that he would shortly insist on Giraud's permitting the subordination of his services to the new centralized intelligence agency, DGSS (*Direction Générale des Services Spéciaux*), of which Soustelle had been director since November. Following this decision, a number of moves led to a new political orientation. Some hint of De Gaulle's intensified antipathy to the Allies was remarked by observers on March 27, when, during the final debate on methods of re-establishing a republican government in France, he stated:

> Several times there has been mention of the importance which the position taken by the Assembly or by the Government could have abroad. In this regard, the Government, certain however of sharing your views, asks you not to take into consideration anything except that which springs from the national will, and that is all. . . . France has no need, in deciding the way in which she will reestablish her own liberty, to consult opinions which come from beyond her frontiers. And, in regard to the Provisional Government of the Republic, which, since June, 1940, has not ceased to take a firm stand in the field of democracy as well as in that of war, it does not heed, I assure you, any lesson which does not come from the French nation which moveover it alone is qualified to lead.

Although De Gaulle had frequently spoken of the FCNL as the "government," this was the first occasion he referred to it publicly as the Provisional government in France, thus revealing that he himself looked for support not among the Allies but among the French. On April 1 the plan for civil administration after liberation, signed on March 14 but kept secret until then, was published in the *Journal Officiel,* and the appointments of Le Trocquer as civil delegate and General Koenig as military delegate were announced. The designation of Koenig, a Gaullist general of great prestige, to replace General François d'Astier revealed De Gaulle's determination to intensify his representation at SHAEF in the hopes of arranging a military, if not a political, understanding before D–Day.

The first three days of April found the FCNL in full crisis. Another pronouncement by the Combined Chiefs of Staff that they would not accept the right of the Committee to appeal at the government level on military matters prompted the Committee, on April 4, to insist once more that in regard to the use of French troops they must retain the right of discussion with the British and American governments. On the same day a new ordinance was promulgated which designated De Gaulle as chief of the armies. The new decree obviously placed the basic authority which General Giraud still possessed in De Gaulle's hands or in the hands of General Béthouart, who was soon appointed chief of the General Staff of National Defense. Had there been an opportunity for Giraud to exercise an active military command in connection with "Anvil," an outlet for his energies could have been found; but since the designation of General Patch as commander of all American, British, and French landing forces, there was no possibility of his assuming a military command commensurate with his rank. To replace Juin or De Lattre would have constituted a demotion. The only activity left for Giraud included the essentially staff functions of administration, co-ordination, and supply, for which the General had consistently demonstrated his lack of interest and ability. The problem of the intelligence services had finally forced De Gaulle to take command of all French armies, and he now consented to raise with the Committee the prospect of using his authority to transfer Giraud to another command.

On April 4, De Gaulle broadcast from Algiers an unprecedented assertion of his authority and an appeal to the French people to recognize no other authority than that of the FCNL:

> The direction of the French people in the war rests with the Provisional Government of the French Republic and with it alone. This Government, which I have the honor to direct and which has its seat on French soil, at Algiers, until it can establish its seat at Paris, is responsible for its acts before the national sovereignty as soon as this can be expressed. It has the exclusive sovereignty as soon as this can be expressed. It has the exclusive responsibility to speak in the name of the country. . . .
>
> National unity requires that all Frenchmen follow their Government. Wherever they may be and no matter what happens, Frenchmen have no orders to receive except from it once the enemy's restrictions are no longer exercised over them. No authority is valid unless it acts in the Government's name. No French effort in the war can count for France unless accomplished under its authority.

These words represented the most extreme and defiant claim that De Gaulle had yet made for authority in France in the face of Allied non-recognition and Communist opposition. It was not until May 12, however, that the Consultative Assembly voted to recognize the FCNL as the French Provisional government.

The next step was to regulate the Giraud question. De Gaulle realized that Giraud, who was now in consultation with General Juin, Duff Cooper, and Selden Chapin, the American chargé d'affaires, was prepared to resign in case his authority as commander in chief was threatened, and for four days De Gaulle debated whether or not to make the move; but on April 8 he finally decided to appoint Giraud to the honorific post of inspector general of the armies.

The crisis which De Gaulle had hoped to avert now quickly developed. Giraud refused to accept the new post and refused to resign. For several more days, while arguments raged within the Committee, Giraud sought allies who would be willing to stand by him, both in the FCNL and out. Robert Murphy, now on the Italian Advisory Commission, made an "indignant verbal protest," but his position was by no means as influential as it had previously been; and although many Americans undoubtedly felt personally sorry for the indomitable old General, no official voice in Washington was raised in Giraud's defense. The President may have been disturbed at De Gaulle's final move, but he took no steps to interfere. It should be remarked that with a British general at Allied headquarters and with no representation other than a chargé d'affaires at Algiers, it would have been difficult for the President to intervene even if he had wished to. Furthermore, exhausted from overwork and illness, Roosevelt had left Washington on April 8 for South Carolina, where for over three weeks he kept himself relatively isolated from political entanglements. Events had by-passed General Giraud, and he was now incapable of doing more than providing pathetic evidence of the fate, so eloquently invoked several years later by General MacArthur, of old soldiers.

On April 12, Béthouart's appointment was confirmed, and two days later appeared the decree which finally and officially placed Giraud on the reserve list and deprived him of his command. Soon afterward, his hopes of leading a victorious French Army shattered, he retired to a small Algerian town near Mostaganem, where he nursed his bitterness at the fate which had brought him so close to great achievements and had then so shabbily abandoned him.[31]

Compared with the crises of June and November, 1943, the crisis of

[31] Four months later, on 28 Aug. 1944, Giraud was wounded by a Moslem soldier in an attempt on his life. Although there were rumors that this had been engineered by

April, 1944, passed with relatively minor repercussions among the Allies. In Algiers forty members of the Consultative Assembly, mostly Communists and delegates from the Resistance, protested against the Giraud dismissal as "ill-timed, maladroit, and not calculated to increase General de Gaulle's prestige," but on the whole there were more protests against the civil administration plan than against Giraud's dismissal.

---

officials in Diethelm's department (Leahy, *I Was There*, 257), no proof was found to show that this was other than an isolated attack. Giraud did not return to France until Oct., 1944, long after De Gaulle had marched triumphantly down the Champs Élysées. Giraud was later given an administrative command in northern France. He died in 1949.

▶ 6. The Liberation of France

Allied Policy before D-Day

AT THE TIME of Giraud's forced resignation, British and American negotiations with regard to the FCNL had come almost to a standstill. Churchill had not rejected Roosevelt's draft directive of March 15, but during the weeks that the Committee crisis unrolled in Algiers he had taken no action on it. Meanwhile, several important military decisions, which would bear directly on aspects of French policy, were being made. These decisions related to the imminent invasion of France and to contacts with the French underground.

On March 20, after various aspects of "Overlord" and "Anvil" had been examined, Allied commanders reached the conclusion that it would be impractical to land in southern France at the same time as in Normandy. It had been hoped that by this time the Italian campaign would have been attained in March. Furthermore, additional aid to the Resistance authorized by Churchill in January had not significantly relieved German pressure in Italy, and there seemed little prospect in the immediate future of operations in the Po Valley which would open the way to Austria. Although Churchill was unsuccessful in persuading the Combined Chiefs of Staff to relinquish "Anvil," he contrived to have the operation postponed, and even a month later no specific date for the invasion of southern France had been established.

It is not unlikely that the postponement of "Anvil" and the failure of the Resistance to divert German divisions from Italy somewhat cooled Churchill's enthusiasm for additional sorties into the Midi. But other considerations also made him reluctant at this time to emphasize a Resistance aid program. First of all, in spite of Churchill's deprecation of the extent of British assistance, reports reached Washington in February from the OSS that British planes were parachuting ten times more equipment to the underground than were the Americans; and De Gaulle had made some allusions to the mediocrity of American aid as compared to British. Secretary Hull, always sensitive about Anglo-Gaullism, became particularly outraged when he learned of a report from North Africa that the United States was opposing aid for political reasons. The Joint Chiefs of Staff wrote Eisenhower on this matter on March 17, and Hull sent a note to Admiral Leahy about it three days later, the same day that "Anvil" was subjected to reconsideration. These American protests, on reaching Churchill, must have given the Prime Minister pause concerning the advisability of continuing a policy which could have unfavorable repercussions in the White House.

Another significant move relating to the Resistance was made on March 23, when SHAEF assumed control of all secret-service and intelligence activity in connection with the Normandy landings. This meant that Eisenhower now controlled "general direction and planning, instruction as to target priorities, reduction or increase of activities to conform to SHAEF plans, and directions as to the effort to be expended on various activities." Under the Allied Commander's general supervision, therefore, came the combined Anglo-American Special Force Headquarters (SFHQ), formed by the unification of the British SOE (Special Operations Executive) and the American SO (Special Operations). Churchill apparently made no objection to turning over to SHAEF the far-flung British connections with the French underground, probably because he saw no further strategic advantage in controlling it, because he wished to avoid altercations with Washington, or because he believed that "Overlord's" success would be better assured by placing operations under military command. Whatever the Prime Minister's motives, the transfer of authority to SHAEF had serious consequences for the French. It meant that although the British sorties for April were already scheduled, further parachuting to the Resistance would have to be worked out not with the British but with SHAEF's G–3 section under Major General H. R. Bull and that decisions on future sorties would be based predominantly on military rather than political considerations. The transfer also raised an interesting point: since SHAEF had not yet been authorized to deal with the FCNL, with which French agency would it now co-operate in connection with underground activities—with Jacques Soustelle, heading the predominantly Gaullist DGSS; with Emmanuel d'Astier, heading the Commissariat of the Interior under which DGSS technically belonged; with the Military Delegate of the FCNL in London; with General Giraud, as commander in chief of the French armies, and with the regular French Army SR and CE chiefs, still not entirely subordinated to DGSS; or directly with Resistance groups in France? It could hardly be expected that Eisenhower personally would comprehend all the nuances of the French situation, nor could he anticipate how his relations with various French agencies would be interpreted at Algiers, London, and Washington.

Eisenhower was understandably confused. He consulted with the Prime Minister in London and told him that in spite of stories current in the press, he had received no official directive regarding his future relations with the French. Churchill admitted that he also knew of no such directive, although, of course, he had received the President's draft, with which he told Eisenhower he concurred. Churchill probably hoped, meanwhile, that the Combined Chiefs of Staff would agree to deal with the FNCL at government level, in which case direct contacts through the Foreign Office would supersede military liaison via SHAEF and SFHQ at Algiers. When Emmanuel d'Astier saw Churchill on April 2, he received the impression that the Prime Minister was favorably disposed toward the Committee and had recovered from his grievances about the purge. D'Astier wrote De Gaulle:

> When I was about to leave, he repeated to me insistently: "It is indispensable that General de Gaulle come here." I have the impression that the Prime Minister would like to have French support and that he sincerely regrets not having complete liberty of action in his foreign policy.[1]

Two decisions in April greatly reduced the capacity of the British to bring about an improvement of relations with Algiers. On April 1 the Combined Chiefs of Staff agreed that no information should be

[1] D'Astier, *Les dieux et les hommes,* 120–21.

released to the French which might compromise "Overlord," and two weeks later, on April 17, the British government itself placed a restriction on all communications coming from or to Great Britain. The practical effect of this ban was to cut off the transmission of messages in French code from Algiers to General Koenig and to Manuel, chief of the London branch of DGSS: the *Bureau de Renseignements et d'Action de Londres* (BRAL). It was ironic that after De Gaulle had taken the drastic step which theoretically gave Soustelle undisputed control of French intelligence services, the head of DGSS could not effectively control contacts with the Resistance via London because of the communications restriction.

If Churchill and the British government were content to advance cautiously on the French question, Washington also moved two steps forward and one step back. Secretary of State Hull, always sensitive about French matters, nettled by hints that the United States planned to deal with Vichy, was not satisfied that his denial, made on March 21, was strong enough to quiet critics who insinuated that American policy was improvised from day to day. Considering the fact that he had acquiesced to an about-face in his antagonism to De Gaulle's Committee and that the President's note of March 15 did in fact purport to grant Eisenhower wide powers, Hull determined to make a speech which would constitute a major clarification of the American position.

On April 7, the day before he left Washington for a rest, President Roosevelt admitted that he had conferred with Hull about his speech, scheduled for delivery two days later, and had seen part of it. One of the correspondents at his press conference asked the President if he had any statement to make about the French situation. "No," answered the President, "I don't think there is anything about the French situation that is not pretty much common property. On the other side they know a lot about it."

A correspondent ventured that not very much was known here. The President went on to elaborate: "We know everything they do. It all comes down to the question as to what is self-determination." He said he could write a good many columns on what is self-determination. "How do we know how the people of France feel?" The President said he did not know and that nobody knew. He did not think anyone in his office had been in France lately, and if they had, could they have gotten around or would they just have been in one place? "Would you," he concluded, "let that determination be made by people who are not in France? That is difficult, isn't it?"

The general tenor of his remarks did not suggest to his listeners that he was any more inclined to recognize or to help De Gaulle than he had ever been or that any change in policy was anticipated. For this reason Hull's speech, which seemed to pronounce an altered policy, was the more surprising. Either the President had not read the speech with much care or the Secretary of State was misinformed about Roosevelt's real views. When Hull delivered his statements on April 9, he formulated a number of ideas that derived from drafts discussed in Washington the previous January but which, as a result of the President's opposition, had never become public. The significant section of Hull's speech was the following:

> We have no purpose or wish to govern France or to administer any affairs save those which are necessary for military operations against the enemy. It is of the utmost importance that civil authority in France should be exercised by Frenchmen, should be swiftly established, and should operate in accordance with advanced planning as fully as military operations will permit. . . .
>
> The President and I are clear, therefore, as to the need, from the outset, of French civil administration—and democratic French administration—in France. We are disposed to see the French Committee of National Liberation exercise leadership to establish law and order under the supervision of the Allied Commander-in-Chief. The Committee has given public assurance that it does not propose to perpetuate its authority. On the contrary, it has given assurance that it wishes at the earliest possible date to have the French people exercise their own sovereign will in accordance with French constitutional processes. The Committee is, of course, not the government of France and we cannot recognize it as such. In accordance with this understanding of mutual purposes the Committee will have every opportunity to undertake civil administration and our co-operation and help in every practicable way in making it successful.

Hull's statement went a long way in the direction of providing a *de facto* recognition of the French Committee, and it was immediately hailed as a desirable and long-delayed step.

In London the statement was received with astonished but pleased interest. The tenor of the Secretary's remarks seemed to revive the conclusions reached several months previously, and the Foreign Office could not help but conclude that the United States must have revised its policy between March 15 and April 9. At the time of Hull's speech, the new undersecretary of state, Edward Stettinius, was in London on a mission which returned the courtesy visit of Eden to the United States the previous March. Stettinius found that Churchill had still taken no action on Roosevelt's draft directive, but, encouraged by the tone of Hull's remarks, the Prime Minister expressed hope that the President might now be willing to concede that Eisenhower should deal exclusively with the FCNL. Churchill also wrote De Gaulle in an attempt to persuade him that a visit to Roosevelt might bring about a new orientation on the part of the President.[2]

It was not until April 15 that Hull learned how adamant Roosevelt could be on the subject of nonrecognition and how stubbornly the President would refuse to alter the draft directive's *may* to the word *should*. With the Normandy landings six weeks away, in spite of the continual and earnest persuasion of Churchill, Ambassador Wilson (who had still not returned to Algiers), and McCloy, the President would not give in. It is not unlikely that De Gaulle's move in eliminating Giraud was having its negative effect on Roosevelt, who, apparently not fully appreciating the content of Hull's declaration, now began to entertain more favorable views toward the War Department thesis of a military approach to French administration.[3]

A question parallel to the one involving SHAEF's authority to negotiate with the FCNL was that concerned with Allied authority over French forces to be used in "Overlord" and "Anvil," a topic that had been the subject of exchanges between the Committee and the Combined Chiefs since January. Negotiations seemed to be deadlocked by the FCNL's insistence that they discuss disposition of French troops

[2] Hull, *Memoirs*, II, 1429–30; De Gaulle, *Mémoires*, II, 219, 624–26.

[3] Roosevelt to Hull, 15 Apr. 1944, State Dept., 851.01/3711; Leahy, *I Was There*, 236. The President also approved granting General Giraud asylum in the United States in case he cared to come.

at governmental level, an arrangement which would, in a sense, provide the Committee with a say in decisions of high strategy. On this point Roosevelt was emphatic, writing Marshall on April 28:

> It is my desire at the present time that the military questions which involve the French forces be handled directly between the Allied Commander-in-Chief and French military authorities and not as one sovereign government in full possession of its sovereignty and another government which has no *de facto* sovereignty.[4]

With Giraud now out of the picture, it would seem that such an arrangement could not have been entirely unsatisfactory to the French. General de Gaulle was now chief of the armies; General Béthouart chief of staff to the Defense Council; General Koenig military delegate in London; General Juin in command of the expeditionary force in Italy; and General de Lattre, since April 18, designated to command the French forces to be used in "Anvil." Arrangements were also being made for General Leclerc's armored division to be transported to Yorkshire with a view toward including it in "Overlord." In spite of the fact that all French forces clearly recognized the FCNL's authority, the Committee continued to insist on the right of appeal at governmental level, with the result that no agreement had been reached on command relationships by D–Day.

Churchill and Eden persisted in hoping, against overwhelming evidence, that Hull's speech represented the American view more accurately than the President's directive. The Prime Minister could not forget the invasion of North Africa, when Eisenhower, lacking adequate instructions, had negotiated with Darlan. Churchill had brushed off some of the acute and embarrassing criticism which followed by pointing out that since the "Torch" expedition had been essentially American, he did not wish to run counter to the President's policy. But the Prime Minister could find no such escape from the problems surrounding D–Day, where it was clear that with SHAEF's staff as much British as American, the expedition against Normandy would be a combined one. Churchill could not place his signature on a directive which granted

[4] Pogue, *Supreme Command*, 151.

authority of political decisions to a military commander, particularly when that commander, being an American, was peculiarly susceptible to influence from the President and the American Chiefs of Staff. Churchill was only too aware of the pressures that had been exerted against Eisenhower when the Supreme Commander had shown evidence of sympathy with the British position on "Anvil," and he had no illusions about his ability to bring the President into sympathy with British policy toward France.

On May 3, when the Foreign Minister was asked in the House of Commons whether an agreement had been reached with the FCNL, he replied:

> I am happy to take this opportunity to emphasize that His Majesty's Government are in full agreement with the statement, made by the United States Secretary of State on the ninth April in regard to the administration of liberated France. In accordance with this, conversations are now in progress between the Supreme Allied Commander and the French Military Mission in this country under General Koenig, with a view to working out detailed arrangements.

When he was asked whether his statement meant that "the authority with which we deal in liberated France will be the French Committee of Liberation," Eden replied:

> Yes, Sir. Incidentally, I do not know of any other authority except Vichy, and, of course, we have no intention of dealing with them, in any circumstances whatever. [Cheers] It will be for the French Nation in due course, as has been repeatedly declared by leaders of the French Committee of National Liberation, to make their own choice of government.

When Hull learned of Eden's remarks, he assumed that the British were trying to twist something out of his statement which the facts, emphasized by the President's stubborn refusal to change his mind, did not justify. He as much as told the British ambassador, Lord Halifax, that it was dangerous to place hopes in outdated remarks in the face of clear evidence that the President's views did not coincide with those of his Secretary of State.[5]

244

With D–Day now one month distant, it appeared that neither London nor Washington could find a way out of the impasse. Eisenhower remained without instructions, and the French at Algiers remained sullen and confused by the Anglo-American stalemate.

French Policy Prior to the Normandy Landings

On April 17, the same day that the British communications ban was imposed, General Koenig started informal discussions with Eisenhower's deputy, General Smith. The restriction, placed in effect as a security measure in view of the coming operation, required that all foreign powers except the major Allies could no longer transmit secret messages by code or diplomatic pouch. Messages of a military nature continued to flow between Algiers and London via British code, but De Gaulle refused to send political dispatches in that manner. When, during his press conference of April 21, he was asked about the significance of recent conversations between Churchill, Eden, and Pierre Viénot, the FCNL representative in London, De Gaulle replied: "I regret to say that because of the state of Inter-Allied communications at the present stage of the war, the French Government learned only through the newspapers that its Ambassador in London had the honor of being received by the Prime Minister and the Minister of Foreign Affairs of Great Britain."

Eisenhower's position in opening negotiations with General Koenig was delicate in the extreme. He had determined to commence the conversations on the strength of Churchill's encouragement that differences on the directive would be resolved, and he undoubtedly received assurances from Stettinius and from Assistant Secretary of War McCloy, who was also in London at the time, that military arrangements ought to be made with the French Mission. Koenig was prepared to go ahead, and on April 19 he prepared an *aide-mémoire,* which Eisenhower agreed to forward to the Combined Chiefs, covering the basic areas for discussion. On the military side, Koenig hoped that Eisenhower would take him into full confidence regarding plans for the employment of French forces in operations in France well in advance of their being

[5] Hull, *Memoirs,* II, 1431. See also De Gaulle, *Mémoires,* II, 639.

committed to those operations. On the civil side, it was hoped that agreement could be reached on the provision of goods and services, civilian labor, treatment of banks and security exchanges, transfer of property, custody of enemy property and that of the United Nations, matters of public safety, public health, distribution of civilian supplies, and displaced persons.

It should be remarked at once that the list of subjects for treatment avoided the most pressing problems: command relationships in regard to the use of French forces, interior and exterior; co-operation with the underground; establishment of civil administration; the question of extraterritorial rights and martial law; methods of requisition; and the issue of emergency currency—all questions of the utmost importance which could hardly be resolved in a month. In spite of the obvious difficulties, discussions proceeded smoothly and effectively. If there was disagreement about the role to be played by the FCNL at high political levels, among the lower echelons at SHAEF there was sincere co-operation among British, American, and French officers. Early in April, Colonel de Boislambert, who had accompanied De Gaulle to the Casablanca Conference, came to England to train over one hundred French liaison officers who were to provide for co-operation between the Allies and the FCNL delegates in liberated areas on matters pertaining to administration.

Formal discussions began in London on April 25 between Koenig and General A. E. Grasett, chief of SHAEF's European Allied Contact Section, together with General F. E. Morgan, Eisenhower's deputy chief of staff. Two days later prospects looked so encouraging that André le Trocquer, the prospective civil delegate, announced in Algiers that he would soon leave for London. But within a few days De Gaulle once more became completely disillusioned about the possibilities of continuing to negotiate with the Allies, for by the end of April the bright hopes fired by Hull's remarks on April 9 had been extinguished by the President's refusal to abandon his original position. At the same time, two of De Gaulle's emissaries, André Philip and Emmanuel d'Astier, were subjected to novel indignities by the Allies.

On April 27 the British government placed a restriction on civilian departures from the British Isles. Philip and D'Astier happened to be among the last who had been able to leave before the regulation went into effect, but they were forced to permit British authorities to examine their personal papers before they were allowed to board their plane. To De Gaulle the action representd a violation of diplomatic privilege—therefore an insult to French sovereignty—and he would apparently have preferred them to remain in London rather than submit to such an affront. The incident seems to have reduced De Gaulle to the final limits of despair. On May 6 he ordered Koenig to break off negotiations and announced that Le Trocquer's trip to London was indefinitely postponed.

On the following day, during a speech delivered in Tunis, De Gaulle gave voice to his pessimism, and at the close of his speech he hinted at a reorientation of French policy in a direction which was certain to catch Churchill's notice:

> In Europe, which remains the great source of human activity and wealth, the French wish, once the enemy is defeated, that there may be in the West a center of direct and practical co-operation and, in regard to the East, that is to say first of all in dear and powerful Russia, a permanent ally.

The reference to Russia was particularly significant in that a little over two weeks earlier, at his press conference, when asked specifically about a formal alliance with Russia, De Gaulle had replied noncommittally: "Of course we are linked with the USSR, although there exists no formal treaty between us." He had also engaged in a long conversation with Bogomolov on April 28. De Gaulle was foreshadowing a policy which would reach fruition seven months later when he flew to Moscow for direct negotiations with Stalin.

The breakdown between the French Committee and the Allies seemed to be so complete that in the opinion of Duff Cooper only a personal contact between De Gaulle and Allied authorities would be capable of breaking the deadlock. On May 8 he wired Churchill and Hull such a suggestion. On learning of Duff Cooper's communication, Eisenhower fell in with the proposal and three days later informed the Combined Chiefs of Staff that a potentially dangerous situation had developed which might be averted by informing Koenig of the date and place of "Overlord" and by inviting De Gaulle to London, where he could be informed about the invasion. On May 13, Roosevelt replied to Eisenhower's suggestion, stating that he had no objection, as long as De Gaulle did not return to Algiers until after the invasion had been launched. He then went on to say:

> I agree that you have full authority to discuss matters with the French Committee on a military level, since I am not able to recognize any government of France until the French people have an opportunity to make a free choice. The French are still in a state of shell-shock from their war experience, and we have no right to color their views or to give any group the sole right to impose one side of a case on them.[6]

On the same day that Roosevelt agreed to personal discussions between Eisenhower and De Gaulle, an innocent-looking announcement appeared in the press which prompted another explosion at Algiers. This item was a SHAEF communiqué, published in London, which announced that:

> General A. E. Grasett, of His Majesty's Army, has been appointed head of the civil department of General Eisenhower's staff. Two Americans are directly under his orders: General J. C. Holmes and General J. F. McSherry. The civil department's duties fall into two categories: (1) operations in the Allied countries of northern Europe (France, Belgium, Luxembourg, Denmark, Holland and Norway; (2) operations in occupied Germany.[7]

To the French at Algiers, lacking knowledge of any other plan to deal with civil administration, the announcement seemed to proclaim the long-feared Allied intention of introducing an AMGOT into France. Rumors abounded in Algiers that De Gaulle would resign. In Washington, John J. McCloy, acting as chairman of the Combined Civil Affairs Committee, attempted somewhat lamely to calm French appre-

---

[6] Adapted from Pogue, *Supreme Command,* 148.

[7] General Grasett had in fact headed G–5 (Civil Affairs) since 22 Apr. and had occupied himself in a reorganization which would make field commanders directly responsible for civil affairs' operations in their areas. Administration in France would come under Montgomery's Twenty-first Army Group (Pogue, *Supreme Command,* 82–83).

hensions on May 15 by pointing out, during a press conference, that civil government for France would be less strict than in Italy. He also permitted himself what the *New York Times* referred to as a "cautious hint" that there might be self-rule through the FCNL. "The Allies," McCloy said, "do not intend to apply military government as such to France and friendly countries." He added that there might be a military zone in France but that the "general tendency" would be against such rule. The French Committee did not find much to reassure them in these declarations, however.

If there had been any truth in the report that De Gaulle considered resigning, no outward evidence of his real intentions in that regard appeared. Meanwhile, from the floor of the Consultative Assembly, which, during the middle of May, was debating foreign policy, emerged some of the strongest statements so far recorded about France's intentions of fulfilling an independent and significant role in the postwar world. On May 12, Foreign Commissioner Massigli delivered a long speech which summarized the FCNL policy at that date. He praised the efforts of French negotiators, especially Jean Monnet, for the success of the complex conversations they were undertaking, but he regretted that discussions on civil administration and revision of the Clark-Darlan Agreement had broken down.

The most dramatic incident to take place during the foreign policy debates was reserved for the final day, May 15, when, in the course of remarks about Italy, Joseph Costa of the Tunisian Resistance expressed regrets that negotiations to modify the Clark-Darlan Agreements had failed. At this point General de Gaulle asked permission to take the floor. He began:

> I wish to say publicly that France does not consider herself at all bound by arrangements that were made a short time ago, by the Allied military authorities on one hand, and Darlan on the other. Furthermore, time has marched on and many *de facto* changes—for it was a case of *de facto* situation—were brought about in the workings of what I still hear called, I do not know why, the Clark-Darlan 'Agreements.'

This was a unilateral declaration of independence which went farther than De Gaulle had yet gone in his relationship with the Allies. It marked his feeling of complete hopelessness that satisfactory arrangements would be reached between the FCNL and the Allied governments. It was not likely, on the eve of the Normandy invasion, that the United States or Great Britain would impose an occupation on North Africa, particularly since its strategic importance as a base was considerably diminished from what it had been a few months previously; but the French action, which went into effect two weeks later, nevertheless imposed the same effect as a sit-down strike in regard to civil administration. De Gaulle's decision did not apply to military operations, but it meant that the French sat no longer in joint committees and that they ceased co-operating with Allied authorities. Lack of co-operation continued until July, when relations with the Allies improved as a result of De Gaulle's visit to Washington.

The Consultative Assembly now went even further. Cheering enthusiastically at the announcement of Juin's successes in Italy, they took the step at which De Gaulle had hinted for several months. Albert Gazier put forth the following motion: "The Provisional Consultative Assembly expresses the hope that the French Committee of National Liberation will officially assume the name: Provisional Government of the French Republic." The Assembly gave Gazier's motion an eager reception and unanimously voted it into effect. Two weeks later, on June 2, the FCNL officially adopted the resolution. While the new title brought about little change in day-to-day activities, it considerably altered the Committee's approach to the Allies and, indeed, to the National Resistance Council. It meant that the Committee would now have to insist even more vigorously that settlements be arranged at governmental level and that recognition as a *"de facto* authority" which had been requested previously would not be sufficient. It placed Roosevelt in a most difficult position. After refusing for a year to recognize the FCNL as the sole representative of French interests because he was not convinced that it represented the French people, he was now asked to recognize it as a government. If he were to remain consistent with his earlier position, he would logically have to insist more strongly than ever that elections be held before he could commit the United States. Since the French people would be unable to go to the polls for months after liberation, the FCNL's action, which incidentally violated its own

ordinance on the restoration of public powers, automatically made
American *de jure* recognition impossible unless the President would
completely and drastically reverse himself.

Arrangements for D–Day

In spite of the difficulties produced by the Assembly's motion of
May 15, the idea that De Gaulle should go to London for D–Day moved
from the realm of suggestion to the more solid area of possibility. On
May 22, Duff Cooper received a wire authorizing him to tell De Gaulle
that he was going to be invited to London at some unspecified date.

Before describing the circumstances under which De Gaulle returned to London, it is necessary to comment on certain aspects of the
preparations connected with the Normandy landings. Of the many arrangements on which no agreement with the FCNL had been reached,
one of the most pressing was an understanding on invasion currency.
It was generally agreed that the Allies would need millions of francs
to launch the invasion, but it was not equally agreed upon the source
of these francs—whether they should come from *Banque de France*
resources held in the United States, from authorization by the FCNL,
or from Allied printing presses. If from the latter, there would be need
for guaranteeing the currency to prevent it from inflicting a spiraling
inflation on the French people; if from the former sources, some prior
agreement with the Committee would have to be reached. The problem
had been anticipated as far back as December, 1943, at the time of
Eisenhower's appointment as supreme commander, but it had not been
solved because of the failure to recognize the FCNL. During January
and February, 1944, negotiations were suspended pending a White
House pronouncement on the Committee's status, but since a decision
was postponed from week to week, so was action on the currency problem. Early in May the question was reborn of necessity, and while
Eisenhower desperately sought a declaration of policy from the Combined Chiefs of Staff, Pierre Mendès-France, finance commissioner on
the FCNL, hurried to Washington to try to settle technical arrangements in connection with monetary problems. His discussions with
State, War, and Treasury Department officials resulted in a new ex-

change rate—49.627 francs to the dollar—but lacking powers recognized by the United States to settle political matters, Mendès-France was unable to reach a firm understanding on the question of financial control during the invasion.

Meanwhile, the notes, coins, and stamps, valued at more than 5,500,000,000 francs, had been prepared and made available to SHAEF; but as late as May 25, Eisenhower had received no authorization concerning their use. He feared, quite reasonably, that if he placed the francs in circulation by proclamation, his action would be considered a flagrant violation of French sovereignty. This action was nevertheless the one which he was required to take, for a monetary policy statement, approved at "the highest American level" and transmitted on May 26, asserted that the "authority for issuing supplemental francs belonged to SHAEF and that any statement by the FCNL would merely be a supporting announcement."

Although Mendès-France did not return immediately to Algiers, De Gaulle soon learned of Allied intentions to issue their own francs. On May 27, Duff Cooper found him "as grumpy and sulky as usual" and far less disposed to come to London than he had been a few days earlier.

Equally troublesome were the negotiations on civil administration and the use of French troops, which since the middle of May had come to a standstill. Since no exterior French troops would be used in the initial stages of "Overlord," the lack of a decision on their employment was not as serious as disagreements over civil affairs. With an improvement in communications between London and Algiers permitted around May 20, there seemed hope in Koenig's headquarters that some meaningful accords might still be reached. Actually, planning and training at the lower levels had continued without interruption in anticipation of a last-minute political agreement which would enable Boislambert's 180 administrative liaison officers to be employed.

On the essentially military level, where Eisenhower believed himself to be on firmer ground, definite arrangements did develop before D–Day. In order to use interior forces most effectively, Koenig wished to concentrate SHAEF agencies that dealt with France, principally the French sections of Special Force Headquarters, within a centralized command for all French Forces of the Interior. Such an arrangement would have given Koenig (and, by implication, De Gaulle) command over British Intelligence, Psychological Warfare, OSS, and other British-American agencies; it would have terminated the long-standing SOE–BCRA rivalry; it would have brought Paillole's quasi autonomous military security agents more firmly under Colonel Passy; and it would have ended the rival claims of the Communist-dominated COMAC in France to military authority over the FFI. On June 2, Eisenhower agreed that Koenig should have command over the FFI, and he agreed to the establishment of an Anglo–French–American staff under Colonel Vernon (Jean Ziegler), but he refused to relinquish control of SFHQ to the French. Firm and satisfactory arrangements over details were still to be negotiated during the next few weeks, but the basic decision on Koenig's command was made before D–Day.

A definite arrangement on counterespionage was also made between SHAEF's G–2 section and the French Service of Military Security under Paillole and Bonnefour. Since French security agents were already operating at Rennes and Angers, it had been essential that such an agreement be reached before D–Day if immediate use of their information was to be made. Authorization was granted by SHAEF that in certain instances arrests of collaborationists, suspected spies, and members of the PPF and *milice française* could be effected by French security officers. It is not without significance that authority to identify collaborationists was thus given by Eisenhower to a non-Gaullist organization.[8]

D–Day: De Gaulle Goes to London

In spite of De Gaulle's peevishness over the currency matter, there remained in his mind a remote hope that if he should go to London, he would be able to consult at a high level with representatives of the British and American governments. For this reason, while planning on the staff to accompany him, he thought not only in terms of military advisers, such as Béthouart and Billotte, but of Massigli to cope with

[8] "Résumé de l'action des services de contre-espionnage," 73–74; "Technical Instructions on the Co-operation between the CE Forces of the Allied Expeditionary Forces and the SSM," drawn up about 1 June 1944, signed 7 June 1944, by Col. H. G. Sheen, head of CE section, G–2, SHAEF, and Cdt. Paillole, head of SSM.

foreign affairs, Le Trocquer to take over his responsibilities as civil delegate, of an economist—Mendès-France or Hervé Alphand—to arrange the currency matter, and for contacts with the underground, D'Astier or Soustelle. But on May 29 statements appeared in the press to the effect that Roosevelt refused to permit an American to participate in talks with the Gaullists. De Gaulle began to wonder what benefit his trip to London would have if he could not discuss outstanding political differences between himself and Washington. Duff Cooper did his utmost to encourage De Gaulle that under British pressure Roosevelt might relent, but De Gaulle nevertheless persisted, not without reason, in his belief that the voyage would be pointless.

It was true that Roosevelt did not want to authorize Winant or Eisenhower to embark on political discussions with De Gaulle, but, on the other hand, he had no objection to meeting De Gaulle himself. This was learned unexpectedly by the head of the French Naval Mission in Washington, Admiral Fenard, during a conversation with the President around May 24. Fenard had learned that American personnel were being trained near Washington to provide military government teams for France after liberation. Deploring the possibility of an AMGOT for France, he sought an interview with the President to persuade him that such measures were unnecessary. In the course of their conversation, Fenard found to his surprise that Roosevelt not only entertained no basic aversion toward talking things over with De Gaulle but felt that the British consistently placed impediments in the way of a Franco-American *rapprochement*. Roosevelt explained that he could not *invite* De Gaulle to Washington as head of a state, but that any time De Gaulle wished to come, he would make arrangements to see him. The President's attitude appeared so favorable to Fenard, and so different from what he expected, that the Admiral made immediate arrangements to go to Algiers, where he arrived on May 28. When he finally relayed his message to De Gaulle, he had to repeat it twice to permit its import to be fully appreciated. However, on the eve of receiving word from London about the possibility of his voyage there, De Gaulle could not well plan on a trip to Washington when his place, as head of the FCNL, was near France. He had not yet decided whether to go to London, but if he left Algiers at all, it would have to be for England rather than America.[9]

On June 1, Duff Cooper learned from London that two planes were being sent to Algiers for De Gaulle's use and that the trip should be made as soon as possible. There was, however, no definite assurance on three points that had major importance to De Gaulle: that he be permitted uninterrupted communication facilities, that the currency question be regulated, and that an American representative be available for discussions. Duff Cooper delayed delivery of the invitation for a day to obtain an assurance that De Gaulle could return to Algiers if the United States was not to be represented at the discussions, and on the following day he received a telegram from Churchill containing an urgent appeal for De Gaulle to come. But the Prime Minister could not have been sanguine about the possibility of American participation. He had just received the following message from the President, sent on May 31:

> I would like to make the matter of de Gaulle clear beyond peradventure of doubt.
>
> It has been suggested that de Gaulle visit Washington. I have told Fenard, who is on his way to see de Gaulle, that I have been hoping the General would send me a message asking if a visit would be welcome. If such a message were received, it would be answered in the affirmative immediately and cordially. I have explained to Fenard, as I think I have made clear to many people before, that I cannot well invite de Gaulle, who is not head of the French Government or the French State, but only the head of a committee.
>
> In general, we must of course do everything we possibly can to encourage French national spirit and to get it working immediately with us at top speed. What the state of this French spirit is, we do not definitely know and won't know until we get to France; but we hope for the best.
>
> Marshall will be in London about four days after D–Day, but we cannot give him plenary powers to negotiate with you and de Gaulle jointly, or with de Gaulle singly, since the matter is wholly in the political and not in the military field. I have no one to send who can represent me at the conversations with de Gaulle.[10]

[9] Details of this mission were told the writer by Admiral Fenard. See also De Gaulle, *Mémoires*, II, 222.

[10] Paraphrased from Hull, *Memoirs*, II, 1431–32.

It must be remarked that with authorization already given Eisenhower to go ahead with the issue of French currency, with Roosevelt's refusal to permit an American political representative to speak with De Gaulle, and with no possibility of reaching an agreement on civil affairs, De Gaulle had no reason for enthusiastic anticipation at the prospect of seeing London once more.

But in Algiers, De Gaulle was subjected to a constant barrage of persuasion from the British Ambassador and from members of the Committee. It took a personal assurance by Duff Cooper that De Gaulle would have complete liberty to communicate with Algiers, and a threat of resignation on the part of Massigli and others, before the General was persuaded to leave. On June 3, however, he departed for London in the plane which the British government had placed at his disposition.

On the same day that De Gaulle left for London the official announcement that the FCNL had assumed the title of Provisional government was made. Thereafter the BBC used the expression in its broadcasts, but American broadcasts, under the Division of Psychological Warfare, were not permitted to refer to the Committee in its self-designated terms. The announcement was peculiarly ill timed to persuade Roosevelt to alter his decision about permitting an American representative to talk with De Gaulle.

De Gaulle had, in any case, resolved to deal essentially with military and economic matters in London, and although he brought Alphand and Soustelle with him, his entourage did not include any other civilian advisers. Neither Massigli, Le Trocquer, nor D'Astier were able to leave Algiers at this time. All political representation in London was left in the hands of Pierre Viénot, the refined FCNL ambassador who was to die a month later.

It was not long after his arrival in England that De Gaulle's optimism was replaced by disillusionment: he was hampered in his communications with Algiers, he learned that invasion currency had already been issued to troops scheduled to disembark in Normandy, and his fears were confirmed that G–5 would handle civil affairs without consulting the FCNL. On the morning of June 4, De Gaulle saw both Churchill and Eisenhower. The Prime Minister was awaiting D–Day in a railway coach not far from Eisenhower's headquarters at Widewing and had

General George C. Marshall is saluted, Gallic fashion, by General de Gaulle, who has just bestowed the *Grande Croix* of the Legion of Honor on him at the French Embassy in Washington (August 24, 1945). Admiral William D. Leahy, whose face is barely visible over De Gaulle's shoulder, also received the decoration.

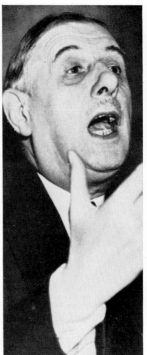

De Gaulle, the speaker, in four poses that span a decade: addressing an Armistice Day observance in Algiers in 1943; adjusting his glasses during a news conference in Paris in 1949; emphasizing a point during a speech before a group of newsmen in 1952; and making a radio attack on the idea of a European defense community in 1953.

agreed to receive De Gaulle at his unorthodox retreat. When he arrived, the Frenchman was bristling.

Churchill, as De Gaulle had anticipated, was mostly interested in the General's broadcasting a public message at the time of the Allied landing. De Gaulle was more interested in reaching an agreement concerning the administration in liberated areas. Discussion between the two men rapidly produced the angry, strained atmosphere which so frequently permeated their discussions; and Churchill, irritated and apprehensive about the impending operation, threatened De Gaulle if any split developed between the United States and the French Committee, he would "almost certainly side with the Americans." He went on to emphasize that Britain would not ask Roosevelt to give De Gaulle the title deeds to France but would go so far as to ask the President to agree that the Committee was "the principal body with whom he should deal in France." Neither the Prime Minister's bluntness nor De Gaulle's sensitivity promised any amelioration of relations, and after De Gaulle angrily pointed out that he realized the United Kingdom would side with the United States against France, Duff Cooper and General Smith were glad to extricate De Gaulle from the Prime Minister's quarters.

After lunch Churchill preceded De Gaulle to Widewing, in order to obtain Eisenhower's help in persuading De Gaulle to deliver a statement. Harry Butcher describes the scene in his engaging style:

> Winston was an hour late getting here, talked quickly to Ike, and along came de Gaulle, it having been decided in the meantime that Ike had to keep de Gaulle sufficiently informed so he could broadcast a word of encouragement to the French. So Ike took them all on a Cook's tour of the war room, and de Gaulle lectured on what he would do. Whereupon Ike and de Gaulle strolled up the shady cinder path in front of the signals tent where there was enough elbow room for de Gaulle to wave his arms and talk. Ike did some too, and in due course they returned, went into the war room, and we heard Anglo-French dictation to one of Churchill's secretaries. De Gaulle was to broadcast when called upon, but had wanted Ike to take out of his speech any reference to his, Ike's, control of law and order amongst his, de Gaulle's, Frenchmen.[11]

[11] *My Three Years with Eisenhower*, 570.

The text of Eisenhower's statement, in order to be palatable to American and British views, had been left vague and noncommittal. The sections of special interest to De Gaulle were as follows:

Citizens of France! I am proud to have again under my command the gallant forces of France. Fighting beside their Allies, they will play a worthy part in the liberation of their homeland. . . . Follow the instructions of your leaders. A premature uprising of all Frenchmen may prevent you from being of maximum help to your country in the critical hour. Be patient. Prepare.

As Supreme Commander of the Allied Expeditionary Forces, there is imposed on me the duty and responsibility of taking all measures necessary to the prosecution of the war. Prompt and willing obedience to the orders that I shall issue is essential. Effective civil administration of France must be provided by Frenchmen. All persons must continue in their present duties unless otherwise instructed. Those who have common cause with the enemy and so betrayed their country will be removed. As France is liberated from her oppressors, you yourselves will choose your representatives and the government under which you wish to live.

There was scarcely a sentence of this announcement which De Gaulle could read with pleasure. It talked about French forces under Allied command, when in fact no agreement had yet been reached about the employment of French troops in "Overlord" or, with the exception of General Koenig as commander of the FFI, concerning command relationships. The speech instructed Frenchmen to follow the instructions of "your leaders." But who were they—Vichy prefects, the Communist-dominated COMAC, or the military delegates of the FCNL? De Gaulle could not fail to remark on the pointed neglect of any reference to himself or to the French Committee in the entire speech. Further in the statement Eisenhower enjoined Frenchmen to obey him as Allied Commander. This appeal was also vague. If Eisenhower meant obedience in the military zone for military expediency, his comment might be justified, but if he meant in all France, the claim for authority could not fail to be disputed by De Gaulle in his capacity as head of the self-designated Provisional government. The next sentences, stating that civil administration must be provided by Frenchmen and that all persons must remain in their present duties, appeared to indicate that Vichy administrators would not be removed "unless otherwise instructed." Instructed by whom? Collaborators would "be removed." By whom? The implication was inescapable that they would be judged by SHAEF presumably on recommendations of Paillole's counterespionage agents. De Gaulle could not object to the final sentence, but one question arose: until the French people chose their representatives, what was to be the government of France? Would it be an AMGOT imposed by Eisenhower, possibly involving a deal with another Darlan, or would it be a provisional regime by a broadened FCNL?

Much has been written about the stubbornness and lack of co-operation which De Gaulle manifested on D–Day, and from the Allied point of view, it is true that he was far from helpful during the trying and nerve-wracking twenty-four hours before the landings. But from De Gaulle's point of view, the picture was entirely different. It was not he who had insisted on coming to London, and he had gone on record consistently and vociferously for the previous six months in opposition to an AMGOT for France. If the Allies insisted on going ahead with their plans, he could not very well prevent them, but it was asking too much to insist that he underwrite them. Particularly difficult from De Gaulle's point of view was the fact that Eisenhower's speech had been approved by Roosevelt and Churchill, had been recorded for broadcast, and had been printed for distribution. Even if it had been physically possible to alter it, Eisenhower could not have changed the text without fresh authorization from London and Washington.

Under the circumstances the only type of speech that De Gaulle deemed possible was one which asserted an authority concerning which nothing had been said in Eisenhower's statement. In the course of June 5, De Gaulle drew up a speech, some of the significant points of which were as follows:

> For a nation which fights bound hand and foot against an oppressor armed to the teeth, battle discipline imposes several conditions. The first is strict obedience to instructions given by the French Government and by French leaders which it has qualified to so act.
> The second condition is that our action in the rear of the enemy shall

be co-ordinated as closely as possible with the action of the Allied and French armies. Now, we must expect that the struggle of the armies will be hard and long. That means that the action of the forces of the Resistance must go on and increase to the moment of the German collapse.

The sentence insisting on obedience to the French government was scarcely compatible with Eisenhower's appeal for obedience to him. De Gaulle concluded that if he broadcast at all, he should not follow immediately after Eisenhower, since this would give the impression that he was corroborating Eisenhower's statements.

De Gaulle also decided not to issue orders to Boislambert and the 180 French administrative liaison officers who had been under instruction in London. From De Gaulle's point of view, these officers had been trained in accordance with Article VI, Section 3 (b) of the March 14 Ordinance on Civil Administration, on which no agreement had been reached with either SHAEF or the Allied governments. If SHAEF was determined to handle civil affairs through its own G–5, it seemed perfectly logical to De Gaulle that officers trained under an agreement that had never been reached would be superfluous.

Confusion and misunderstanding marked the day prior to the invasion. De Gaulle had labored under the misapprehension that there was a possibility of revising or modifying Eisenhower's text and that his suggestions for changes would be sympathetically received. Churchill was unclear about the purpose of the liaison officers and seems to have believed they were interpreters absolutely vital to the operation. Confusion also resulted from a report that De Gaulle had refused to broadcast, when he had only refused to broadcast directly after Eisenhower. Much of the thankless work of calming irritated spirits in both camps fell on Charles Peake, the British political adviser assigned to SHAEF, and to the French ambassador, Viénot. At one point during the protracted altercation, Churchill dictated a letter to De Gaulle in which he threatened to send him back to Algiers and to denounce him by stating that he had refused to associate himself with the liberation. The note was fortunately never sent, and in the small hours of the morning the question of the speech was finally resolved.

By broadcasting a speech under Allied auspices, in which he admonished Frenchmen to obey the government which he represented, De Gaulle was able to achieve at least one of his objectives. He could not alter the remarks made by Eisenhower, but he had been able to countermand them in a sense by formulating an order which affirmed that there was but one French authority to be heeded. The question of the liaison officers was not as easy to regulate. Viénot saw Duff Cooper on D–Day, June 6, and asked him to try to persuade De Gaulle to change his mind. In his diary, Duff Cooper wrote:

> I saw de Gaulle at three o'clock. I pointed out to him that in his own interest he ought to agree to the officers going, as otherwise it would be said of him that he had refused to help us in the battle itself. He would not accept the logic of this argument but eventually said that to please *me* he would agree to send at least some of the officers, if not all.

De Gaulle then permitted twenty officers to leave for France, but beyond that he would not co-operate.

As the Allies struggled for a foothold on French soil and as French areas began to be freed of German occupying forces, De Gaulle stood firm in the face of an urgent need to settle basic questions. He had no alternative. Having drawn the sword which invested him as president of the Provisional government, he had of necessity to discard the scabbard. If he had been unwilling to surrender the rights of sovereignty in 1941 as chairman of the National Committee, he could much less abandon a defense of French rights, with the force of the National Resistance Council and the Consultative Assembly behind him. To De Gaulle the question was more than a matter of several hundred liaison officers. Since these officers were not combat troops, their presence or absence in France would not jeopardize military aspects of the invasion, but whether the sovereign authority in France became SHAEF or Vichy or the NRC or the FCNL was a fundamental matter of such importance to De Gaulle that compromise was unthinkable. Vast questions had still to be regulated: currency, civil administration, relief and rehabilitation, the establishing and broadening of a provisional government, and control of the Resistance. Their sane and sensible regulation might avert the civil war which seemed by some to be inevitable. Whether the Allies co-operated with him or not, De Gaulle could see no other course than to seek a solution for French problems by means of the facilities which he controlled. From his point of view, co-operation with the Allies now had two basic prerequisites: that negotiations proceed at governmental level and that the United States be a party to any future discussions.

American Policy after D–Day

As bitter fighting to gain control of the Normandy beachhead continued, reports on De Gaulle's actions in London were eclipsed by the headlines devoted to tactical details. Four days after D–Day, when Eisenhower issued a proclamation guaranteeing representative government in France, De Gaulle broke into the news with an interview he gave to war correspondents in London. He revealed that his attitude toward the Allies' unilateral policy in France, especially in regard to civil administration and currency, had not altered.

Although Washington's reaction was one of injured pride—that De Gaulle should have questioned the Allied right to issue currency—there was one hopeful possibility that emerged from the welter of accusations recorded in Washington, London, and Algiers. When Admiral Fenard returned to the United States from his mission to De Gaulle, he was received by the President, who told him that he was still anxious to talk over matters personally with De Gaulle even though he was unwilling to authorize a representative to enter into conversations at London. Fenard immediately flew to England and repeated the President's invitation for De Gaulle to see him between June 22 and June 30 or between July 6 and July 14. At this time Roosevelt could not have been unaware of the political value of a satisfactory settlement of French matters before the November elections or, better still, before the party conventions during the summer. The premier of the Polish government-in-exile, Mikolajczky, was visiting Roosevelt at the time he issued his invitation to De Gaulle, and while their conversations did not solve Poland's problems, they may have encouraged the Polish vote to back the President. French affairs were not so delicately oriented in relation to the Soviet Union, and a friendly chat with De Gaulle could do no harm in any quarter. At his press conference on June 10, De Gaulle announced that he would be happy to see the President.

At the moment, the currency issue seemed to provide the major obstacle to agreement. By ignoring the FCNL, the Allies had placed themselves in a dilemma: if De Gaulle was invited to back the notes, he would gain a sort of *de facto* recognition; but, on the other hand, as Churchill pointed out to the President, "the only alternative is to guarantee the money ourselves." Roosevelt, refusing to be bullied into a conciliatory gesture toward De Gaulle, replied to the Prime Minister on June 12 in these terms:

> I suggest we tell de Gaulle that if the French people will not accept the invasion currency, Eisenhower be authorized to use UK Military Authority money and yellow-seal dollars. Thus, if de Gaulle encourages the French to refuse invasion money, he will be responsible for the certain depreciation of the franc which will follow. I do not favor any effort to press de Gaulle for a statement in support of the new currency, but if he wants to issue something on his individual responsibility, he can put his signature on any currency statement in any capacity that he desires, even to that of the King of Siam.[12]

Three days after the landings, General Marshall, Admiral King, and General Arnold arrived in London to obtain a firsthand view of "Overlord's" progress. In the course of their inquiries, they encountered the American political adviser to SHAEF, William Phillips, and asked his opinion on the French situation. Concerned about the deterioration of relations between SHAEF and De Gaulle's Committee, Phillips elaborated on the potentially dangerous situation that was developing because of the lack of a sound policy governing Eisenhower's contacts with Resistance forces. He endeavored to point out that there was strong opposition in the Foreign Office to Churchill's policy of following Roosevelt's lead and that a definite directive should be given to SHAEF. The tenor of Phillips' opinions was drawn up in the form of a memorandum by him and General Julius Holmes and forwarded by Marshall, King, and Arnold to the President, with copies to Stimson and Eisenhower. Roose-

---

[12] Paraphrased from Pogue, *Supreme Command*, 233.

velt replied to the communication in terms similar to those used many times before:

> While I am not inclined to do any favors for de Gaulle, I am willing to make full use of any organization or influence the General may have which would aid the Allied military effort, provided the result is not to impose the FCNL on the French people by force of United States or British arms.[13]

Secretary of War Stimson, who, in spite of his predilection for military government, tended to take realities into account, saw in Marshall's report an opportunity to influence the President into a rethinking of his French policy. Stimson did not believe it would be wise for the United States to assume the responsibility for a democratic French election. The only authority capable of accomplishing this was now De Gaulle, and the best the United States could do would be to get pledges from him concerning his democratic intentions. Stimson wrote in his diary:

> No matter what we do, if he tries to use his preferred position to win further rewards from the French people at the election we really cannot stop it and it is better not to run the risk of bickerings now which will serve not only to divide us from de Gaulle but will divide us from the British who more and more are supporting de Gaulle. It is this latter situation, namely the cleft between us and the British, which most alarms me.[14]

After Stimson had studied the Marshall memorandum, which he received on June 14, he discussed it with McCloy, and they both decided on the importance of persuading the President to grant De Gaulle some degree of recognition. Before getting in touch with Roosevelt, Stimson attempted to obtain backing from the Secretary of State, but Hull was pointedly reluctant to interfere in what he insisted was a matter for the military forces, and Stimson telephoned the President without Hull's support. Stimson recorded his conversation in his diary as follows:

[13] Pogue, *Supreme Command*, 234.
[14] Stimson and Bundy, *On Active Service*, 549.

At nine o'clock I got a telephone connection with the White House and talked with the President. He had already received the telegram from Marshall, King and Arnold but gave it scant attention. He was adamant in his refusal to depart from his position taken in the directive, that is now waiting in London, and considered it would be a departure from moral standards to do so. I patiently went over the different steps above enumerated in a talk which lasted on the telephone for nearly an hour, but I made very little advance. I pointed out the impossibility of actually supervising French elections and he fully agreed. But he believes that de Gaulle will crumple and that the British supporters of de Gaulle will be confounded by the progress of events. This is contrary to everything that I hear. I think de Gaulle is daily gaining strength as the invasion goes on and that is to be expected. He has become the symbol of deliverance to the French people. The President thinks that other parties will spring up as the liberation goes on and that de Gaulle will become a very little figure. He said that he already knew of some such parties. . . .

Our conversation, while it was clear and the issue plainly stated on both sides, was perfectly friendly and . . . the President not only took no offense at my persistence but apparently wished himself to argue the matter out because he kept the conversation going even when I gave him several opportunities to stop.[15]

A Recapitulation of Roosevelt's Attitudes

The Presidential opposition to De Gaulle, which was now entering its final phase, possessed as much stubborn vigor as it ever had, but it now began to base itself on somewhat different arguments. Roosevelt had built up a picture of what was going to happen in France. He apparently believed that when the restrictive authority of the Axis was released, France would divide herself into her latent revolutionary forces and plunge into the morass of civil war. The remnants of Pétainism, it must be assumed, would be aligned into a reorganized right, which would embark on an ugly internecine conflict with the Socialist-Communist-dominated Gaullist Resistance. Roosevelt was so obsessed with his conviction of imminent civil war in France that he vigorously at-

[15] *Ibid.*, 550–51.

tempted to avoid accepting an occupation zone in Germany which would require communication lines across France. It must be admitted that a certain amount of evidence could be adduced to support the President's conclusions. The pattern of civil war had developed in Yugoslavia between Partisans and Chetniks and in Greece between ELAS and EDES; an analogy could easily be drawn between those countries and France: occupation by German troops, a vigorous Communist-dominated Resistance, and a government-in-exile. And by early 1944 revolutionary developments in Yugoslavia and Greece did provide prototypes which the President may have felt to be applicable to France. Had Pétain's regime been less unstable than it proved to be, had Gaullism been less moderate than it was, and had revolutionary ideas in the Resistance been stronger than events were to demonstrate, Roosevelt's hypothesis might have possessed greater validity. It is a curious fact that Roosevelt's views were shared by virtually no one outside the White House.[16] If the President believed that De Gaulle held the same radical approach to politics as Communists (or indeed as some Gaullists) or that the presence of two Communists and a fellow traveler in the FCNL meant Communist domination, either he was misinformed about De Gaulle or he seriously underrated him. The State Department, the War Department, OSS, and SHAEF all made more realistic assessments of De Gaulle's capabilities and objectives than the White House, yet they were apparently unable to divest the President of his conviction that De Gaulle's entry into France would be the precursor of revolution.[17]

It is noteworthy that in the months following liberation there did exist in France a critical rivalry for power, but the dichotomy was not Pétainist-Gaullist but Gaullist-Communist. The interior Resistance, dominated by the National Resistance Council through its action committee, COMAC, its military hierarchies, its committees of liberation, and its irregular forces, was thoroughly infiltered with Communists and

[16] According to Stimson (*On Active Service,* 595), it was Leahy who principally warned Roosevelt about the dangers of revolution. Gaullists generally believed that Chautemps and Léger gave the President similar warnings.

[17] Nothing said here is meant to infer that revolutionary ideas were lacking among Gaullist and other non-Communist resistance groups. See, for example, the section "Résistance et Révolution" in Henri Michel and B. Mirkine-Guetzevitch (eds.), *Les idées politiques et sociales de la Résistance,* 139-75. Only after liberation were events to reveal how readily France would slip back into the well-worn grooves of the Third Republic.

their sympathizers. If it had not been outclassed by De Gaulle, the NRC might have served as the nucleus for France's post-liberation provisional government. When the President told Stimson that "other parties will spring up" and that "he already knew of some such parties," he perhaps referred to reports available to him of Resistance groups in which a lively anti-Gaullism already existed. But if he knew that many of these groups were oriented farther to the left than Gaullism and would be much less likely to insure stability than De Gaulle, it is hardly conceivable that he would have been so anxious to eliminate De Gaulle's influence from the political vacuum that would follow the *Wehrmacht's* withdrawal. Or perhaps the President referred to contacts that had been made with men like Albert Lebrun and Edouard Herriot, whom the Allies were trying to persuade to come out of retirement and participate in a political movement that would not be tied to Gaullism. It is, of course, much easier to criticize in retrospect than to formulate policy for the future on the basis of scanty and unreliable evidence. No one in 1944 could estimate the extent of Communist infiltration in the Resistance or could know what policies would be followed by the party. Nor could anyone before the invasion have foretold the tremendous personal prestige which De Gaulle would possess as symbol of the Resistance. No figure—certainly not Bidault, head of the NRC—was to approach De Gaulle in stature for many months. Perhaps Roosevelt, had he lived to witness De Gaulle's resignation in 1946, would have remarked triumphantly that his estimate of De Gaulle had been right— that De Gaulle was too egocentric, too rigid, and too dictatorial to survive the hurly-burly of democratic politics. In 1944, however, De Gaulle's prestige was the only force other than Allied power that could guarantee stability and order in France.

There is evidence that, in the spring of 1944, Roosevelt was becoming more and more convinced of the dangers of postwar imperialism and more certain about the value of trusteeships as a device to mitigate the worst measures of colonialism. That the White House was seriously thinking along these lines was brought to public notice by an article published in David Lawrence's *United States News* on April 14, 1944. Lawrence writes with such confidence about the President's attitudes that he must have obtained his material from sources not far distant from the White House, and his article reflects ideas that had long circulated in Washington but had never been formulated so positively. Some of the sections of the article pertaining especially to the French follow:

> Mr. Roosevelt and his advisers do not forget that the French, without a fight, turned over to Japan the big French naval base at Saigon in Indo-China, thereby enabling Japan to out-flank and reduce Singapore, and to cut U. S. access to rubber and tin. The President remembers that, when the U. S. was hardest pressed by German submarines, the French island of Martinique served as a hostile dagger aimed at the vitals of our defences in the Caribbean. He has said definitely that French Dakar cannot again be left under a control that will threaten the approaches to this Hemisphere.
>
> The President is concerned over the future of these strategic spots. He is thinking of other French possessions also—Madagascar, New Caledonia, French Guiana, the islands of Miquelon and St. Pierre. He is unwilling to see the whole French empire restored intact, without guarantees that will protect the security of the U. S. General de Gaulle, on the other hand, insists on the restoration of France as a sovereign world power. He claims full rights to all French possessions. He is adamant in his demands. The unyielding attitude of General de Gaulle regarding these possessions is said to be the real explanation for Mr. Roosevelt's reluctance to give complete recognition to the de Gaulle committee as the government of France.

Lawrence's article received more comment in June, when it was abridged and republished in the *Reader's Digest* under the title "Our Postwar Stake in the World's Strategic Outposts"; and when it appeared on June 15 in a supplement to *Stars and Stripes,* it was picked up by French journalists and given wide distribution in North Africa. There were protests by the French, and with no clear-cut denial issued in Washington, French apprehension grew into mistrust that the United States had designs on the French Empire. There was never a question of the United States' wishing to annex French territory; but, on the other hand, it is certain that the President lacked enthusiasm for an unimpaired French Empire, and he hoped that the trusteeship principle would be widely applied. On January 24, 1944, he sent Hull the following forthright memorandum:

I saw Halifax last week and told him quite frankly that it was perfectly true that I had, for over a year, expressed the opinion that Indo-China should not go back to France but that it should be administered by an international trusteeship. France has had the country—30,000,000 inhabitants—for nearly 100 years, and the people are worse off than they were at the beginning.

As a matter of interest, I am wholeheartedly supported in this view by Generalissimo Chiang Kai-Shek and by Marshal Stalin. I see no reason to play in with the British Foreign Office in this matter. The only reason they seem to oppose it is that they fear the effect it would have on their own possessions and those of the Dutch. They have never liked the idea of trusteeships because it is, in some instances, aimed at future independence. This is true in the case of Indo-China.

Each case must, of course, stand on its own feet, but the case of Indo-China is perfectly clear. France has milked it for 100 years. The people of Indo-China are entitled to something better than that.[18]

This memorandum is worth comparing with De Gaulle's reply to a blunt inquiry, "Do you hope to recover the Empire intact? I am thinking particularly in Indochina," which was put to him during a press conference on July 10, 1944:

France is certain that she will recover intact everything that belongs to her, but France is certain that after this war and the human experiences which have been undergone, the form of the French world organization and especially for Indochina will not be the same as before the tragedy we have experienced.

In other words, De Gaulle was willing to admit that France should adopt a more liberal policy toward the French Empire, but he was not going to relinquish any parcel of land which he considered as rightfully belonging to France.

The considerations which convinced President Roosevelt that he must continue to oppose De Gaulle have been touched on frequently in the foregoing pages, but it has been impossible to find a complete, logical statement, in the President's own words, which satisfactorily accounts

[18] Hull, *Memoirs,* II, 1597.

for his attitude toward the Free French. As Edwin Lahey, writing in the *Chicago Daily News* on June 14, 1944, put it:

> One of the most fascinating, if not the most important, mysteries of this war is the precise reason for Mr. Roosevelt's obvious dislike for General de Gaulle. Despite all the inside stories that are related at the cocktail hour, the only safe conclusion one arrives at is that when Mr. Big doesn't like a party, he's very thoroughgoing about it.

Before proceeding with a description of Franco-American relations after D–Day, a recapitulation of the considerations which the President bore in mind in formulating his French policy may prove of value.

Roosevelt's antipathy toward De Gaulle derived basically from four sources. These were:

First, his attitude toward France. In Roosevelt's judgment, France was an exhausted, defeatist, confused country which did not correspond to De Gaulle's perorations about historical glory and grandeur. Because of the few thousand Frenchmen who had left their homes to join him, De Gaulle had no right to speak on behalf of the forty million who appeared to be satisfied with Marshal Pétain. If, indeed, De Gaulle represented the French people, they should have the right to say so after the country was liberated, but De Gaulle should not meanwhile be given the "title deeds" to France. This aspect of his policy coincided with Roosevelt's habitual wartime insistence on postponing political decisions until the peace conference and subordinating civil to military problems.

Second, his personal mistrust of De Gaulle. Although the President enjoyed mimicking De Gaulle's Joan of Arc attitude as he had encountered it at Casablanca, it is not likely that Roosevelt's mistrust derived solely from his brief interviews with the General in January, 1943. But he did not trust De Gaulle's judgment or his tactics. There was a long history: the difficulties following the Anglo-Free French invasion of Syria; the Gestapo methods of Colonel Passy's BCRA; the vindictive anti-American editorials in the Gaullist newspaper *La Marseillaise;* the violence of André Philip; the dictatorial attitudes, the exaggerated claims, and the prima donna-like demeanor of De Gaulle; the Giraud ouster; and the methods employed to obtain representation on the Italian Commission. Stimson wrote: "To the President, de Gaulle was a narrow-minded French zealot with too much ambition for his own good and some rather dubious views on democracy."[19] As time went on, it would become more and more difficult for the President to reverse himself. Duff Cooper explained Roosevelt's stubbornness in regard to De Gaulle by pointing out that the President had backed two losers, Darlan and Giraud, and was understandably reluctant to admit that he had been wrong all along.[20] Such an about-face would come hard to the man who sometimes referred to himself as "a pigheaded Dutchman." In 1954 the present writer had the opportunity to ask De Gaulle how he interpreted the President's antagonism. De Gaulle commented on the difference between his and Roosevelt's concept of France and then went on to say: "Roosevelt was a star—*une vedette*—and he disliked sharing the spotlight. He had difficulties in getting along with anyone, like Churchill, for example, who was also a star, but whom Roosevelt did not like, although both made great pretense of friendship. With his physical handicap to overcome, Roosevelt was obsessed with a psychological requirement of rising above his difficulties, of being the principal in the show." De Gaulle made a point of insisting that he thought his personal relations with Roosevelt were extremely cordial; "But our policies were entirely different."

Third, his concept of the postwar world. Roosevelt believed that collective security, implemented by friendly accord among the great powers, would put an end to the international friction generated by balance of power, spheres of influence, and imperialism. He believed he would find in Stalin an ally to impose this concept on Churchill, but he was convinced that De Gaulle would place himself in the opposition. Roosevelt was not inclined to give power to a man who might stubbornly oppose postwar efforts of the United Nations to establish trusteeships over Indochina and other colonial areas.

Fourth, his employment of unsound premises and misinformation in formulating his French policy. Roosevelt was wrong in his belief that civil war would develop in France, wrong in thinking that De Gaulle would establish a dictatorship, and wrong in his estimate of De Gaulle's

[19] *On Active Service,* 546.
[20] *Old Men Forget,* 316.

relationship to the "revolutionary" elements of the Resistance. When one realizes that Stimson and Eisenhower, and later Secretary Hull and Robert Murphy, favored co-operation with De Gaulle and when one takes cognizance of the fact that virtually all reputable newspapers, including the *New York Times,* opposed the President, it is difficult to understand how he could have insisted on his policy unless he had access to information not generally known, on which he placed great reliance. It is not unlikely that intelligence from OSS and Psychological Warfare failed to reach or influence the President; on the other hand, reports from Admiral Leahy, from General Giraud, and from other sources may have convinced him that he possessed "inside" information unavailable at other levels.

Altogether, the considerations enumerated above massed themselves into a syndrome which, whether adequately diagnosed or not, suggests why Roosevelt was reluctant to accord anything but minimum recognition to De Gaulle and the French Committee. The firmness with which he adhered to his attitudes would result in continued antagonism for months after D–Day, in the face of the entire world's recognition of the fact that De Gaulle in reality headed the French government.

British Attempts to Initiate Negotiations

If post-Normandy bickerings with the French gave Stimson cause for alarm, they brought Eden to despair. After a week of attempting to get negotiations started with De Gaulle, Eden told Duff Cooper that he had never been so unhappy or so perplexed by anything as he was by the French situation and that he could not see what was going to be the result. On June 14, Churchill was confronted with embarrassing questions in the House of Commons about relationships with France. It had been reported in the press that Roosevelt had told newspapermen that the United States and Great Britain would back French currency. When asked about this, the Prime Minister, knowing that Roosevelt was at the moment disinclined to settle the matter, refused to discuss it. Many Labor representatives wanted to debate a policy that would grant British recognition of the French Provisional government; but Churchill entertained hopes that a better solution could be achieved after several

De Gaulle, fifteen years later, as French premier.

Almost to the day, fifteen years later (June 4, 1958), De Gaulle returns to Algiers. Saluting him is Admiral Philippe Auboyneau, commander of French naval forces in the Mediterranean. In the foreground is Jacques Soustelle, French deputy and one of the leaders of the Gaullist movement.

weeks had elapsed, and he declined to be drawn into argument. "I think," he told the House, "it would be better to allow the relationship between General De Gaulle and the United States to proceed further before we have a formidable debate on these questions." The Prime Minister had his way and the debate was postponed.

Meanwhile, the Foreign Office was endeavoring to persuade De Gaulle that it would be to his advantage to permit discussions with the British government on civil administration in France. Although any agreement between London and Algiers would not have validity unless approved by Roosevelt and adopted by SHAEF, a concrete understanding would provide the President with an example of the sort of instrument that could be drawn up. After the middle of June, as French administrators in Normandy found general acceptance by Allied authorities, De Gaulle became more amenable to the British suggestion, and before he left for Algiers on June 17, he authorized Viénot to begin discussions with the British.[21]

The negotiations were initiated in London on June 19. Viénot was supported by the FCNL economic expert, Hervé Alphand, and by Foreign Minister Massigli; the British delegation was headed by the judge advocate general, Sir Henry MacGeaugh. With the beginning of conversations between their representatives, both Churchill and De Gaulle, although they had not spoken to each other since D–Day, had reason to be hopeful of the future, and De Gaulle returned to Algiers well pleased with the ultimate results of his visit to London.

The French in Normandy and Algiers

The great test of the soundness of the President's policy, which had prevented top-level agreement with the FCNL on civil administration, came when the liberation of parts of Normandy necessitated the rapid establishment of administrative organs. It soon appeared that most of

[21] De Gaulle, *Mémoires*, II, 231. A precedent for such an agreement existed in the implements that had been signed by SHAEF and representatives of Norway, Belgium, and Holland on 16 May 1944. These agreements gave Eisenhower authority over liberated areas until such time as he felt it permissible to turn over control to the various governments. Provisions were included to establish jurisdiction of national tribunals as against Allied military courts and to regulate Allied rights of requisition, claims, and the use of facilities necessary for military operations. See Pogue, *Supreme Command,* 140.

the confusion and misunderstandings existed in the rarefied atmosphere of policy-making levels and failed to affect the men who were responsible for routine operations in the field. In spite of French fears, SHAEF's G-5 was not prepared to carry on a complete administration for France; not only was its personnel too limited, but its civil affairs program was directed at supervision, help, and co-ordination in technical areas rather than at political control. When a town like Bayeux or Isigny was liberated and had passed behind the actual military zone, an Anglo-American civil affairs team, consisting usually of a doctor, a public utilities expert, and one or two administrative specialists, would enter the area and, co-operating with the French local authorities, attempt to insure the health, provisioning, and services of the locality. As the first liberated areas fell within the authority of Montgomery's Twenty-first Army Group, there was a preponderance of British officers who, generally more sympathetic to Gaullism than were the Americans, made no objection to allowing members of the Resistance to handle the political end of affairs. Most civil affairs officers were not interested in French politics and assiduously avoided embroiling themselves in political matters. Some weeks after the landings Emmanuel d'Astier, having made a tour of Normandy in July, told newspapermen that he was impressed by the excellent relations between the Allied armies, especially the British, and the French civilian population. "British officials in France," he said, "have distinguished themselves by their scrupulous respect for French sovereignty."

In spite of his lack of agreement with the Allies, De Gaulle saw no reason why he should hesitate to put into effect as soon as possible the administrative arrangements envisaged by the March 14 ordinance. De Gaulle was deeply concerned over the question of which French agency would dominate a purged civil administration. In almost every French department there were local committees of liberation, made up of Resistance and Labor representatives, loosely co-ordinated with the National Resistance Council and in many instances dominated by Communists. The liberation committees possessed a strong ally in De Gaulle's minister of the interior, D'Astier, who, seeing in them the true Resistance, insisted that they should bear the responsibility for purging and remaking the local administration. The FCNL, on the other hand, planned to honeycomb France with regional commissioners, appointed by the FCNL and responsible to it. Regional commissioners, not departmental committees of liberation, would then have authority, under the laws of a state of siege, to remove and appoint prefects, subprefects, and other officials; the local committees would serve them in an advisory capacity only.

One week after D–Day, De Gaulle received approval from SHAEF to visit Normandy. He insisted on crossing aboard a French destroyer, *La Combattante,* and on June 14 once again stood on French soil, almost four years to a day since he had made his first appeal to Frenchmen to resist. Accompanying De Gaulle on his visit to General Montgomery was François Coulet, designated commissioner for the Normandy region. Montgomery raised no objection to his remaining in France, and Coulet established his headquarters in newly liberated Bayeux. Backed by General de Gaulle's authority and not hindered by the Allies, Coulet had no difficulty in establishing a regime which was hierarchically related to the Algiers Committee, and as the front widened, the Provisional government's authority became more and more extensive. Coulet's good sense, efficiency, and moderation went a long way toward establishing respect for the sort of administration which the Provisional government intended to impose. Although the committee of liberation protested that Algiers did not consult sufficiently with them or with the National Resistance Council, there was surprisingly little unrest or defiance during the first weeks that the Gaullist administration was gradually imposed. Least of all was there any protest from administrators who felt more comfortable under the shadow of Marshal Pétain. There was no sign of civil war, and the collaborationist elements of the administration quietly disappeared or attempted to make themselves inconspicuous. By the beginning of July it was entirely clear that Roosevelt's major apprehensions about France and De Gaulle were ill grounded.

Co-operation between Eisenhower and Koenig progressed rapidly and satisfactorily. SHAEF had long been somewhat skeptical about the underground's value from a military point of view and had not counted greatly on its assistance. But in Brittany, even before the breakthrough, French guerrilla forces began to sabotage railroads, slowing the movement of trains, and even to engage in pitched battles. At

Malestroit, on June 18, two thousand troops of the FFI fought heroically against the Germans. Quickly recognizing the FFI's value, Eisenhower placed his tentative arrangements with General Koenig on a firmer foundation: on June 17 he provided him with basic orders on the control of the FFI and six days later issued a second directive which gave General Koenig, as commander of the French Forces of the Interior, the same status enjoyed by all Allied commanders. In this capacity Koenig now received the consideration which the FCNL had long attempted to obtain, namely, the right of a military commander to refer to his government any orders which appeared in conflict with national interest. Thus Eisenhower's directive of June 23 provided a *de facto* recognition which was the most advanced step so far taken toward Allied acceptance of the FCNL. That General de Gaulle considered the new directive satisfactory was given definite proof by his agreement to permit some two hundred French liaison officers to proceed across the Channel in fulfillment of the duties for which they had been trained. Gradually, control of military intelligence networks in France, thus far invested in SFHQ, were transferred to General Koenig; although not until August 21, a few days before Paris was liberated, did Koenig obtain really effective control. Transfer of authority over SFHQ provided an important move in the direction not only of recognition but of control over the physical means through which De Gaulle's authority could be effectively established in France. Many of the agents, codes, records, dossiers, and communication facilities which had been scattered among a variety of agencies—British Intelligence, OSS, G-2, regular French Army—now would come via General Koenig to Soustelle's DGSS (which now obtained a new name, *Direction Générale des Études et Recherches* [DGER]) or under André Diethelm's Ministry of War. The objective of Passy and Soustelle, of constructing a central intelligence agency under Gaullist control, was on the threshold of realization.

The week following General de Gaulle's return to Algiers (he arrived there on June 17) brought such an improvement of relations with the Allies that for the first time in many months the General could hope for a speedy resolution of differences. The official designation of Koenig as FFI commander on June 23 was succeeded by reports from

London that Anglo-French negotiations had virtually terminated and that it only remained to put finishing touches on the official drafts. By June 26, De Gaulle had made up his mind that the Washington trip should not be delayed, and he inquired of Roosevelt whether a visit between July 5 and July 9 would be acceptable.

De Gaulle Finally Goes to Washington

De Gaulle now had a week to prepare for his voyage to Washington. While waiting for Alphand to bring the Anglo-French draft agreement from London, he made a hurried trip to the Italian front and to newly liberated Rome. Meanwhile, Jean Monnet, who had been in the United States since the previous October carrying on technical negotiations in connection with Lend-Lease, transportation, relief, and rehabilitation, returned to Algiers for consultation. It is worth remarking that just as Eisenhower had been able to make valuable practical military arrangements with Koenig, so had American financial experts been able to negotiate practical economic arrangements with Monnet.[22] At every level except the highest, *de facto* recognition of the FCNL had been accorded long before the official governmental pronouncement, and practical administrative problems often found satisfactory solutions in common-sense negotiations.

The tentative agreement which Alphand brought from London early in July was much more detailed than the Clark-Darlan Agreement, and its clauses provided for a variety of procedures which took into account French demands that the sovereignty of France be respected.[23] The basis for discussions had been the FCNL ordinance of March 14, which

[22] On 15 July, UNRRA announced that R. L. Cochran, former governor of Nebraska, had arrived in Algiers to work with the "Provisional Government of the French Republic." While UNRRA was an international rather than a purely United States' agency, the recognition testified to the success of Monnet's work in Washington. An arrangement known as "Plan A," concluded on 10 Aug. 1944, provided for over one million tons of provisions to be imported to France.

[23] The following analysis is based on the final version of the agreement, which was signed on 25 Aug. 1944. The preliminary drafts have not been available to the writer, but it seems logical to describe the terms of the agreement at this point rather than later in the narrative. The text is available in "Civil Administration and Jurisdiction in Liberated French Territory: Agreement between the U.S.A. and France . . . Dated August 25, 1944," *Department of State Publication 4395,* U.S. Treaties Series, No. 2313.

was now essentially accepted with the understanding, however, that "in areas in which military operations take place the Supreme Allied Commander will possess the necessary authority to ensure that all measures are taken which in his judgment are essential for the successful conduct of his operations (Art. 1)." The French plan of dividing liberated France into a forward zone and an interior zone was accepted, although where the French ordinance gave the power to fix the zones to the FCNL, the new agreement reached a compromise by granting this authority to the French delegate (André le Trocquer) who would effect the delimitation "in accordance with French law in such manner as to meet the requirements stated by the Supreme Allied Commander (Art. 2)."

The delegate and the military delegate were acknowledged to have the authority granted to them by the FCNL, but clauses had been added which guaranteed that in the forward zone the delegate would take measures "deemed necessary" by the Supreme Commander for military operations; also, in emergencies affecting military operations, Eisenhower could take steps "as a temporary and exceptional measure" which he considered necessary. In the interior zone administration was to be "entirely a matter for the French authorities," although the French authorities, when requested by the Allied Commander, would take such measures as they considered necessary for the conduct of military operations. The right of requisition, which had been so criticized in the Clark-Darlan Agreement, was granted to the Supreme Commander, but in the event that areas such as ports or forfeited areas were taken over, the conduct of territorial administration was to be solely a matter for French authorities. Furthermore, supplies, facilities, and services which the Allies required were to be requisitioned by the French authorities at the request of the Allied Commander, and in order to have the "least possible disruptive effect on the economy of France, the Allied military authorities and the French authorities" were to consult together over the services and supplies the Allies might wish to employ.

The question of extraterritorial rights, another grievance in the Clark-Darlan Agreement, was covered by a series of articles which generally granted jurisdiction in most cases to the French. Allied military courts retained jurisdiction over members of their own forces, although military personnel could be "arrested by the French Police for offenses against French law, and detained until they can be handed over for disposal to the appropriate Allied service authority." Other sections of the agreement delineated the procedures for handling French and Allied property and releasing French property which fell into Allied hands; for censorship, which in the forward zone was controlled by SHAEF and in the interior zone by the French in consultation with the Supreme Commander and in accordance with his instructions; and for the distribution of relief supplies to the civil population. The thorny question of currency issue was also regulated by an agreement whereby the French Central Treasury would issue all future funds but would accept those already placed in circulation.

It should be noted that nothing in the agreement provided for recognition of De Gaulle's Provisional government. In order to preserve their freedom in regard to recognition, the American authorities would insist on maintaining the fiction that the agreement was a purely military instrument drawn up between SHAEF and the French Military Delegate, in spite of the fact that the basic negotiations had been carried out by representatives of the British government with Frenchmen who were acknowledged to be representatives of the French Provisional government. The document did little more than describe the *de facto* situation which had existed since D–Day, and most of its terms could have been drawn up, like those in the Belgian and Dutch agreements, long before the invasion became an actuality.

Armed with the draft agreement and accompanied by Hervé Alphand and General Béthouart but by no member of the FCNL, General de Gaulle arrived in Washington in the early afternoon of July 6. The choice of companions revealed his anticipation that discussions would be economic and military, involving the Departments of the Treasury and of War rather than of State. President Roosevelt had already made it clear that recognition would not be discussed, and General de Gaulle insisted that his trip to Washington should not have as its object the negotiation of a civil affairs agreement; he hoped, however, that an atmosphere would be created which would permit the opening of such negotiations.

Ironically, the same sort of enthusiastic reception given to General

Giraud exactly one year earlier was now tendered to the man who had replaced him. De Gaulle was immediately escorted to the White House, where he was received by a smiling President surrounded by his cabinet. De Gaulle comported himself with a dignity and cordiality which surprised many officials who had been led to expect a temperamental prima donna encrusted with suspicious anti-Americanism. Even Admiral Leahy grudgingly admitted that he found De Gaulle, whom he had not previously met, "more agreeable in manner and appearance than I had expected. . . . De Gaulle made a very good impression upon the people he met during his brief stay in our capital, including myself."[24] Cordell Hull was also impressed. "[De Gaulle] went out of his way," wrote the Secretary of State, "to make himself agreeable to the President, to me, and to other members of the Government, and to assure us emphatically and repeatedly that he had no intention of forcing himself or his committee upon France as her future government."[25]

President Roosevelt and the General ran into none of the misunderstandings that had hampered their first encounter, a year and a half earlier at Casablanca. During the morning of July 7 they discussed a wide range of subjects which included not only specifically French problems but matters of general postwar import. De Gaulle elaborated on his concept of the France which would emerge after liberation, and Roosevelt raised one of the questions which absorbed him, the need for some strategic bases such as Dakar to safeguard American security. While he had no intention of surrendering any part of the French Empire, De Gaulle showed himself sympathetic to the possibility of discussing questions of international security and of moving in the direction of a French union. In regard to Indochina he expressed his intention of elevating the country and of bringing its representation within a federal system. It appeared that Roosevelt and De Gaulle, while possessing different points of view, did not stand so far apart that the gulf between them was unbridgeable. De Gaulle then raised the question of Germany's future. Ever since publication of the Atlantic Charter he had maintained reservations about aggrandizement, feeling that France possessed both the right and need to achieve some sort of control over the

24 *I Was There*, 244.
25 *Memoirs*, II, 1433.

Rhineland. Talks about Germany, however, comprised nothing more than an exchange of views, for at this time no firm arrangements had been reached among the Big Three, or in the European Advisory Commission, on the partition and occupation of Germany. Roosevelt, fearful about disorder in France, still hoped to obtain northern Germany as the American zone, but the matter was not to be settled for several months.

After his private conversation with the President, De Gaulle was his guest for lunch at the White House. Roosevelt was in fine humor and spoke about Franco-American relations in the most optimistic terms:

> . . . There are all kinds of problems, most of them what might be called technical, or detailed, or local, which can be resolved by the meeting of the leaders—the old idea that if you get around the table with a man you can solve anything.
>
> There are no great problems between the French and the Americans, or between General de Gaulle and myself. They are going to work out all right, if they will just leave a few of us alone to sit around the table.

He continued by mentioning that he and the General had talked that morning about many things—some controversial and some not dealing with France. "We can work these problems out," he concluded, "if we keep on meeting the way we are meeting now."[26] One can only speculate on whether earlier discussions of the two men "around the table" might have prevented the long unhappy series of misunderstandings and conflicts that makes the political history of Franco-American wartime relations such a sorry one. When it is borne in mind that discord at the top was in contrast with general harmony at more modest levels, the record appears particularly unfortunate—even tragic—in the sense that conflict among the protagonists inflicted avoidable hardships on thousands who fought and suffered and could not understand.

From the date of their meeting and talks in Washington, relations between Roosevelt and De Gaulle, while never warm and always restricted by considerations of high strategy, continued in a more cordial

[26] Rosenman, comp., *Public Papers and Addresses of F. D. Roosevelt, 1944–45,* 195; Leahy, *I Was There,* 244.

vein than previously. Churchill was quite enchanted by the President's "honeymoon with De Gaulle," writing Eden on July 10:

> Clearly we shall have to go as far as the United States go, and after their decision is declared we may press them to go farther. Should the President make a *volte-face* and come to terms with de Gaulle we shall have a very good case to present to Parliament, showing how foolish it would have been to have had a premature debate which might have spoiled all this happy kissing.[27]

On the date Churchill penned the foregoing note, word had reached London that the United States was prepared to recognize the FCNL as the *de facto* authority in France, and on the following day, at his press conference, Roosevelt elaborated on the new American policy. He pointed out that while the FCNL would be accepted as the civil authority for all liberated areas, this did not mean recognition, and Eisenhower remained the final judge of which areas would be placed under civil control and would exercise a military veto over civil appointees.

Although De Gaulle insisted that he had not come to Washington to press for recognition, the Anglo-French draft agreement had in fact been submitted to the Treasury and War Departments upon De Gaulle's arrival. On July 7, Daniel W. Bell, representing Treasury, and McCloy from the War Department brought the draft to Leahy for submission to the President, who received it on the following day (after De Gaulle had left Washington for Ottawa) and used it as the basis of his pronouncement on July 11. Hervé Alphand remained in Washington and, with Hoppenot of the French Mission, continued to work out the details of the agreement.

In contrast to Giraud's visit of the previous year, De Gaulle achieved his poorest success in the military area. At the Pentagon, General Béthouart brought up two questions for which the French were anxious to find answers: would the United States, having completed the eight-division Anfa program, undertake to arm five additional divisions, the man power for which, estimated at 100,000, would come from France; and would the United States assist in the arming and transporting of a

[27] Churchill, *Triumph and Tragedy* (vol. VI of *The Second World War*), 244–45.

French expeditionary force to fight in the Far East—particularly to participate in the liberation of Indochina? On both of these questions Béthouart failed to obtain satisfaction. Neither Eisenhower nor the other field commanders believed that they needed additional combat forces, although they were willing to equip 172,000 men, of whom 140,000 would be French, for garrison and service purposes. Faced with negative recommendations from the theater, the Joint Chiefs concluded that French rearmament thus became a postwar, and automatically a political, affair; and they refused to commit themselves, putting the French proposals aside for decision by higher authority. But the President was in no hurry to tackle new armament questions until developments in France proceeded further and until he had consulted with Churchill. Two months were to pass before Churchill and Roosevelt met, and by then the entire French problem would be altered by the fact that two-thirds of France would be liberated and De Gaulle would be head of a government established in Paris.

▶ 7. Paris

The Return to France

THE RAPID ADVANCE of Allied forces in the two weeks following the breakthrough upset much of the FCNL's careful planning. Before July 24 it had not seemed probable that the Committee could enter France unless "Anvil" eliminated Axis domination in the south; then, with Marseilles or Toulouse in French hands, it might be possible to administer a limited section of French soil. Or in the north, with the Germans pushed out of Normandy and Brittany, it might have been possible to install the government in Rennes or Nantes. But by August 15, when "Anvil" was finally launched, the Third U. S. Army was at Chartres, fifty miles from Paris, and in the week following, with the elimination of the Falaise pocket, the Germans had fallen back to the Seine. Towns were being liberated with such rapidity that it was impossible to find administrators who had even heard of the ordinances of March 14 and April 21, and with the lack of representatives from Algiers, local despots and liberation committees began to take over the administration. Should Paris he liberated before De Gaulle and the Algiers government arrived, it was not impossible that Parodi and his interim government might have difficulty in making their voices heard. To De Gaulle it was evident by mid-August that his presence, and the presence of his government, was required in France as soon as possible.

Difficulties over transportation ensued. General Bedell Smith wanted three days' advance notice and wished De Gaulle to come by way of London. He even offered a plane for the General's use. But De Gaulle insisted that he fly in a French plane with a French crew and without elaborate precautions which he suspected had been devised to prevent or delay his arrival in France. De Gaulle's firmness finally prevailed, and after receiving clearance from the Combined Chiefs of Staff, he flew into France from Algiers on August 18, joining Leclerc's armored division which had disembarked in France over two weeks previously. De Gaulle was received two days later by Koenig, Admiral d'Argenlieu, and General Juin (who had replaced Béthouart as chief of staff of national defense) at Cherbourg, where he addressed a crowd of 7,000 enthusiastic citizens. Also, as Allied forces continued the rapid march toward Paris, he conferred with Eisenhower and discussed the progress of the campaign in northern France. In areas under Allied control the acceptance of De Gaulle was so widespread and spontaneous that last-minute efforts of Pétain to enter into relations with the Free French had no significance in providing for political stability. It had not proved necessary to enter into deals with any aspect of the Vichy regime.

On August 21, De Gaulle wrote Eisenhower and urged him strongly to occupy Paris. By this time the Resistance had risen against the Germans occupying the capital and had seized the Prefecture and most of the governmental offices. Since August 19 a truce had existed between the Parisian forces and General von Choltitz, the German commander, but no one could predict whether, on August 23, when the truce was to terminate, German troops would withdraw or plunge Paris into bloody destruction. From the point of view of over-all strategy, Eisenhower had little interest in the French capital, which he hoped to by-pass. Had there been no insurrection within the city, Choltitz would in any case have soon found himself in a completely intolerable situation. But for the French the liberation of Paris was much more complex. What developed in Paris would affect all France, and a long drawn-out struggle between the Germans and the Resistance could well enhance Communist prestige, since the FTP was bearing the brunt of the actual fighting. In the confusion of the Paris conflict it was not clear whether the Communists, the National Resistance Council, or the Provisional government of secretaries-general appointed by Parodi would emerge as the repository of sovereign power.

De Gaulle was successful in his efforts to persuade Eisenhower to send troops into Paris, and by so doing he insured for himself and his government rapid control of the capital with its attendant administrative agencies. Although to Parisians, Koenig and Leclerc will forever be considered the liberators of Paris, from the Allied command's point of view, the operation, under over-all supervision of General Bradley, was entrusted to General Gerow, commander of the V Corps. Under Gerow's orders advance units of Leclerc's Second Armored Division moved into the city on the evening of August 24 and on the following day, with the help of the U. S. Fourth Division, brought about Choltitz's surrender. By late afternoon General de Gaulle had established headquarters in the War Ministry and had appointed General Koenig as military governor.

It was at this dramatic point that the *de facto* agreement approved by Roosevelt in July was finally signed. The text had been completed on August 15, the same day that French troops disembarked in southern France, but ten days had elapsed before the documents could be prepared for the formalities of signing. Hervé Alphand had first to bring the drafts to London, where Massigli had come to sign them on behalf of the French government. Then the more difficult task, entrusted to General Julius Holmes, of bringing the document to Eisenhower and Koenig, had to be accomplished so that the Anglo-French text, to be signed in London by Eden and Massigli, would be put into effect at the same time that the Franco-American text was signed in Paris. The Anglo-French agreement was signed on August 25 in London, but it was not until a day later that Eisenhower and Koenig were able to place their signatures to the other text. Once signed, the agreement held the peculiar status in international law of being a treaty between the British and French governments but only a working arrangement between American and French military commands.[1]

In exchanging ratifications with Koenig, Eisenhower notified the French Commander:

> I have been authorized to deal with the French Committee of National Liberation as the *de facto* authority in France, which will assume the leadership of and responsibility for the administration of the liberated areas of France. This action is taken on the understanding that the Supreme Commander, Allied Expeditionary Force, must possess what-

[1] For an analysis of the agreement see Chap. VI, above. De Gaulle believed that the delay in signing resulted from Roosevelt's anti-Gaullist prejudices (*Mémoires*, II, 307–16).

ever authority he may need for the unimpeded conduct of military operations as well as in recognition of the fact that the civil administration
in France, pending the full liberation of the country, should be exercised,
in so far as it is practicable, by Frenchmen.

In authorizing me to take this action, my government also understands
that it is the intention of the Committee that as soon as the military
situation permits, the French people will be given an opportunity to
select a government of their own free choice. My dealing with the Committee as above outlined is based upon the support which the Committee
continues to receive from the majority of Frenchmen who are fighting
for the defeat of Germany and the liberation of France.

The fact that Paris had been liberated and De Gaulle placed in a
position to install his government in the ministry buildings of the
capital provided a new and unanticipated turn to the French situation.
De Gaulle had only to insure control of Paris, and extension of the
Provisional government's authority over the rest of France would undoubtedly follow as a matter of course. De Gaulle, who arrived in Paris
a week before his colleagues in the Algiers government could find ways
to reach the capital, realized that his first task was to establish his authority, i. e., the authority of the State, to maintain order and to leave
no question in the minds of the NCR, the CGT, and the FTP that he
was invested with sovereign power in France. In order to help accomplish this he ordered a victory parade down the Champs Élysées on
August 26, counter to the advice of General Gerow, who, as Allied
commander in the area, was responsible to SHAEF for security and
order. The tremendous ovation which De Gaulle obtained from the
Parisians, and the admiration generated for his cool demeanor when
shots were fired during his entry into Notre Dame, undoubtedly helped
to cement his authority in the city and give pause to Communist leaders
who had to estimate their chances in pitting themselves against him.
But the difference with General Gerow over the parade was sympto-
matic of a new source of friction between the Allies and De Gaulle,
who insisted that decisions in the French interest must come before the
interests of SHAEF. When General Gerow a few days later turned over
his command to Koenig, he was unceremoniously informed that such
a transfer was meaningless because Koenig had already been exercis-

ing this authority since August 25, the day he had been appointed military governor of Paris.

To further cement his authority De Gaulle requested Eisenhower not only to permit Leclerc's division to remain in Paris but also to order two additional United States divisions to the city. Although no American units could be spared for garrison duty, two U. S. divisions made a demonstration of force by marching through Paris on August 29 en route to the front, and Leclerc was ordered to remain in Paris until the end of the month.[2]

With the beginning of September, as almost all of France was abandoned by the Nazis, De Gaulle emerged as undisputed leader of France. He had refused to meet with the National Resistance Council as a body, but by receiving its members individually, he recognized their achievement in the liberation without according them any sanctions other than a guarantee of places in the Consultative Assembly. By insisting that the FFI should be incorporated into the regular army as rapidly as possible, he served notice to the Communists that no private militias would be tolerated, and the COMAC's politico-military role was terminated. When the Algiers Committee arrived in Paris on September 2, De Gaulle at first added only three members to it—Aimé Lepercq, Pierre Tanguy-Prigent, and Robert Lacoste—and opened himself to charges that he unjustly favored his Algiers colleagues at the expense of the Resistance. In the week that followed De Gaulle modified his course and reconstituted his cabinet in such a way that while a nucleus of old comrades—Catroux, Tixier, Diethelm, Pleven, Capitant (and Soustelle as head of Intelligence)—remained in office, a sprinkling of representation from other elements in France was provided. A connection with republican tradition was established by inclusion of the venerable Jules Jeanneney as minister of state. Two Communists remained in the government—Billoux and Charles Tillon, who replaced Grenier as minister of air—and three Socialists (although De Gaulle did not reappoint Philip, Le Trocquer, or Queuille). His one gesture toward the National Resistance Council was to hand its president, Georges

---

[2] Dwight D. Eisenhower, *Crusade in Europe*, 297–98. De Gaulle has denied that he requested these divisions (*N.Y. Times*, 7 Dec. 1948), and he does not refer to them in his *Mémoires*.

Bidault, the portfolio of foreign affairs, while Massigli moved to London as ambassador. Yet at the same time he failed to reappoint another member of the NRC, Emmanuel d'Astier, whose important Ministry of the Interior was turned over to hard-working Adrien Tixier, a Socialist and a more efficient administrator than D'Astier. The elimination of D'Astier suggested that De Gaulle now felt assured that he had sufficient support without the backing of Communist-dominated Resistance elements. Other Resistance leaders were brought in—Pierre-Henri Teitgen and Augustin Laurent—but, placed in the Ministries of Information and Communications, they did not wield a power comparable to that controlled by the Minister of the Interior.

Jean Monnet, now heading a Commission on Imports, avoided the spotlight of publicity but continued to exercise great influence on the trend of negotiations for American economic aid. All together, with two Communists, three Socialists, three Popular Democrats, four Radical Socialists, and representatives of the CGT and the Resistance, the new government, announced on September 9, was fairly representative of non-Vichy France. It did not seem reasonable to suppose that Allied recognition would be delayed much longer.

Final Steps Toward Recognition

An opportunity for Anglo-American discussion of recognition was provided by the meeting of Churchill and Roosevelt at Quebec on September 11, but if the French held any hopes that further moves in the direction of recognition would be made, they were destined to disappointment. Roosevelt could no longer put confidence in his fears that revolution or civil war would break out in France, but he was not willing to relinquish his argument that De Gaulle's authority was self-imposed. At Quebec discussions on France were restricted and indecisive, while arguments over Pacific strategy and the German occupation had high priority. Roosevelt finally withdrew his reluctance to accept a southern occupation zone in Germany, but there was no serious thought at this time of assigning a zone to the French. Indeed, the whole question of the occupation was confused by extended discussions over the Morgenthau Plan, which upset and postponed workable arrangements concerning what the Allies should do when they moved into Germany. In regard to French participation in the Far Eastern campaign, no decision was reached, nor was any commitment made in regard to further arming of French troops.

President Roosevelt was disinclined to take any positive steps in regard to France. It should be remembered that at the time of the Quebec Conference his health was far from good and that he tired easily and did not examine issues with his usual vigor. At Quebec he had neither Hopkins, Stimson, nor Hull at his side to exert a pressure that might have made him inclined to grant recognition, and even Churchill seems to have sensed the danger of pressing Roosevelt too hard. The President seemed unequal to the effort of striking out on new, untried policies, and even though he and Churchill spent a few days at Hyde Park after the formal work of the Conference had been concluded, he did not change his mind. On September 19 he sent Hull a memorandum:

> I have had lengthy talks with the Prime Minister in regard to recognition of the Provisional Government of France. He and I are both very much opposed to it at this time. The Provisional Government has no direct authority from the people. It is best to let things go along as they are for the present.[3]

Three days later, however, the President did acquiesce to the announcement that Jefferson Caffery, former ambassador to Brazil, would shortly go to France as American representative, with the rank of ambassador, to the *de facto* government. It should be noted that since Edwin Wilson had returned from Algiers nine months previously, he had never gone back, on account of his wife's illness, and he had ultimately been reassigned to work in the State Department. Meanwhile, the chargé d'affaires, Selden Chapin, had carried on the routine work of representation and on September 8 had re-established the American Mission in France. Liaison with De Gaulle had also been provided through SHAEF's Military Mission in France, headed, after September 15, by Major General John T. Lewis. Thus while Russia continued to

[3] E. Roosevelt, ed., *F.D.R.: His Personal Letters*, II, 1542.

be represented by Bogomolov, and Great Britain by Duff Cooper (who moved to Paris on September 13), the United States lacked an ambassador until October 15, when Caffery finally arrived in the French capital. Yet while the appointment of Caffery was a good omen, the State Department, in accordance with the President's wishes, emphasized the fact that no change in policy was to be assumed.

To Georges Bidault, the new French foreign minister, the situation verged on the ridiculous. He first learned of Caffery's appointment by reading about it in the newspaper. On the same day that the announcement was made, Bidault held his first press conference. He told newspapermen that postponement of recognition by the Allies was particularly annoying by reason of the fact that there was no rival claimant—between the government and France there was no difference. "You must take us," he said, "as we are." The logic was so indisputable that only the White House could fail to acknowledge it.

If Winston Churchill had been reluctant at Quebec to press the President into further recognition, he did not conceal his desire to see France emerge as a great power. Before the House of Commons, which he addressed on September 28, three days after his return to London from the United States, the Prime Minister reiterated his hope of seeing France erected into a strong, friendly, and independent state which would participate in all discussions affecting the Rhine frontiers and the general settlement of Germany. He hailed the recent broadening of the Provisional government and suggested that Allied recognition might follow if the legislative assembly were transformed into an elected body reinforced by the addition of new elements drawn from inside France.

Whether or not as a direct result of Churchill's suggestion, De Gaulle's government on October 6 passed an ordinance which provided for the broadening and enlarging of the Consultative Assembly, which, it was announced, would meet in Paris in a month's time. This was not quite the same as calling for elections, but a committee headed by Adrien Tixier had concluded that for technical reasons it would be impossible to hold elections prior to February, 1945. Meanwhile, the Consultative Assembly, enlarged to contain the entire National Resistance Council, 129 other delegates from the French Resistance, and representatives of the parties, labor groups, and other organizations, would be the closest practical counterpart of an elected body. If the move did not fulfill Churchill's requirements, it provided at least a gesture which could not fail to have some influence in Washington.

American refusal to recognize the De Gaulle government had now reached the point where further reluctance to take cognizance of reality was prejudicial to United States interests. The French newspaper *Franc-Tireur* made capital of the situation in an editorial on October 5:

> The United States and Britain have recognized the Italian Government. That is good news for the latest country to join the United Nations.
>
> It is probable that the Rumanian Government which succeeded Antonescu's will also be recognized. Then it will be the turn of Bulgaria, and one day, let us hope, of Hungary.
>
> It goes without saying that after the final victory the Governments that are set up in Berlin and Tokyo will also be recognized.
>
> It will then only remain for our Anglo-American Allies to establish normal relations with the Papuans, the Hottentots and the Lapps.
>
> After which, who knows, we French may at last get a look in.

In actual fact, the situation was not quite so black as it appeared. General Juin, chief of staff of national defense, had been discussing with representatives of SHAEF, since the end of September, the boundaries for the zone of the interior, which, according to the *de facto* agreement of August 25, would be primarily under French administration. By October 13 a tentative agreement had been reached at SHAEF to the effect that about three-fourths of France, including Paris, should be incorporated into the interior zone. This agreement placed Washington in an impossible dilemma: it would be difficult to grant virtually the whole of France to De Gaulle for administration and then fail to recognize the organs which he had established for this purpose.

This logic was not lost on the Prime Minister when the status of these negotiations was forwarded to him at Moscow, where he was discussing Balkan affairs with Stalin. On October 14 he dispatched a long memorandum to Roosevelt. He commented on his own suggestion about the Assembly and about the successful negotiations concerning the zone of the interior. He then continued:

The enlargement of the Consultative Assembly is also making good progress. Duff Cooper reports that owing to very real difficulties of communications in France the French have found it impracticable to proceed with the original Algiers plan of getting members of an enlarged Assembly confirmed in their mandates by elections in liberated departments. They propose instead to add selected delegates from the Resistance Movement Parliamentary groups. I understand it is hoped to settle the matter shortly and publish a new decree defining attributions of the reformed Assembly and giving it increased powers over the Executive. It is thought that the enlarged Assembly should be able to meet at the end of this month.

There is no doubt that the French have been co-operating with Supreme Headquarters and that their Provisional Government has the support of the majority of the French people. I suggest therefore that we can now safely recognize General de Gaulle's Administration as the Provisional Government of France.[4]

Although the President was not unwilling to entertain proposals for recognition, he was still in no hurry to take action. By this time all of his advisers, including Admiral Leahy, were in favor of recognizing De Gaulle. Freeman Matthews of the State Department had urged upon Leahy that he should attempt to persuade Roosevelt to take the final step, and Leahy finally and reluctantly concluded that it would be advantageous to the Allied cause. Eisenhower had written the Joint Chiefs of Staff on October 20 urging formal recognition of the De Gaulle group as the Provisional government. (Since the zone-of-interior arrangement went into practical effect on that same day, he could scarcely make any other recommendation.) Yet as late as October 20 there was little evidence that the President had changed his mind. At his press conference he told journalists that the military were still studying the question of turning over more civil affairs to the French and whether that could be a basis of recognition. He described the situation as "iffy." On the same day he wrote Churchill:

I think until the French set up a real zone of interior that we should make no move towards recognizing them as a Provisional Government. The enlargement of the Consultative Assembly, which has already been

4 Churchill, *Triumph and Tragedy*, 246–47.

extended and made more representative, is almost as important, and I should be inclined to hand recognition on the effective completion of both these acts. I would not be satisfied with de Gaulle merely saying that he was going to do it.

I agree with you that there must be no implication, if and when we do recognize a Provisional Government, that this means a seat on the European Advisory Council, etc. These matters can be taken up later on their merits.

I am anxious to handle this matter, for the present, directly between you and me, and would prefer, for the moment, that the "modus operandi" should not become a matter of discussion between the State Department and your Foreign Office.[5]

Within two days, however, Roosevelt had reversed himself and given his approval to recognition. As Leahy comments, it must have been a difficult decision for the President. For the previous nine months, after Hull had come to believe that nonrecognition of De Gaulle would no longer serve American interests, Roosevelt had himself borne the burden of stubborn opposition to the French leader. All of his arguments for the opposition had proved unfounded: De Gaulle had not proclaimed a dictatorship; civil war had not broken out; rival parties and leaders had not come forward; and to all observers, De Gaulle was wholeheartedly, spontaneously, and enthusiastically the choice of Frenchmen as head of their Provisional governmnent. By October 20 the President was forced to acknowledge that De Gaulle had broadened his cabinet and the Consultative Assembly and that Eisenhower had agreed to turn over three-fourths of France to French administrators appointed by De Gaulle. It is perhaps significant that on that same day Roosevelt left Washington on a speaking tour in connection with his fourth-term campaign, and he could not have avoided the realization that recognition would be received with approval in many quarters.

On October 23 the announcement of recognition was made in a statement by acting Secretary of State Stettinius. Churchill, still at Moscow, was "surprised at the very sharp turn taken by the State Department" and feared that the Russians would take offense, for the rapid American action would make it appear that the Soviet Union had ob-

[5] *Ibid.,* 247–48.

structed recognition, when the contrary was the case. At the last moment, however, agreements were reached which permitted all three powers to publish their statements of recognition on the same day. With an awkwardness that had become habitual when its French policy was concerned, the United States pronounced that "this action is in harmony with its policy toward France as publicly enunciated from time to time by the President and the Secretary of State." The statement referred to Hull's declaration of April 9 as if the Secretary of State had in fact pronounced American policy at that time. When every informed Frenchman knew that recognition in any form had been the antithesis of the American attitude and that Hull's statement had been overruled by the President, it was indeed ungracious, even guileful, to introduce the fatuous implication that the State Department's French policy had been a continuous and resounding success, now fittingly climaxed by the triumphant recognition of October 23.

It is difficult to point out advantages in the policy which the President had so long and so obstinately pursued. A case can be made for nonacceptance of De Gaulle during 1940 and 1941, and it is even arguable that introduction of De Gaulle into North Africa at the time of the landings would have served no purpose; but a point had been reached toward the end of 1943 when further by-passing of De Gaulle and the FCNL operated against rather than for Allied interests. Particularly after January, 1944, when the State and War Departments concurred in a policy of recognition, did the President's intransigence become indefensible. His inaction resulted in lack of guidance and confusion among those whose task was to implement policy, and it led to a series of *de facto* arrangements which could have been brought about sooner and more easily with intelligent leadership at top levels.

As Churchill had long since pointed out, *recognition* is simply a word, and it has no meaning except in terms of practical results. Recognized or not, De Gaulle's government was coping day by day with France's internal problems; without recognition the Provisional government had been able to negotiate Lend-Lease agreements, arrange for arms' deliveries, regulate currency matters, and participate in some international conferences. Now the question uppermost in the minds of Frenchmen, who accepted the long-delayed recognition with complacency, was the extent to which it would mean entry into higher Allied councils. If France would have to persist in standing at the door outside the council chamber, obtaining news from the syndicated press, she might as well be unrecognized. As he had done a year earlier after the formulas resulting from the first Quebec Conference had been announced, De Gaulle waited, not without cynicism, to learn what "recognition" might really mean to his government.

An Estimate of United States Relations with the Dissident French

With recognition of De Gaulle's Provisional government, the long and involved story of relations with the French Committee of National Liberation came to an end. For De Gaulle it would no longer be necessary to cope with the familiar questions of Giraudist versus Gaullist, BCRA versus *Deuxième Bureau,* or FCNL versus National Resistance Council. Nor would the Allies have to worry about which dissident group represented France. Charles de Gaulle was in France, in control of the French Armies, chief of the French government, and so recognized by all the Allied powers. That is not to say that he had become the peer of Roosevelt, Churchill, or Stalin or that France was recognized as an equal of the principal belligerents. But France stood once more upon her feet, and in 1944 and 1945, De Gaulle would make tremendous progress in bringing his defeated and broken France back to a position of European influence. In spite of these accomplishments, the peculiarities of De Gaulle's temperament would continue to lead him perversely into conflict with those whom it was frequently unwise, or at least undiplomatic, to alienate. The postwar years would reveal no alteration in this Gaullist tendency, and it would irk President Truman when he succeeded to the Presidency, even as it had annoyed his predecessor.

The personal conflicts and misunderstandings that developed during the war years must not obscure the real accomplishments which grew out of contacts between the United States and the dissident French. Whatever his shortcomings, General de Gaulle did weld the diverse elements which resisted Hitler's aggression into a centralized force whose achievements ultimately made a significant contribution to the over-all war effort. Even though the early United States policy of dealing with local groups found some justification in the first few years of the war, arrangements made through a central responsible agency tremendously increased the efficiency and effectiveness of such arrangements. It was unrealistic for Lend-Lease contracts to be made separately with the controlling officials of Martinique, North Africa, Madagascar, New Caledonia, and the various French colonies. Once the Committee of National Liberation was recognized—however reluctantly and hesitatingly—it was possible to enter into negotiations for providing civilian and military supplies with a central organization that could facilitate local arrangements in the colonies or in France itself.

However dramatic the temperamental clashes of Roosevelt, Churchill, and De Gaulle may have been, one should never overlook America's material contribution, arranged for with little bickering or headlines, in helping French forces re-enter the war. Roosevelt's personal antipathy to De Gaulle's politics did not stand in the way of American economic assistance to the French people. Such assistance was negotiated at a level lower than that of chiefs of state, and a vast program of aid was carried out more or less smoothly. In the long view, the humdrum facts of Lend-Lease, buried in masses of figures and reports which rarely made the front pages, provide realistic proofs of fundamental Franco-American good will which in over-all importance eclipsed the ephemeral tiffs between the President and De Gaulle.

It may be useful and instructive at this point to recapitulate the amount of American aid which, up until the end of 1944, had been assigned to France. Under the Anfa program, the United States had equipped eight French divisions at a cost estimated at $700,000,000. For this sum the French had received 1,091 planes, plus $14,000,000 of spare parts and accessories, 802 small antiaircraft guns, 800 antitank guns, 484 pieces of heavy artillery, 1,100 light and medium tanks, 2,300 armored cars, 255,000 guns and pistols, 9,500 machine guns, 1,200 mortars, 8,800 jeeps, 5,400 cars and ambulances, 20,000 trucks, and 14,000 trailers. The United States had also brought to North Africa and France 125,000 tons of rails, 130,000 tons of material for bridges, and 1,000,000 tons of construction material, including 4,000 tractors and 500 cranes. To the French railroad system the Americans brought 1,150 locomotives and 13,600 cars and shipped for civilian use 175,000 tons of food, clothing, medications, and other goods valued at $30,000,000. In a later report of Lend-Lease operations, it was estimated that France had received $3,-235,000,000 in Lend-Lease aid, against reciprocal Lend-Lease assistance calculated at $868,000,000.[6]

But whatever material benefits the French may have obtained from their relations with the United States and the other Allies, De Gaulle never was able to achieve what he most earnestly desired, acceptance as a cobelligerent by the Big Three. Some years after the war, De Gaulle told a group of his adherents that France must never again sit on the edge of her chair when invited to Allied war councils. The obligation of receiving crumbs from the table, of being excluded from meaningful deliberations on strategy, and of not being trusted to receive vital information tremendously irritated De Gaulle and his colleagues. The French leaders were brought to Casablanca virtually under guard and were not even invited to Quebec, Cairo, Teheran, Yalta, Potsdam, or the sessions of the Combined Chiefs of Staff. Small comfort emerged from French participation at conferences like UNRRA, to which representatives of all the United Nations, large and small, had been invited. Even membership in the Italian Advisory Commission proved a shallow accomplishment when it became apparent that the Commission possessed no real influence in determining policy on Italian administration.

French exclusion from Big Three deliberations by no means resulted simply from Roosevelt's hostility to De Gaulle. No belligerent making a minor contribution in men and materials was invited to these discussions. All three chiefs of state agreed that the Big Three was a very exclusive club, the entrance fee being 5,000,000 soldiers or the equivalent. Because it was obvious that France, even with additional man power available after liberation, could not equip and train more than a minute fraction of that number before the end of the war, neither Churchill, Roosevelt, nor Stalin entertained the slightest thought of bringing France into their strategic conferences.

It cannot, of course, be denied, in reviewing Franco-American wartime relations, that a significant factor in determining the course of

[6] Report released 3 Feb. 1945 by the Office of War Information. See *Business Week*, No. 806 (10 Feb. 1945), 113–14. Also *Twenty-third Report to Congress on Lend-Lease Operations*, for the period ended Sept. 30, 1946, 8–10. France was third in recipients of Lend-Lease. Great Britain received $31,392,361,000 and the Soviet Union $11,297,833,000.

policy was the personal intervention and concern of the American President. But there were other factors as well. At the beginning of the war, regardless of the White House attitude, the strong State Department devotion to Vichy would probably have required a maintenance of relations with Marshal Pétain at least until December, 1941, when the United States entered the war. After Pearl Harbor, in the course of 1942, as recognition of the Vichy regime became less and less defensible, a vigorous Presidential decision to deviate sharply from the traditional attitude could easily have been made. There was no public pressure to hinder such a decision—on the contrary—and while effective support of De Gaulle might have irritated Cordell Hull, whose judgment, nettled by bitter memories of Saint Pierre and Miquelon, fell short of impartiality, it must be recalled that General Donovan's OSS and members of the War Department recognized, even at that time, the significance and value of Fighting France to the war effort. That the Vichy policy prevailed, and that De Gaulle found the door unceremoniously shut in 1942, was in part the consequence of a series of fortuitous but related circumstances. If the Anglo-American decision to launch a cross-Channel offensive had not been subverted by the adoption of "Torch," the entire North African political fiasco might have been avoided. It is of course idle, however fascinating, to wonder whether, in the event that original plans for a Roosevelt–De Gaulle meeting in 1942 had been adhered to, the President might have developed a more favorable outlook toward the Free French. But once it had been decided to move into North Africa, where Robert Murphy's groundwork with anti-German, anti-Gaullist elements made a *rapprochement* with the Fighting French impossible, the break with De Gaulle became inevitable. To the extent that Roosevelt was personally responsible for the "Torch" decision he was responsible for an anti–De Gaulle attitude's becoming official United States policy. One could not work simultaneously with Darlan and De Gaulle; one could work simultaneously with Giraud and De Gaulle only with the greatest difficulty. All of Roosevelt's great gifts for compromising extremes and for exerting his personal charm to erase misunderstandings among subordinates failed in the face of a gap as unbridgeable as that which stretched between the dissidence of De Gaulle and the dissidence of Giraud.

One positive advantage to France emerged from the North African imbroglio. If the De Gaulle–Giraud controversy had not developed, France might have received far less military equipment from the United States than she did. When Roosevelt approved the Anfa program of eleven divisions, he personally and singlehandedly committed the United States to a policy which, had it been left to the labored deliberations of the Joint Chiefs of Staff, might never have been adopted. Without Presidential backing, the program most certainly would have been delayed or sidetracked by the Combined Chiefs, whose British members registered small enthusiasm over arms for Giraud. Many field commanders were equally unsympathetic; for no matter how much they appreciated the fighting qualities of French units, American theater commanders experienced difficulties enough in fighting coalition war without adding new troops, unfamiliar methods, and a new language to their problems. Many U. S. officers at Allied headquarters in North Africa, who wished to employ French troops solely for garrison purposes, would have opposed the Anfa program of combat divisions for military reasons. The Anfa decision was a political one, and it was urged for political ends. But once adopted, it was never reversed for political reasons; although he was tempted when he saw De Gaulle obtaining control of the new divisions, Roosevelt never took measures to impede deliveries in order to undermine De Gaulle's authority. When the number of divisions was reduced from eleven to eight, it was not the President but military commanders who, for military considerations, reduced the program. And when, at the end of 1944, the Combined Chiefs of Staff, as a military requirement, recommended that eight additional divisions be equipped, Roosevelt instantly approved the new program. Much as De Gaulle may have railed against the slowness and reluctance with which the United States undertook to provide him with tanks and guns, France's postwar military accomplishments point to the accuracy of American estimates that the Provisional government was incapable of administering more than sixteen divisions. There is no evidence that Roosevelt, for the sake of his postwar plans, endeavored to keep France weak; on the contrary, he permitted maximum military and civilian shipments commensurate with other American commitments, the availability of shipping, and the capacity of France to accept deliveries.

It is not so easy to exonerate Roosevelt of charges that his reluctance to recognize a De Gaulle–headed government was unrealistic and contrary to the best interests of the United States and the war effort. If exclusion of De Gaulle from North Africa was thrust upon the Allies by the nature of the invasion, acceptance of De Gaulle, once he had achieved domination of the French Committee of Liberation, was logical and inevitable. The question was not whether De Gaulle and the FCNL should be recognized but how soon—in other words, at what time did De Gaulle exercise such control over the Committee and over Resistance elements in France that failure to work with him produced disadvantages far outweighing the benefits? By October, 1943, there was good evidence that De Gaulle, not Giraud, was the man to work with; by December this evidence was conclusive; and by January, 1944, virtually every responsible officer in the North African theater and in Washington, including Eisenhower, Murphy, Wilson, McCloy, Stimson, and even Hull, had become convinced that closer relations with the FCNL were imperative. The responsibility for denying the Committee falls squarely on the shoulders of the President, who, for month after month —from January to July, 1944—stubbornly refused to submit. It can be pointed out that during these months Roosevelt's vitality was sapped by illness and that Harry Hopkins, also ill, was not available to provide the President with that sensible counsel which sometimes served to mitigate his chief's carelessness and obstinacy. But this defense can in no wise excuse the President for so centralizing control of foreign policy that in case of his disability no other agency could serve to reach necessary decisions.

To be sure, De Gaulle did nothing to make the President's task easier. Scarcely did American policy show signs of softening, when the General would initiate a crisis—over Corsica, Italy, the Mediterranean Commission, the Levant states, or Giraud—and act with such arrogance, refusing to descend from his Olympian heights, that serious misgivings were of necessity entertained in Washington about the possibility of working effectively with him. It may be that Roosevelt's offhand comments about the future of Morocco and Indochina, or his often-repeated statements on "local arrangements," were not calculated to calm Gaullist apprehensions; but power is accompanied by privilege, and De Gaulle as much as anyone had reason to be aware of that fact of political life.

If Roosevelt, in February, 1944, had approved the directive empowering Eisenhower to make arrangements exclusively with the FCNL, he would have enormously facilitated administrative questions connected with the Normandy landings: the awkward problems of liaison, currency, co-ordination with the Resistance, and civil affairs could all have found solutions—and essentially the same solutions which time in any event imposed—much earlier and much easier. Even more important, friction with the British over French policy would have been avoided. Considering Churchill's wise efforts to minimize where he could the differences between Washington and London over De Gaulle, it is not likely that the French issue would under any circumstances have driven a wedge between the Western Allies or between the West and Russia; but controversy about France provided only one of many problems—including Poland, Yugoslavia, and Greece, Mediterranean strategy, operations in Burma and the Far East, and postwar colonialism—which were subjects of lively altercation between the United States and Britain. Any effort to reduce Anglo-American differences would have helped the war effort. If vital American interests found themselves jeopardized by recognition of De Gaulle, it would have been right and just to oppose the British position; but when the White House opposition was misdirected, sometimes perhaps pigheadedly holding its position merely to prove that it did not slavishly follow a British lead, it can be neither justified nor condoned.

None of President Roosevelt's expressed fears about De Gaulle and the Free French materialized. It may be that Roosevelt opposed Free France because no proof could be adduced that De Gaulle was the French people's choice, it may be that he was lukewarm about De Gaulle because he believed he saw in him an opponent of collective security; or it may be that he was loath to furnish him his "white horse" because he distrusted and disliked him; but when it became clear that in spite of the President's personal opinion De Gaulle was to become the French chief of state, the better part of political wisdom should have dictated that Roosevelt could achieve his ends more successfully—as in the contest between the Sun and the Wind to make the Traveller remove his coat—by means more subtle than forceful antagonism. Roosevelt feared that De Gaulle would make himself a dictator, but De Gaulle, as he had promised, surrendered his powers to the first elected Assembly at the end of 1945; Roosevelt found De Gaulle unsympathetic to the trusteeship idea, but the original trusteeship concept never achieved fruition; Roosevelt feared civil war in France, but De Gaulle proved to be the best possible safeguard against internal disturbance; Roosevelt believed that other political leaders from inside France would emerge, but they did not. For a host of groundless fears the President interposed his solitary but powerful opposition to a policy which would have been, as events proved, in the American interest; and for the first half of 1944 no positive action in regard to the French could be taken by interested agencies in Washington as a result of Roosevelt's negative and indefensible attitude.

Relations with De Gaulle until Roosevelt's Death

In the six-month interval between *de jure* recognition of De Gaulle's Provisional government and the President's death, the United States' attitude toward France must be considered, even more than in the earlier years of the war, within the framework of general policy. Until 1944 the American propensity to subordinate all political thinking to the philosophy of "win the war" had operated to make the French problem an essentially military one; and even in 1945 the triple concept of "win the war," "save American lives," and "postpone political decisions until the peace conference" exercised such weighty influence on American thinking that an unrealistic ostrich attitude had developed in Washington. It was not untypical that as late as October, 1944, Roosevelt had written to Hull about occupation plans for Germany: "I dislike making detailed plans for a country we do not yet occupy."[7] There is little evidence that Roosevelt gave much thought to a peculiarly French policy during the final months of his life. Just as De Gaulle frequently commented that *"France balayera tout ça,"* so the President hoped the UN would sweep away the petty nationalist quarrels which for centuries had imposed balances of power on Europe. In the course of postwar

[7] Hull, *Memoirs,* II, 1621.

events, France would take her appropriate place in the new and better world.

It must never be forgotten that month after month, and never seriously impeded by political events, the steady and unspectacular deliveries of military and civilian supplies continued to be made in North Africa and France. On the French side there was constant reciprocal assistance to America—ports in Nouméa and Africa, and the use of installations and transportation and communication facilities throughout the French Empire. Historical justice can scarcely be done to a type of relationship which is catalogued in inventories and statistics, but mutual economic and military assistance in the war effort comprises the solid and massive substance of United States relations with the dissident French. Unflattering as it may be to Frenchmen, French policy did not occupy an enormous proportion of President Roosevelt's time and thought; compared to domestic affairs, military strategy, and relations with England and Russia, the French problem was for Roosevelt a relatively small one. Any estimate of Roosevelt's French policy must be made in relation to his other tasks and in relation to his over-all accomplishments; some of the petty friction then disappears before the positive and vast results of an assistance program that was as much American as Rooseveltian. If the President was responsible for nonrecognition of De Gaulle, he was equally the architect of Lend-Lease; and this alone should justify the final estimate that his policy, on the whole, benefited rather than handicapped French interests.

This post-recognition period, from October, 1944, until the war's end, revealed some significant progress in Franco-American relations. It should be recalled that while Lend-Lease and relief arrangements had been concluded with the French Committee of National Liberation in September, 1943, and in August, 1944, no commitment had been made with France. The recognition of October 23 rendered it now advisable to place Lend-Lease on a permanent footing through an agreement to be signed with the French Provisional government. Negotiations were entrusted to Jean Monnet, now head of the French Import Mission, who came to Washington late in December, 1944, to discuss France's needs with officials of the Foreign Economic Administration. Monnet had already drawn up a plan calling for large amounts of food, chemicals, and machinery to be shipped to France in the following eight months. By February 8, 1945, a basic Lend-Lease understanding was reached, and a few weeks later, on February 28, the agreement was officially signed which became the fundamental document on further aid to France. By this instrument the United States undertook to ship $1,675,-000,000 worth of raw materials, food, and petroleum and $900,000,000 worth of heavy equipment, such as rolling stock, heavy machinery, and harbor equipment. In return, France guaranteed under a reciprocal program to provide for American military needs in France. It is noteworthy that this basic agreement, a solid manifestation of Franco-American harmony, was concluded at the precise moment that the Yalta Conference, from which France had been excluded, prompted De Gaulle to utter renewed complaints that France had been by-passed and slighted.

Also in this post-recognition period France received from the United States a promise to equip eight more divisions. It is possible, however, that if Hitler's defenses had not stiffened in September and October, and if von Rundstedt had not launched his counteroffensive in December, French rearmament might have remained at the original Anfa level. But at the end of October, Eisenhower recommended rearmament of two additional French divisions, and in November the French were invited to formulate a program commensurate with their current capacities. Minister of War Diethelm drew up a schedule, submitted to the Allies on November 30, which called for eight new combat divisions involving 207,000 men, together with other programs to equip security battalions and troops for use in the Far East. Negotiations with Allied officials over the November 30 proposals might have dragged on for several month if it had not been for the Ardennes counteroffensive launched on December 15 by Marshal von Rundstedt.

Although the attack was curbed by December 28, the threat of German countermoves made Eisenhower painfully aware of the desirability of additional Allied forces in France. On that day he notified the Combined Chiefs that he approved an immediate equipping of five additional French divisions. The Combined Chiefs of Staff outdid themselves in supporting the Supreme Commander and on the following day approved in principle the entire eight-division program requested by the French on November 30. The CCS recommendations were immediately approved by the President, and De Gaulle became the astonished recipient of a New Year's gift of equipment he could scarcely have anticipated receiving so soon.[8]

While arrangements of Lend-Lease and military equipment seemed to point toward improved Franco-American understanding, De Gaulle's personal relations with Roosevelt, up to the moment of the President's death, never took an important turn for the better. Whether it was conflict with SHAEF over control of French troops or personal pique at his exclusion from Big Three councils, De Gaulle apparently could not restrain his disturbing habit of throwing stones into frog ponds in such a way that the troubled waters of American-French diplomacy never completely calmed down.

Around New Year's, 1945, a near-crisis developed between De Gaulle and SHAEF as a result of the Rundstedt counteroffensive. As Allied troops were withdrawn to the west, Eisenhower's north Alsatian defenses were so seriously weakened that Hitler determined to launch an offensive from the north between Saarbrücken and the Rhine. Such an attack would head directly for recently liberated Strasbourg. If the Germans succeeded in their northern attack and joined forces with units pushing up from Colmar, they could surround any Allied troops left in northeastern Alsace. Under these conditions, Eisenhower on January 1 ordered a strategic withdrawal to the Vosges, which would have shortened his lines and increased his reserve but would have abandoned Strasbourg to German reprisals.

De Gaulle and General Juin were aghast at the implications of Strasbourg's possible loss. Not only would there be German vengeance on the Alsatians but danger of revulsion and reaction throughout France against a government which would abandon the city without a fight. So strongly did De Gaulle feel about the matter that he appealed over Eisenhower's head to Roosevelt and Churchill, and he also informed Eisenhower that in case the Americans withdrew he would be forced to order De Lattre to operate independently in defending the city. De Gaulle argued his case in person before Eisenhower, who finally concluded that unrest in France would provide a greater danger to the war effort than his overextended line. He decided to try to hold a front

[8] Vigneras, *Rearming the French*, 336.

north of Strasbourg from the Vosges to the Rhine and turned over to
the French the major responsibility for defending the city. Ultimately
the German attack was repulsed before Strasbourg was reached, and
by the end of January the Allies had resumed the offensive.

A crisis which would have been deplorable on all counts had been
averted. But the incident demonstrated with illuminating clarity how
intensely De Gaulle would insist that French interests should take precedence over blind allegiance to the Allied supreme command. While this
position proved annoying to British and American authorities, it must
be admitted that without representation in the Combined Chiefs of
Staff or at top-level conferences, De Gaulle had no other means of
making his point of view felt. To criticize De Gaulle for this stubborn
defense of French interests is to overlook the many differences between
Roosevelt and Churchill, Eisenhower, and Montgomery over a multitude
of strategic and national idiosyncrasies.

The Strasbourg incident may not have been important in itself, but
on the eve of the Yalta Conference it did nothing to suggest to Roosevelt that he should reverse his earlier decision to exclude De Gaulle
from the forthcoming meeting. On December 6 he had told Churchill:
"I still adhere to my position that any attempt to include de Gaulle in
the meeting of the three of us would merely introduce a complicating
and undesirable factor." Neither Roosevelt nor De Gaulle, however,
rejected out of hand the possibility of conferring together after the Conference was over.[9]

Since the Yalta settlements, although in some instances affecting
France, are not central to the issues with which this study is concerned,
it is neither appropriate nor necessary to discuss the deliberations in
detail. It is pertinent, however, to mention the decisions briefly and to
remark upon the influence of the Conference in bringing a further deterioration, at a time so close to the President's final illness, of De Gaulle's
and Roosevelt's personal relations. Although absent from the Conference,
France did not fare badly. She received a German occupation zone, she
was granted a seat on the Allied Control Council for Germany, and she
was invited to become one of the powers sponsoring the San Francisco

[9] A formal request to participate in the Yalta Conference had been drafted by the
French government on 13 Jan. 1945 (*The Conferences at Malta and Yalta*, 296–97).

Conference. That she was given so much authority in the future disposition of Germany and of world affairs provides a good indication of the success with which France, even though unrepresented, was regaining recognition among the powers. De Gaulle might have been surprised, and undoubtedly somewhat dismayed, had he been in a position to remark how strongly his country was defended by Roosevelt and Churchill and with what reluctance his new Soviet ally (France and Russia had concluded a mutual defense pact the previous December) agreed that an occupation zone should be reserved for France.

With the formal work of the Conference completed by February 10, Roosevelt turned his attention to plans which would enable him to visit several Near Eastern heads of state on his return from Yalta. He also sent a message to De Gaulle: he regretted that he was unable to come to Paris but hoped that an alternate proposal, that De Gaulle should come to Algiers to see him, would be satisfactory. This communication was delivered to General de Gaulle by Ambassador Caffery on February 12, the same day that the Yalta communiqué was made public. Upon noting the terms of the President's proposal, General de Gaulle saw fit to refuse the invitation, stating that he continued to hope that President Roosevelt would visit Paris, where the government and the whole population would be extremely happy to receive him at any time.[10]

Once again Franco-American relations, at least on the highest level, took a sharp, sudden plunge. The President was extremely irritated at De Gaulle's brusque rejection of his proposal, and the final opportunity for the two men to develop better personal relations collapsed. Roosevelt had only two months to live. De Gaulle's curiously misguided pride had once more forced him into a move which, while entirely consistent with his handling of his foreign relations since 1940, emphasized French independence rather than good sense. To explain this decision, one has only to recall the sensitiveness with which De Gaulle responded to any action violating French national rights. He had exploded with wrath in 1944 when Churchill, after his illness in Cairo, settled himself in Marra-

10 Communiqué of the French and United States' governments, 21 Feb. 1945. It had been assumed that the incident would remain secret, but it leaked to the press and statements from the two governments became necessary.

kech, a French city, without so much as a by-your-leave from De Gaulle. He had later refused to see Churchill at Algiers when the Prime Minister arrived there without invitation, and he had been furious when Churchill showed up in Corsica during the "Anvil" landings. According to the rights and dignities of international protocol, the head of one state should not arrive in a city of a foreign state without invitation from the head of that state; thus it was one thing for De Gaulle to invite Roosevelt to Paris, but quite another for Roosevelt to invite De Gaulle to Algiers. If it had been irritating to be summoned in 1943 to Casablanca when he headed the Fighting French, it was intolerable for De Gaulle to be summoned to a French city when he was head of the French government and had been so recognized by the United States. Probably these considerations did not occur to Roosevelt or his advisers. It may never have crossed his mind that protocol need be respected in regard to travel in areas which where still military theaters. It is regrettable that such misunderstandings on both sides should have arisen; a little care, a more thoughtfully worded message, or concern for opposing points of view might have altered a sorry incident into a helpful and much-needed friendly exchange of views.

With only two months remaining in Roosevelt's life, there could now be no possibility of ameliorating the relations of the two men. But there was still at least one important problem affecting the French that required the President's personal attention. This was a decision on the question of whether the United States would continue to equip French divisions after the war ended. French hopes were pinned on the President's taking favorable action on an appeal, made by De Gaulle on New Year's Day, for matériel capable of equipping fifty divisions. It was not until March 24, 1945, that the President replied to De Gaulle, and his letter was couched in formal and unhelpful terms:

> It is believed that due to limitations of personnel and equipment, the commitment to arm the French should be limited to the sixteen divisions and supporting troops already approved.
>
> In view of all the factors involved, you will appreciate the fact that attempts at French rearmament beyond the commitments which can clearly be met by France and the United States would interfere with the prosecution of the war.[11]

[11] Vigneras, *Rearming the French,* 387.

To the writer's knowledge, this communication was President Roosevelt's last pronouncement on French policy. Several days later Roosevelt left for Warm Springs, and nineteen days after he signed the dispatch to De Gaulle he was dead. It is perhaps symbolic, and certainly ironic, that Roosevelt's gesture toward De Gaulle should have been a refusal to concur in a policy which the General believed to be vital to French interests.

Truman and De Gaulle

A few words suffice for commentary on De Gaulle's relations with the United States after Harry Truman succeeded to the Presidency. It was during Truman's first year in office that De Gaulle made his second trip to the United States. Since the visit developed into a triumphal tour, erasing many of the ill feelings engendered during the war years, it appropriately sounds the note on which this study concludes. Before he arrived in Washington, however, De Gaulle had managed to present the new President with samples of his intransigence and had incurred, in fact, sharper reprisals than any Roosevelt had seen fit to make.

One incident, occurring in April, 1945, was reminiscent of the Strasbourg affair. On April 23, French elements occupied the strategically located city of Stuttgart. But in the rapid advance made by the Sixth Army Group, the supply lines of the U. S. Third Army and Seventh Army, and the French First Army, had crisscrossed. With traffic jams on the roads to Stuttgart, Ulm, and Austria threatening Allied operations almost as much as enemy action, General Devers decided to shift control of Stuttgart to the Seventh Army.

De Gaulle's sensitivity immediately caused him to interpret the order as an Allied move to shunt the French out of an area which they might claim as part of their occupation zone. He ordered the French not to evacuate the city and told De Lattre that he should hold and administer territory conquered by his troops until the French zone of occupation had been fixed. As soon as the Stuttgart impasse was brought to Eisenhower's attention, he wrote De Gaulle that while he refused to make an issue of the incident, he had no alternative but to report to the Combined Chiefs of Staff that he could no longer rely on the operational employment of any French forces which they might contemplate equipping in the future. He then forwarded his recommendations to the Combined Chiefs, through whom, via Admiral Leahy, they reached President Truman. Truman immediately wrote De Gaulle that he was shocked at the General's action and warned him that if the time had come when the French Army was to be considered as carrying out only French political designs, the command structure would then have to be rearranged. Truman's threat might have matured into a curtailment of equipment, but friction over the Stuttgart incident was outdated a week later by the end of hostilities against Germany. All wartime military aid programs, except those actually in process of delivery, automatically ceased; their resumption would have to involve governmental discussions on postwar problems.

Even after the war was ended, Truman found himself involved in further manifestations of De Gaulle's efforts to insure French independence and sovereignty. In April, during the last days of the Italian campaign, a co-ordinated attack was made simultaneously from Italy and France against German forces in the Alps along the Franco-Italian border. From the French side the offensive was entrusted to French units under Lieutenant General Paul Doyen, who advanced beyond the 1939 border into the Italian province of Cuneo. Since the Franco-Italian frontier marked the boundary between the Fifteenth Army Group and the Sixth Army Group, General Devers ordered Doyen on April 28 to arrest his advance and withdraw into France. Doyen refused to withdraw without orders from the French government, and throughout the month of May, with the war then at an end, he would not move.

On May 30, General Doyen, following De Gaulle's instructions, announced to the Allied command that he had been ordered by the French government to occupy and administer the Cuneo area and that he would be compelled to oppose the installation of any Allied administrative agency. When this communication was received by the Joint Chiefs of Staff in Washington, Admiral Leahy did not delay in reporting its contents to the President. Several alternative lines of action were considered, one of which was to publicize the incident; but after extended cabinet discussion, the President decided to transmit a firm letter to De Gaulle. On June 6, Ambassador Caffery was directed to deliver a communication along the following lines:

I feel deep concern over the action of the French Army in ignoring orders issued by representatives of the Combined Chiefs of Staff. General Doyen's letter of 30 May contained the unbelievable threat that the French might fight the Americans. The American people would be shocked if they knew of this threat. I urge you to reconsider your stand in this matter. Meanwhile I have no alternative but to order the stoppage of issue of military equipment and munitions.

Acting Secretary of State Joseph Grew (Stettinius was in San Francisco) thought the message was masterly. "Masterly is not quite the word," retorted the President, "that note was a sledge hammer."[12] Shortly after the message was delivered, Bidault reported that General Juin would proceed to General Alexander's headquarters to deal with the matter in the "broadest spirit of conciliation"; and by June 10 it was learned that De Gaulle had consented to the withdrawal of French troops.

Yet, if De Gaulle's actions tended to render Washington and London somewhat unsympathetic to certain French aspirations, not all of France's enterprises evolved hostile responses from the Allies. For example, even though De Gaulle was barred from conferences like Yalta and Potsdam, France was not excluded from United Nations conferences, and at San Francisco, represented by newly appointed Foreign Minister Georges Bidault, she made major contributions to the re-establishment of world order. Misgivings which the French had entertained about several matters to be aired at San Francisco soon proved to be largely ungrounded. In two areas where French doubts had been paramount the French delegation learned that the United States and Russia shared the French position. One of these doubts involved the matter of trusteeships, which had for so long seemed directed in State Department thinking at separating France from her colonies. By the spring of 1945, however, Americans were not talking so firmly about permitting all of the world's subject peoples to achieve independence after a period of international sponsorship. As the United States began to feel and comprehend the implications of world-wide power, her military chiefs, seeing the strategic requirements of Pacific bases, put pressure on State Department planners to modify their visionary proposals. After Hull left the Depart-

12 Joseph C. Grew, *Turbulent Era,* ed. by Walter Johnson, II, 1512-17.

ment, and after Roosevelt's death, no one at a high level of the government was prepared to carry the burden of the original trusteeship idea in the face of British, French, and his own military opposition. By the time of the San Francisco Conference the concept had been watered down to apply only to former League of Nations mandates, former Axis territories, and areas voluntarily placed under the United Nations by the colonial power. Strategic areas like Dakar would be the subject of separate and further negotiation. No one threatened France with any more "intolerable suggestions" (the phrase was Bidault's) that Indochina or New Caledonia should be taken from France. After long months of apprehension on the part of De Gaulle that Roosevelt intended to put the French Empire on trial before the United Nations, the threats evaporated when subjected to the disabusing rays of postwar reality.

De Gaulle's Second Visit to the United States

By the summer of 1945, in full possession of her ancestral territory, with control of an occupation zone and representation in the United Nations, France had essentially re-established her sovereignty. Under these circumstances it seemed fitting to President Truman in July to invite General de Gaulle to pay another visit to Washington. Since De Gaulle had not been asked to the Potsdam Conference, the President may have believed that personal conversations in the United States would compensate for the slight which the General believed—rightly or wrongly—had been inflicted on him.

General de Gaulle's reception in the United States during the last week of August, 1945, marked a high point in Franco-American relations. The grievances and irritations of the war years were forgotten in exuberant outbursts of friendliness and good will. At the White House, President Truman pinned the Legion of Merit insignia on the tunic of a smiling De Gaulle, while the American Chiefs of Staff were comparably honored by the French government. Even that doughty antagonist of Gaullism, Admiral Leahy, who scarcely two months previously had remarked that the fall of the "irascible" and "difficult" De Gaulle would have been very pleasing to all the Allied governments,[13] was awarded the *Grande Croix de la Légion d'Honneur.*

[13] *I Was There,* 374.

There were now few outstanding differences between the two governments, and conversations between Truman, De Gaulle, and their experts reached much common ground. De Gaulle was greatly concerned about Germany, particularly as the evolution of Poland into a Russian satellite moved the German political center of gravity westward. He also expressed concern about political unification in Germany but was assured that economic centralization, which in the American view was to be given high priority, did not necessarily imply that Germany would become immediately unified. The Americans appeared to be sympathetic with the French position but felt that faith should be placed above all in the United Nations as the agency which would dispose of troubled Europe's problems. De Gaulle was not convinced.

Questions concerning the Pacific were also brought up, but they failed, as usual, to achieve clear-cut or final solutions. Since the Japanese had then capitulated, a tentative agreement made at Potsdam to continue military deliveries and to use French troops in the Far East had been suspended. De Gaulle seemed not to be worried that the United States intended to annex Nouméa or Dakar. He pointed out to correspondents that American troops still used bases in New Caledonia but added that the French government had not been informed of any request for the establishment of a permanent base there. "This is a problem of collective security," he stated, "and exchanges of views among the Allied powers are necessary." When the time came for the United States to consider bases involving her own security, the Cold War would force her to think more in terms of airfields in Morocco and France than of naval bases 4,000 miles from Okinawa and Formosa.

Behind the scenes there were conversations connected with French financial and economic rehabilitation. It was recognized that the Lend-Lease agreement signed the previous February would not be carried out in its entirety, and that President Truman, as a result of the Japanese capitulation, would shortly terminate the entire program. Since it was estimated that deliveries under the agreement would ultimately amount to about $1,000,000,000, the French hoped to obtain credits in that amount in order to achieve a final Lend-Lease settlement. The press, emphasizing that De Gaulle brought no financial experts with him, overlooked the fact that Jean Monnet had already been in Washington for some time carrying on negotiations with officials of the State Department and the Export-Import Bank. The good feeling generated by De Gaulle's visit facilitated continuation of these talks, which led to American collaboration in the French program on reconstruction and modernization which came to be known as the Monnet Plan. By December, 1945, France agreed to support the Bretton Woods Agreement establishing the World Bank and to participate in discussions on the proposed International Trade Organization; the United States, for its part, approved the general structure of the Monnet Plan and agreed, through the Export-Import Bank, to extend $550,000,000 in credits. In the course of the first months of 1946 further conversations led to a final settlement of Lend-Lease at $720,000,000, and in May, 1946, additional credits of $650,000,000 were extended through the Export-Import Bank.

After his talks in Washington, De Gaulle proceeded on his triumphal tour. He visited Annapolis and West Point; he laid a wreath on Roosevelt's grave at Hyde Park; he received a tremendous ovation in New York, where he was made an honorary citizen; and he was hailed by enthusiastic and noisy crowds in Chicago. If there had ever been misgivings about De Gaulle on the part of Washington officialdom, there could be no doubt about the effusive good will borne by the American people toward France and her liberator. This agreeable mood was shared by the General, who surpassed himself in manifesting his own amicable feelings about America. At his press conference on August 24 he told correspondents:

> France . . . is fully resolved most actively and sincerely to participate with the great powers in international co-operation. In this co-operation . . . I believe that long-standing Franco-American friendship is one of the principal elements. I say Franco-American friendship, for I know that no question of interest has ever divided us and, even today, no interests divide us. My old country has made war—don't repeat this—on every country in turn except the United States. Today I affirm with immense satisfaction that those elements of friendship which have always existed between us—that is, no divergence of interest on the one hand, and on the other, an identical way of looking at things, of looking at the rights of men and women in this world, at freedom, democracy and justice—have never altered and are forever alive. I repeat, the under-

standing between your great country and mine, an understanding animated by our friendship, is and must be a useful and essential element
in international co-operation.

No more appropriate note could be struck to terminate a five-year history of difficulties and misunderstandings, underneath which, however,
had always existed a spirit of friendliness and co-operation marred only
by tensions created in high places. No more remarkable feature of the
greatest of all coalition wars can be found than the spirit of collaboration
at lower echelons, where Americans, Russians, Englishmen, and men
of other races and nationalities struggled together in common effort
against the Axis. General de Gaulle's words emphasized what is sometimes overlooked: that disagreement was spectacular and newsworthy,
whereas the real achievement, which escaped the headlines, should be
sought in terms of the millions who worked together and in so doing
paid more than lip service to the ideal of co-operative enterprise.

There is no need to question whether France benefited from De
Gaulle's spectacular career; in the time of her moral and material bankruptcy, France found in De Gaulle the unique voice which summoned
her to believe in the magnificent heritage of her past. Without De Gaulle
to rally the French Empire and to serve as focal point and symbol of
the Resistance, France might have fumbled throughout the war for
means to unify her actions and failing, could have emerged hopelessly
divided, seething with internal dissension. In spite of President Roosevelt's snide anecdotes, De Gaulle's place in French history, by the side
of Joan of Arc, is undeniably secure.

De Gaulle's wisdom in choosing his methods of collaborating with
the Allies is another matter. By scrupulously insisting that every French
sovereign right be respected, De Gaulle forced England and America
into recognition of the fact that even though defeated and deficient in
power, France continued to exist. But let us suppose that De Gaulle had
acted more pliantly regarding French interests: would the consequences
have been such as to assist or weaken his aims? One may put in question
De Gaulle's fundamental assumption that he must achieve the heights
and never descend from them—the basic conviction of the idealist that
forever stands in opposition to the pragmatist's concern for consequences.

The opposition of idealism to pragmatism, ancient as the arguments of Plato and Aristotle, is vividly expressed in French history by the devotion of St. Joan and the cynical "Paris is worth a Mass" of Henry IV. Charles de Gaulle steered his course closer to Joan than to Henry, but he might have served France better by occasionally casting a tactful glance in the opposite direction when French issues were concerned. A more tolerant attitude in regard to Saint Pierre and Miquelon and the Levant states would have been worth cultivating even at the expense of neglecting French "rights." All the fury and bad blood developed over Syria and Lebanon did not alter the destiny of those states nor preserve French prerogatives within them. One can even propound the cynical suggestion that Vichy's strong-arm methods were more capable of preserving France's privileged position in Moslem areas than the liberalism (and military feebleness) of Free France. De Gaulle could easily and profitably have demonstrated better manners in regard to Churchill and Roosevelt. Anger at the Prime Minister and the President for trespassing on French soil was hardly worth cultivating at the expense of alienating the heads of two powerful states. And granted that De Gaulle stood within his rights over Strasbourg, the French stand on Stuttgart and the Italo-French boundary affairs could hardly be justified from the point of view of enabling France to gain her ultimate objectives, which could be achieved better with assistance than with protests from London and Washington. With Allied good will and co-operation De Gaulle might have achieved a position which would have enabled him to protect French interests far more successfully than he could do when he butted headlong against the stone wall of Allied indignation.

The pattern of De Gaulle's relationship with the Allies, and especially with Roosevelt, is not without elements of tragedy, in its profoundest and grandest sense. Like Antigone, standing consistently, stubbornly, and proudly in defense of her convictions, De Gaulle aroused the world's admiration even as the implementation of his ideals foundered before the implacable opposition of great powers, corridor maneuvers, the importunity of human nature, and the reality of French political life. De Gaulle was at his best in 1940 when he called upon the French people to resist and at his most inexpert when faced five years later by the necessity of leading France through a complex of economic, political, and social reforms. Between 1940 and 1945, De Gaulle developed enormously from the unknown specialist in tank warfare to the statesman coping with international and domestic affairs; but in spite of a considerable and often unacknowledged diplomatic skill, he never acquired that magnanimity, that breadth of view, or that sense of humor which might have altered the tragic course of his career and rendered his achievement far greater than it was.

Whatever his defects, had there been no De Gaulle, there might have been no consistent pattern to American relations with France in World War II. Lacking the centralized force which De Gaulle brought to French dissidence, the historian would be compelled to describe a series of isolated incidents—the story of Pétain, of Admiral Robert, of Darlan, of Godefroy, of Giraud—with no unified pattern such as that provided by De Gaulle's personality and the program of Free France. De Gaulle's consistent adherence to his ideal imposed on the United States and the other Allies, in spite of themselves, the necessity of recognizing a France which, without his challenging leadership, might have been overlooked. To France, the loss of Charles de Gaulle would have been inestimable.

▶ Bibliography

Note on official sources. The *Journal officiel de la République Française* normally constitutes the basic repository of official acts and debates for France, just as the *Parliamentary Debates* serve for Great Britain and the *Congressional Record* for the United States, but French dissident movements also produced official publications. De Gaulle's headquarters published the *Journal officiel de la France Libre (Journal officiel de la France Combattante* after August, 1942), and Darlan (later Giraud) at Algiers published the *Journal officiel du haut commissariat de France en Afrique* (changed in February, 1943, to *Journal officiel du Commandement en Chef Français*). After formation of the Committee of National Liberation, De Gaulle and Giraud jointly sponsored the *Journal officiel de la République Française,* printed in Algiers from June 10, 1943; it continued in France after the liberation and replaced Vichy's *Journal officiel de l'état français.*

The Fighting French movement was an indefatigable distributer of information and propaganda. It published in London a bimonthly periodical called *Documents d'information* until June, 1942; *Les documents* until May 15, 1943; and thereafter *Les cahiers français.* A comparable publication in English, called *Free France,* was published by the French Press and Information Service in New York. Useful official information was published by the FCNL after June, 1943, in the *Bulletin d'information et de documentation.* Since liberation, the European, International, and Colonial Series of the official *Notes et études documentaires* has contained helpful data. Official papers of the Fighting French, having been deposited in the Archives Nationales, are unavailable to historians. However, a selected group of these documents appears as appendices to General de Gaulle's *Mémoires de guerre,* and other documents have been made available in memoirs by Soustelle, Catroux, Passy, Muselier, Giraud, Emmanuel d'Astier, and others.

On the British and American side, several official and semiofficial collections are invaluable. Several documents concerning American-French relations are found in *The Public Papers and Addresses of Franklin D. Roosevelt,* compiled by Judge Samuel I. Rosenman, and an occasional item appears in *F.D.R.: His Personal Letters,* edited by Elliott Roosevelt. For high-level documentation of the British position, Winston Churchill's six volumes of *The Second World War* are, of course, indispensable, granted the record is far from complete. Useful collections of official and other documents are found in *Documents on American Foreign Relations,* edited by L. M. Goodrich and M. J. Carroll annually for the World Peace Foundation; in *A Decade of American Foreign Policy: Basic Documents, 1941–1949,* and *Postwar Foreign Policy Preparation,* both published by the U.S. Government Printing Office in 1950; and in various issues of the State Department *Bulletin.* Documents published by the Royal Institute of International Affairs form an easily available collection.

Note on the Press. Several French-language newspapers were published outside France during the war, and their pages provided sounding boards for extremely partisan coverage of controversial issues. In London the newspaper *France* expressed a French, but not necessarily Gaullist, point of view. The principal Gaullist organ was *La marseillaise* (not to be confused with a Front National [*Communist*] journal of the same name), edited by François Quilici, whose continual denunciations of American policy greatly disturbed Secretary of State Hull. *La marseillaise* was forced to suspend publication in England. Quilici later became editor of the rightist, Gaullist *La bataille.* Several other Gaullist papers, most important of which was the South American *France nouvelle,* were published in various parts of the world.

In America, French sentiments found expression in *Pour la Victoire,* edited by Geneviève Tabouis and Henri de Kerillis. At first Gaullist, *Pour la victoire* became strongly Giraudist after the beginning of 1943. The Gaullist position was continually reflected by *La voix de France,* and after its absorption by *Pour la victoire,* it could be seen in *France-Amérique,* edited by Henry Torrès.

La France Libre, published first in London and later in Algiers, expressed Free French views until 1941 when its editor, André Labarthe, broke with De Gaulle. The paper's policy, in spite of its name, became anti-Gaullist and later pro-Giraud.

After North Africa became the center of French dissidence, the Algerian newspapers *L'echo d'Alger* and *Alger républicain* gained in importance, and gradually a variety of newspapers and journals appeared in Algiers, such as: *Combat,* the Gaullist underground paper which was published openly after February, 1943; *TAM,* in which Lemaigre-Dubreuil had an interest; *Liberté,* organ of the Communist party; and *Le canard dissident,* published by a group associated with the University of Algiers, which continued the tradition of *Le canard enchaîné.*

Books and Articles Cited

1. *Relating to the Allies*

Butcher, Harry C. *My Three Years with Eisenhower.* New York, 1946.

Carroll, Wallace. *Persuade or Perish.* Boston, 1948.

Churchill, Winston S. *The Second World War:* I, *The Gathering Storm* (Boston, 1948); II, *Their Finest Hour* (Boston, 1949); III, *The Grand Alliance* (Boston, 1950); IV, *The Hinge of Fate* (Boston, 1950); V, *Closing the Ring* (Boston, 1951); VI, *Triumph and Tragedy* (Boston, 1952).

Clark, Mark W. *Calculated Risk.* New York, 1950.

Cunningham, Admiral Andrew Browne, Viscount of Hyndhope. *A Sailor's Odyssey.* London, 1951.

Duff Cooper (Viscount Norwich). *Old Men Forget.* London, 1953.

Eisenhower, Dwight D. *Crusade in Europe.* Garden City, 1948.

Funk, A. L. "The 'Anfa Memorandum': An Incident of the Casablanca Conference," *Journal of Modern History,* Vol. XXVI, No. 3 (Sept., 1954).

Grew, Joseph C. *Turbulent Era,* ed. by Walter Johnson. 2 vols. Boston, 1952.

Hull, Cordell. *The Memoirs of Cordell Hull.* 2 vols. New York, 1948.

Langer, William L. *Our Vichy Gamble.* New York, 1947.

———, and Gleason, S. Everett. *The Undeclared War, 1940–1941.* New York, 1953.

Leahy, William D. *I Was There.* New York, 1950.

Pendar, Kenneth. *Adventure in Diplomacy: Our French Dilemma.* New York, 1945.

Roosevelt, Elliott. *As He Saw It.* New York, 1946.

Sherwood, Robert E. *Roosevelt and Hopkins: An Intimate History.* New York, 1948.

Smith, Kingsbury, "Unrevealed Facts about Robert Murphy," *American Mercury,* Vol. LIX, No. 251 (Nov., 1944).

Spellman, Francis J. (Cardinal). *Action This Day.* New York, 1943.

Stettinius, Edward R., Jr. *Roosevelt and the Russians: The Yalta Conference,* ed. by Walter Johnson. Garden City, 1949.

Stimson, Henry L., and Bundy, McGeorge. *On Active Service in Peace and War.* New York, 1948.

Twenty-third Report to Congress on Lend-Lease Operations. Washington, 1946.

2. *Relating to Intelligence Activities, Resistance, and French Dissidence*

Aron, Robert. *Le piège où nous a pris l'histoire.* Paris, 1950.

Astier de la Vigerie, Emmanuel d'. *Des dieux et les hommes, 1943–1944.* Paris, 1952.

———. *Sept fois sept jours.* Paris, 1947.

Barlone, Daniel. *La route des sommets.* Monte Carlo, 1953.

Catroux, General Georges. *Dans la bataille de Méditerranée.* Paris, 1949.

Crusoe (*nom de guerre* of Jacques Lemaigre-Dubreuil). *Vicissitudes d'une victoire.* Paris, 1946.

Gaulle, Charles de. *Mémoires de guerre:* I: *L'appel, 1940–1942* (Paris, 1954); II, *L'unité, 1942–1944* (Paris, 1956).

Giraud, Henri. *Un seul but, la victoire.* Paris, 1949.

Kammerer, Albert. *Du débarquement africain au meurtre de Darlan.* Paris, 1949.

Marshall, Bruce. *The White Rabbit.* Boston, 1953.

Michel, Henri, and Mirkine-Guetzévitch, B., eds. *Les idées politiques et sociales de la Résistance.* Paris, 1954.

Nord, Pierre (Colonel Brouillard). *Mes camarades sont morts:* I, *La guerre du renseignement* (Paris, 1947); II, *Le contre-espionnage* (Paris, 1947); III, *La préparation du débarquement* (Paris, 1949).

Passy, Colonel (Wavrin, André de). *Souvenirs.* Monte Carlo, 1947. (I, *Deuxième Bureau à Londres.* II, *10, Duke Street, Londres (le B.C.R.A.).* III, *Missions secrètes en France.*)

Richard, René, and Sérigny, Alain de. *La bissectrice de la guerre. Alger, 8 Novembre 1942.* Algiers, 1946.

Roussy de Sales, Raoul de. *L'Amérique entre en guerre (Journal d'un Français aux États-Unis).* Paris, 1948.

Sandahl, Pierre. *De Gaulle sans képi.* Paris, 1948.

Soustelle, Jacques. *Envers et contre tout:* I, *De Londres à Alger* (Paris, 1947); II, *D'Alger à Paris* (Paris, 1950).

3. *Relating to Military Affairs*

Lattre de Tassigny, General de. *Histoire de la première armée française: Rhin et Danube.* Paris, 1949.

Marey, Georges. "Le réarmement français en Afrique du Nord, 1942–44," *Revue politique et parlementaire* (Oct., Nov., 1947).

Pogue, Forrest C. *The Supreme Command,* vol. III, pt. 4 of *U.S. Army in World War II.* Washington, 1954.

Vigneras, Marcel. *Rearming the French.* Special Study in *U.S. Army in World War II.* Washington, 1957.

4. *Relating to France, the Third Republic, Vichy, and the Fourth Republic*

Conferences at Malta and Yalta. Washington, 1955.

Dansette, Adrien. *Histoire de la libération de Paris.* Paris, 1946.

Gosset, Pierre and Renée. *La deuxième guerre; les secrets de la paix manquée.* Paris, 1950.

Kerillis, Henri de. *I Accuse De Gaulle* (translation of *De Gaulle, Dictateur.*) New York, 1946.

Peyrouton, Marcel. *Du service public à la prison commune. Souvenirs.* Paris, 1950.

Robert, Amiral Georges. *La France aux Antilles de 1939 à 1943.* Paris, 1950.

▶ *Index*